ENGLISH SAGA
(1840-1940)

By the Same Author

SAMUEL PEPYS
CHARLES II
ETC., ETC.

ARTHUR BRYANT

ENGLISH SAGA

(1840-1940)

COLLINS
with
EYRE & SPOTTISWOODE
LONDON

THIS BOOK IS SET IN FONTANA, A NEW TYPE FACE DESIGNED
FOR THE EXCLUSIVE USE OF THE HOUSE OF COLLINS, AND
PRINTED BY THEM IN GREAT BRITAIN

First Impression	-	-	-	-	December, 1940
Second ,,	-	-	-	-	December, 1940
Third ,,	-	-	-	-	January, 1941
Fourth ,,	-	-	-	-	February, 1941
Fifth ,,	-	-	-	-	July, 1941

COLLINS CLEAR-TYPE PRESS : LONDON AND GLASGOW
COPYRIGHT

To
LORD QUEENBOROUGH,
ENGLISHMAN

"Their children also shall be as aforetime, and their congregation shall be established before me, and I will punish all that oppress them. And their nobles shall be of themselves, and their governor shall proceed from the midst of them; and I will cause him to draw near, and he shall approach unto me. . . . And ye shall be my people, and I will be your God."

Jeremiah xxx.

CONTENTS

PREFACE

THOSE fighting have a right to the answer to a question now forming in millions of minds. *What is going to happen after the War?* For we know what happened after the last. In a wartime broadcast Mr. J. B. Priestley, contrasting a visit to a deserted Margate with one taken a few years ago, asked himself whether, had he a magician's power, he would bring back that happier peacetime scene in place of the grisly present. And he answered, No. For by making such a choice he would forgo the right to make a better future—a Margate and an England which no man can at present even visualise.

The key to a nation's future is in her past. A nation that loses it has no future. For men's deepest desires—the instrument by which a continuing society moulds its destiny—spring from their own inherited experience. We cannot recreate the past, but we cannot escape it. It is in our blood and bone. To understand the temperament of a people, a statesman has first to know its history.

This record of a hundred years of crowded social evolution has been written at a turning point in England's existence. At the time it opens an old society was dying largely through its inability to adapt itself to revolutionary change. The new nation which took its place never understood it. The England of the rationalists and the money-makers had no time to consider the England of the "yeoman and the ale house on the heath." It thus lost the key to its own past and future. Its divided posterity has been seeking it ever since.

The social conditions of that older England—Christian, rural, half-democratic and half-authoritarian—were the outcome of centuries of evolution. They combined diversity with great cohesion and strength. Within their strong but narrow confines the English had developed the capacity for compromise, ordered freedom and toleration which is the core of modern democracy, defeated the attempts of the Spanish and French Empires to dominate the world by force and established, with the aid of sister kingdoms, the British Empire in their stead. They left posterity, the English village and countryside, the parliamentary system,

the genius of Shakespeare and Newton and the London of
Wren.   The present may still have something to learn from a
community that could achieve so much out of so little.

Its virtues sprang from nature, but also from conscious will.
The English were what they were because they had long wished
to be. Their tradition derived from the Catholic past of Europe.
Its purpose was to make Christian men—gentle, generous,
humble, valiant and chivalrous. Its ideals were justice, mercy
and charity. Shakespeare was not writing fantasy when he put
into the mouth of John of Gaunt his vision of a

> "land of such dear souls, this dear, dear land:
> Dear for her reputation through the world."

He was merely defining the character of his country.

Her institutions were moulded to make it easier for her people
to attain that character. Within their framework they could live
Christian lives without denying human needs and without
constant conflict between their conscience and their circumstance.
A squire or merchant who treated his neighbours with a sense of
responsibility could still prosper. As a result of long and unbroken Christian usage, it became native to the English to live
and work in a society in which moral responsibility existed. And
when England broke with the Catholic past—partly out of a
critical sense of its human imperfections—she still cherished the
old ideal of a nation dedicated to the task of breeding just and
gentle men. All that was best in Puritanism was an attempt to
restate it. Without justice and charity there can be no England.
That is the historic and eternal English vision.

A nation, unlike a man who is subject to death, can get what it
wants if it wants it long and strongly enough. With her unbroken island tradition, England more than any other Christian
nation consistently tried to make herself a land of decent men
and women esteeming justice, honesty and freedom. Her success
in the fulness of time brought her unparalleled prosperity. The
virtues of her people gave them opportunities of wealth and power
greater than men had ever known before.

They were only human and they in part misused them. Their
very sense of the value of liberty and of the significance of the
individual for a time tempted them to condone selfishness and to
forget the historic purpose of their commonwealth. This book
is the story of what happened when they did so.

CHAPTER ONE

Green Land Far Away

"A' babbled of green fields."
Shakespeare.

A HUNDRED YEARS AGO, within the life-time of a few old men and women still living, the population of England and Wales, now more than forty million, scarcely exceeded fifteen. That of Scotland numbered another two and a half million and Ireland—a restless subject state—a further eight millions or very nearly twice what it is to-day. Of these twenty-six millions, two million lived in London and another million and a half in seven cities of over 100,000 inhabitants. Scarcely more than a quarter of the population lived in towns of over 20,000. The rest dwelt, as their fathers before them, among the fields or in towns from which the fields were only a few minutes walk. At least half the British race were engaged in rural or semi-rural pursuits. The overwhelming majority were the sons or grandsons of farmers, yeomen, peasants and craftsmen.

This comparatively small community comprised the wealthiest, most vigorous and most powerful national unit in the world. Its rule was acknowledged by more than a tenth of the earth's twelve hundred million inhabitants. In less than a century England had conquered an Asiatic peninsula of 1,800,000 square miles, thirty-four times her size, subjecting nearly half of its two hundred million to her dominion and the remainder to her virtual control, a still vaster tract of land in North America inhabited by a sprinkling of British and French settlers and indigenous Red Indians, and at the far side of the world, separated from her ports by a sea voyage of six months, an entirely new continent nearly forty times her own size. Scattered about the world were other countries, islands and ports which flew the British flag and acknowledged the sovereignty of the King of England.

In all this vast dominion overseas, there were only two million men and women of British race, apart from the professional army which was far smaller than that of any other major power. They ruled by measure of their complete mastery over the seas, won for them in a series of seven great European and world wars which, covering sixty-seven out of a hundred and twenty-six years between 1689 and 1815, had culminated in the defeat and exhaustion of a rival with a population nearly three times as great. Since then, apart from punitive expeditions against the heathen, the British had lived in peace with their fellow Christians.

The continent of Europe, of which Britain was geographically a part, consisted of thirteen Christian nations, the Mahomedan and partially Asian Ottoman Empire, and forty-one minor German and Italian states which, though enjoying sovereign independence, lacked national status in the modern sense. Four only were major powers, the still semi-revolutionary French kingdom with thirty-five million inhabitants—a source of perpetual fear to its neighbours; the old multi-racial Empire of Austria with a slightly smaller population; the parvenu north German Kingdom of Prussia with about sixteen millions and the barbaric Empire of Russia with more than sixty millions of whom seven millions inhabited the Siberian plains. The once powerful Kingdom of Spain and the Ottoman Empire, still exercising an uneasy and despotic sway over the semi-Christian tribesmen of the Balkans, no longer played any part in the councils of Europe.

Of the other continents, Africa was a savage *terra incognita* with a fringe of decadent Mahomedan states littering its Mediterranean shore, one of which, Algiers, had recently been annexed by France, and a few scattered British, Dutch and Portuguese outposts along its ocean coasts. Round the latter passed the ships which carried the trade of Europe to the East. Asia, with more than two-thirds of the world's population, had become a European trading preserve, though still mainly unexploited, with its southern peninsula British, its vast northern deserts Russian, and only the moribund Empire of China preserving a semblance of loose independence while British traders and gunboats injected western commerce and culture into her eastern ports and creeks. Japan was a group of dreamy islands, still unopened to European trade and innocent alike of western idealism and material progress.

Only in North America was there any civilisation comparable to that of Europe. Here seventeen vigorous millions of British descent, who had broken with the too rigid rule of Westminster sixty years before, were furiously engaged in developing and throwing open to European emigration an uninhabited continent. In central and southern America, seventeen scantily populated and ramshackle Latin states, recently revolted from Spanish and Portuguese rule, offered an almost illimitable field to the exploiter. Here also Britain with her sea power and her growing manufacturing and banking supremacy was first among her trading rivals.

. . . .

Such was the planet in which for that moment in time rustic England held vigorous but kindly mastery. Her capital, London was the symbol of that supremacy. With its two million inhabitants it was by far the largest and richest city in the world and like the nation itself had more than doubled its size since the beginning of the century. Stretching from Shadwell and Wapping in the east it extended along both banks of the Thames as far as outer Chelsea and Battersea: thence a double line of villas ensconced among trees and large gardens continued almost to Hampton Court. For the first time in its history the city was venturing away from the river; houses, skirting the new Regent's Park, strayed into the fields and farms of Primrose Hill where children still gathered the flowers which gave it its name. Everywhere bricks and mortar were rising: the removal of the Court from St. James's to Buckingham Palace had stimulated an outburst of building on the marshy fields and market gardens of Pimlico, soon to be renamed after its Cheshire owners, Belgravia. The red brick of which Wren and his successors had re-created London after the great fire was giving place to white and potentially grimy stucco:

"Augustus at Rome was for building renowned
And of marble he left what of brick he had found;
But is not our Nash, too, a very great master,
He finds us all brick and leaves us all plaster."

Standing on top of the Duke of York's column on an early summer day of 1842, the downward-glancing eye lighted on a jumble of old houses and red-tiled roofs mingling with the foliage and blossom of Spring Gardens. Along the Mall the trees still straggled anyhow, unregimented into their modern columns, while cows thrust their horned heads over the wooden palings of Carlton House Terrace. Trafalgar Square was building on the recently cleared site of the old Royal Mews, where untidy advertisement-pasted hoardings concealed the stump of Nelson's slow-rising column and the Percy lion, with its straight tail poker, roared defiance above the Tudor brick palace of the Dukes of Northumberland[1]. Farther afield loomed the great Pantechnicon in Belgrave Square, and Apsley House, with its world-famous inhabitant and its ferruginous shutters defying reform and revolution, standing solitary against the country setting of Hyde Park. Beyond lay Kensington village and the first rising mansions of Bayswater. Southwards towards the river were the Abbey and the long straight line of Westminster Hall, but Barry's Houses of Parliament were still only rising from the scaffolded ashes of old St. Stephens. Opposite that empty spot stood the eighteenth-century houses of Bridge Street and Westminster Bridge; beyond tall chimneys, bespeaking the industrial employments of the dwellers in the Lambeth and Southwark suburbs, and the virgin heights of woody Penge and Norwood.

This city, multiplying itself in every generation, was still governed on the rustic model of its own past. Side by side with the medieval Lord Mayor and Corporation were three hundred parish and other authorities, mostly Vestries, whose functions overlapped in the most inextricable manner and whose members, self-elected or holding office for life under no less than 250 Acts of Parliament, interpreted democracy in their own jovial way by almost ceaseless entertainment at the public expense. The hammering and plastering that daily enlarged London's circumference went on without control or interference: except for the new west-end squares which Cubitt was raising for the Marquis of Westminster, the small speculating builder built as he felt fit. It was the age of "superior Dosset," carrying his yeoman frugality and peasant notions of propriety into the building of a new Rome. Nobody had time or money to plan: there were no broad avenues or boulevards: the town, free from continental fortifications, grew outwards not upwards and on the principle that the best place to build was the nearest available space. The brand new suburbs which housed the City clerks over the former village pastures and

---

[1]Thirty years later, it was still there, standing high above Landseer's lions in the Square, and was reputed by mothers in their nursery tales to wag its tail as Big Ben struck midnight.

gardens of Islington, Hoxton and Camberwell, were monotonous agglomerations of mean streets and terraces marked by pathetic Cockney attempts at gentility and country ways of living wherever there was room for a vine, a carpet-sized flower garden or a fan-light over the narrow hall.

That was the new London; it was still overshadowed by the old. Past the great white invitations to "Try Warren's" or "Day and Martin's Blacking" and the castellated summer houses and villas of the outer bourgeoisie, the traveller entering London felt the shock and heard the roar of the cobble stones and saw elm trees and winkle stalls giving way to continuous lines of houses and gas lamps. The narrow streets through which the coaches and drays forced their way were thronged with the human material from which Dickens and Cruikshank derived their inspiration. Women in fringed shawls and straw bonnets, pock-marked and ragged beggars and pickpockets, clean-shaven and tightly-stocked young men with mutton-chop whiskers and tall fluffy beaver hats, clerks, also crowned with the universal stove-pipe, flowing inwards to the counter or back to suburban villages —"preceded by a ripple of errand boys and light porters and followed by an ebb of plethoric elderly gentlemen in drab gaiters" —and, as one reached the fashionable squares and roadways of Mayfair, a wealth of coloured and gilded liveried servants with stuffed white calves, cockaded hats and gold aigulets, emulating prize cattle in their rotund solemnity. These not only mixed with the crowds on the pavements and appeared sunning them-selves at innumerable doorways but flowed majestically along the streets at a higher level, as they sat red-nosed on the draped boxes or stood erect with tall silver-crowned canes on the swing-ing platforms of crested coaches. And behind the double doors of the great houses of Grosvenor Square and Piccadilly were their brethren, the hall porters, sitting in vast hooded chairs, sometimes with a foot-rest and a foaming tankard as witness of their master's absence in the country.

These were the rank and file of the private armies of the privileged, sleeping in truckle beds in tiny dusty attics or dark basement pantries but sharing their master's glory and living on the cream of the land. At the great routs of High Society and at the Levées of St. James's, the populace crowding about the flambeau-lit doorways could see them in all their magnificence, enacting their well-rehearsed parts in the cavalcade

of the last age in which the English rich expended their wealth on
public pageantry instead of on personal comfort. The bedizened
flunkeys and the elegant, disdainful beings they attended never
lacked spectators: a nimbus of ragged wide-eyed urchins, sometimes jeering, always half-admiring, attended them wherever
they went—gamin school and spawn of the true Cockney with his
love of splendour and his delight in derision.

Here the ages mingled—the past and the future. The great
country houses of Piccadilly behind their high stone walls,
ignoring London and dreaming of the shires from which the rosy
country-bred lords and legislators who governed England
hailed, were washed by the ceaseless tides of the London
of commerce. Jogging past those tall brocaded eighteenth-
century windows, the fathers of the Forsytes sat crowded and
upright within or sprawled, long-legged and check-trousered, on
the narrow knife-edged roofs of the little sixpenny buses that,
driving a resolute way among the crested barouches, chariots and
landaus of the fashionable west-end, plied between the Bank and
outer Paddington and Brompton or the Yorkshire Stingo close by
leafy Lisson Grove. At the back, straw in his mouth and ribaldry
on his lips, stood the outrageous cad, loudly touting for passengers against the conductors of rival machines and pushing his
clients through the narrow door into his hot, swaying straw-
strewn pen.[1] There they sat, six aside on the dirty plush cushions,
glaring suspiciously while their thoughts ranged ahead of the
steaming horses on schemes of money-making which never
troubled the fine pates of the great lords and ladies whose
residences they were humbly passing. For in the first days of the
young Queen new England was on the make and old England was
on the spend. The nation's growing wealth offered scope for both.

Looking back across the first forty years of our own century
and the long prosperous reign that preceded it, we know how
vigorously and inevitably that young England was advancing to
victory, how doomed was the antique pomp and stately policy it
supplanted. At the time the battle seemed undecided: the foundations of the old world looked firm and brassy and the busy,
vulgar confusion of the new rootless and evanescent. The teeming

---

[1]In May 1842 the stipendiary magistrate at the Marlborough Street Police Court
sentencing the conductor of one of Powell's Brentford omnibuses for an assault on a
passenger, "observed in very indignant tones that it was necessary to protect the public
and females in particular against the ruffianly conduct of omnibus conductors."
—*Illustrated London News*, I, 46.

legions of the money-makers were there on sufferance: back in
the shires from which they or their fathers came, they paid the
common immemorial tribute to the lords of hereditary status
and acre. Down in his native Wessex by the sea, superior Dosset,
master of London bricks and mortar, touched his cap with his
yeoman cousinry to the squire of Lulworth or Osmington. Here
in London he fought for a footing in a crowded hurly-burly from
which status was lacking for all but the richest. Even for his
place in the omnibus—the advancing chariot of democracy—he
had to rise betimes and struggle: for in the race for money,
many were called and few chosen and the prize was only to the
assiduous, the pertinacious and the thrifty. In 1837 London only
boasted 400 narrow, three-windowed, two-horse buses and 1200
dirty hooded gigs or cabs, with a total carrying capacity of less
than ten thousand.

Other public conveyances there were none. The river, whose
scourings the tides could no longer cleanse, had ceased to be the
city's waterway: the watermen who had ferried the generations
of the past between the stone stairs were dying out. Mostly
London tramped over the cobbles to its labour, nearly a hundred
thousand pedestrians daily crossing London Bridge. In those
narrow crowded streets Shanks's pony generally proved the
swiftest mount: with long swinging strides the Londoner
covered his morning and evening miles and went abroad for
country rambles after his midday Sunday dinner: the studious
Macaulay thought nothing of walking for recreation from his
chambers in the Albany to New Cross or riverside Greenwich.

It was a London that still had a country appetite. It ate not
because it wanted vitamins but because it was hungry. At midday
the new London sat down in a panelled steaming chop-house—at
Cock, Rainbow or Cheshire Cheese and many a humbler horse-box
hostlery—to devour steaks, joints, chops and porter, cheese,
potatoes and greens, usually with hot spirits and water to follow.
Off liver and bacon at 10d., a pint of stout at 4½d., potatoes, bread,
cheese and celery one could dine very comfortably for 2/- and
leave a pile of coppers for that loquacious piece of old England,
the waiter. Men whose immediate forebears had been hale and
hearty farmers would think nothing of tackling at a sitting a
boiled leg of mutton with carrots, turnips and dumplings,
black pudding of pigs' and sheeps' trotters, tripe and faggots and
pease pudding. In their appetites the gentry were at one with the

rising commercial classes: at Lord Grey's house Creevey sat down
with five or six others to a luncheon of two hot roast fowls, two
partridges, a dish of hot beef steaks and a cold pheasant, and to a
"double" dinner of two soups, two fishes, a round of beef at one
end of the table and a leg of mutton at the other with a roast
turkey on the sideboard, followed by entrees of woodcocks,
snipes and plovers, with devilled herring and cream cheese to lay
the last despairing stirrings of appetite. Dinner was followed,
after due time allowed for the gentlemen's port, by tea, and,
where late nights were in contemplation, by the supper
tray—Melton pie, oysters, sandwiches and anchovy toast with
sherry, bottled stout and Seltzer-water and the usual mahogany case with its four cut-glass decanters labelled Rum, Brandy,
Whisky, Gin. The London poor, few of whom tasted butcher's
meat more than once a week, had to content themselves with
envying the well-filled forms and rosy faces of their betters.

The poor—the flotsam and jetsam of casual labour and the
ne'er-do-wells who lacked the status and solider fare of the skilled
artisan class—were somewhat of a problem in that great city, and
the bigger it grew the more of them there were. The magnet of
wealth seeking more wealth drew them from the dissolving world
of status and the hedgerow, and from the old trades which the
new were paralysing. To house them the jerry builders worked
ceaselessly, raising innumerable straight streets of plain two-
storied houses with slated roofs, the cheapest that could be built.
Here, and in the regions where older and grander buildings had
decayed to verminous tenements, they lived and died and multiplied, for despite filth and cholera and typhus life proved stronger
than death. Even the down-and-outs and the homeless urchins,
sleeping in their thousands under the arches of the Adelphi and
Waterloo Bridge, lived.

Many of the worst slums jostled the dwellings of the rich and
the haunts of fashion. There were rookeries of thieves and
prostitutes under the very noses of the lawyers in the Temple and
the legislators in Westminster, and behind the new plate-glass
windows of the fine shops of Regent and Oxford Streets
the urban poor squatted in worse than farmyard filth and
squalor. But few troubled much about the poor who were left
to the Vestries and Providence: every one was too busy making
money or spending it. Only sometimes a wretched creature,
rising from the shadowy recesses of London or Waterloo Bridge,

would mount the parapet and, sliding into the water, take swift dramatic leave of a world that knew small pity for failures.

Strangely contrasted, the life of rich and poor yet mingled. In Tothill fields, the scholars of Westminster took almost daily part in gigantic battles against gangs of young roughs from the adjoining slums. And the street walkers on their promenade from Temple Bar to Westminster Hall knew more of the good and great who ruled the aristo-democracy of England than the good and great would have cared to admit. Many of the traditions of the Regency died hard, paying tardy deference to the more squeamish and frugal morals of the money makers. Fine gentlemen of the shires, accustomed of ancient use and lusty living to take their pleasure of the willing wives and daughters of their tenantry—and no one, in their estimation, the worse in thought or fact—kept dual establishments in town: a house in Portland Place or Berkeley Square for family and *haut ton* and a pretty box for some charmer, promoted from ballet or millinery shop, in one of the little Chelsea or Brompton Squares that were ever rising on the sites of the western market gardens. At night the young bucks and their hangers-on would assemble at the Cavendish or some neighbouring Piccadilly hostelry. When the white damask was strewn with empty jugs of Chateau Margaux and broken decanters of port, they would sally out to wrench off the knockers and bell handles of Sackville Street and Vigo Lane, make merry with the blackguard democracy of the London under-world on comic songs, roast kidneys, cigars and gin and water in the smoky haunts of Leicester Fields and the Haymarket, and finish the night in riotous harmony amid the dishevelled Cyprian delights of the Piccadilly Saloon, or at Vauxhall gardens, watching the fireworks and the dances in the Rotunda from a leafy grotto and lingering long into the morning over sliced ham and bowl of arrack with the nymphs of the place. The sleepy turnpike men on the Bridge and the newly-formed Metropolitan Police, in their tall hats and clumsy belted coats, treated such privileged revellers with respect so long as they kept their amuse-ments from assuming too dangerous a shape. The "Peelers" had been brought into the world not to molest but to protect property and its owners. For on the untrammelled use of property, it was held, the nation's liberties depended.

A rough natural democracy governed by an aristocracy and landed gentry was the English model with plenty of scope for

folk who wished to be free and easy. But already the shades of a
more prim and decorous age were falling: the new police and
the new passion for making laws had began to trace on the
nation's ruddy face the sober lineaments of a more formal society.
In Oxford Street the first wood blocks had already taken the place
of the cobbles and in the larger thoroughfares the stone posts on
the pavements were being crowned with spikes to discourage the
urchins of the streets from their interminable leapfrog. The day-
long music of the London street cries was beginning to grow
fainter.

Within the great club-houses of Pall Mall and St James's, a
new life for the rich, based on decorum and silent comfort,
was taking the place of the noisy gambling and drinking of the
unregenerate past. By 1837 there were twenty-five of these great
institutions from behind whose windows warm men with broad
acres or money in the Funds could sit over their *Quarterly* or
Edinburgh Review and watch a safer and remoter world than their
fathers had ever known. Here the old and the new were already
learning to mingle, and the successful man of commerce who had
negotiated the terrors of the black ball might hope to strike an
acquaintance with the quieter sort of lord or squire. There was
even a special club dedicated to Reform with the most famous
chef in London installed among tin-lined copper pots and gas
ovens to teach old England the way to live after a new French
model.

At night the march of progress was symbolised by the lighting
of the London streets. Gas lighting had come in a couple of
decades back, and was now being slowly extended from the
main thoroughfares into the courts and alleys of the older London
that besieged them. The great gasometers rose like fortresses
above the drab rows of working-class dwellings, and from dusk till
dawn the flaring gas jets made a peculiar humming that was the
musical background to the nocturnal activities of the Londoner.
Judged by modern standards the light they gave was dim and
little diffused: to our rustic forefathers it seemed a prodigious
illumination. Yet four years were to elapse before the main
road from Hyde Park Corner to Kensington was lit by a single
lamp.

The essential services of life were still supplied to the Londoner
after a country model. Donkeys carried vegetables to Covent

Garden and colliers or "Geordies" brought their "best Wallsend" from Tyne and Wear by sail: a prolonged west wind could cause a fuel shortage in the capital. And the wintry streets were perambulated by tall-hatted coalheavers peddling their wares. Here, too, the old cries of London were still heard: in winter crossing-sweepers sat by braziers to gather toll of familiar clients for keeping their pitch clean. In her rough white cottage in Hyde Park opposite Knightsbridge, old Ann Hicks sold gilt gingerbreads and curds and whey and took her modest toll, won by half a century of prescription, of Park brushwood and hurdles to make her fire. In the new Bayswater road one could watch haymakers in the open fields to the north: a little farther on, where the gravel Oxford turnpike fell into Notting Dale, the pig-keepers who supplied the London hotels squatted in rustic confusion. In the cellars of Westminster as well as in the suburbs Londoners still kept cows: the metropolis' milk supply was mainly home-made with, so it was hinted, liberal assistance from the pump.[1] And on any Monday morning herds of cattle were driven by drovers armed with cudgels and iron goads through the narrow streets to Smithfield: pedestrians were sometimes gored by the poor beasts. In Smithfield Tellus kept his unsavoury rustic court: a nasty, filthy, dangerous country Bastille in the heart of London and a great offence to sensitive and progressive persons. Vested interests defended it stubbornly against all assaults: *Punch* depicted a proprietary Alderman taking his wife and family for a walk there. "Oh! how delicious," he declares, "the drains are this morning!"

How rustic London still was could be seen from its summer greenery. The west-end was full of trees and green squares and courts. The fields were half-a-mile away from Buckingham Palace and Grosvenor Square, and snipe were occasionally shot in the Pimlico marshes. In St. James's Park long rough untrimmed grass ran down to the water's edge, and there were no railings to keep people from wandering on it. Sometimes on wintry evenings the scarlet of a huntsman's coat could be seen in the fading light ascending the slope of Piccadilly or entering the Albany courtyard. In Chelsea, where the old brown roofs and twisted high chimneys of the houses almost tumbled into the un-

---

[1] Cynics sometimes went further. "A great *fall* of chalk occurred at Mertsham on the Brighton Railway . . .; a corresponding *fall* of milk took place in London on the following day."—*Punch, I, 202, 6th Nov., 1841.*

embanked river, the sage Carlyle rode down eighteenth-century lanes to improve his digestion. Here on Saturdays would come bowling by many "a spicy turn-out and horse of mettle and breed," with the little liveried top-hatted tiger swinging on the footboard behind and his gay bachelor master smoking his cheroot and flicking his whip as he sped to his riverside villa, with its fairy-like grounds, cellar of recherché wines, pictures, statues, and "many a gem of virtue."

Elegant London of royal Victoria's virgin days where Jullien, the Napoleon of Quadrille, "saucily served Mozart with *sauce-piquant*" and Taglioni danced like a spirit in Rossini's newest ballet! For all its ragged hungry urchins, its fever-stricken alleys and crushing poverty, there was still music and gaiety in it. In August, 1842, Mozart's *Così fan tutte* was being sung at His Majesty's and Rossini's *Semiramide* at Covent Garden under the direction of Benedict, while Purcell's *King Arthur* was rehearsing at Drury Lane and Spohr's new opera, *The Fall of Babylon*, at the Hanover Rooms.

.   .   .   .

There was a pastoral quality about the amusements of our great-grandparents. The great summer regattas on the Thames between London Bridge and Hammersmith were attended by paddle steamers with brass bands and boats full of fluttering flags and pretty girls giggling in the sunlight under painted awnings, while the banks were thronged with runners and riders and convivial parties watching from the festooned balconies and gardens of riverside pubs. At Putney Fair were Fat Ladies and Learned Pigs, much "firing of cannon, jollity, shouting, jangling of street pianos and popping of ginger beer," and many a pull at Finch's ale. Every Whit Tuesday the Cockneys went *en masse* to Greenwich, cargo after cargo going down the river singing and cheering and devouring stout and sandwiches, to sample the traditional delights of the great fair—its rows of booths hung with dolls, gilt gingerbreads and brandy balls, its raree-shows and performing pigs, its giants and its dwarfs. Here prentices and shop boys pushed about with whistles, penny trumpets, false noses and rolled twopenny scrapers—in sound simulating tearing material—down the backs of their elders. And the park was filled with young people and hoydens—playing at kiss-in-the-ring, riding donkeys, or, more simply, tumbling head over heels down the hill.

For though London was the greatest city in the world its people still had their roots in the country or were separated only by a generation or two from country ways. They were scarcely yet sophisticated. The poorer streets were frequented by gigantic brown dancing bears led by picturesque, seedy-looking Italians. Barry, the clown at Astley's Circus, went down the Thames in a washing tub drawn by geese, and a lady rider at Vauxhall could draw all London. For children the chief sights of the town were the Tower, the Elgin Marbles and Mr. Cross's Surrey Zoo, recently moved from the old Royal Mews to make way for Trafalgar Square. Here in the grounds of Walworth Manor lions and tigers perambulated in a circular glass conservatory more than a hundred yards wide and a giant tortoise carried children on his back. Another popular treat was the Panorama. At the Colosseum on the east side of Regent's Park one could view the Fire of London with canvas scenery and fireworks and the Alps with a real Swiss and a real eagle. Athens and the Himalayas were also shown for a shilling—"the Ganges glittering a hundred and fifty miles off, and far away the snowy peak of the mountain it rises from." A little later a new Royal Panorama was opened in Leicester Square, where scenes from England's contemporary colonial wars were presented in the manner of a modern news reel. The battle of Waterloo—the chief title-deed, with Trafalgar, of an Englishman's innate superiority to all foreigners—was a permanent exhibit.

For sport the well-to-do Londoner affected the pastimes of squires and farmers. Cricket was already established at Lord's suburban ground and was played vigorously in top-hats: but shooting parties, steeplechases, hunting with the Queen's, the Old Berkeley or the Epping Hunt, and fishing up the river were far more widely patronised. At Richmond the well-to-do merchant and shopkeeper, arrayed in top-hat, white tie and long tail coat, would sit in a punt of a Saturday afternoon perched on a chair with rod and line, dining afterwards at the Star and Garter and calling on the way home at the pastrycook's to buy his wife six-penniworth of Maids of Honour. The Englishman, though immersed in low commerce, liked above all to think of himself as a man of potential acres—a younger son who might one day come into his heritage. His, as Mr. R. H. Mottram has written, was "that almost divine snobbery of very strong motive power that keeps the Englishman from being content ever to be classed as

a workman or labourer, a priest or soldier or scholar, as men of
other civilisations are, and makes him always desire to be a
gentleman, a word without equivalent in any other language."[1]

The old Chelsea bun house, the ale-house standing solitary in
the Kensington road between Hyde Park Corner and the royal
gardens, the ox that was roasted whole in the park on Coronation
Day, were all reminders that the capital of a great empire had not
wholly shaken off the village. So were the established bad
characters who frequented its shady gambling-houses and saloons,
the imitation bucks and dandies, the bankrupts, bullies and half-
pay captains who still, in the last age before the railway came in,
sometimes emulated Macheath and Turpin by robbing the be-
nighted traveller in Epping Forest or on the Surrey heaths. On
an execution morning at Newgate one saw the rough old London
of the landless squatter—greasy, verminous and grimy—gathered
outside the gaol; ribaldry, coarse jokes, reckless drinking and
unashamed debauchery continued uproariously until the chimes
of St. Sepulchre's striking eight and the tolling of the prison bell
brought a momentary hush as the prisoner mounted the steps and
the sickly jerk of the rope gave the signal for an unearthly yell
of execration. For countrymen deprived of their land and status
soon degenerated.

So rough and ill-disciplined was that London that until
Home Secretary Peel had established his Metropolitan Police in
1829, St. James's Park had been patrolled by Household Cavalry.
Many still living could remember the terrible week when the
mob, emerging from its filthy lairs in the cellars and crazy
tenements of Blackfriars and St. Giles's, had surrounded Parliament and all but burnt the capital. When in the winter before her
coronation the little Queen, with pretty pink cheeks and pouting
mouth, drove behind her emblazoned guards through the streets,
the crowd gaped but scarcely a hat was raised or a cheer heard.
"The people of England," wrote Greville, "seemed inclined to
hurrah no more." Even at Ascot in the following summer only a
few hats were raised as the royal barouche drove down the
course.

There were some in that age who thought England was
driving to a republic. For a hundred and fifty years the innate
English loyalty to the monarchic principle had been under-

[1] *Early Victorian England (Edited G. M. Young) I, 185.*

mined by the iconoclastic Whig contempt for royalty[1] and its pomps and geegaws, by a race of foreign rulers on the throne and during the last four decades by the vagaries and indecorums of the royal family. These had reached their climax in 1821 in the spectacle of a stout, vulgar and hysterical German Queen vainly attempting amid the plaudits of the mob to force an entry into the Abbey at the coronation of her adulterous and bigamous spouse. Since the death of Charles II. the royal England of Elizabeth and the Plantagenets had been transformed almost unknowingly into a oligarchy. A sovereign sat on the throne and went through ancient forms, but an aristocracy governed. Though the dignity with which the young Queen bore her part in the ceremonies of coronation in the summer of 1838 did something to stir deeper and latent national instincts[2], the general feeling was expressed by William Dyott when he wrote, "A very young Queen coming to the throne of this mighty empire (just eighteen years of age) brought up and subject to the control of a weak and capricious mother, surrounded by the parent's chosen advisers . . . gives token of unpropitious times to come."

The real rulers of England were still the greater squires. In the course of a century and a half of monopoly and splendid, unblushing corruption they had inch by inch pared the powers both of the Crown and of the smaller squirearchy. In the latter eighteenth century, in their hunger for ever more land, they had even destroyed the English peasantry. They were the most accomplished and cultured aristocracy the world has ever seen: by their great houses and avenues, their libraries and noble possessions and their likenesses limned by Reynolds or Gainsborough, one can see the manner of men they were. They left their mark on English literature and art as the Athenian aristocracy did on that of ancient Greece—a mark that was both lovely and imperishable. They increased the wealth and power of their country beyond measure, extended her dominions into every sea, gave her arts and industries that enriched the human race for generations, and confronted by superior force, humbled by their inspired use of English courage and manhood the tyranny alike of Grand

[1] "Is it true," Queen Victoria is reported to have asked the last great Whig, Lord John Russell, "that you hold that a subject is justified in certain circumstances in disobeying his Sovereign?" "Speaking to a sovereign of the House of Hanover, your Majesty," he replied, "I can only say that I suppose it is."

[2] When, pale and tremulous, she took her sceptre and declared before the crowded Abbey, "I have it and none shall wrest it from me," even the misanthropic Jeremiah, Carlyle, uttered a grudging blessing.

Monarque, Revolutionary Tribune and Military Empire.
They had almost untrammelled power; they gambled, hunted, drank and whored, they feared no man, they did what was good in their own eyes, yet they did it with some measure of moderation and restraint. In this they differed from other tyrants and were like the ancient Athenians. By the time our chapter of English history begins, they were already past their prime and starting to decline. One sees them in the tell-tale pages of Mr. Creevey: with their rentals multiplied out of all measure by improved agriculture and urban expansion,[1] but already divorced by their staggering wealth from that close contact with reality and their humbler fellow citizens which had enabled their forebears to obtain power. Their ruling passion was the chase. Their tragedy was that they were getting spoilt by their own excessive wealth and power. Such a one was the great Lambton of Durham—a man who in his lightning moods beat his footmen, insulted his guests and declaimed against the very privileges which enabled him to do these things with impunity. He was called King Jog having once remarked that a man could always "jog along" on £70,000 a year.

At its best the ruling caste was exemplified in the Duke of Wellington. The younger son of a music-loving, dilettante lord, a colonel at twenty-four and a major-general at thirty-three, privilege—unasked and unsought—had enabled him to turn a forlorn Iberian adventure into one of the most glorious chapters of British military history, to fling back the hordes of advancing Revolution and humble Napoleon himself on the field of Waterloo. All this had happened before his forty-seventh year; since then he had served his country as selflessly in the senate as in the field. Now at the age of seventy-one he was the greatest public figure in the nation. Without any of the arts that sway popular opinion—which he unreservedly despised—he had accustomed himself from his earliest years to a fearlessness in speech that took the form of a literal and uncompromising truth on every occasion. Eight years before at the time of the Reform Bill—a measure he had opposed in the teeth of popular frenzy on the grounds that sooner or later it must lead to a suicidal scramble for power—he had had his windows broken by the very mob who a little while before had acclaimed him as the victor of Waterloo. But he was

[1] Those of the Shakerleys, a typical north country family, increased tenfold between 1760 and 1830.

equally indifferent to the adulation and the abuse of the multitude: his steady heart valued only the respect of his fellow aristocrats, the preservation of the national heritage which he had fought for, and the understanding and society of lively and beautiful women. He liked only the best. For the second-rate and the unformed he had nothing but disdain. Even the hardbitten, hard-used men who had fought under his command on the battlefields of Spain and Flanders he sometimes spoke of as the scum of the earth.

Over himself and all he did he exercised an iron mastery, long rendered second nature by proud tradition and unceasing practice. He devoted that mastery without reserve to the service of his country. He had one political principle: that the King's government must at all costs be carried on. He had one unfailing rule: that the work of the day must be done in the day. Despite the radical Brougham's ill-tempered remark that Westminster Abbey was yawning for him, the lingering final act of his long life was one of unbroken glory. When he appeared at the Hullah choral concert at Exeter Hall in 1842, the choir stopped singing and the whole audience rose, cheering and waving handkerchiefs to salute "the great old man . . . now the idol of the people. It was grand and affecting," wrote an onlooker, "and seemed to move everybody but himself."

Such men were cold in their Olympian calm and detachment; passionate like all their countrymen in their robust vitality and the intensity of their personal feelings. Aristocratic statesmen reproaching one another on the floor of the House did not at times restrain their tears: and a burst of momentary indignation could create life-long and unappeasable enmities. In 1828, Wellington, then Prime Minister, fought a duel because a fellow peer in the heat of political controversy had charged him with corruption. Lord George Bentinck was reported to have lost £27,000 in a single race: Jack Mytton—climax of English aristocratic eccentricity—went out for a bet stark naked on a winter's night to shoot duck and drank a bottle of port before breakfast. The breed was as vigorous in its loves as in its hates and wagers: another Prime Minister was cited as co-respondent in the Divorce Courts when approaching the age of sixty. A great lady in her eighties, asked by her son-in-law when a woman ceased to feel passion, replied, " You must ask a woman older than I am." Intellects were as tough as passions, strength; natural and quite unconscious, was the distinguishing mark of the race.

Even at its worst—and sometimes in men like the Marquis of Hertford, Thackeray's Lord Steyne and Disraeli's Monmouth, it was very bad indeed—the standard of that aristocracy was bound up with a sense of *noblesse oblige*. They were landowners and they were hereditary legislators, and as both they had traditional duties to perform which they felt they could not leave undone without shaming themselves and their caste. " The Duke of Rutland," wrote Greville, "is as selfish a man as any of his class —that is, he never does what he does not like, and spends his whole life in a round of such pleasures as suits his taste, but he is neither a foolish nor a bad man ; and partly from a sense of duty, partly from inclination, he devotes time and labour to the interest and welfare of the people who live and labour on his estate. He is a Guardian of a very large Union, and he not only attends regularly the meetings of the Poor Law Guardians every week or fortnight, and takes an active part in their proceedings, but he visits those paupers who receive out-of-door relief, sits and converses with them, invites them to complain to him if they have anything to complain of, and tells them that he is not only their friend but their representative at the assembly of Guardians, and it is his duty to see that they are nourished and protected." His fellow Duke of Richmond made it his business to visit the sick room of the Workhouse of which he was Guardian when cholera and typhus were raging among the inmates: he had been in the army, he said, and did not fear these contagions.

The English aristocracy and the country gentry ruled by virtue of the fact that they were the focus on which the national society centred. Wherever they did so—in the village, in the small country town, in London—their position seemed strong and assured. Wherever that focus was lacking—in the great industrial cities and on the absentee estates of dispossessed Ireland —aristocracy was already in eclipse and decay. But it still kept a substantial measure of its ancient hold on the mind of England. In its salons in London the intelligentsia were still welcome: middle-class Mr. Macaulay might talk like ten parrots and a chime of bells but he took his place by right of intellect among the beeches and princely patronage of Bowood and in the rooms of Holland House. "The world has never seen and never will see again," wrote Greville, "anything like Holland House." In that society almost everybody who was conspicuous, remarkable or agreeable was expected automatically to bear a part.

. . . .

The instrument of authority through which the landed classes governed was the House of Commons. Since the seventeenth century, the greater landowners had preferred to rule through the lower House in preference to their own. In this they showed unconscious wisdom, since those set in authority over the English usually in the end provoke their jealousy and incorrigible sense of independence. The power of the nobles, established over the Crown in 1688, had been preserved by being concealed. Throughout the eighteenth century the Lords did little more than record the decisions of the Commons. But they exercised their authority by their control of the electoral machinery of the old unreformed Parliament and by the presence of their relations and dependents in the lower House. Thus before the Reform Bill, the Duke of Buckingham alone is said to have controlled the votes of a dozen members of the House of Commons. Such a man had as much parliamentary power as a great city like Manchester to-day.

The Reform Bill of 1832, long delayed by the struggle with revolutionary France, broke this power. Henceforward it was not the landed magnates of England who controlled its urban franchise. They still continued to wield considerable interest, both through their presence in successive governments and through their family and social ties in the House of Commons. In Lord Melbourne's Whig Cabinet of 1835, eleven out of fourteen members were Lords or the sons of Lords: in its Tory successor of 1841 nine. But ultimate power was soon to pass into other hands—to the voters of the growing cities and towns of industrial England.

Not that it was yet realised. The £10 householders enfranchised in 1832 scarcely constituted a revolutionary body. They were a respectable and to those of superior station who troubled to approach them rightly, an even deferential body, as Macaulay, deprived of Lord Lansdowne's rotten borough of Calne by the Reform Bill, discovered when he contested Leeds in 1832. "My leading friends," he wrote to his sister, "are very honest, substantial manufacturers. They feed me on roast-beef and Yorkshire pudding: at night they put me into capital bedrooms; and the only plague which they give me is that they are always begging me to mention some food or wine for which I have a fancy, or some article of comfort and convenience which I may wish them to procure." The wealth, power and culture of an ancient and complex community continued to be represented by those who possessed them. In 1840 nobody in Parliament, and few outside, would have questioned the propriety of this.

But, though this attitude to the art of Government was subconsciously held by almost every member of the two ruling assemblies, they were far from all of them admitting to it. The prevailing majority in the House of Commons was Whig, and it was the unspoken philosophy of the Whigs that property should be maintained and their own importance preserved by a liberal advocacy of advanced and popular sentiments. Seven years before they had brought to an end a long period of Tory predominance by championing the cause of parliamentary reform, which they had represented as the sure cure for the grave social and economic troubles from which the lower orders in the new industrial towns were suffering. As a result, after a brief period of furious agitation, an electorate of 300,000 had been discreetly widened into a slightly less submissive one of about 800,000.

Though to many timorous folk the Reform Bill of 1832 seemed the prelude to bloody revolution, the new electors, like the old, continued to return men of substance to the House of Commons. Nor had the change in the system of representation brought about any improvement in the condition of the poor. The popular force of the Whigs was therefore expended, and they remained in office with the cynical support of a small body of Radical reformers for no better reason than that the Tories were not quite strong enough to turn them out. Neither party had any strong basis of support in the country, which tended to distrust them both, the Tories because they were supposed to oppose all change—a view which their opponents lost no chance of fostering—and the Whigs because they were popularly suspected, with perhaps greater justice, of using office to feather their own nests. "What son, what brother, what nephew, what cousin, what remote unconjectural relative in the genesis of the Greys," wrote a contemporary of the family of the Premier who had carried the Reform Bill, "has not fastened his limpet to the rock of the national expenditure?" The civil service, such as it was, was still staffed almost exclusively by the fortunate nominees of high political personages, and opportunities for nepotism were considerable. They were almost universally taken.

As put by one of their supporters, the object of the Whigs was to remain in office, keep down their dangerous Radical allies and gradually and safely bring about such reforms as should end—though no one was clear how—the discontent of the industrial working-classes. The only object of the Tories seemed to be to turn out the Whigs, though they had little really to gain save office by doing so. Every few years a general election took place, and the party battle was then transferred to the constituencies. Here it took on a form peculiarly English, with mobs processing through the streets with flags and banners, with party devices and mottos and special tunes—"Bonnets of Blue" for the Tories and "Old Dan Ducker" for the Whigs—with companies of hired boxers and cabmen and paid toughs to intimidate the electors, with free beer and breakfasts at the expense of the candidate in every tavern, with the wooden hustings on which fine gentlemen who sought the suffrages of a free people grinned and suffered, while rotten eggs, oranges and rude shouts whizzed over, under and sometimes at them. This popular saturnalia, which was the special prerogative of the poorest and roughest elements of the community, served no apparent electoral purpose, for only a comparatively few quiet and well-conducted persons possessed the vote and elections were decided mainly by local territorial influence and the state of current opinion among the reading classes.[1] But it served the ancient English purpose of letting off steam in a rough human way, and it helped to give uneducated people a sense that they were taking part in the government of the country without any of the disturbing consequences of their actually doing so. It gave a great deal of happiness and excitement, not to the rich and discreet, but to the uncalculating majority. It was becoming an increasing annoyance to respectable citizens of a liberal and reforming turn, who took every opportunity of attacking its abuses and trying to do away with it in the name of purer and more rational politics. For this reason, despite all its noise, roughness and drunkenness, it was already a dying institution.

From the bacchic tumult of the unenfranchised multitude which attended its election, Parliament itself was far removed. No boisterous breath of democracy would have been tolerated

---

[1] Bribery, though universally practised, had a far smaller effect on eighteenth and early nineteenth century elections than is popularly supposed. For one thing, the bribes of the rival candidates tended to cancel each other out.

in the House of Commons which was still almost the most exclusive club in England. A number of northern manufacturers and eccentrics with radical hobby horses were tolerated with humorous or contemptuous resignation by the well-groomed majority, who viewed them as they would have viewed the few odd slovens and cranks at a fashionable public school. The House was a place where the gentlemen of England sat or lolled at their ease, with feet stretched out before them, arms akimbo, and top hats tilted over their eyes or pushed comfortably to the back of their heads while papers and blue books were strewn idly on the floor before them. When, as often happened, the course of debate flowed languidly, many would stretch themselves out on the benches and sleep or watch the familiar proceedings of their House with half-closed eyes, some face downwards, others with legs in the air. Honourable Members could not see anything incongruous in such a method of conducting their business: the House was as much their property as their own library or club, and to have questioned what they did there would have been the highest presumption. Only within the last few years had the right of the public to read first-hand reports of its debates in the press been tacitly admitted by the provision of a press gallery. Centuries of struggle and, more recently, of unchallenged supremacy had given the House its arrogant and serene assurance: the government was upon its shoulders and it carried the burden with nonchalance.

On its benches sat many men of talent and one or two of genius, for any male member of the governing class who possessed ability could if he wished be sure of a seat. The system put him there and kept him there without effort on his part. He was thus able to apply all the powers of his mind, fortified by the most cultured and scholarly education afforded on earth, to the art of politics and the parliamentary game. Of such was Lord John Russell, a cadet of the great Whig House of Bedford, who, in the absense of the Prime Minister in the Lords, led the Commons. He was a sharp, delicate little man with a mild voice and great dignity of manner, who somehow contrived to appeal to the imagination of the middle classes. This was the more curious because he was a scholar of distinction with a taste in epigram, and like all his race something of a crank. His particular political hobby was reform of the franchise, which his colleagues liked to think had been settled for all time by the measure of

1832 but which retained for John Russell a personal and almost mystical fascination. Whenever this subject came before a reluctant House, he would rise to considerable heights of fervour: those were the hours when "languid Johnny glowed to glorious John." He was never, however, a master orator: indeed since the death of Canning ten years before, parliamentary eloquence, which had reached its zenith in the days of Fox and Pitt, had been in something of a decline.

The first parliamentarian in the House, though his greatest triumphs were still ahead of him, was Robert Peel, the leader of the Tories. The son of a famous cotton manufacturer, he had graduated into the legislative class by way of Harrow and Oxford. For twenty years he had made it his business to master the legislative requirements of the new industrial interest, which still remained so much of a mystery to the country gentlemen who formed the bulk of his fellow-members. In doing so he had made himself indispensable to the Tory Party whose captaincy he had taken over from the Duke of Wellington. His name was already identified in the public mind with the smart new constabulary force which he had given to London during his tenure of the Home Office. He was a fine if rather uninspiring speaker, who occasionally repelled by his lack of aristocratic grace but who always spoke from a profound and well-digested knowledge of his subject. In this respect he had no equal in the House. Outside in the country his bluntness was well liked: it was said that when Minister to King George IV, that master of courtly etiquette, repelled by his awkward manners, had addressed him with a "Damn you, sir, don't stand there pawing the air, put your hands in your pockets," only to be answered with a nettled "Damn you, sir, I have no pockets!"

At Peel's side on the front Opposition Bench was his lieutenant and successor, Lord Stanley. The eldest son of the House of Derby, he was heir to one of the greatest fortunes in the world, created almost automatically in half a century through the fabulous rise in the land values of industrial Lancashire. He belonged to a family which, it was said, did not marry but only contracted alliances, and he was by universal acclaim the second orator in the House of Commons—the "Rupert of Debate"—and a classical translator of no mean order. But in his native Lancashire, or in the betting-room at Newmarket, chaffing and shouting among a crowd of jockies and blacklegs, he was, with the eccentric perversity of the English, a good deal of an overgrown schoolboy—"a lively, rattling sportsman apparently devoted to racing and rabbit shooting, gay, boisterous, almost rustic in his manners, without refinement." Seeing and hearing him among his country friends and neighbours, it was difficult to believe oneself in the presence of the haughty aristocrat and scholar who, at his Peel's side, marshalled the gentlemen of England against the Whigs and Radicals.

In contrast was Lord Melbourne, the Whig Prime Minister. Of all who had held supreme office, none was ever so thoroughly a man of the world. He never dined at home, talked with a rollicking laugh and refused to take anything—even his own loss of office —too seriously. It was his creed that it was best to try to do no good and then one could do no harm: his favourite remark, "Why not leave it alone?" He had been a great roué in his day and was still a favourite with the ladies: the escapades of his wife, Lady Caroline Lamb, had once set the whole kingdom talking. But in his old age he had reformed his manners and curbed his speech—which was of the old English School—to suit the tastes and needs of a bread and butter miss promoted from the governess room to the throne.[1] Under his easy and accomplished teaching his little sovereign had developed with almost startling rapidity. Her marriage to Prince Albert in 1840 transferred her education into other hands. It was characteristic of aristocratic England that the Prince's painstaking German ways met at first with little favour. It was freely noted that the royal couple rose early on the first morning of their honeymoon: "strange that the bridal night should be so short," wrote the Clerk of the Council, "I told Lady Palmerston that this was not the way to provide us with a Prince of Wales."[2]

To express criticism of what one did not approve, and in no unmeasured terms, were the prerogative and habit of an English aristocrat. The *genus* held strong views on a great variety of subjects and never hesitated to voice them. They had their own standards, many of them eccentric and peculiar, but such as they were they seldom modified them. They saw no reason why they should. "They are born wicked and grow up worse," was a Whig lady's uncompromising reply when asked by her children

---

[1] ". . . a little tit of 18 made all at once into a Queen." Creevey to Miss Ord, 5th Aug., 1837. *Creevey's Life and Times (ed. J. Gore), 427.*
[2] *Greville.*

whether Tories were born wicked or merely grew up that way. Passionate, instinctive and, when action was demanded, unreflecting, such beings never doubted themselves or their right to do and say whatever they thought proper.

. . . .

The gentlemen of England carried the same downright and frank assurance into their administration of public affairs. "Goose! goose! goose!" wrote Palmerston across a diplomatic despatch. The great Foreign Secretary treated what he regarded as the literary lapses of his country's representatives abroad like an outraged schoolmaster: one received back a despatch with an injunction that it was "to be re-written in blacker ink," while another was forbidden to use the un-English gallicism "corps diplomatique" and reminded that the expression "to resume" did not mean "to sum up" or "to recapitulate" but to "take back." "Sentences," he wrote on another occasion, "should . . . begin with the nominative, go on with the verb and end with the accusative."[1] Such men were accustomed to leave no doubt as to what they meant in the minds of those they ruled.

In all this they represented, not inadequately, the people of rural England whose homely lands gave them their titles and wealth. They were rough and ready in their ways, brave and independent. Cock fights and cock-shies, dog fights, bull and bear baiting—though these were already dying out in most parts of the country—"purring" matches in Lancashire where men and women vied in kicking each other with clogs, bespoke the love of contest for its own sake that ran right through the nation. At Oxford sporting undergraduates, in ancient rooms lined with pictures of prize-fighters, race-horses and dogs, would amuse themselves by opening a cageful of rats for their terriers to worry.

Boxing was the national sport *in excelsis*. Boys were brought up on tales of the classic exponents of the Science—of Tom Cribb, Gentleman Jackson, Gully who rose to the House of Commons, Mendoza and Molineux the negro. Young noblemen had their pet prize-fighters: every village its "best man," who had won his title in some homeric contest with his predecessor. There were no Queensberry rules and men fought with their bare fists, sometimes to the death. In June, 1830, the Irishman, Simon Byrne, and the Scottish champion, Sandy McKay, met in the

[1] *H. C. F. Bell, Lord Palmerston, I, 261.*

Buckinghamshire village of Hanslope: in the forty-seventh round the Scot fell unconsicious to the ground never to rise again. His victor perished in the ring a few years later at the end of ninety-nine rounds.

Game to the death, such men bore little malice. Bad blood was not allowed to grow rancid: it was let after the fashion of the day on the green sward. A "mill" brought all the neighbours running to see fair play and courage: afterwards the combatants were ready enough to be friends. There was something intensely good-humoured about that open-air, fighting England. It was rough but it was healthy. Borrow has left us a picture of an old prize fighter, his battles over, keeping open house in his "public" down Holborn way, "sharp as winter, kind as spring . . . There sits the yeoman at the end of his long room, surrounded by his friends. Glasses are filled and a song is the cry, and a song is sung well suited to the place; it finds an echo in every heart— fists are clenched, arms are waved, and the portraits of the mighty fighting men of yore, Broughton and Slack and Ben, which adorn the walls appear to smile grim approbation, whilst many a manly voice joins in the bold chorus:

> "' Here's a health to old honest John Bull,
>   When he's gone we shan't find such another,
>   And with hearts and with glasses brim full,
>   We will drink to old England his mother.'"

The independence of the national type matched its pugnacity. For all the deference of traditional England to its superiors, it was a deference strictly based on established right and custom. It yielded little to claims based on anything else. A man owed certain duties to Church, state and society to be performed according to his station: when they had been fulfilled, he owed no others. Lord Palmerston, in attendance as Foreign Secretary at Windsor Castle, rode as befitted his office beside her Majesty's carriage: when, however, she embarked on Virginia Water he did not accompany her but left the royal barge to row about in a dinghy, not choosing to miss his daily exercise. The skilled craftsmen of Birmingham disposed of their hours of labour in a similar spirit: when they had earned enough, they would take a day or even a week off to drink. Even the clerks of the Bank of England—though the new powers that were beginning to rule

English society were fast taming them[1]—insisted on their ancient rights of private trading and of receiving tips from clients, kept shops and pubs and drank spirits in office hours. For according to the old English reckoning a man who did his duty had a right to do it as he pleased.

Any interference by the State not established by prescription was viewed with abhorrence. This explains the ease with which the urban and radical doctrine of *laissez-faire* captured the mind of the older England. A magistrate told some poor pavement vendors, arrested by an officious policeman for selling water-cress in Marylebone High Street, that they had as good a right to sell their wares as other people to dispose of anything else. When Income Tax, abolished after the Napoleonic Wars amid the loudest cheering ever recorded in the history of the House of Commons, was reintroduced in 1842 at 7d. in the £ it was regarded as an almost intolerable inquisition which struck at the freedom and privacy of every respectable Englishman. "Private affairs must be divulged," commented a newspaper, "private feelings outraged—malicious curiosity gratified —poor shrinking pride, be it never so honest, humbled and put to the blush—deceit and the meanness of petty trickery, encouraged in evasion—and much appalling immorality spread with the abandonment of truth. Many a gentleman will sicken over the forms he has to bear with; and many a tradesman will become either ruined or a rogue."

The more rustic the scene, the stronger this almost exaggerated passion for independence. Fred Bettesworth, farmer's boy, wishing to see the world, left a master with whom he was perfectly happy without a word and waited on Staines Bridge till he found a carter to give him new employment. A year or two later, sooner than be tied, and feeling he had "a kind o' roamin' commission," he left another master and tramped forty miles into Sussex to see the country.[2] Every summer for many years he did the same. In the villages of Whittlebury Forest, almost every householder was a poacher: a decade or two back when the game-keepers of the enclosing lords had failed in the face of local opinion to make an arrest for nutting in the forest, the whole village of Silverstone turned out armed with staves to repel

---

[1]Their traditional holidays, forty-two a year in 1830, were reduced by 1834 to four. —*Early Victorian England* 1, 178.
[2]W. Notestein, *English Folk* 40.

the Bow Street runners in pitched battle and assert their ancient privileges. A yeoman farmer of the same place left a sum of money to cover his grave with spikes pointing upwards, swearing that he had never been trodden on when alive and would not be so when dead.

Such a type was well content with its own forms of life: it had no wish to oppress others but had small use for foreigners or their ways. At the Egham races William IV called out to Lord Albemarle to tell him the name of a passing dandy whose was face unfamiliar. Albemarle replied that it was Count D'Orsay. "I had no notion it was," replied the King: then, mustering all his energy, gave vent to the natural feelings of an honest English sailor in a loud "Damn him." "If the French attempt to bully and intimidate us," wrote the Foreign Secretary to the Prime Minister in 1840, "the only way of meeting their menaces is by quietly telling them we are not afraid, and by showing them, first, that we are stronger than they are and, secondly, that they have more vulnerable points than we have." And to the British Ambassador in Paris, the same organ voice of England spoke more expressly, "If Thiers should again hold to you the language of menace . . . convey to him in the most friendly and in-offensive manner possible, that if France . . . begins a war, she will to a certainty lose her ships, colonies and commerce before she sees the end of it; that her army of Algiers will cease to give her anxiety and that Mehemet Ali"—the French protégé— "will just be chucked into the Nile."[1]

To a man like Palmerston—and his very Englishness made him the idol of England—abuse of the foreigner was no more than a national prerogative which only a scoundrelly trouble-seeker would take amiss. When he favoured his Devonshire constituents with his views on French colonisation he was cheered to the echo.

> "There is a contrast of which we may have reason to be proud, between the progress of our arms in the East, and the operations which a neighbouring power, France, is now carrying on in Africa. The progress of the British Army in Asia has been marked by a scrupulous reference to justice, an inviolable respect for property, an abstinence from any-thing which could tend to wound the feelings and prejudices of the people . . . The different system pursued in Africa

[1] *Bell, Palmerston, I, 303-4.*

by the French has been productive of very different results; there the French army, I am sorry to say, is tarnished by the character of their operations. They sally forth unawares on the villagers of the country; they put to death every man who cannot escape by flight, and they carry off into captivity the women and children (*shame! shame!*). They carry away every head of cattle, every sheep, and every horse, and they burn what they cannot carry off. The crop on the ground and the corn in the granaries are consumed by the fire."[1]

The leading article of a popular weekly commented even more freely, as was its right and duty, on the glaring delinquencies of the foreigner.

"Selfishness, inconsistency, tyranny, caprice, and insolence characterise the whole bearing of France. . . . We have the half consolation, half disgust of knowing that France arrogates herself, whenever selfishness dictates, the false pride and the bad principle of being always in the wrong."[2]

Yet though often absurd and offensive in expression, the proud imperialism of England was founded on a very real love of liberty and on a certain innate if vigorous humanity which the Englishman, and the English gentleman in particular, possessed as his distinguishing trait. The nation which had led the world in abolishing the slave trade and forbidding slavery in its dominions, which had produced the pioneers of prison reform and of every branch of humanitarianism, had at least a *prima facie* right to lecture others. When English statesmen rebuked harassed foreign rulers, with a tithe of their wealth, security and opportunity, for aggression towards their weaker neighbours or oppression of their subjects, it was because the English of all classes thoroughly disliked aggression and oppression. They might in their rough and vigorous way indulge in a certain amount of it themselves but it was nearly always unconscious. If the already vast empire of Britain continued to expand, it was more than arguable that in a world where all virtue is comparative the outward march of the Union Jack brought enduring benefits that easily compensated for any temporary suffering and injustice. Palmerston, in a speech in the House in 1841, well expressed this feeling.

[1] *Bell, Palmerston, I, 316-17.* [2] *Illustrated London News, I, 523 (24th Dec., 1842).*

"As long as England shall ride pre-eminent on the ocean of human affairs, there can be none whose fortunes shall be so shipwrecked, there can be none whose condition shall be so desperate and forlorn that they may not cast a look of hope towards the light that beams from hence; and though they may be beyond the reach of our power, our moral support and our sympathy shall cheer them in their adversity. . . . But if ever by the assault of overpowering enemies, or by the errors of her misguided sons, England should fall, . . . for a long period of time, would the hope of the African . . . be buried in the darkness of despair. I know well that in such case, Providence would, in due course of time, raise up some other nation to inherit our principles, and to imitate our practice. But . . . I do not know any nation that is now ready in this respect to supply our place."[1]

.   .   .   .

It was because it had so strong a sense of its own strength, sanity and inherent decency that the England of character and tradition felt it had so little to learn of foreigners. Gladstone loved to tell the story of the dying Admiral who, when assured by his spiritual pastor of the glories of Heaven, cried out, "Aye, aye—it may be as you say—but ould England for me!" The patriotism of the English was founded on their unbroken past. They felt themselves to be an historical people, "generation linked with generation by ancestral reputation, by tradition, by heraldry." In the remoter parts of the country all shared in this feeling: the first Lord Redesdale in his *Memoirs* recalled an old peasant couple who lived in the tower of a ruined manor house at Mitford. "Their beautifully chiselled features, no less than their proud bearing and dignified manners, might have befitted the descendants of crusaders. She was always clad in an old-fashioned lilac print gown, with the square of shepherd's plaid crossed over the bosom. Her delicate, high-bred face, with blue eyes, still bright and beautiful, was framed in the frills of an immaculate mutch covering her ears and almost hiding the snow-white hair: her small feet were always daintily cased in grey worsted stockings and scrupulously blacked shoes. She must have been nearly eighty years old when I used to sit with her in her kitchen —the aged dame on one side of the hearth, the little boy on the other, listening to her old-world tales of the past glories of

[1] *H. C. F. Bell, Lord Palmerston, I, 232.*

Mitford. There were always a few old-fashioned flowers in the kitchen parlour, and she herself sweetly reminded one of lavender. The good soul was always stout for the rights and honour of the family."[1]

Such folk, like the old England they belonged to, were living on the momentum of a past tradition. It was now dying and in many places already dead. Its purpose had been to produce virtuous men and women. It had been rooted in the Christian morality of the medieval church which, believing that the purpose of life was to save and prepare man's soul for Heaven, taught that worldly laws and institutions should be based as far as possible on the gospel of Christ. The medieval state—though its practise fell far short of its theory—had therefore condemned usury, forbidden divorce and offences against the family, and endeavoured to fix a "just" level of wages and prices and an "honest" standard of workmanship. It had done so not only to protect the public from greedy egotists but because it was believed that the practise of anti-social activities debased the human soul.

A society founded on such principles did not, of course, succeed in establishing the rule of righteousness on earth. But it made it easier for the ordinary citizen to live a Christian life and taught him to revere just and honest dealing. When the corruptions inherent in the medieval ecclesiastical system resulted in the Reformation, the island English—more conservative than their fellow protestants of the Continent—carried the old ideal into the secular organisation of the new state. The idea of moral justice continued to haunt the English mind. The king as head of the national church at his coronation still swore to "do justice, stop the growth of iniquity, protect the Holy Church of God, help and defend widows and orphans, restore things that are gone to decay, maintain the things that are restored, punish and reform what is amiss and confirm what is in good order." For nearly three hundred years after the repudiation of papal authority, a protestant but Christian Parliament, though with diminishing faith and vigour, continued to enact moral and sumptuary laws, to forbid usury, regulate labour and fix prices. For it was held that the business of the statesman was to make England strong, healthy and content by rendering her people so. His first consideration was the elevation and maintenance of the national character.

[1] *Lord Redesdale, Memoirs, I, 13-14.*

Yet the momentum behind such paternal legislation had long been running down. Among the intellectual leaders of the nation, faith in a divinely appointed order was giving way to a new belief in the unaided power of human reason. Men, it was felt, could live best, not by adherence to traditional standards of aggregate wisdom and justice, but by their own sharp wits. And with the weakening of the authority of the central government that followed the defeat of the Crown by the aristocracy, the rich and powerful grew restive at any interference with their freedom of action. In every place where the old forms of organised life were giving place to new—in the capital, in the ports and the industrial towns—the vigorous and stubborn Anglo-Saxon temperament, so tenacious for personal rights and jealous of freedom, responded to appeals to shake off the trammels of the feudal and priestly past.

Thus over an ever-widening circle the will and interest of the individual came to be regarded as more important than Christian justice and the community. The profit motive superseded the communal conscience as the ultimate arbiter of national policy. The consequence was quickly reflected in legislation and administration. Yet in the countryside where the old forms of an ordered life still lingered, there was an instinctive conviction, or prejudice, as some called it, that man was more important than money and moral health than reason. The state might divest itself of moral authority: but the individual conscience, moulded by the unbroken centuries of Christian rule, remained. Whatever bagmen might practise and economists preach, the ordinary Englishman clung to an ideal that had nothing to do with profit-making and little with abstract reason—that of a "gentleman." He most valued the man whose word was as good as his bond, whose purse was ever open to the needy, whose heart was above calculation and meanness, and who was fearless toward the strong and tender and chivalrous towards the weak—in other words a Christian. When Squire Brown sent his son to Rugby, he asked himself before giving him his final injunctions what he wanted of him:

"Shall I tell him to mind his work, and say he's sent to school to make himself a good scholar? Well, but he isn't sent to school for that—at any rate, not for that mainly. I don't care a straw for Greek particles, or the digamma, no more does his mother. . . . If he'll only turn out a brave, helpful, truth-telling Englishman, and a gentleman and a Christian, that's all we want."[1]

A few years later, Tom, unconsciously answering his father's question, defined his scholastic ambition as being, "I want to leave behind me the name of a fellow who never bullied a little boy or turned his back on a big one." It was still that of nine Englishmen out of ten.

.   .   .   .

The forms of an organised religion, though increasingly neglected in the towns, helped to keep alive this noble temper in the country. In most villages the Church was still the centre of communal life, its Sunday service, with its gathering of the rustic hierarchy, churchyard gossip and interchange of news, the chief social event of the week. Until the old string and brass choirs were superseded by the new-fangled organs and harmoniums, the village played as great a part in the exercise of communal worship as the parson. Standing each Sunday in the west gallery these rustic instrumentalists, with their copper key-bugles, trombones, clarionets, trumpets, flutes, fiddles and bass viol, represented a folk tradition that was older than squire or clergy. Yet for all their tenacious clinging to old forms and ritual—"it allus has bin sung an' sung it shall be"—the string choir was doomed and the conservative democracy of the English village with it. It was suppressed by the reforming vicar just as the landed peasantry of the old unenclosed parish had been by the reforming squire a generation or two before. The effects of this iconoclasm were not yet fully perceived; it took long to transform the habits and character of a tenacious people. But the chain once broken could not be repaired.

Already in many villages the established church had lost its hold on the rustic heart. Pluralism, though recently abolished by ecclesiastical reformers, had long accustomed country folk to the spectacle of neglected churches,[2] perfunctory services and clergymen who seemed more interested in foxes and sometimes in the bottle than the cure of souls. An old man living at the end of the last war could recall a clergyman who was so drunk at a

[1] T. Hughes, *Tom Brown's Schooldays.*
[2] Edward Fitzgerald told Tennyson in 1843 that he always wore his thickest great-coat in his parish church as the fungi grew in great numbers about the communion table.—*Letters and Remains of Edward Fitzgerald, I, 119.*

funeral that he had to be held by his coat-tails to prevent him
falling into the grave: another who dropped heavily asleep on
the cushion in the middle of his own sermon. Left to themselves
the parishioners of such men lapsed into a strong native paganism
that the Church, even in the age of faith, had never wholly
eradicated. A heathen folk-lore and tradition that died hard took
the place of a half-hearted theology. More than one eighteenth-
century church was clandestinely dedicated to the Devil by the
local morris-dancers. If many through the apathy of their
spiritual pastors had ceased to believe in Christ, they had not
ceased to believe in his great adversary: "Old Scraper" could
almost be heard by the imaginative on moonlight nights patter-
ing through the undergrowth. Every village had its tales of
ghosts and witches, of bygone murders and haunted cross-
roads and gibbets. Many of these old wives' tales had a ring
that went back to the past of fairy-lore and border ballad:

> "One lonely night, as I sat high,
> Instead of one there two passed by.
> The boughs did bend, my soul did quake,
> To see the hole that Fox did make."

In such an atmosphere, no country child could grow up wholly
lacking in a sense of poetry.

Christian as apart from pagan faith among humbler folk was
by 1840 more often to be found in the Methodist congregations
which had spread like wildfire through the countryside since
Wesley's missionary journeys of the previous century as well as in
the Baptist and Independent congregations of the older nonconformity. It was often of a somewhat primitive and uncritical
kind but made up in fervour and homely force what it lacked in
subtlety. Incidentally it had a stimulating effect on the Establishment, provoking a strong rivalry between "Church and
King" and "Dissent." To the adherents of the former the
"Methodies" were "long eared 'uns,"—ignorant and cantankerous
fanatics—while to the Methodists, churchgoers seemed little
better than damned. Yet even the most enthusiastic adherent
of the meeting-house still preferred to be buried like his father
in the churchyard. The historic community of the village was
not quite dead.

Its dying flame burnt brightly at the traditional festivals of
the Christian and pastoral year still kept in the countryside. At

Christmas the mummers came round to hall and farm-house with their age-long drama and unchanging characters—

"A room, a room, for me and my broom,
And all my merry men beside,
I must have room and I *wull* have room
All round this Christmastide."

On Oak Apple Day the inns were decorated with oak boughs and the village lads wore oak apples in their buttonholes and cried "Shickshack" to those who wore none. There were morris-dancers in duck trousers and white ribboned shirts and handker-chiefs at Whitsun, the summer Sunday School Treat when the gifts of home-brewed wine were divided by the teachers into two classes, the less alcoholic to be drunk by the children and the stronger by themselves when the children had gone to bed. Many villages had their annual Feast—a relic of the old pagan Whitsun Ale—when the lads and lasses out on service came home, the travelling fiddler appeared, the inns were crowded and the Feast Ale tapped. Akin to it was the farm Harvest Home, eagerly looked forward to by many a hungry labourer, with its lit barns and groaning tables, its "churchwardens" and beer jugs, its traditional songs—"The Jolly Ploughman," "The Fox has gone through the Town O!", "Poor old Horse"—and its crowning toast, "Here's health to master and missus, the founders of this feast!"

The pride and patriotism that sprang from these things, however naïve and even pathetic they may appear to modern minds, attached not only to England but to every separate part of it. A countryman was thrice citizen of his country, of his shire, of his native town or village. All three were steeped in accumu-lated tradition and custom. Seldom has England been more rich in the proud consciousness of her history than in 1840. Every country place had its own peculiar memorials and celebrations and every place thought its own the best, yet recognised the validity of its neighbours'. The provincial capitals—York, Norwich, Exeter, Shrewsbury, Bristol—each had its own peculiar society, civic lore and culture: its special crafts, domestic indus-tries and style of architecture, its cherished monuments and legends, its theatre, assembly rooms and musical festival, its hereditary merchant and professional class and neighbouring gentry, in some places such as Norwich its own school of art.

The smaller towns and villages of England were as marked in their distinguishing differences. At Abbot's Bromley in Staffordshire on the first Monday after September 4th, the Deer Men with their hobby horses danced the Horn Dance in painted reindeer heads and ancient costumes of red and green. In May, at the Furry Festival at Helston, any person who would not join the dance and remained at work was set astride a pole and carried to the river there to leap or compound in cash for the good of the community.

> "Where are those Spaniards
> That made so great a boast, O?
> They shall eat the grey goose feather,
> And we will eat the roast, O!"

There was a wonderful wealth and diversity in the local manner of celebrating the great Christian, and still older than Christian feasts. On Christmas Eve in the villages of the New Forest libations of spiced ale were poured out to the orchards and meadows: at Huddersfield the children on their wassailing bore evergreens hung with oranges and apples:

> "We are not daily beggars
> That beg from door to door,
> But we are neighbours' children
> Whom you have seen before.

> "Call up the butler of this house,
> Put on his golden ring;
> Let him bring us a glass of beer,
> And the better we shall sing."

And after service on Christmas morning in many parts of the north country the whole people ran through the streets crying—

> "Ule! Ule! Ule! Ule!
> Three puddings in a pule,
> Crack nuts and cry Ule."

In Wiltshire Shrove Tuesday was kept by bands of children marching three times about the churches with joined hands.

In Suffolk the farm lass who could bring home a branch of haw-thorn in full blossom on May Day received a dish of cream for breakfast. At Polebrook, Northamptonshire, during the last days of April, the May Queen and her attendants gathered posies in the meadows and begged the loan of ribbons, handkerchiefs and dolls from their neighbours to carry on garlanded hoops round the village to a song that came out of the depths of antiquity. In other places they sang:

> "The life of man is but a span
> It flourishes like a flower,
> We are here to-day and gone to-morrow,
> And are dead in an hour.

> "The moon shines bright and the stars give a light
> A little before it is day,
> So God bless you all, both great and small,
> And send you a joyful May."

All this betokened a culture that was not founded on Courts and cities but on the green fields and the growing earth. Like a tree it spread upwards. Walking among the water meadows at Bemerton one could see its roots: the spire of Salisbury Cathedral tapered skywards out of the cup of the downs and the cottage folk spoke of a pious man named George Herbert whose grave was forgotten but whose books they still read. In men's hearts there dwelt a novel called the Past: its chapters were their own earliest memories, hallowed by repetition and loving association, and the tales their fathers and the old wives of the village had told them.

Like bees the country English gathered honey from the flowers of their own history. The combs in which they stored it were the manifold institutions in which they expressed their social life. Church and State were only the greatest of these—prototype and symbol of all the others. Every parish was an institution—a living organism from which successive generations derived purpose and inspiration. When the parish bounds were beaten each year the whole community attended in witness of its own existence: the beer-laden wagons, the rough practical jokes, the unchanging rituals and chants were the shrew-bread on the altar of Christian neighbourhood. A diary-keeping parish clerk records these homely pieties: "stopt on the mount

in the lane and cut X cross, put Osgood on end upon his head, and
done unto him as was necessary to be done by way of remembrance
. . . Old Kit Nation was turned on end upon his head and well
spanked in the corner of Northcroft and upon the Wash."[1]

So, too, were schools and charities, walking by ancient beacons
lit by the piety of men of old and tended by a long procession of
successors. The Blue Coat boys of Christ's Hospital passed
through the London streets in the belted gown of Edward VI's
England and in the knee-breeches and shining shoe buckles of that
of George I: the children of the parish school of St. Botolph's
Bishopsgate still wore silver badges and muffin caps. At Eton,
under elms planted in the days of Charles I, the boys, celebrating
the martial heroes of antiquity, kept the old feast of Montem—
the tenure by which the College held its domains. All that
human courage, quixotry and goodness had achieved in the long
sordid struggle of man against the stubborn forces of nature was,
however crudely and imperfectly, treasured and commemorated
as though to remind the successive generations of their continuing heritage and nobler destiny. Few could see unmoved the
heroic pageantry of the Trooping of the Colour or the great
annual spectacle of six thousand London Charity children assembled under the dome of St. Paul's, singing with that "honest old
English roughness that no man need feel ashamed of " while their
eyes shone with the thought of the feast before them. As after
the prayers thousands of glossy aprons fell simultaneously, it
seemed to one watching like the fall of snow.

It was not only its own tradition that England celebrated, but
those of the two great peoples of the ancient world—the Hebrew
and the Greek. Those who stood Sunday after Sunday in the
parish church identified the songs and faith of Zion with their
own rustic life. The manger in which Christ was born stood in
the byre where the friendly beasts of the field crowded on wintry
nights: the green pastures into which the Good Shepherd led his
flock were the meadows of home. Men who could not write
their names but whose memories were unimpaired, knew every
collect in the prayer book by heart and were as familiar with the
Bible names as with those of their own fields. So for the more
sophisticated the images of the classics were superimposed on
those of their own England: an Eton boy recalled his first May
Day walking by Fellow's Pond through a half-Grecian haze, "the

---

[1] W. E. Adams, Memoirs of a Social Atom, I, 54-6.

fairies tripping in rings on the turf, the dryads tempted out of their barken hiding-places, the water-nymphs making high festival on the silver flood."

Knowledge of the classics was still a universal passport. It opened the doors of intellectual society. On that solid foundation of common effort and allusion, the culture of a gentleman rested. Statesmen quoted Latin in the Commons and even on the hustings: and busy men of the world found relaxation in the evenings or on holiday in re-reading the authors of the old pagan world whom they had first encountered at school or college. Macaulay defined an independent scholar as one who read Plato with his feet on the fender. In the characters of the ancient world such men recognised themselves, their own failings and virtues. "I am reading Plutarch's lives," wrote Edward Fitzgerald, "one of the most delightful books I have ever read: he must have been a gentleman." The common experiences of life constantly recalled to such readers the reflections of their fellow men who had passed the same way under other skies many hundreds of years before.

"I took down a Juvenal," one of them wrote to a friend, "to look for a passage about the Loaded Wagon rolling through the Roman streets. I couldn't find it. Do you know where it is?"[1] The absorption of their degenerate descendants in cross-word puzzles and detective novels is a faint and attenuated reflection of this bygone passion. Sometimes the incongruity of it struck them with a glow of pleasure: "think," wrote one, "of the rocococity of a gentleman studying Seneca in the middle of February, 1844, in a remarkably damp cottage." The pleasure once acquired never deserted them, and death found them with their thumbed Homer or Horace by their side. Forty years later an English poet who had grown up with the century, crossing Lake Garda on a summer's evening, put into his native verse the innate love of his generation for the classical learning of his youth:

> "Row us out from Desenzano, to your Sirmione row!
> So they row'd, and there we landed—' O venusta Sirmio '—
> There to me thro' all the groves of olive in the summer
>   glow,
> There beneath the Roman ruin where the purple
>   flowers grow,

[1] *Letters and Literary Remains of Edward Fitzgerald*, I. 288.

> Came the ' *Ave atque Vale* ' of the Poet's hopeless woe,
> Tenderest of the Roman poets, nineteen hundred years
> ago,
> ' *Frater Ave atque Vale* '—as we wandered to and fro
> Gazing at the Lydian laughter of the Garda Lake below
> Sweet Catullus' all-but-island, olive-silvery Sirmio!"[1]

The great country houses with the classical colonnades and porticos and their parks recalling some gentle Sicilian or Thracian scene were a natural setting for these gentlemen scholars. Here the law of primogeniture afforded a nursery for the higher branches of the national culture. Their library walls were lined with the golden volumes of two centuries of English and more of classical thought and learning: the child who grew up in those stately rooms knew, subconsciously, that he was heir to the ages. Even when, as often happened, the eldest son abjured books for the superior charms of horse, rod and dog, it was almost certain that one or other of his numerous younger brothers would acquire in the freedom of his father's library the scholarly tastes that he would carry with him into a wider world.

.   .   .   .

Here in the country-house was the accumulated tradition not only of culture but of order. The life of a great country-house afforded a microcosm of the state: no fitter training ground could have been devised for those called upon by birth and wealth to rule. An English landed estate in the first half of the nineteenth century was a masterpiece of smooth and intricate organisation with its carefully-graded hierarchy of servants, indoor and out-door, and its machinery for satisfying most of the normal wants of communal life—farms, gardens, dairies, brewhouses, gran-aries, stables, laundries and workshops; carpenters, ironmongers, painters, masons, smiths and glaziers; its kitchens, larders, and sculleries, beer and wine cellars, gunrooms and stores. At Wo-burn the Duke of Bedford directly employed nearly 600 persons, 300 artificers being regularly paid every Saturday night, and his bill for domestic pensions alone amounted to over £2000 a year. Here, Greville reported, "is order, economy, grandeur, comfort and general content . . . with inexhaustible resources for every taste—a capital library, all the most curious and costly books,

---

[1] *Tennyson,* **Catullus Ode.**

pictures, prints, interesting portraits, gallery of sculpture, gardens, with the rarest exotics, collected and maintained at a vast expense." Almost every county had at least one Woburn and a dozen or score of hereditary mansions on a smaller but comparable scale.

Such houses were the headquarters of what was still the chief industry of England—agriculture. From their estate offices a great national interest was directed. During the past eighty years its productivity had been immeasurably increased. New and revolutionary methods of farming and stockbreeding had been introduced and nearly seven million acres of waste land reclaimed by enclosure. A German traveller in the eighteen-twenties was amazed on each successive visit to England to see vast tracts of formerly uncultivated land transformed into fine corn-bearing fields. It was during these years that Tennyson's northern farmer was engaged on his long and manly task of "the stubbling of Thornaby weäste." It was all part of a tremendous national achievement. Though the population had doubled itself since 1760 and England had ceased to be a corn exporting country, more than three-quarters of its total wheat and nearly all its barley consumption were being met by the home producer.

By their agricultural activity and inventiveness the English had not only given an example to the world but saved themselves. The new methods of breeding stock, the increase of grazing, the use of fodder crops on lands formerly left fallow, fencing, building and draining, contributed as much to the defeat of a militant and revolutionary France as the broadsides of Trafalgar and the stubborn squares of Waterloo. Without them the rising populations of the new manufacturing towns could never have been fed nor the power of Napoleon humbled. The accumulated experience of all this mighty effort had now been elevated into a science: the annual gatherings at Holkham to toast the great Coke of Norfolk who had turned thousands of acres of rabbit warren into a smiling countryside, the ceaseless output of books on improved methods of farming and the foundation of the Royal Agricultural Society in 1838 were among its many symptoms.

One best saw the industry in its corporate capacity on market day in any country town—the old market hall, the country women's stalls and baskets spread about the roadway, the gentry and tenant farmers in their John Bull top-hats, loose open frock-coats, vast collars, white waistcoats and breeches and heavy top boots. One saw it, too, in the great fairs that sprang up annually throughout the countryside, where a whole neighbourhood of peasant and farmer folk would assemble to buy, gossip and junket and when those who wished to be hired for service for the coming year proudly carried the symbols of their trade—the carter his whip, the milkmaid her pail and the cook her ladle. The lads or lassies hired received a shilling as testimony of acceptance and stuck a ribbon in cap or hair in honour of the bargain. "I took the shilling, put a bit of ribbon in mi' hat to show as I were hired like 'tuthers," said an old farm labourer recalling the days of his strength and pride, "and went and spent the rest of the day at the pleasure fee-ar." And as night fell and the drums and bugles outside the painted, lit booths sounded over lonely down and far watching valley, the rustic fun waxed fast and furious. A national industry was relaxing.

It had its statelier moments. When Queen Victoria and her young husband came to Stowe in 1845, the farmers of the Bucks Yeomanry escorted the royal carriage from the Wolverton terminus, a cavalcade of five hundred of the Duke's mounted tenantry awaited them in Buckingham and six hundred more in white smocks and green ribbons lined the avenue to the Corinthian Arch. That night delegations from all the neighbouring villages and from the county Friendly Societies waited on their sovereign with banners and torches, while the church bells pealed for twenty miles round and two thousand rosy-cheeked children sat down to feast in Buckingham town hall.

If the apex of the agricultural community and of its ordered industry and culture was the country house, its basis was the cottage. It was here that those who reaped and sowed were born and bred. Their homely virtues were as vital to their country's splendid achievement as the genius and assurance of the hereditary aristocrats who led them. On the field of Waterloo the great Duke gave his calm orders, and with equal calm and fortitude the rustics who manned the battered squares obeyed.

Of the 961,000 families engaged in agriculture in 1831, 686,000 were those of labourers who worked the land for others. The recent enclosures of the common lands had increased their numbers with many small-holders who, finding their hereditary tenures less valuable through loss of common rights or more onerous through heavy charges for enclosure or drainage, had disposed of them to their richer neighbours. In other ways the enclosures had operated against the interests of the labourer who, by legal processes little understood by him, had been deprived of certain prescriptive rights which had never had the formal recognition of law. As Arthur Young put it, "The poor in these parishes may say, *Parliament may be tender of property; all I know is I had a cow, and an Act of Parliament has taken it from me.*" More often the cow was only a mangy donkey or a few straggling geese, but the right to keep them on the common and to gather firewood there had been an important item in a poor country-man's budget.

Yet if partially deprived, particularly in the southern counties, of his former and inadequately recognised stake in the land, robbed of his share in the dwindling wild food supply of the open countryside by cruel Game Laws and of a market for the products of his domestic handicrafts by the new machines, the peasant still clung to his hereditary standards and virtues. An intense confidence in his skill and capacity for work sustained him through a life of hardship—that and love of the land he tended. He was never so happy as when working regularly under a good master. Such men were neither the fantastic and passion-ate creatures of modern regional novelists nor the down-trodden puppets of sentimental social historians. Their intellects were naïvely elementary, their passions (as proper to those who worked hard on the soil) unobtrusive, their instinctive feelings profound. They conformed to the natural rhythm of life, and in this lay their enduring strength. Love of the soil, love of food—"bee-acon wi' fat about three inches thick, tha's the tackul!"—pride in their own strength and skill—"I 'eeant very big but I can carry a sack of whait ur wuts ur beeans wi' anybody"[1]—and unshakable integrity and conservatism were the attributes of the English peasantry.

"Wurken an the land is lovely wurk," was the ungrudging verdict of an old Buckinghamshire labourer after a life of cease-less labour, "and in mi time I wurked furteen and fifteen hours a day, but that was afuur the machines come about. We sowed by hand, ripped by hand, and threshed wi' the thraiul. It was lovely wurk, and that was how it done when I was a young man. We used to dibble the sayd in, and I a' dibbled many a aiacre of wheeat, beeans, wuts and barley. Sometimes we used to sow bradcast.

[1] *H. Harman, Sketches of the Bucks Countryside.*

At harvist we cut wi' a sickle." At times the same witness spoke
in the language of poetry of his feeling for the land.

"Some people think they can git summut out a nauthing—
but they can't, and nivver wull. All me life I a noaticed that
land wi' no dress gis very poour craps—short straa, little
eeurs, and little kurnuls; but land well dressed always gis
good craps—long straa, long eeurs, and big kurnuls: and I
nivver yit sin big eeurs wi' fat kurnuls an thin short straa,
and nobody else nivver did. When carn is sold by weight,
ant it beeter to taiak a peck out a the sack, than put a peck
in? That's the difference atween good and bad farmin'. You
must a cleean land, plenty a dress, and plenty a laiabour to
git th' increeas and when ye a got these, the increeas comes."[1]

Such a man when his time to die came could look round on an
entire countryside which he had helped to cultivate.

A rough, simple, pastoral people, of great staying power,
invincible good humour and delicate natural justice, such were
the labourers of rural England. "Here lies," runs a Gloucestershire epitaph,

"JOHN HIGGS
A famous man for killing pigs,
For killing pigs was his delight
Both morning, afternoon and night."

Set against the background of their industry, their homely
pleasures assume an almost epic dignity. One loves to think of
them in the taproom of the thatched ale house in the evening
over their modest pint of mild when their day's work was done—
the high settles in the chimney corner, the bacon rack on the oaken
beam, the sanded floor, the old brightly-worn furniture gleaming
in the flickering firelight.

Higher in the economic scale than the labourer was the small-
holder. He still represented a substantial element in the rural
community. With the village craftsman—a numerous class—he
constituted the social and moral backbone of the parish. In 1831
one countryman in three possessed a stake in the land. One in
seven worked his own land without hiring labour. Such a

[1] *H. Harman, Buckinghamshire Dialect, 110-111.*

man—often a yeoman who held his tenure for life—was still the standard rustic Englishman.

The old cottage folk of England were very tenacious of the good things of life they had been brought up by their fathers to honour. They liked to keep a bright fire burning on the hearth, choice old china on spotless shelves, smoked flitches of bacon and ham hanging from the ceiling and home-brewed wine to offer their neighbours. They took pride in their mastery of oven and vat: in their skill in keeping garden: in raising poultry and bees. Above all they valued the virtues of decent living and good neighbourhood—honesty, truth and purity of word and life.

Though the process was a more gradual one than has been generally realised, the yeoman type was slowly disappearing. It was too conservative to compete successfully with the more ruthless and greedier values set by urban and industrial commerce. And the tendency of landlords was to allow the old tenures for life—a rustic economy based not on accountant's statistics but on the rhythm of the human heart—to expire when they fell in. In their place they offered annual or determinable leases. The number of lifehold properties and copyholds of inheritance was therefore every year diminishing.

The older, smaller type of squire was also departing—killed by the violent fluctuations which followed in the wake of the Napoleonic wars and by the rising standard of social expense set by rich neighbours.[1] But he was still to be found in considerable numbers in the remoter parts of the country—particularly in Devonshire, Wales and Clun Forest, in the Fens and in the Yorkshire and Cumberland dales. Like the old hero of Scawen Blunt's poem he liked the hunting of the hare better than that of the fox, spoke in dialect, dined at six and spent his evenings over a long pipe and a tankard in the village inn. The pride of his house was the gun-room which he called his hunting parlour. In white breeches and buckled shoes, fawn-coloured leathers, tight double-breasted, brass-buttoned, bright blue coat, buff vest and low top hat—for he inclined to the "old Anglesey school of dressers"—he was still an essential part of the English landscape.

To him and his kind, defying the sombre black of the encroaching towns, that landscape owed at least a part of its enchantment. He supplied it with pageantry. The lovely primary colours of

[1] "The French Revolution produced a war which doubled the cost and trebled the difficulty of genteel living."—*The Lady's Keepsake and Maternal Monitor, 1835.*

the English past that to-day only survive in the dress uniform of the Guards and the huntsman's coat shone in front of the vivid greenery of May or glowed through the mists of autumn. So, too, long afterwards when England had grown drab and urban, old men recalled with a thrill of pleasure the sight of the coaches, thirty or forty a day in any fair-sized main-road town: "the dashing steeds, the fanfaronades on the horn, the scarlet coats of the coachmen and the guard."

. . . .

Down by the coasts the country looked out on the sea. In white Jane Austen houses along the Solent one could see through the vistas in the trees the great battleships with their bellying sails and the stately West Indiamen "sailing between worlds and worlds with steady wing." Here was the watery highway from which the new England drew its ever expanding wealth, with clippers bringing tribute from Pagoda Bay and the far ends of the earth, and the rough, passionate sailors whom coastwise England bred, singing as they pulled on the ropes how soon they would

> "be in London city,
> Blow my bully boys blow!
> And see the girls all dressed so pretty,
> Blow! boys, blow!"

Such men, by modern standards, lived lives of almost indescribable hardship, spending years afloat before they set foot on shore and, cleaned out by a single gargantuan and open-handed debauch, signing on again a few days later for another voyage. They were ready, like their fathers who fought under Nelson, to dare and do almost anything, and the safety and wealth of England rested on their rude, unconscious shoulders. For them the great shipbuilding yards on the Thames still turned out wooden ships of a quality unmatched throughout the world, made by men who had learnt their craft—part of England's hereditary wealth—from their forebears. "His father's name before him was Chips, and his father's name before him was Chips, and they were all Chipses."

Pride in craftsmanship and skill handed down the generations were the attributes that made the products of English manufacture sought and honoured throughout the earth. Their hallmark was quality, and they bore the unmistakable stamp of a nation of aristocrats. In the Lancashire cotton mills and the London slums a proletarian labouring class was fast emerging, but its significance was still hidden from contemporaries by the multitude of skilled craftsmen who constituted the rank and file of British industry. Except for cotton, no textile trade had been radically affected by machinery before 1830; wool-combing was still governed by skill of hand as was the hardware industry of the Midlands and the cutlery of Sheffield. The old trades were still more extensive than the new: at the time of the Reform Bill, there were more shoemakers in England than coal-miners. The unit of industry was very small: apprentices frequently lived with their employers over their own workshop, and every craftsman might aspire to be a master. The Spitalfields weavers of London, who on summer evenings could be seen seated in the porticos of their houses enjoying their pipes or digging their allotments in Saunderson's Gardens, the 200,000 bricklayers, masons, carpenters, house-painters, slaters, plumbers, plasterers and glaziers who made up the close corporation of the building trade, the serge and cloth workers of the West Country, Gloucestershire and East Anglia, the bootmakers of Northampton, the blanketers of Witney, the chair-turners of the southern Chilterns and the cabinet makers and clock makers of almost every country town were—for all the threat of the new machines to their employment and standards of living—men with a status in the country based on personal skill and character.

So were the rural handicraftsmen—blacksmiths, wheelwrights, carpenters, millers, cobblers—the fishermen and sailors of the coast towns and the engineers who were coming into existence to make and tend the new machines of steel and iron. North of the border in Lanarkshire, a French traveller found the Scottish craftsmen the best educated in Europe, "well-informed, appreciating with sagacity the practice of their trade and judging rationally of the power of their tools and the efficiency of their machinery."[1] Such men—even the Durham miners whose working conditions so distressed Cobbet—enjoyed solid houses, substantial fare and fine sturdy furniture made by craftsmen worthy of themselves. Pride in their domestic establishment was the hall-mark of the British artisan and his wife: the Handloom Weavers' Commissioners' Reports of 1838 speak of the Midland weavers' cottages as good and comfortable and much superior

[1] *Baron Dupin. The Commercial Power of Great Britain, 1825, II, 237.*

to those of the surrounding agricultural labourers, with a solid dower of nice clocks, beds and drawers and ornamented with prints. Within was cleanliness, good order and fine frugal cooking.

Such was the old English system. It was based on the home, and home spelt contentment. Here was the seat of man's love—of his birth and his continuance. Here, too, he did his work. For the cottage, so long as the old economy persisted, was often both home and factory. Yarn was spun and woven under a single roof: "the wife and daughter spun the yarn and the father wove." Cottage labour for the womenfolk, such as the beautiful lace industry of old Buckinghamshire, implemented the household income and gave an additional pride and interest to family life. In his leisure hours the good man, home from farm or smithy, cultivated his own little piece of land. "He was no proletarian, he had a stake in the country, he was permanently settled and stood one step higher in society than the English workman of to-day." Such men, as Engels wrote in the changed world of 1844, "did not need to overwork; they did no more than they chose to do, and yet earned what they needed."

They were rooted fast in their own soil. They had faith, they had home and they had love. They were freemen, for within their narrow bounds they had freedom of choice. "But intellectually, they were dead; lived only for their petty private interest, for their looms and gardens, and knew nothing of the mighty movement which, beyond their horizon, was sweeping through mankind. They were comfortable in their silent vegetation and but for the industrial revolution they would never have emerged from this existence, which, cosily romantic as it was, was nevertheless not worthy of human beings." For to the pure but rootless intellect of the German radical, Engels, they did not seem human beings.[1]

.   .   .   .

For those who were fortunate enough to inherit a share in that vanished rural England—for all not imprisoned in the great industrial towns or disinherited by the poverty that followed the enclosures—there was a sober joy in it. It came from healthy living, from quietude begotten of continuity, from the perceiving eye and the undulled sense. In the letters of Edward Fitzgerald

[1] "In truth they were not human beings." *F. Engels, The Condition of the Working Class in England, in 1844. 3.*

one sees green England sunning herself in her immemorial peace
—"the same level meadow with geese upon it . . . the same
pollard oaks, with now and then the butcher or the washer-
women trundling by in their carts." "I read of mornings the
same old books over and over again," he writes, "walk with my
great dog of an afternoon and at evening sit with open window,
up to which China roses climb, with my pipe while the black-
birds and thrushes begin to rustle bedwards in the garden."
"We have had," he wrote on another occasion, "glorious weather,
new pease and young potatoes, fresh milk (how good!) and a cool
library to sit in of mornings." Down in his native Suffolk this
gentle patriot found the heart of England beating healthily:
whenever he returned from sophisticated London he was amazed
at "the humour and worth and noble feeling in the country."
Fishing in "the land of old Bunyan . . . and the perennial Ouse,
making many a fantastic winding . . . to fertilize and adorn,"
he stayed at an inn, "the cleanest, the sweetest, the civillest, the
quietest, the liveliest and the cheapest that was ever built or
conducted. . . . On one side it has a garden, then the meadows
through which winds the Ouse: on the other the public road,
with its coaches hurrying on to London, its market people halting
to drink, its farmers, horsemen and foot travellers. So, as
one's humour is, one can have whichever phase of life one pleases:
quietude or bustle; solitude or the busy hum of men: one can
sit in the principal room with a tankard and a pipe and see both
these phases at once through the windows that open upon either."[1]

To such a one the changing seasons only brought new contentment—spring "Tacitus lying at full length on a bench in the
garden, a nightingale singing and some red anemones eyeing
the sun manfully," and autumn "howling winds and pelting
rains and leaves already turned yellow" with a book before a great
fire in the evening. "In this big London," Fitzgerald wrote to
Bernard Barton, "all full of intellect and pleasure and business,
I feel pleasure in dipping down into the country and rubbing
my hand over the cool dew upon the pastures, as it were. . . .
I should like to live in a small house just outside a pleasant
English town all the days of my life, making myself useful in a
humble way, reading my books and playing a rubber of whist

---

[1] "Through all these delightful places they talk of leading railroads; a sad thing, I
am sure; quite impolitic. But Mammon is blind." *Letters and Literary Remains of
Edward Fitzgerald, I, 62.*

at night. But England cannot expect long such a reign of inward quiet as to suffer men to dwell so easily to themselves."

For he knew that it could not last. The portents of change were already blazing in the northern and midland sky. "The sun shines very bright, and there is a kind of bustle in these clean streets, because there is to be a grand True Blue dinner in the Town Hall. Not that I am going: in an hour or two I shall be out in the fields rambling alone. I read *Burnet's History*—*ex pede Herculem*. Well, say as you will, there is not, and never was, such a country as old England—never were there such a gentry as the English. They will be the distinguishing mark and glory of England in history, as the arts were of Greece, and war of Rome. I am sure no travel would carry me to any land so beautiful as the good sense, justice, and liberality of my good countrymen make this. And I cling the closer to it, because I feel that we are going down the hill, and shall perhaps live ourselves to talk of all this independence as a thing that has been."

CHAPTER TWO

Dark Satanic Mills

"We have game laws, corn laws, cotton factories, Spitalfields, the tillers of the land paid by poor rates, and the remainder of the population mechanised into engines for the manufactory of new rich men; yea the machinery of the wealth of the nation made up of the wretchedness, disease and depravity of those who should constitute the strength of the nation."

S. T. Coleridge.

IN MAY, 1842, four men—Southwood Smith a doctor, Thomas Tooke an economist, and R. J. Saunders and Leonard Horner, factory inspectors—published a document which profoundly troubled the conscience of England. It was called the First Report of the Children's Employment Commission. It dealt with the conditions of labour of children and young persons working in coal mines. The commission had been set up two years before by Lord Melbourne's government, largely through the pertinacity of Lord Ashley, an inconveniently well-connected young Tory[1] of strong evangelical tendencies who had taken up the cause of the north-country factory operatives with an enthusiasm which seemed to some of his contemporaries to border on the hysterical.

Everybody knew that the conditions of life and labour in the new factory towns of the north and midlands, until now a remote, barren and little visited part of the country, were of a rough and primitive character. There had always been rough and primitive Englishmen, and in these smoky and unsavoury districts they were undoubtedly on the increase. It was part of the price that had to be paid for the nation's growing wealth. But the revelations of the Commissioners' pages took the country by surprise.

From this document it appeared that the employment of children of seven or eight years old in coal mines was almost universal. In some pits they began work at a still earlier age: a case was even recorded of a child of three. Some were employed as "trappers," others for pushing or drawing coal trucks along

[1] He was Palmerston's son-in-law.

the pit tunnels. A trapper, who operated the ventilation doors on which the safety of the mines depended, would often spend as many as sixteen hours a day crouching in solitude in a small dark hole. "Although this employment scarcely deserves the name of labour," ran the Commission's report, "yet as the children engaged in it are commonly excluded from light and are always without companions, it would, were it not for the passing and repassing of the coal carriages, amount to solitary confinement of the worst order."

Those who drew the trucks were "harnessed like dogs in a go-cart" and crawled on all-fours down passages in some places only eighteen inches high. Other children worked at the pumps in the under-bottom of the pits, standing ankle deep in water for twelve hours. One who was cited, only six years of age, carried or dragged half a hundredweight every day up a distance equivalent to the height of St. Paul's Cathedral.

What struck the conscience of early Victorian England with especial horror was the fact that girls as well as boys were employed in these tasks. Naked to the waist, and with chains drawn between their legs, the future mothers of Englishmen crawled on all-fours down tunnels under the earth drawing Egyptian burdens. Women by the age of 30 were old and infirm cripples. Such labour, degrading all who engaged in it, was often accompanied by debauchery and sickening cruelty: one witness before the Commission described how he had seen a boy beaten with a pick-axe. Lord Ashley in a speech in the Commons mentioned another whose master was in the habit of thrashing him with a stick through which a nail had been driven: the child's back and loins were beaten to a jelly, his arm was broken and his head covered with the mark of old wounds. To add to its horrors the Report was illustrated with pictures.

Here was something never contemplated by Church and State. "We in England," wrote a leading journal, "have put ourselves forward in every possible way that could savour of ostentation as champions of the whole human race; and we are now, on our own showing, exhibited to the world as empty braggarts and shallow pretenders to virtues which we do not possess. . . . We have listened to the cries of the slave afar off, but we have shut our ears to the moaning of the slave at our feet." When Ashley, striking while the iron was hot, rose in the Commons a month later to introduce a Bill excluding all women and girls from the pits and boys under thirteen, he found himself almost a national hero.

. . . . . .

Yet there was nothing new in what the Report revealed or Ashley described: these things had been going on for years. They had been defended, as they were even defended on this occasion, with all conscientiousness by many honourable men in positions of responsibility on the ground that they were the unavoidable result of the laws of supply and demand. Since the publication of Malthus' treatises, serious minds had been haunted by a fear that the staggering increase of population rendered possible by the advance of machinery and medical science would outgrow the earth's productive capacity and culminate in famine. They were equally possessed of the belief so brilliantly propounded by Adam Smith more than half a century before and revered by every living economist that the wealth of men and nations depended on the unimpeded operation of economic law. " It is not from the benevolence of the butcher, the brewer or the baker," he wrote, " that we expect our dinner, but from their regard to their own self interest. We address ourselves, not to their humanity, but to their self-love, and never talk to them of our necessities, but of their advantage." Only by leaving every man free to pursue his own interest could production in such a revolutionary age keep pace with the rise in consumption. The more the population increased and the greater the consequent suffering of the poor, the more incumbent it became on those who governed to refrain from any interference with economic processes. For it could only end in calamity. The most one could hope for, in the view of the professors of "the dismal science," was that the poor should be fed at all. Hardships suffered by them in the course of obtaining food were in reality blessings, since without them they and all mankind would starve.

This belief was widely held by humane and enlightened reformers who were passionately anxious to eradicate ancient abuses, of which there were many, and to mitigate human suffering. The English individualists who subscribed with such uncritical zeal to the doctrine of *laissez-faire* in economic matters were among the world's greatest humanitarians. They led a reluctant mankind in every philanthropic crusade: by their unflagging efforts they had abolished slavery in the British dominions, removed from the statute book the barbarous laws that condemned men to the pillory and women to the lash, reduced from more than a hundred and fifty to six the crimes punishable by death and rendered illegal the cruel sports of cock-fighting and bull-baiting. These humanitarians rigidly opposed the infliction of all needless pain except in the factories and mines of England. For here, in their view, it could not be avoided.

This melancholy and fatalistic attitude towards industrial suffering was bound up with the high hopes which had been formed of human nature by the idealists of the eighteenth century. It was this that made it so formidable. The age of reason saw the birth of a belief that challenged the older notion of revealed religion and morality. By the light of the untram-melled mind, man would be able to attain to perfection. Only two things were necessary: that he should strictly observe natural law and be freed from every antiquated legal shackle, supersti-tion and custom that prevented him from following his will according to the light of his own reason. The emancipation of the individual reason was the key to a new era of happiness and perfection. Man was born free: he had only to rid himself of his chains to enter into his heritage.

In France this theory, first preached by philosophers and later accepted as a social truism, had resulted in the storming of the Bastille, the Declaration of the Rights of Man and the Revolutionary and Napoleonic armies. In sober commercial England it had taken a more prosaic form. Expounded for more than half a century by a rich and respectable philanthropist of genius, the promotion of "the greatest happiness of the greatest number" had become the polite faith of nine "enlightened" English reformers out of ten. It was Jeremy Bentham's belief that that happiness could most readily be realised by the free exercise on the part of every individual of enlightened self-interest. Complete freedom of contract was the very core of the utilitarian creed. Any denial of it by the State could only delay and perhaps defeat the bene-ficent purposes of Providence.

A theory, running counter to the whole course of English social history, was thus employed both by members of the government and by manufacturers, as well as by academic economists, to justify almost any suffering or inhumanity. Employers and employed must be left free to make whatever bargains they chose: legislative interference could only make confusion worse confounded. Nine years before the Report of 1842, when Ashley had been struggling to get a bill through Parliament limiting the hours of children in textile mills to ten a day, he was opposed on the ground that the measure would hamstring one-sixth of the nation's producing power and, by weakening British industry in competition abroad, react fatally on the wages and employment of the adult worker. Even so humane a man as Lord Althorp, then leader of the Commons, argued it would make famine inevitable. Cobbett's common-sense remark that the House had discovered that the stay and bulwark of England lay, not as was hitherto supposed in her navy, maritime commerce or colonies, but in the labour of 30,000 little factory girls, was regarded as perverse nonsense.

For the English being bad theorists, though masters of practice and adaptation, overlooked the fatal error in the logic of *laissez-faire*, which accorded so readily with their own stubborn hatred of tyranny and love of independence. That liberty was a sacred blessing never to be lightly infringed and that every man should be free were propositions that appealed to their deepest instincts. What in their passion for liberty they failed to see was that men were not rendered free merely because they ought to be, or by the removal of artificial legal restrictions on trade and contract. A child, a cripple, a pregnant woman, an epileptic or a neurasthenic was not free but was the slave of circumstances over which he or she had no control. The theory that the economic price for services and commodities could only be determined by the unimpeded bargaining of buyer and seller assumed a different aspect when the buyer was a rich man in no hurry to buy and the seller a hungry wretch with a sick wife and family. Unfortunately the English could not grasp this in theory: it was only after they had been brought face to face with its cruel and degrading consequences that they reacted against it. Even then, they failed to detect the cause of the effect they deplored.

That the ruling classes were so slow to perceive the evil that was sapping the nation's health and unity was due to a combination of causes unique in history. The social changes wrought by the English inventions of the eighteenth and early nineteenth century—themselves the product of a glorious vitality, ingenuity and disciplined activity of mind—were so far-reaching that men already absorbed by the problems of an ancient, vigorous and

intricate society had some excuse for not grasping their significance. For they happened with bewildering rapidity. They took
place in remote and little frequented parts of the country which,
having formally been scantily populated, were without parliamentary representation. And at first they only affected an
insignificant minority. At the beginning of the century factory
and mine-workers formed only a small fraction of the population.
The speed at which their numbers increased upset all normal
calculations of statecraft.

But the chief cause for the failure of the English government
—aggravated as it was by the prevailing *laissez-faire* theory—was
the overwhelming pressure of external events. From the outbreak
of the French Revolution—itself following only six years after
the disastrous war with the American colonies—to the fall
of Napoleon, England had no time for reflection. It was
in circumstances of continual peril and while facing a
dangerous revolutionary theory abroad and bewildering changes
at home that the hideous problem, which came to be called the
Condition-of-England question, arose in the new manufacturing
areas. What the menace of Nazi ideology and aggression is to-day,
that of French Jacobinism seemed to our stubborn forefathers as
they fought for their threatened homes and the liberties of
Europe. To them every sign of discontent was a symptom
of revolutionary terror and the most legitimate criticism the
blackest treason. With all the obstinacy of Englishmen in time
of duress, the rulers of George III.'s England clamped down
the hatches of the ship of state against change. For more than
a quarter of a century reform was driven under ground and
a new population, growing up amid unprecedented social
phenomena, was deprived of leadership. Humane and kindly
men, at their wits' ends how to feed a besieged island and taught
by the economists that in such matters sentiment would prove
fatal, accepted as inevitable the spectacle of women with blackened
faces and tears coursing down their eyes as they dragged their
loads up pit ladders, of work-dizzy cotton spinners mangled in
the shafts of unfenced machinery, of workhouse children rented
by frugal-minded overseers to rough north country millowners
who treated them like beasts of burden. They treated them worse,
for while only a fool would maltreat his horse, a manufacturer could always replace crippled or prematurely senile human
workers by further supplies of cheap labour that cost him nothing

but their keep. An American cotton planter who bought and bred his own slaves had an interest in being careful of his "Labour." A Lancashire cotton manufacturer only hired his; his responsibility for it began and ended at the factory gates.[1] He was merely concerned with paying as little for it and getting as much out of it as possible. And this was precisely what the economists—the "feelosophers" of Cobbett's indignant phrase— told him to do. Selfishness had been elevated by the theorists of the study into a public virtue.

There were many manufacturers whose consciences were repelled by these methods of conducting business. But not only were they told by those learned in such matters that to question economic law was folly, but the competition of rivals who had no such scruples about underpaying and overworking their wretched employees compelled them under pain of bankruptcy to do the same. A kind of Gresham's law operated to debase the standard of the best employer to that of the lowest. Among the small millowners—and even in capitalist Lancashire the unit of employment was still by modern standards very small—were many of humble origin who had achieved wealth by their talent for using their elbows. Though men often of splendid vigour, courage and independence, they were without the ruling tradition of responsibility and *noblesse oblige*, and the professors of economic science told them that such scruples were in any case antiquated and useless. They had one main concern, to get rich, and by every legitimate method available. As is often the way with servants turned master, they tended to confuse discipline with terror. Their own manners and habits were rough and brutal,[2] and they saw no reason to soften them in their relations with employees.

Machinery gave them their chance. Every new invention by simplifying the processes of manufacture and multiplying the rate of output increased their opportunities for growing rich. They took them with all the boisterous energy of their race. All that was needed by the new "manufacturer," working not by his own hand but by machine and proxy, was capital enough

---

[1] "A man may assemble five hundred workmen one week and dismiss them the next, without having any further connection with them than to receive a week's work for a week's wages, nor any further solicitude about their future fate than if they were so many old shuttles." *Sir W. Scott, Familiar Letters, Vol. II, 19th May, 1820.* The practise still seemed shocking to any one nursed in the older social system.

[2] In the early years of the nineteenth century the publican of a famous Manchester tavern patronised by the town's leading manufacturers used to expel his customers at closing time with the help of a lash. *A. F. Fremantle, England in the Nineteenth Century, 42.*

to buy or hire a roomful of power looms, a resolve to keep his expenses and consequently his prices down against all rivals and a plentiful supply of cheap labour. The machine took the place of the domestic craftsman whose hereditary skill it rendered useless, whose price it undercut and whose ancient markets it captured. If continued unemployment did not drive him to lower his wage demands, women and children could be hired for the factories at half or a third of his price. So could filthy, barefooted Irish paupers who were always ready to leave their own overcrowded and half-starving island at almost any wage. They were shipped into Liverpool and Glasgow in tens of thousands to feed the mills. By a curious nemesis, their ways of life—little better than those of the pigstye—still further depressed the wages and social standards of England and Scotland.

. . . .

The first great surge of invention affected the textile trade and principally the manufacture of cotton goods. It was in the humid valleys of south Lancashire that the factory system appeared. The earliest cotton mills, worked by water power though later by steam, were largely operated by apprentice pauper children from the urban slums who, consigned by the Guardians to the millowners in cartloads, were housed or rather packed in barrack-like 'prentice houses (where they slept in shifts) and kept more or less continuously at work until they either died or reached an age at which their labour ceased to be profitable. The working hours of one mill in 1815 were from 5 a.m. till 8 p.m. with half an hour's grace for breakfast and dinner. There were no Saturday half-holidays, and Sundays were partly devoted to cleaning the machinery. One instance is is recorded of unwanted children being taken when the mill was idle to a neighbouring common and turned loose to shift for themselves.[1]

The early factory reformers—a little minority of humane men, several of them millowners like the first Sir Robert Peel— concentrated their efforts on regulating the worst abuses of indentured child labour in the cotton mills. Later they were able to extend their tentative reforms to what was ironically

[1] The proprietors denied that the children were "turned adrift"; they were merely "set at liberty." " To be sure, they would not be well off; they would have to beg their way or something of that sort." *Report on Children in Manufactures, 1816* (*Peel's Committee, 288-93, cit. J. L. & H. Hammond, The Town Labourer, 148-9*).

termed "free" child labour and to other branches of manufacture. But they received small encouragement from the bulk of their well-to-do countrymen who in a stay-at-home age were not given to trips to smoky and remotely situated factory towns and were unable to imagine what they had not seen. The isolation of the industrial areas before the coming of the railways created a deep gulf between one-part of the nation and the other. The only reforms philanthropists could smuggle on to the Statute Book were of the most rudimentary kind, such as the prohibition of the employment of children under nine in cotton mills and the limitation of hours of labour for young persons under sixteen to twelve a day. Even these were avoided in practice. The Factories' Inquiry Commission of 1833 showed that many manufacturers were still employing children of six and seven and that the hours of labour were sometimes as high as sixteen a day. Flogging was regarded as a necessary part of the process of production. Harassed parents, with their eye on the family budget, accepted all this as inevitable and even desirable: many fathers acted as sub-contractors for the employment of their own children.

Nor did the reforms, such as they were, keep pace with the growth of the system. The victims of the factory—at first only an insignificant fraction of the population—increased by leaps and bounds. Every year new inventions widened the scope of machinery, offered new opportunities for growing rich and forced more hungry craftsmen to seek employment for their wives and children in the factory towns. What had hitherto been a localised evil became a national one.

During the period of transition from cottage to factory labour, the course of nature was reversed. The breadwinner was left idle in the home, the wife and her little ones driven by want to the mill. In 1833 the cotton mills employed about 60,000 adult males, 65,000 adult females, and 84,000 young persons of whom half were boys and girls of under fourteen. By 1844, of 420,000 operatives, less than a quarter were men over eighteen and 242,000 were women and girls.

The result was appalling. A wife who worked twelve or thirteen hours a day in a factory had no time to give to her children who grew up, in Engels' tragic words, like wild weeds. Put out to nurse with some half-savage creature for a few pence a week until old enough to become wage-earners, they learnt nothing from their mothers of the arts of domestic life and little of its charities. Even immediately after confinement women were forced out of sheer necessity to return to the mills. Lord Ashley made English gentlemen in the House of Commons listen to evidence that revealed their misery: "H. W. has three children, goes away Monday morning at five o'clock and comes back Saturday evening: has so much to do for the children then that she cannot get to bed before three o'clock in the morning; often wet through to the skin, and obliged to work in that state. She said: ' My breasts have given me the most frightful pain, and I have been dripping wet with milk.' "

The effect on the children can be imagined. The home to which they returned at night, often too weary even to eat, was an untended hovel. The machines to which they hurried back before dawn never tired as they did. In the country which had abolished slavery and was vigorously opposing the slave trade in every corner of the world, "strappers" were kept to flog drowsy factory children lest they dropped asleep at their work, and groups of pallid mites could be seen supporting each other home as they dragged their limbs up the dark cobbled lanes of the Lancashire and Yorkshire valleys.

Many were crippled for life: few grew to mature and healthy manhood or womanhood. Long, monotonous and unnatural working positions resulted in permanent curvature of the limbs. Whole families went about with crooked legs or twisted shoulders. Knees bent inwards and backwards, ankles were thickened and deformed and spinal columns pressed forward or to one side. Every street had its company of cripples, of prematurely aged and arthritic youths bent double and limping, of hag-like girls with deformed backs and hips. Constitutions were permanently enfeebled: long hours in hot, damp, crowded rooms and foul and vitiated air left debilitated bodies and listless minds. The factory population of Lancashire and the West Riding was discoloured and stunted and seemed more like some ill-fated race of pigmies than normal human beings. A Leeds surgeon testified that but for the constant new recruits from healthy country stock, the race of mill-hands would soon be wholly degenerate.

On no one did the tragedy of factory life fall more heavily than on the old craftsmen class of northern England—the finest artisans in the world. Accustomed to independence, to the regulation of their own hours of labour, to a solid standard of

comfort and to the environment of the countryside, they found
themselves through causes beyond their ken deprived of their
wonted markets, undersold by cheap machine-made wares and
finally driven in desperation into the close air and foetid lanes of
the new towns where their wives and children could sell their
labour. The bottom had fallen out of their world. In a letter to
Oastler, the factory reformer, a Yorkshire workman described
how a fellow artisan, tramping Lancashire in search of work,
had come across an old acquaintance of his in a cellar in St.
Helens.

"There sat poor Jack near the fire, and what did he,
think you? why he sat and mended his wife's stockings
with the bodkin; and as soon as he saw his old friend at
the doorpost he tried to hide them. But Joe had seen it, and
said: 'Jack, what the devil art thou doing? Where is the
missus? Why, is that thy work?' and poor Jack was ashamed,
and said: 'No, I know this is not my work, but my poor
missus is i' the factory; she has to leave at half-past five
and works till eight at night, and then she is so knocked up
that she cannot do aught when she gets home, so I have to
do everything for her what I can, for I have no work, nor
had any for more nor three years, and I shall never have any
more work while I live;' and then he wept a big tear. Jack
again said: 'there is work enough for women folks and
childer hereabouts, but none for men; thou mayest sooner
find a hundred pound on the road than work for men—but
I should never have believed that either thou or any one
else would have seen me mending my wife's stockings, for
it is bad work. But she can hardly stand on her feet; I am
afraid she will be laid up, and then I don't know what is to
become of us, for it's a good bit that she had been the man
in the house and I the woman; it is bad work, Joe;' and he
cried bitterly. . . . Now when Joe heard this, he told me
that he had cursed and damned the factories, and the masters,
and the Government, with all the curses that he had learned
while he was in the factory from a child."[1]

When such simple Englishmen, feeling themselves cheated
and lost, turned for relief to their rulers they received little

[1] *Engels, 145-6.*

comfort. It had formerly been regarded as part of the duty of society to ensure at the expense of its principal beneficiaries a "fair wage" to every Englishman willing to labour. But a cold and alien philosophy now ruled the conduct of those in power. A Realm of England that denied the validity of its own authority announced that it could no longer help the People of England to preserve their traditional rights and status. Those who were submerged in the factory towns responded by forgetting that they had any part in the tradition of the realm. There was nothing to remind them that they had.

The new spirit informed the Poor Law which was enacted in 1834 to remedy the disastrous effects of the well-intentioned but makeshift system—known as Speenhamland—of subsidising wages out of rates. It bore the cold impress of the mathematical mind. It was based on the principle that the smaller the burden placed by the relief of poverty on the taxpayer the greater the country's wealth. Itself a contradication of the strict letter of that economic law, it adhered as closely to it as was compatible with the traditional and obstinate English dislike of allowing a man to die of hunger. Outdoor relief, with all its kindly charities, was sternly discouraged: in its place the Workhouse, built with sombre economy by the administrative Unions of parishes formed under the new Act, offered to the needy poor the maximum of deterrent with the minimum of subsistence.

It was this austere form of charity that was doled out to the dispossessed weaver, the hungry handcraftsman deprived of his employment and the agricultural labourer who had simultaneously lost his grazing rights on the common and the supplementary earnings of the traditional home industries which the machines had destroyed. To men and women nursed in a kindlier tradition it seemed an outrage that old folk who had laboured all their lives and had become destitute through no fault of their own should be torn from their homes, separated from each other's company and herded in sexes into prison-like institutions.

For the economists did not see Labour as a body of men and women with individual needs and rights but only as a statistical abstraction. Labour was a commodity of value on which the man of Capital, with whom all initiative lay, could draw as the state of the market demanded. And as that market—a world one—was at the mercy of accident and fluctuated unpredictably, a "reserve" of labour was indispensable. In exceptionally good times the whole "reserve" could be quickly absorbed by productive industry: in normal or bad ones, it must remain unemployed and subsist on poor relief or beggary.[1] Engels writing in 1844, reckoned the surplus in England and Wales at a million and a half or about a tenth of the entire population.

The economic justification of all this was that the factories were giving to the country a wealth she had never before possessed and bringing within the purchasing power of the poor articles which had hitherto been available only to princes. The evils that were inseparable from that system were merely transitional; the nation had only to be patient, to refrain from palliative and wasteful measures and observe the laws of supply and demand, and all would be well. The general body of the middle class accepted this comforting proposition. To any one with capital the mechanical multiplication of productive processes offered unprecedented opportunities: never had there been such a chance for the far-seeing investor. The same processes by cheapening the price and multiplying the quantity of goods must surely benefit labour too. The march of progress was irresistible. "Our fields," declared Macaulay, voicing the buoyant sentiment of his class, "are cultivated with a skill unknown elsewhere, with a skill which has extracted rich harvests from moors and morasses. Our houses are filled with conveniences which the kings of former times might have envied. Our bridges, our canals, our roads, our modes of communication fill every stranger with wonder. Nowhere are manufactures carried to such perfection. Nowhere does man exercise such a dominion over matter."

The spirit of the age—that is, of the readers and writers of books, newspapers and journals—was preoccupied with the getting of material wealth and a purely mechanical organisation of society. It preferred a quantitative to a qualitative ideal of production. It was opposed to that older and more catholic con-

---

[1] ' At the gates of all the London docks,' says the Rev. W. Champney, preacher of the East End, ' hundreds of the poor appear every morning in winter before daybreak, in the hope of getting a day's work. They await the opening of the gates; and, when the youngest and strongest and best known have been engaged, hundreds. cast down by disappointed hope, go back to their wretched homes.' When these people find no work and will not rebel against society, what remains for them but to beg? And surely no one can wonder at the great army of beggars, most of them able-bodied men, with whom the police carries on perpetual war." F. Engels, *The Condition of the Working Class in England* iv, *1844, 86-7.*

ception in which rural and traditional England still lingered. It was pragmatic, vigorous and vocal. The other England was passive and unthinking. The few who set its ancient and forgotten philosophy against the spirit of the age were dismissed by the intellectuals as dreamers and mischievous meddlers.

That those few included some of the profoundest minds of the time was not realised. No one heeded Coleridge's warning that the price of neglecting human health, breeding and character for the sake of profits would have to be paid with heavy interest in the future. "You talk," he wrote, "about making this article cheaper by reducing its price in the market from 8d. to 6d. But suppose in so doing, you have rendered your country weaker against a foreign foe; suppose you have demoralised thousands of your fellow-countrymen and have sown discontent between one class of society and another, your article is tolerably dear, I take it, after all." Persons were not "things." The latter found their level, as the economists maintained, but after starvation, loss of home and employment, "neither in body nor in soul does man find his level." Man was not an unchanging and measurable commodity but a variable and creative creature intensely sensitive not only to his immediate environment but to that of his progenitors from whom he inherited many of his attributes.

The wealth and power of Britain to which the economists and their middle-class disciples loved to draw attention was not merely the result of machinery and the laws of supply and demand. It was based on the skill, discipline, industry and social cohesion of the British people—qualities which they had derived from generations of healthy living and sound social organisation. It was these invisible assets that enabled British manufacturers to sell their goods in every corner of the world. To destroy them by ignoring human rights and needs for the sake of an excessive and impatient expansion of material wealth was to deprive coming generations of the very advantages they had enjoyed and exploited. Such improvidence could only end in killing the goose that laid the golden eggs. The early Forsytes for all their private integrity and frugality never comprehended this, and, unknowingly, committed waste on the national estate.

. . . .

The new England they built was housed not so much in towns as in barracks. These were grouped round the new factories, on the least expensive and therefore most congested model attainable. Unrestrained individualism was the order of the day. Since the rate of profits was not affected if their inhabitants died prematurely no consideration was paid to matters of sanitation and health. The dwellings which housed the factory population were run up by small jerry builders and local carpenters, who like the millowners were out for the maximum of profit with the minimum of responsibility. They were erected back to back and on the cheapest available site, in many cases marshes. There was no ventilation and no drainage. The intervals between the houses which passed for streets were unpaved and often followed the line of streams serving a conduit for excrement.

The appearance of such towns was dark and forbidding. Many years had now passed since the first factories appeared among the northern hills. Now the tall chimneys and gaunt mills had been multiplied a hundredfold, and armies of grimy, grey-slated houses had encamped around them. Overhead hung a perpetual pall of smoke so that their inhabitants groped to their work as in a fog. There were no parks or trees: nothing to remind men of the green fields from which they came or to break the squalid monotony of the houses and factories. From the open drains and ditches that flowed beneath the shade of sulphurous chimneys and between pestilential hovels arose a foetid smell. The only symbols of normal human society were the gin shops. Here on the rare days of leisure the entire population would repair, men, women and children, to suck themselves into insensibility on "Cream of the Valley" or Godfrey's Cordial.

In a terrible passage in one of his novels of the 'forties, Disraeli described such a town. "Wodgate had the appearance of a vast squalid suburb. As you advanced, leaving behind you long lines of little dingy tenements, with infants lying about the road, you expected every moment to emerge into some streets, and encounter buildings bearing some correspondence, in their size and comfort, to the considerable population swarming and busied around you. Nothing of the kind. There were no public buildings of any sort; no churches, chapels, town-hall, institute, theatre; and the principal streets in the heart of the town in which were situated the coarse and grimy shops . . . were equally narrow, and if possible more dirty. At every fourth or fifth house, alleys seldom above a yard wide, and streaming with filth, opened out of the street. . . . Here, during the days of business, the sound of the hammer and the file never ceased, amid gutters of abomination, and piles of foulness, and stagnant pools of filth; reservoirs of leprosy and plague, whose exhalations were sufficient to taint the atmosphere of the whole of the kingdom and fill the country with fever and pestilence."

Reality was more terrible than art. Disraeli did not exaggerate but, out of deference to Victorian proprieties, toned down the horror of his picture. The official reports of the Royal Health of Towns Commission of 1845 were more graphic for they were more exact. In 442 dwellings examined in Preston, 2400 people slept in 852 beds. In 84 cases four shared a bed, in 28 five, in 13 six, in 3 seven, and in 1 eight. The cellar populations of Manchester and Liverpool, nearly 18,000 in the former and more in the latter, were without any means of removing night-soil from the habitations. Even for those who lived above ground water-closets were unknown and the privies, shared in common by hundreds, were generally without doors. A doctor in his report on the Lancashire towns testified:

"I have known instances where the wall of a dwelling-house has been constantly wet with foetid fluid which has filtered through from a midden and poisoned the air with its intolerable stench: and the family was never free from sickness during the six months they endured the nuisance. Instances in which foetid air finds its way into the next dwelling-house are not infrequent. I know an instance (and I believe there are many such), where it is impossible to keep food without its being tainted for even a single night in the cupboards on the side of the house next the public necessary, and where the foetor is offensively perceptible always and oppressive in the morning before the door is opened. In this instance the woman of the house told me she had never been well since she came to it, and the only reason she gave for her living in it was, the house was 6d. a week cheaper than others free from the nuisance."[1]

Such horrors, intolerable to modern minds, must be judged in proper proportion: it was only the unprecedented rapidity

[1] *Dr. Lyon Playfair, Health of Towns Commission, I. Report on the State of Large Towns in Lancashire, 1845.*

and extent of their growth which made them seem terrible to contemporaries. There had always been filthy slums in the small, semi-rural cities of the older England; nobody had dreamt of regulating them. Nor was sanitary carelessness confined to the poor of the new towns. Even at royal Windsor the footmen in the pantry suffered perpetually from sore throats until 1844 when more than fifty unemptied cesspits were discovered under the castle. A people still rustic regarded bad drains as a joke in the same category as high cheese and "old grouse in gunroom," and even welcomed their stench as a useful warning of bad weather. But those of the better-to-do classes who had to pass through the new factory towns found the nuisance there beyond a joke. It had become, as Disraeli later reminded the House of Commons, not a matter of sewerage but a question of life and death.

In Little Ireland, Ancoats, Engels, seeking material for his great work on the proletariat of south Lancashire, described the standing pools, full of refuse, offal and sickening filth, that poisoned the atmosphere of the densely populated valley of the Medlock. Here "a horde of ragged women and children swarm about, as filthy as the swine that thrive upon the garbage heaps and in the puddles. . . . The race that lives in these ruinous cottages behind broken windows mended with oilskin, sprung doors and rotten door-posts, or in dark wet cellars in measureless filth and stench . . . must really have reached the lowest stage of humanity. . . . In each of these pens, containing at most two rooms, a garret and perhaps a cellar, on the average twenty human beings live. . . . For each one hundred and twenty persons, one usually inaccessible privy is provided; and in spite of all the preachings of the physicians, in spite of the excitement into which the cholera epidemic plunged the sanitary police by reason of the condition of Little Ireland, in spite of everything, in this year of grace, 1844, it is in almost the same state as in 1831."[1]

But Engels encountered worse. Groping along the maze of narrow covered passages that led from the streets of the old town of Manchester into the yards and alleys that lined the south bank of the Irk, he found a courtyard at whose entrance there stood a doorless privy so dirty that the inhabitants could only pass in and out of the court by wading through stagnant pools of excrement. In this district, where one group of thirty

[1] *Engels, 60.*

hovels housing three hundred and eighty people boasted not even a single privy, the joint founder of modern Communism obtained his famous view of the Irk from Ducie Bridge:

"The view from this bridge, mercifully concealed from mortals of small stature by a parapet as high as a man, is characteristic for the whole district. At the bottom flows, or rather stagnates, the Irk, a narrow, coal-black, foul-smelling stream full of debris and refuse which it deposits on the shallower right bank. In dry weather, a long string of the most disgusting, blackish-green, slime pools are left standing on this bank, from the depths of which bubbles of miasmatic gas constantly arise and give forth a stench unendurable even on the bridge forty or fifty feet above the surface of the stream. . . . It may be easily imagined, therefore, what sort of residue the stream deposits. Below the bridge you look upon the piles of debris, the refuse, filth, and offal from the courts on the steep left bank; here each house is packed close behind its neighbour and a piece of each is visible, all black, smoky, crumbling, ancient, with broken panes and window frames. . . . Here the background embraces the pauper burial-ground, the station of the Liverpool and Leeds Railway, and in the rear of this, the Workhouse, the ' Poor-Law Bastille ' of Manchester, which, like a citadel, looks threateningly down from behind its high walls and parapets on the hilltop upon the working people's quarter below."[1]

To comprehend the dual nature of early nineteenth century Britain and the legacy of discontent and social division we still inherit from its tragic dualism, this picture drawn by Engels from Ducie Bridge must be set against Wordsworth's sonnet written on its fellow English bridge at Westminster.

As Engels justly asked, how could people who were compelled to live in such pigstyes, and who were dependent for their water supply on this pestilential stream, live natural and human lives or bring up their children as anything but savages? And what kind of posterity was England, in her feverish search for wealth, breeding to preserve and enjoy that wealth? It was a question to which economists gave no answer.

[1] *Engels, 49-50.*

There were more urgent ones to answer which concerned not posterity but the present. If reflection could not teach the intellect that men who inhabited the same country were dependent on one another, germs could. Typhus and putrid fever took a less individualist view of man's nature than the economists. The microbes of infection never acknowledged the law that every man could find and maintain his own separate level. Asiatic cholera in 1831 and typhus in 1837 and 1843 from their strongholds in the industrial towns defied every effort of hastily improvised sanitary police and chloride of lime to dislodge them and threatened to devastate the whole country.

There were other warnings that a nation could not neglect a substantial part of its population without endangering its safety. A sullen and savage proletariat, growing in numbers, was turning against the rest of the community, its symbols and traditions. Carlyle, with his poet's sensitiveness, felt from the seclusion of his Chelsea study the imminence of some terrible explosion among the northern workers. "Black, mutinous discontent devours them. . . . English commerce, with its world-wide, convulsive fluctuations, with its immeasurable Proteus steam demon, makes all paths uncertain for them, all life a bewilderment; society, steadfastness, peaceable continuance, the first blessings of man are not theirs. This world is for them no home, but a dingy prison-house, of reckless unthrift, rebellion, rancour, indignation against themselves and against all men. . . ."[1]

In such a soil the orator of social revolution and the agitator could look for speedy returns. In the year of Victoria's accession a People's Charter was put forward by a small group of radical members of Parliament, dissenting ministers and Irish and Cornish orators. It demanded the immediate transfer of electoral power from the middle-class electorate of 1832 to the numerically superior labouring class through universal franchise, the ballot, annual parliaments, the abolition of the property qualification, payment of members and equal electoral districts.

The Charter, which was submitted to mass meetings in Birmingham and London in the following year, caught on like wildfire in the industrial towns. The agitation soon assumed an alarming aspect. At meetings arms were called for by excited

[1] *T. Carlyle, Chartism.*

Celtic orators, and forests of oak saplings were brandished by grimy sons of toil. Stories were whispered about the country of how the master workmen of Birmingham—the savage bishops of heathen Midland tradition—were manufacturing pikes which, smuggled out in the aprons of Staffordshire chain and nail makers, were being sold to honest revolutionaries at 1/8 a piece or 2/6 polished. Men spoke of kidnapping the wives and children of the aristocracy and carrying them into the northern towns as hostages, of the secret manufacture of shells and hand grenades and caltrops for strewing in the path of the hated yeomanry. Newcastle was to be reduced to ashes: "if the magistrates *Peterloo* us," the cry went round, "we will *Moscow* England." In 1839 the principal town of Monmouthshire was attacked by miners with muskets and pitchforks. Here and in riots at Birmingham many lost their lives.

The ruling class ignored the movement. The violence of its spokesmen[1] rendered it ridiculous in the eyes of responsible persons. The House of Commons, with its hatred of exaggeration, refused to receive its petitions. During the debate on one, purporting to bear the signatures of millions of operatives, the House was half empty: though a Tory back-bencher, who one day as Prime Minister was to take more than one step towards the fulfilment of the People's Charter, contended that the rights of labour were as sacred as those of property. Those within the movement who advocated violence were correspondingly strengthened. For it seemed that the rulers of England had no interest in the sufferings of its disinherited people.

The climax came in 1842, the year which saw the publication of the Report on the employment of children in the coal mines. One of those prolonged and periodic depressions that attended industrialisation had culminated in almost unbearable hardship in the midlands and north: factories were closing and the families of the operatives starving. Through the previous winter stories

[1] Feargus O'Connor, the Chartist leader, who claimed to be descended from the Irish Kings, thus addressed his followers in Palace Yard, Westminster. "It was said the working classes were dirty fellows, and that among them they could not get six hundred and fifty-eight who were fit to sit in the House of Commons. Indeed! He would soon alter that. He would pick out that number from the present meeting, and the first he chose he would take down to Mr. Hawes's soap factory; then he would take them where they should reform their tailors' bills; he would next take them to the hairdresser and perfumer, where they should be anointed with the fashionable stink; and having done that by way of preparation, he would quickly take them into the House of Commons, when they would be the best six hundred and fifty-eight that ever sat within its walls."

had been reaching the breakfast tables of the well-to-do and respectable of the sufferings of their human brethren in such remote places as Bolton and Paisley. The growth of the newspaper-reading habit and the introduction of the penny post, was beginning to open the eyes of the middle class to what was happening in other parts of the country. That year the first illustrated weekly appeared in London and the pages of its earliest issues were full of sombre pictures of the distress of the manufacturing districts.

In the spring Sir Robert Peel's Conservative government, faced by a serious budget deficit, resorted to its revolutionary device (for peacetime) of an income tax of sevenpence in the pound on all incomes of over £150 a year. At Buckingham Palace that May a Bal Masque was held in the hope of stimulating trade. The Queen, who was dressed as Queen Philippa, accompanied by Prince Albert in the costume of the chivalrous Edward III., wore a pendant stomacher valued at £60,000. Several nobles, inspired by the Gothic revival, commissioned suits of full armour for the occasion. Another hired £10,000 worth of jewellery for the night from Storr and Mortimer. Under the soft glare of five hundred and thirty gas jets the spectacle continued till long after three in the morning. A few days later, as the Queen returned down Constitution Hill from her afternoon drive in Hyde Park, a crazy youth tried to assassinate her with a pocket pistol. As he was seized by the police he was heard to cry out: "Damn the Queen; why should she be such an expense to the nation!"[1]

Meanwhile the news from the north grew worse. At Burnley the Guardians, with a quarter of the population destitute, were forced to appeal to the government for help. Here the weavers were working for 7½d. a day. Idlers with faces haggard with famine stood in the streets their eyes wearing the fierce and uneasy expression of despair. A doctor who visited the town in June found in eighty-three houses, selected at hazard, no furniture but old boxes, stone boulders (for chairs) and beds of straw and sacking. The whole population was living on oatmeal, water and skimmed milk.

Revolution was in the air. The workers were talking openly of burning down the mills in order to enforce a nation-wide strike. In Colne and Bolton hands were clenched, teeth set and

[1] *Illustrated London News, I,* 67.

fearful curses uttered. Haggard orators bade starving audiences take cheer, for soon "Captain Swing" would rule the manufacturing districts. At a Chartist gathering on Enfield moor near Blackburn, a speaker announced that the industrial North would soon be marching on Buckingham Palace ; if the Queen refused the Charter, every man would know what to do.[1]

Across St. George's Channel, Ireland—herself the mother of many an English factory operative—starved and rioted. In Ennis the mob attacked the flour mills; at Cork, growing weary of a diet of old cabbage leaves, it stormed the potato markets. Dear corn—popularly believed to be the price of the time-honoured Corn Laws which protected the landowner at the expense of the poor—the new machines and the middle-class franchise were alike indicted by bitter and angry men as the cause of their sufferings. As the uneasy parliamentary session of the summer of 1842 drew to a close, the authorities reinforced the troops in the industrial areas.

The first rumblings of the storm came from Staffordshire. Here towards the end of July the colliers, following a reduction of their wages to 2/6 a day, turned out and, marching on every works in the neighbourhood, compelled their comrades to do likewise. Those who refused were flung into the canals, plugs were hammered out of the boilers and furnaces extinguished. The word went round that all labour was to cease until the Charter had become the law of the land. The markets in the towns of the western midlands were deserted and every workhouse besieged by vast queues of gaunt woman and children and idle men.

The Lord Lieutenant, sitting with the magistrates at the Dartmouth Hotel, West Bromwich, called out the county yeomanry. The 3rd Dragoon Guards, stationed in Walsall, endeavoured to restore order. Shopkeepers and farmers were enrolled as special constables, and the old England was pitted against the new. But in the industrial areas the dispossessed had the advantage of numbers and they were desperate. At Wolverhampton strikers surrounded the workhouse and established virtual mob-law. Farther north a procession of 6000 workmen surged down on collieries, iron-works and potteries until every chimney in the district had ceased to smoke. There

[1] Another speaker on Pendlehill referred to the Queen as "a dawdling useless thing." (*Annual Register, June, 1842.*)

was little physical violence for only in a few places was there any resistance. Under threat of crowbar and torch, the owners of bakeries, groceries and public houses distributed provisions with the best face they could. Bills appeared on the walls calling the "Toiling Slaves" to monster demonstrations: others, issued by alarmed authorities, threatened transportation to those who destroyed machinery or used intimidation.

Such was the position as the parliamentary session of 1842 drew to a close and Ministers, who doubted their ability to keep the peace for more than a few days longer, prepared after the imperturbable manner of England for the customary Cabinet fish dinner at the Crown and Sceptre tavern, Greenwich. In the seaports there were signs of a slight improvement in trade. But the reports that poured in from every manufacturing district continued menacing. The whole population was in a state of intense excitement. It was difficult to say whether the cause was hunger, wage reductions, Chartism or the popular demand for cheap bread and repeal of the Corn Laws.

The explosion came on August 4th at Staleybridge, where the employees of Messrs. Bayley's mill had received notice of a further reduction in wages. The strikers, as though acting on prearranged orders, turned out the workers at every factory in Ashton and Oldham. Next morning they marched on Manchester. For a few noisy hours the main body was held up by a small detachment of police and troops at Holt Town. But other rioters swarming out from the streets on either flank, the authorities were forced to fall back leaving factories and provision shops at their mercy. At Messrs. Birley's mill, where momentary resistance was encountered, the roof was stormed, every window broken, and two policemen and an onlooker killed. On Saturday, 6th, while Sir Robert and his fellow Ministers were embarking at Hungerford Pier on the *Prince of Wales* steam packet for their outing at Greenwich, riots were raging in every district of Manchester. Police stations were demolished and more officers killed.

The great "Turn Out," long threatened by heady orators and whispered among the people, had come at last. The workers were on the march. On Sunday the rioting spread to Stockport and other parts of Cheshire. Mills were attacked, bakeries looted and the police pelted with stones. At Preston the mob attacked the military, and several lost their lives. In the Potteries some colliers arrested by the police were rescued by their fellow miners who subsequently stormed the Burslem Town Hall, burnt its records and rate books, and sacked the George Inn and the principal shops. Afterwards the town looked as though an invading army had passed through it.

The scene of the insurrection would not have been England had its grim and starving landscape not been lightened by flashes of humour. At one place where a band of marauding Amazons from the cotton mills threatened to burn down a farm, the farmer turned the tables by loosing his bull. In another—it was at Wigan—the local miners insisted on keeping guard round Lord Crawford's park against their fellow strikers so that, as one of them put it, the old Lord could drink his port in peace.[1]

Work throughout the industrial north was now at a complete standstill. In Manchester all the shops were shuttered and the streets thronged with thousands of workmen who besieged the sidewalks demanding money and food from passers by. Similar scenes were enacted in almost every industrial town from Leicester to Tyneside, and in western Scotland. At Stoke-on-Trent the mob gutted the Court of Requests, the Police Station and the larger houses; at Leeds the Chief of Police was seriously wounded, and fatal casualties occurred at Salford, Blackburn and Halifax. The wildest rumours circulated: that in Manchester the police had been cut to pieces with volleys of brickbats; that the redcoats, welcomed by the hungry populace as brothers, had risen against their officers; that the Queen who had "set her face against gals working in mills" was ready to grant the Charter and open the ports to cheap corn.

The alarm of the well-to-do classes in the adjacent rural areas was by now intense. In the factory towns of Lancashire 6000 millowners and shopkeepers enrolled as special constables to defend their menaced interests. The Government decided to act with vigour. In every northern and midland county the yeomanry were called out, and farmers' sons sharpened sabres on the grindstone at the village smithy before riding off to patrol the grimy streets of a world they did not understand. Tall-hatted magistrates rode beside them ready to mumble through the Riot Act and loose the forces that had triumphed at Peterloo over the urban savagery their own neglect had created.

On Saturday, August 13th, there was fierce rioting in

[1]Communicated by the present Earl of Crawford and Balcarres.

Rochdale, Tolmorden, Bury, Macclesfield, Bolton, Stockport, Burslem and Hanley. At the latter place 5000 strikers marched on a neighbouring country mansion and left it blazing. Hordes of rough-looking men in fur caps carrying clubs and faggots patrolled the squalid unpaved roads around the idle mills; others attempted to hold up the mail and tear up the permanent way on the Manchester-Leeds railway. Next morning, though Sunday, the Cabinet met and issued urgent orders to the Guards and the Artillery at Woolwich to hold themselves in readiness for Manchester. That evening as the 3rd battalion of the Grenadiers debouched with band playing through the gates of St. George's Barracks into Trafalgar Square, vast numbers of working men and boys closed in and tried to obstruct its progress. In Regent Street the crowd became so menacing that the order was given to fix bayonets; all the way to Euston Square Station, which was packed with police, hisses and groans continued. The 34th Foot, summoned in haste from Portsmouth, was also continuously hooted on its march across London.

By the evening of the 16th, Manchester was held by three regular infantry battalions, the 1st Royal Dragoons and artillery detachments with howitzers and six-pounders. A few miles away the streets of Bolton were patrolled by companies of the 72nd Highlanders. Other troops poured in by the new railroads with such rapidity that the rebellion quickly began to lose its dangerous appearance. All that week the magistrates and police, protected by the military, were busy arresting ringleaders and detachments of rioters, and every main road and railway was watched by mounted constables and dragoons.

After that the insurrection crumbled. Further resort to force was useless. Hunger did the rest. Anger and hectic excitement gave place to weakness and despair. The shops were guarded and, with the mills closed, even the miserable wages of the past year of want ceased. The poor rates in every Lancashire town soared as pale, famished multitudes besieged the workhouses, and ruined householders, unable to pay their rent, abandoned their homes. In November Engels saw gaunt, listless men at every street corner in Manchester, and whole streets of houses in Stockport standing empty.

Gradually the factories reopened and a defeated people crept back to work. The insurrection had failed. Yet, like the

Report on the employment of children in coal mines, it had done something to awaken the conscience of England. It had added to pity fear, and, as is the way with the English in times of trial, a sober resolve to remove the cause of the evil. So long as the rioting continued, worthy and peace-loving folk set their faces resolutely against the rioters. But when it was over they took counsel of their consciences.[1]

Many, particularly the manufacturers and the new middle-class, who had nothing to gain by the protection of agriculture and much by the cheapening of provisions, laid the blame on the Corn Laws. Others, like the country landowners, condemned the inhumanity of the millowners, who retaliated by pointing to the low wages and neglected hovels of the agricultural workers in the southern counties. As Ashley, the factory reformer, knew to his misery, none were worse than those on the Dorset estate of his father, Lord Shaftesbury. The economists and the states-men who subscribed to their theories continued to reiterate the importance of non-interference with the laws of supply and demand.

But with the general thinking public the view gained ground that there were limits to the efficacy of *laissez-faire*, where public health and the employment of children were concerned. Sanitary reform and factory regulation began for the first time to be taken seriously. Early in 1843 Ashley was able to carry without opposition an address to the Crown for the diffusion of moral and religious education among the working classes. In the following year a new Factory Bill became law limiting the hours of children under sixteen to six and a half a day and establishing further regulations for the fencing of machinery and the inspection of industrial premises. In the same year a commission on the Health of Towns was appointed. Its Report written by Edwin Chadwick revealed that of fifty large towns examined, only six had a good water supply and not one an adequate drainage system.

Public opinion was by now far ahead of parliamentary

---

[1] "It is certainly a very dismal matter for reflection, and well worthy of the considera-tion of the profoundest political philosophers, that the possession of such a Constitution, all our wealth, industry, ingenuity, peace, and that superiority in wisdom and virtue which we so confidently claim, are not sufficient to prevent the existence of a large mountain of human misery, of one stratum in society in the most deplorable state, both moral and physical, to which mankind can be reduced, and that all our advantages do not secure us against the occurrence of evils and mischiefs so great as to threaten a mighty social and political convulsion." *Greville Memoirs, Part II, Vol. II, 119-20.*

action. During the middle and latter forties the novels of
Dickens, Disraeli and Charles Kingsley, the pamphlets of Carlyle
and the poems of Elizabeth Barrett Browning educated the
reading classes in the Condition of the People question and
stimulated their desire for social reform. Intelligent England
had become conscious of the new towns. Even Tennyson turned
from his dreams of a remote chivalry to confront the inescapable
problem of his age:

"Slowly comes a hungry people, as a lion creeping nigher,
   Glares at one that nods and winks behind a slowly dying fire."

The thought of a new generation was crystallised in Ashley's
unanswerable question, "Let me ask the House, what was it
gave birth to Jack Cade? Was it not that the people were writhing
under oppressions which they were not able to bear? It was
because the Government refused to redress their grievances that
the people took the law into their own hands."

So inspired by pity and purged by the fear of some new and
more terrible arising, the conscience and commonsense of
England addressed themselves to the redress of great wrongs.
They received little direction from the responsible rulers of the
nation who were blinded by a theory.[1] The urge for social
reform was spontaneous and its first fruits were mainly voluntary
and unofficial. It took the form of numberless remedial activities
of a private or only semi-public nature, from feverish church
building and the foundation of industrial schools for the waifs
and strays of the urban slums to the "poor peopling" which
became so fashionable an occupation for well-to-do young
ladies in the late 'forties: it was in this work that Florence
Nightingale began her life of voluntary service. All over
England and Scotland isolated individuals began to tackle self-
imposed tasks, each striving to cleanse his or her own small
local corner of the Augean stable. Such were provincial doctors
who faced fever and vested interest in a tireless campaign against
insanitary conditions, devoted clergymen and nonconformist
ministers, city missionaries and temperance workers, and young
men and women of comfortable circumstances—often evangeli-

---

[1] In later years men like Sir James Graham, the Home Secretary, and John Roebuck,
the Radical economist, admitted that they had been wrong in their fear that the limitation of hours of labour would ruin the country.

cals or quakers—who gave up their leisure hours to teach in ragged schools or to organise clubs, sports and benefit societies for their poorer neighbours. In this way, not for the first time in England's history, the destruction wrought by her own tumultuous vitality, was redeemed in part by the operation of her own generous conscience.

But the evil was deeply rooted, and the remedy, for all the energy and enthusiasm behind it, so ill-co-ordinated and tardy that those who prophesied revolution and social chaos[1] might have been proved right had it not been for one over-riding factor. The social maladies that provoked revolt were not destroyed though they were henceforward slowly but steadily mitigated. On the other hand, while diminishing in intensity, they continued to grow in extent through further urbanisation. Revolution was avoided by extending the area of exploitation. But the very factor which most hastened that process ended the isolation of the industrial areas from the rest of the community. The railways had already been decisive in the suppression of the rebellion: an express train had brought a critical appeal for help from Preston to Manchester, and the Guards had been transferred from London to Lancashire in the course of a single night. Rapid internal communication and a new habit of travel, born of cheap transport, was within a few years to transform England and give her a new unity and orientation.

[1]Engels expected a further and probably decisive revolutionary crisis in 1847, or at latest 1853. *The Condition of the Working Class in England* 296.

CHAPTER THREE

Iron Horse

> "And along the iron veins that traverse the frame of
> our country, beat and flow the fiery pulses of its exertion,
> hotter and faster every hour. All vitality is concentrated
> through those throbbing arteries into the central cities;
> the country is passed over like a green sea by narrow
> bridges, and we are thrown back in continually closer
> crowds on the city gates."
>
> *John Ruskin, The Seven Lamps of Architecture.*

To TURN OVER the pages of the early volumes of the *Illustrated London News*, which was founded in 1842, is to experience a social revolution. The first volume depicts an England that, apart from the capital, is mainly rural—a land of cathedral spires embowered in trees ; fairs and markets ; fat cattle, gaitered farmers and squires and smocked peasants. Where the manufacturing districts appear they do so as an almost savage *terra incognita*, with rough unpaved roads, grim gaol-like factories and men and women of sullen and brutish appearance. Even here one feels the country has only been occupied by a horde of nomad invaders: on the outskirts of the Manchester of 1842 there were still sloping wooded valleys with girls keeping sheep a stone's throw from the flat slate roofs and tall smoking chimneys.

Yet before the end of the 'forties the scene has completely changed. It is an urban England that is engraved on the crowded page. The stress is now on paved streets, vast Gothic town halls, the latest machinery, above all the railroad. The iron horse, with its towering, belching funnel and its long load of roaring coaches plunging through culvert and riding viaduct, had spanned the land, eliminating distance and reducing all men to a common denominator. And the iron horse did not go from village to village: it went from industrial town to town. The England of Winchester and Canterbury and Chester was a thing of the past. The England of smoking Rotherham and Hull and colonial Crewe had arrived.

This revolution in transport came with an extraordinary rapidity. In 1830, and in most places in 1840, a man who wanted to take a journey did so on the roof of a stage coach. Tom Brown went to Rugby of all places in the old Tally-ho! To travel by the London Tantivy mail to Birmingham along the macadamised turnpike, a distance of 120 miles, took twelve hours; to Liverpool another eleven. One left London shortly before eight in the morning, changed in the course of ten minutes into the Birmingham-Liverpool Mail at the same hour in the evening, and reached one's destination, bleary-eyed and exhausted, at seven next day.

That was the very fastest travel. And what travelling it was! On a cold, damp, raw December morning one waited in the dark at the posting-house for the Highflyer or Old True Blue Independent coach "coming hup " and when the muddied, steaming horses drew up in the courtyard, took one's "preference" seat in the hot, suffocating, straw-strewn box. There one sat in cramped darkness for many hours of creaking, lumbering and jolting until the "many-coated, brandy-faced, blear-eyed guard let in a whole hurricane of wind" with the glad tidings that the coach had reached another inn "wot 'oss'd it," where the company was allowed half an hour's grace to dine. The only alternative was to travel on the roof, in dust and glare in summer, and muffled to the nose in a frozen eternity in winter. It had its romantic side, of course, but no man would undertake such travel lightly. And what with the fare of sixpence a mile for inside accommodation, the cost of meals at the posting inns, and the tips to ostler, boots, guard, post-boy and waiter, it was beyond the means of all but a small minority.

In what seemed to our ancestors only a few years all this was changed. The first tentative[1] steam railway from Stockton to Darlington had been opened in 1825, and the Liverpool and Manchester line had followed in 1830. A year after Queen Victoria's accession there were only 500 miles of operating railway in the British Isles. The first railway boom in 1830-9, following a run of good harvests and financed mainly by provincial money, added another 5,000 miles of projected track. Of these 1,900 miles were open by the summer of 1843. They included the lines from London to Birmingham, Manchester, Brighton and Bristol.

---

[1]For long it was an open question whether horses or steam engines should draw railed traffic, and, after the final triumph of steam, whether the new engines would be most serviceable on iron tracks or as unrailed coaches on the turnpike road. *J. H. Clapham, An Economic History of Modern Britain, I, 382, 386.*

Travellers, once they had got over the first shock of noise, sulphur and speed, were entranced by the railroad. Greville in 1837 travelled in four and a half hours from Birmingham to Liverpool to the races, sitting in a sort of chariot with two places and finding nothing disagreeable about it but the whiffs of stinking air. His first sensation, he admitted, was one of slight nervousness and of being run away with, but a feeling of security soon supervened and the velocity was delightful. "Town after town, one park and *chateau* after another are left behind with the rapid variety of a moving panorama." At every stop all heads appeared at the windows, while the platform resounded with astonished cries of "How on earth came you here?" The most surprising feature of it all, apart from the speed[1] and smoothness of motion, was the wonderful punctuality. It gave to man something of the precision and power of the machine.

At first, of course, until people got used to the idea, there was a certain amount of opposition. Landowners, corporations and venerable Cathedral clergy and dons were at pains to keep the vulgar, snorting intruders away from their domains, thus both impoverishing and inconveniencing their successors. Gentlemen resented their noisy intrusion on their parks and huntsmen on their favourite gorses. Poets like Wordsworth thought them hideous, and farmers complained of frightened horses and cattle; keepers of posting-houses, stage coachmen and canal proprietors also naturally hated the puffing billies. "I thought likewise," wrote Jasper Petulengro, "of the danger to which one's family would be exposed of being run over and severely scorched by these same flying fiery vehicles." Such opponents found a doughty champion in the Tory M.P. for Lincoln, Colonel Sibthorpe, who "abominated all railroads soever" and made it his business to oppose every bill for their promotion.

These efforts could not avert the march of progress. The taste for railway travel once acquired continued to grow. In 1842 the linking of England by rail was still very incomplete. When a Chartist agitator was arrested in Northumberland for a seditious speech at Birmingham, he was taken by hackney coach to Newcastle, by ferry across the Tyne to Gateshead, by

---

[1] One "engineer" on the Liverpool-Birmingham line in 1837 reached the astonishing rate of 45 miles an hour, after which he was promptly dismissed by a prudent company. *Greville Memoirs, Part II, Vol. I, 13.*

rail to Carlisle, by stage coach over Shap Fell to Preston, and
thence by what was soon to become the North-Western Railway
to Birmingham. In this fashion a man could travel from Euston
to Glasgow in twenty-four hours—by rail to Fleetwood, by
steamer to Ardrossan and by rail on to Glasgow. "What more
can any reasonable man want?" asked the *Railway Times*. Yet
the reasonable man and the railroad speculators who catered for
his needs wanted more.

Of the latter the most famous was George Hudson, the York
linen-draper. Under his dynamic and sanguine leadership a
railway mania developed that rivalled the South Sea Bubble.[1]
During the period of cheap money after 1843 nearly ten thousand
miles of new railway were sanctioned by private parliamentary
acts. Much speculative money was lost in the process—the
sudden slump of 1847 was a minor social calamity—but amalgamation of the smaller and more hare-brained ventures by the
larger resulted in ultimate stabilisation. By 1849 the railway
system of England had taken on the general form we know
to-day.

All this involved a revolution in English life and organisation.
For many years the country was covered by armies of "navi-
gators" or "navvies," whom contractors employed to translate
the grandiose dreams of the railway projectors and the capital
of their shareholders into solid cutting, embankment, tunnel
and permanent way. In 1848 nearly 200,000 labourers, many of
them Irish, were engaged in this vast task. With their rough
habits and speech, high wages—pay day was usually a brutal
debauch—and their generous taste in steak, plush waistcoats and
whisky,[2] they uprooted ancient ways of living in every place
where they encamped. To many of the older skilled workers in
the country districts their square-tailed coats of velveteen, their
soiled white felt hats and spotted scarlet vests symbolised the
"accursed wages of savagery and sin": for the younger villagers
their sojourn had an exciting, unsettling quality that in after
years caused many to follow them to the great cities along
the gleaming lines they had laid.

In 1840 England was still regional in its outlook: by 1850
it was national. Save in the remoter shires where there was

---

[1] *Punch* depicted a crowd of citizens throwing themselves and their money-bags in
front of an iron "puffing billy" while parliamentary lawyers in the shape of crocodiles
waited hungrily in the foreground and gulls hovered overhead. *Punch IX*, (*1845*), *47.*
[2] They called it "white beer."

still no puff of smoke in the valleys to mar the soft horizons, it had become the common lot of an Englishman to live near a railroad. And the new travel had been made accessible to the poorest. In 1845 Gladstone, then President of the Board of Trade in Sir Robert Peel's Conservative administration, brought in a measure compelling every railway company to run at least one train daily over its system with covered third class accommodation at a penny a mile. Within a few years the receipts of such cheap travel had become almost the most valuable part of the companies' revenue. With the railroad came also cheap coal and cheap food, linking mine, port and countryside to the all-consuming town, and the creation of a vested interest carrying the capital of thousands of shareholders and employing a growing multitude of workers. All these were henceforward dependent on the continued industrialisation of their country.

In other ways England had become more closely knit internally, as well as better connected with the outer world. The first electric telegraph was tried in 1838; eight years later the Electric Telegraph Company was formed to exploit it commercially. Within two years there were nearly 2,000 miles of public telegraph with offices open day and night. Meanwhile the Penny Post, introduced by Rowland Hill in 1840, had led to a far-reaching change in social habit: in three years the weekly delivery of letters in the United Kingdom rose from a million and a half to nearly four millions. Correspondence, hitherto an activity of the well-to-do classes alone, became common to all who could read and write. The prepaid adhesive stamps, affixed to the new paper bags or envelopes which took the place of folded sheets and wafers, were the symbols of a new conception of life, less local and more universal.

So were the trails of smoke that marked every sea-coast horizon. The first British steamboat had been launched on the Clyde in 1811: in the next thirty years over six hundred were built. In 1838 the first iron sailing vessel crossed the Atlantic. Four years later the *Great Western* steamship arrived one June morning in King's Road, Bristol, from New York, having performed in twelve and a half days a passage which until then had normally taken a month. The world of which industrial Britain was the centre was daily growing smaller.

To grasp it she stretched out eager and vigorous hands. Despite trade slumps and periodic fluctuations with all their attendant miseries, the exports of the country were rising fast. History had never recorded such an expansion of wealth and opportunity as came to island Britain in the first half of the nineteenth century: even the golden Spanish discoveries in the Americas three centuries before paled beside it. Exports of unmanufactured iron soared from under 30,000 tons in 1815 to five times as much in 1830, ten times in 1840, and nearly twenty times in 1850. In the first half of the century coal exports were multiplied fifteen-fold. Between 1839 and 1849 alone the exports of mixed wool and cotton fabrics from the West Riding expanded from 2,400,000 to 42,115,000 yards. It was so in almost everything else.

In that torrent of opportunity nothing seemed to matter but getting rich. Whoever could do so was honoured: whoever failed was passed by and trampled under foot. In Merthyr Tydvil, where an army of iron-workers lived, sleeping sometimes sixteen in a room, there were no drains, the water supply came from the open gutters and the filthy streets were unpaved. At the palace of Cyfarthfa Castle a few miles away stood, in Mr. and Mrs. Hammond's significant phrase, "the home and monument of the man who had started life on the road to London with all his fortune in his stout arm and his active brain, and had died worth a million and a half." "Persons in humble life," wrote the editor of the *Mechanic's Magazine* "should be the last— though, we regret to say, they are the first—to speak disrespectfully of the elevation of individuals of their own class, since in nine cases out of ten the individual is the architect of his own good fortune, and the rise of one man by honest means furnishes a ground of hope to all that they may by a proper exertion of the powers which Nature has given them be equally successful."[1] It was the model which the early Victorian moralist held out to his countrymen. Self-help was almost divine.

Of all avenues to individual wealth—as well as to misery, pauperism and degradation—the chief was cotton. In the late eighteen-twenties Britain imported annually an average of 100,000 tons of cotton, ten years later of 200,000 tons, and in 1849 of nearly 350,000 tons. Cotton came to represent nearly a third of the nation's trade. It seemed to many that the national centre of gravity must shift from London to Manchester. The railways

[1] C. Wilkins, *History of the Iron, Steel and Tinplate Trades of Wales.*

underlined the change. What cotton, in other words Lancashire needed, England could no longer deny.

That which cotton needed it asked for. Even in adversity Lancashire was wont to speak out its mind: and Lancashire with brass in its pocket spoke it very loud. And what was in its vigorous mind—in that, that is to say, of its many capitalists great and small—was the wish to make more and ever more money. Everything that stood in the way of its doing so was bad: everything that hastened the process, even by a day, was good.

What Lancashire needed most was to import and export more cotton. Any policy that tended, for whatever reason, to check its imports of raw cotton was opposed to its interests. For centuries the policy of England had been based on the protection of the industry on which the health, social well-being and safety of the bulk of its people depended—agriculture. But to Lancashire the corn-laws which afforded this protection were an impediment and an affront. By restricting imports, they restricted the growth of the industries which manufactured for export. They blocked the channel of expanding profits for Lancashire.

What Manchester thought to-day, it was said, England would think to-morrow. As the power of Lancashire grew, a nation-wide campaign was begun for the abolition of the corn-laws. It enlisted the services of two cotton-spinners of genius, both of whom entered Parliament, Richard Cobden and John Bright. They and the sturdy middle-class voters whose interests they so brilliantly championed held that the proper organisation of human society was one in which Britain devoted herself to the production of manufactured goods, and the rest of mankind supplied her with food and raw materials in exchange. The cheaper the latter, the cheaper and therefore the larger the quantity of goods sold. In this view, the maintenance of duties on foreign corn was a form of national insanity. For they restricted the foreign sales of Lancashire cotton. They could only be explained by the power of monopoly possessed by a few effete and reactionary landowners.

The case for the repeal of the corn laws received new strength from the misery of the industrial proletariat and the rural worker caused by industrial change. Both, confronted by the refusal of the authorities to relieve their sufferings, felt a sense of grievance. The fine gentlemen in Parliament and the land-owners on the Board of Guardians who refused outdoor relief and ignored the promptings of common humanity in the name of *laissez-faire*, themselves enjoyed a protection that was the antithesis of *laissez-faire*. In the shape of a tax on food, protection wore its most odious and therefore most vulnerable form. Wages being low and employment uncertain, the obvious remedy was to remove the impost and cheapen the workers' bread. A Tudor statesman, viewing the interests of the nation as a whole, might have deemed it wiser to seek the same end through minimum wage rates and political action stabilising markets and trade. But to a student of *laissez-faire* such a course could only seem a flagrant breach of immutable economic law.

The cry for cheap bread, therefore, had a triple force. It respected hallowed and eternal truths. It appealed to the needs of the hungry and the hearts of the charitable. It offered enhanced industrial profits. Instead of having to pay higher wages, the north-country manufacturer could reasonably expect, through a fall in the cost of living, to pay lower, and at the same time, by selling more, to increase his returns. That this gain would be at the expense of the landed interest did not trouble him. In the view of Manchester—and as Manchester grew richer, its social consciousness became almost aggressively acute—the landed interest was composed of stupid and anti-quated feudal snobs. The sooner they could be swept away to leave room for the unhampered rule of progressive talent, the better.

But despite the Reform Bill of 1832 the benches of Parliament were still mainly occupied by country gentlemen. The Whig aristocrats who had passed the Reform Bill were landowners like the Tory squires who had opposed it. Neither were yet ready to dispense with a principle on which their own wealth and power, and as they therefore believed, the security of the constitution, depended. The Conservative majority which supported Sir Robert Peel had pledged itself to maintain the existing agricultural duties. The most the Government of 1841 would concede to the reformers was a modification of the sliding scale of 1828 and the fixing of a maximum duty of 20/- a quarter. Even this, to many of its back-bench supporters, seemed too much. A corn-law reformer's motion for total repeal was rejected in 1842 by a majority of more than four to one.

But when Lancashire made up its mind, it took more than a Parliament of squires to stop it. If the House would not see its duty, the electorate would teach it. The power of the vote should be mobilised to destroy the vested interest of the past and, incidentally, to create a new and better one in its place. From its Manchester headquarters, the Anti-Corn Law League had already started on its famous eight-year campaign to arouse the voting middle-class against the protective system and the "corn law monopolists." The agitation was brilliantly successful. In 1841 "Free Trade" was still a panacea of a minority of radical idealists. In 1846, in the face of ever-growing clamour, it was officially adopted by the Conservative Government which had pledged itself to oppose it. By 1850 it had become the classic creed of the country.

There were many reasons for this. The chief were the spirit of the age and the underlying economic dogma which had so curiously captured the imagination of the educated classes. Free Trade was the logical application of Benthamite *laissez-faire*. In the past the English had been little given to abstract speculation: the descendants of farmers, peasants and sailors who had tilled the earth and sailed the seas with an adaptable eye for ever cocked at their changing island skies, they had distrusted logical theories and based their lives on constant and instinctive improvisation—an art in which they excelled all others.

But in the latter eighteenth and early nineteenth centuries the most vigorous elements in Britain had deserted the land. Divorced from the traditional forms of rustic social life of which by long practice they had become past masters, and cut off as it were by the pavements from their own instinctive roots, the English "progressives" fell an easy prey to theory. Before abstract ideas they were as helpless as South Sea islanders before a new disease. They absorbed them uncritically and enthusiastically. Many of them they borrowed from their neighbours, the Scots, whose long training in Calvinism had given them a liking for logic. A Glasgow professor's book, *The Wealth of Nations*, formed the English economic outlook for more than a century.

The early Forsytes, fresh from generations of thought-free and instinctive living in country loam, and their northern prototypes, the Lancashire and West Riding capitalists, were particularly susceptible to the beguilements of abstract political theory, provided it was put to them in a simple form and one likely to benefit their pockets. It was England's fate that the leader of her great traditionalist party during the second quarter of the nineteenth century was himself a man of this class. For all his Harrow and Oxford gloss of classical learning, the leader of the gentlemen of England in the fatal crisis of their history was a Lancashire millowner's son. Sir Robert Peel was a man of splendid talents and industry but, like those from whom he sprang, he was not at home with original ideas. And finding himself in an age of rapid and revolutionary change called upon to steer a course in which his instinct would give him little guide, he was compelled periodically to borrow ideas from others. He did so unconsciously and for that reason with uncritical zeal.

His betrayal of the traditional system he had been elected to defend was as unconscious as it was gradual. Because of his English incapacity for grasping theoretical principles, Peel never saw the corn laws and the protective system of which they were the core as anything but a collection of fiscal instruments. That underlying them might be an enduring principle of government giving continuity to national life, and strength and security to unborn generations, never occurred to his mind. Like most of his countrymen, he began by accepting the corn laws as a matter of course, and ended by swallowing whole the doctrine that destroyed them. The theory of Free Trade was novel, easy to understand and ably and persistently expounded: the ancient principle of state it ignored remained unstated.

Throughout the first half of the nineteenth century the country, largely as a result of the anarchy created by its own feverish pursuit of quick profits in foreign markets, suffered from a series of commercial crises. These increased in intensity with the growth of the system. Various attempts were made to explain them. At one time they were attributed to the unrepresentative nature of the unreformed House of Commons. After the Reform Bill a new scapegoat was sought. It was on the Corn Laws, now assailed by the brilliant oratory and pamphleteering of the League, that the blame was laid. The same simple explanation was held to cover every suffering endured by the industrial masses. Cheap bread was the open sesame which would solve all difficulties. The selfish and stupid

landlord with his antiquated corn laws alone stood between the
nation and perpetual peace and prosperity.

In 1842 Peel, faced by an acute trade slump and the threat
of a revolution in the starving north, met the situation by
reducing the sliding scale duties on corn. During the trade
revival of the next three years he left matters as they were. But
all the while the doctrine of the Anti-Corn Law League was
gaining on his mind,[1] and though he continued dutifully to
regard himself as bound by his electoral pledge to maintain the
existing duties and even denounced Cobden as a dangerous
agitator, he was already his unconscious disciple. When in the
autumn of 1845—one of the wettest and most miserable in
human memory—the Irish potato crop was affected by disease,
he was ready to adopt immediate repeal as the only remedy.

For to feed Ireland, England would have to import surplus
corn from abroad, and neither the English nor the starving
Irish could be expected to pay duty on it. Yet as was pointed out
by Stanley—the only leading member of Peel's cabinet not to be
carried away—abolition of the corn laws only took from the
starving Irish peasant with one hand what it gave with the other.
Having by an act of God been robbed of the first of his two
staple crops, potatoes, he could only be further injured by a
reduction in the price of the second, oats. In the climax of their
own industrial revolution the political rulers of Britain, now
suddenly and almost wholly obsessed by an urban viewpoint,
forgot that the people of Ireland were country, not town
producers. For the remedies they offered were calculated to
relieve the latter at the expense of the former.

Peel, like so many of his countrymen, was in the grip of an
economic theory. He saw the corn laws as a challenge to that
theory and wished to remove them. Having given his electoral
pledge to maintain them, he had regretfully decided that they
would have to stay on the Statute book until the election of a
new Parliament. But the "potato cholera," with its threat to
the Irish food supply, gave him, the first public servant of
Britain, the chance to effect the great change himself—one
which, as he now fervently believed, would set his country and
the world on the path to lasting economic prosperity. It gave
him not a reason for his action—he needed none—but a pretext.

---

[1] As early as 1842 Peel told Gladstone "that in future he questioned whether he could
undertake the defence of the Corn Laws on principle."

For he was seeking not a mere suspension to meet the emergency of the moment, but permanent repeal. It was not, as the Duke of Wellington thought, "rotten potatoes" that put "Peel in his damned fright!" Peel was not in a fright at all, but having been subjugated, as public men in a democracy are apt to be, by continuous pressure and propaganda, he was able to use the Irish calamity to carry a measure in which he now profoundly believed.

It is one of the purposes of a parliamentary constitution to render government sensitive to the larger changes of popular opinion. Before the Reform Bill that of Britain, as a result of a long and gradual redistribution of population, was not sufficiently so. But when the history of our age can be seen in its final perspective, it may come to be held that after the Reform Bill, British parliaments became too sensitive not to the permanent convictions of the nation but to the ephemeral opinion of the hour. For public opinion is not infallible in its pursuit of popular interests. In the early nineteenth century it was assumed by many learned and hopeful persons that it was. The thesis of Bentham and the Utilitarians that the object of all government was the greatest good of the greatest number, was accompanied by the more dubious assumption that that good could always be achieved by the popular decision of the moment. The Reform Bill of 1832, however imperceptibly, began the slow and unconscious transformation of British statesmen from representatives into delegates. Henceforward instead of leading public opinion they tended increasingly to seek votes by following it.

For public opinion, being susceptible of leadership, needs to be wisely led. If it is not led by wise men, it may be led by fools or knaves. Its greatest weakness is that, being imperfectly informed on the complicated issues of government, it is too easily swayed by the specious—by the plausible pretender and the man of limited vision. Cobden, though possessing genius and high integrity, was a man of very short views. He offered his countrymen, in the throes of great and bewildering changes, a panacea for their immediate ills. He explained with brilliant clarity that Free Trade would bring growing wealth to all men and the reign of peace. By removing the cause of discord between nations, it would abolish war. Cobden offered an economic proposition—within certain limits a sound and beneficient one—as an unchanging principle of government. But this no economic proposition can ever be, for economics are governed by the rules of mathematics, and politics by those of inconstant human nature.

It is the highest function of the parliamentary statesman to correct the volatile tendency of public opinion to fall a prey to the ephemeral. To do so he must possess a mind which is proof against plausible fallacy and the clamour of the hour. He must possess the courage of his convictions, the prudence and patience necessary to translate them into achievable policies and the genius to expound them to his countrymen. The more democratic a constitution and the more sensitive its machinery to the changing gusts of popular feeling, the greater becomes the necessity for true leadership and the harder its exercise. It was the misfortune of Britain that at a crisis of her history she did not possess a leader of such calibre. In 1846 she stood, breathless and eager to proceed, at a turning of the road. Without reflection she took what at that moment in time seemed the easiest.

The change in Britain's historic policy came with startling suddenness. Early in November, 1845, Peel proposed in Cabinet that the ports should be opened by immediate Order of Council and that a bill for the permanent modification of the corn laws should be introduced in the new year. Before this decision became public, the leader of the Opposition, Lord John Russell, fearing that the Tories by reversing their policy would steal the electoral tide to power a second time, issued a hasty manifesto to his constituents abandoning the old Whig principle of a fixed duty on corn and declaring for total repeal. This was capped in early December by a Cabinet decision for immediate repeal and an unauthorised announcement in next day's *Times* which precipitated such a crisis in the betrayed Tory ranks that the Government resigned and the Queen sent for Russell. But the latter, prevented from forming an administration by party intrigues centring round the stormy personality of Palmerston, was unable to make use of his opportunity. Instead he "handed back with courtesy the poisoned chalice to Sir Robert."

Peel took it gratefully. He was convinced that he, as the most experienced administrator in the country and the leader of its strongest party, was the proper man to carry the measure. That he had been accredited by the electorate and his own

followers to pursue a contrary policy did not trouble his conscience. For like many other zealous and over-worked public
servants, he had never understood the nature of the English
constitution. He had forgotten that its essence is that a politician
should identify himself with a principle and resign when that
principle is defeated or out of favour. In a speech in which
he declared that he would no longer resist the inference that
employment, low prices and abundance contributed to the
diminution of crime—"as if any human being ever resisted the
inference"[1]—Peel made known his intention to the House when
it reassembled in January. His prestige was such, and the popular
agitation against the Corn Laws so bitter, that a sufficient
number of his own betrayed and shattered Party followed him
with the Opposition into the lobbies on May 15, 1846, to secure
a majority of 98 for repeal. When two months later rising Tory
anger culminated in the fall of his government, he justified
himself in a speech which has gone down to history:

> "I shall leave a name execrated, I know, by every mono-
> polist.... But it may be that I shall be sometimes remembered
> with expressions of goodwill in those places which are the
> abodes of men whose lot it is to labour and earn their daily
> bread by the sweat of their brow; in such places, perhaps,
> my name may be remembered with expressions of good-
> will when they who inhabit them recruit their exhausted
> strength with abundant and untaxed food, the sweeter
> because no longer leavened with a sense of injustice."

It takes a great man to oppose the tide of his age. Benjamin
Disraeli was a great man. Alone among statesmen of his generation he perceived the fallacy of the Manchester School and of
the departure in national policy which it had initiated. The
immediate interests of the factory owner, the worker and the
investor might be served by a free trade policy. But in the long
run he knew that the policy must leave the nation at the mercy
of world-wide forces beyond its control.

A back-bencher when the agitation for the repeal of the
Corn Laws began, a Jew with brilliant but flashy literary antecedents and for that reason denied office in Peel's Government,

[1] *Disraeli, Lord George Bentinck,* Ch. 3.

a parvenu without territorial or commercial influence, Disraeli nevertheless saw with the superior vision of genius the flaw in the logic of the Manchester School—"a body of men . . . eminent for their eloquence, distinguished for their energy, but more distinguished . . . for their energy and eloquence than for their knowledge of human nature or for the extent of their political information.[1] The weakness of their economic reasoning, as of all logical abstraction when applied to human affairs, lay in its lack of elasticity. It was too doctrinaire to withstand the shock of time and the changes wrought by time in human ideas and circumstances. A nation, however powerful, which staked its future on a policy so rigid, might one day suffer a terrible awakening.

The free traders, with their eye on the living individual, rightly assumed that it was the present interest of the British manufacturer and urban worker to sell manufactured goods to a mainly agricultural world and of the world to purchase them by sending its primary products untaxed to Britain. They also assumed that such a favourable situation, once created, would always and automatically continue. But having the historical sense, and not being tied to a formula like Peel and Cobden, Disraeli realised that other nations would not always acquiesce in a British monopoly of industry. They might wish to extend their own industrial markets just as Lancashire had done. If they found their British rivals could undersell them at home, they would put pressure on their governments to raise prohibitive and uneconomic tariffs behind which their growing industries could shelter.

For, as Disraeli reminded his unheeding countrymen, governments were swayed by other considerations than the economic gain of the living individual which Adam Smith had enshrined as the wealth of nations. They might deliberately restrict the course of commerce and limit profits to increase their country's strategic and military strength, safeguard its health and social stability or advance some religious or other ideological conception of national life to which economics were subordinate. Swayed by such reasons, for all Cobden's confident prophecies, they might refuse to follow the British lead and adopt free trade. In place of a world liberated from commercial restrictions and growing ever richer and more peaceable, Britain might one

[1] *Monypenny & Buckle, Disraeli, I, 781.*

day find herself confronted by "a species of Berlin decrees, more stringent even than those of Napoleon."

Disraeli therefore pleaded, though in vain, that his country should hesitate before abandoning the ancient protective and reciprocal commercial principle under which she had so long thrived for one of unrestricted imports. Her aim, he argued, should not be free trade, whose attainment, however desirable, must always depend on constantly varying human factors, but fair trade giving a just and stable reward to the producer. Protection of native industry in the broadest sense was a permanent duty of all rulers and should be "avowed, acknowledged and only limited because . . . protection should be practical . . . and such as should not allow the energies of the country to merge and moulder into a spirit of monopoly."

Human nature being what it was, fair trade could only be achieved through reciprocity. Hostile tariffs could not be fought as Cobden supposed, with free imports. "You cannot have free trade," Disraeli argued, "unless the person you deal with is as liberal as yourself. If I saw a prize-fighter encountering a galley-slave in irons, I should consider the combat equally as fair as to make England fight hostile tariffs with free imports."[1]

Unlike his machine-struck contemporaries, he refused to see cotton-spinning as the final end of British policy. Agriculture, the source of man's nourishment, was still the most vital of national industries. To sacrifice it for the sake of profits, however vast, was to mortgage the country's future security. Three years before the repeal of the Corn Laws, Disraeli, then 38, recalled in the House of Commons the words of a Venetian Doge and merchant prince, "who, looking out from the windows of his Adriatic palace on the commerce of the world anchored in the lagoons beneath, exclaimed, 'This Venice without terra firma is an eagle with one wing!'"[2]

Many of the Corn Law reformers maintained that so far from injuring British agriculture, free trade would benefit it. By reducing the price of bread, it would increase the demand for wheat and so put money even into the pockets of the stupid, reactionary farmer and landlord. It was a mere protectionist's bugbear to imagine that native agriculture would be ruined by cheap surplus wheat from abroad since no such surpluses

[1] Monypenny & Buckle, I, 538.
[2] Hansard, 14th Feb., 1843.

existed. Taking the short view, the Cobdenites were right and fully justified by the events of the next quarter of a century.

But Disraeli was not taking the short view. Wiser than the economists in their own wisdom, he knew that the productive capacity of British farms could not be stimulated indefinitely like that of machinery merely by reducing the price of their products. The unsatisfied demand of the ever-growing towns would increasingly have to be met elsewhere. For a time the virgin corn lands of Asia and the New World, with their vast areas and dependable climates, might lack capital and transport. But with a market in urban Britain for their surplus, permanently guaranteed by an unchanging principle, capital would inevitably be forthcoming to develop their farms and build railways and ships. It would be supplied by British capitalists.

Disraeli not only believed that the decline of British agriculture, at that time the finest in the world, would weaken the country in time of war. He felt that it would undermine the health and happiness of its people and those constitutional liberties which, in his view, rested in the last resort on the strength and independence of the landed interest. By this he did not mean, as his critics supposed, the monopoly of the squires who sat with him on the benches of Parliament. "I am looking in that phrase," he told the House, "to the population of our innumerable villages, to the crowds in our rural towns: I mean that estate of the poor which, in my opinion, has been already dangerously tampered with; I mean the great estate of the Church, which has before this time secured our liberty, and may . . . still secure our civilisation . . . that great judicial fabric, that great building up of our laws and manners, which is, in fact, the ancient polity of the realm."[1]

To the mind of this half-alien patriot the Corn Laws were no mere plank of fiscal policy but an outwork of an historic system which protected a priceless civilisation. That system had based the possession of wealth on the performance of social duty— "the noblest principle that was ever conceived by sage or practised by patriot." Understanding human nature, Disraeli knew how hard it was "to impress upon society that there is such a thing as duty." "The feudal system may have worn out," he wrote, "but its main principle—that the tenure of property

[1] *Monypenny & Buckle, Disraeli, I, 539.*

should be the fulfilment of duty—is the essence of good government."[1]

The idea of private wealth not based on the fulfilment of social duty was repugnant to him because it was contrary to nature. The vice of the *laissez-faire* economists was that they regarded capital as an economic commodity divorced from political and social activity. They treated its use as a purely private affair. Disraeli saw capital not as a commodity of value but as political and social power: as something to be used as a trust. He therefore wished to see its possession permanently associated with social obligations. The ownership of land was capable of giving such association. That of stocks and shares was not.

In all this Disraeli was a Socialist before Socialism became a political force. He told his constituents in 1844 that he had long been aware that there was "something rotten in the core of the social system." Like Coleridge, he held that the State should have the right to invalidate trespasses on "its own inalienable and untransferrable property—the health, strength, honesty and filial love of its children." Rather than an England dominated by the possessors of irresponsible capital, he declared that he would prefer a real revolution in the distribution of national power.

"If there is to be this great change, I for one hope that the foundations of it may be deep, the scheme comprehensive, and that, instead of falling under . . .the thraldom of capital, under the thraldom of those who, while they boast of their intelligence, are more proud of their wealth —if we must find new forces to maintain the ancient throne and immemorial monarchy of England, I for one hope we may find that novel power in the invigorating energies of an educated and enfranchised people."[2]

But Disraeli did not want a revolution. He had not for nothing been nursed in the beech groves of Buckinghamshire amid scenes dear to Hampden and Burke. He was deeply imbued with the spirit of England's history and institutions. He knew that in the last resort the survival of liberty depended on the

---

[1] *General Preface to the Novels, 1870, cit. Monypenny & Buckle, I, 699.*
[2] *Hansard, 20th Feb., 1846, cit. Monypenny & Buckle, I, 767.*

maintenance of private property and on the sense of individual responsibility which its possession could alone engender. Though he did not want a capitalist's England—"a sort of spinning-jenny machine kind of nation"—he did not want a bureaucrat's. Therefore he used all his powers of speech and pen—and it is his country's tragedy that, great as they were, they were limited by his circumstances—to impress on a forgetful generation the twin truths that privilege and property must never be exclusive and that rights must always be accompanied by duties. The greater the privileges, the greater the obligations.

Against the radical and levelling tendencies of his age, Disraeli reacted not because he was opposed to popular rights and social amelioration which he desired to extend, but because he wished to base both on something more stable than the despotic will of an all-powerful popular assembly and an attendant bureaucracy. At the time when almost every social activity of government, national and local, was dormant, he foresaw that the very abuses of irresponsible capital which he exposed would ultimately provoke a central despotism capable of stifling all liberty. Knowing how many nations centralisation had enslaved and devitalised in the name of efficient administration, he wished to insure against it by strengthening local self-government and restoring national institutions.[1]

At the back of Disraeli's mind lay always certain ancient English ideals—the one Tudor and the other medieval—of a united nation and of a continuing community composed of men and women possessing inalienable privileges and rights secured by a stronger tenure than that of their own lives. His conception of society was essentially religious and humane—an ordered hierarchy based on a universal recognition of human needs and rights. He wished to restore dignity, romance and personal influence to the throne, responsibility to the nobility and gentry, moral authority to the Church, above all, status, pride of craft and security to the peasant and worker. In his home in the Wycombe woods he loved to speak of the Buckinghamshire

[1] "In the great struggle between popular principles and liberal opinions, which is characteristic of our age, I hope ever to be found on the side of the people, and of the Institutions of England. It is our Institutions that have made us free, and can alone keep us so; by the bulwark which they offer to the insidious encroachments of a convenient, yet enverating system of centralisation, which, if left unchecked, will prove fatal to the national character. Therefore I have ever endeavoured to cherish our happy habit of self-government, as sustained by a prudent distribution of local authority." *Monypenny & Buckle, I, 837-9.*

peasant's right to his triple estate of the porch, the oven and the tank. His policy, utterly misunderstood by his contemporaries and almost as much by his successors, was defined by himself as being:

"To change back the oligarchy into a generous aristocracy round a real throne; to infuse life and vigour into the Church as the trainer of the nation, . . . to establish a commercial code on the principles successfully negotiated by Lord Bolingbroke at Utrecht, and which, though baffled at the time by a Whig Parliament, were subsequently and triumphantly vindicated by his political pupil and heir, Mr. Pitt; to govern Ireland according to the policy of Charles I, and not of Oliver Cromwell; to emancipate the political constituency of 1832 from its sectarian bondage and contracted sympathies; to elevate the physical as well as the moral condition of the people, by establishing that labour required regulation as much as property, and all this rather by the use of ancient forms and the restoration of the past than by political revolutions founded on abstract ideas."[1]

An England, obsessed by material wealth and the economic formulas of Manchester, naturally did not understand what he was talking about.

His contemporaries took the strength, assurance and vital character of England for granted. Disraeli, a half-foreigner viewing the land of his adoption with detachment, knew that the virtues which made her people great and prosperous were nourished by institutions and principles whose relinquishment must bring about a gradual national decay and ultimate defeat and ruin. He could not share the easy optimism of reformers who supposed that they had only to rationalise to improve. He distrusted human reason, knew it to be fallible and its conclusions subject to ceaseless and unpredictable change. Like Burke he preferred the instinctive wisdom and prejudice of the older England. An intellectual himself, he fell back on instinct and precedent: on the accumulated reason of generations tested by experience. "A precedent," he once said, "embalms a principle." It was a rational opinion, widely held by economists, that

[1] *Monypenny & Buckle, I, 569-70.*

the capacity to make profits was the proper test of all economic activity. It was an ancient national principle and a popular prejudice that a man should receive a fair price for the product of his labour, that he should be protected in his employment, his enjoyment of home and his dignity as a man, however great the potential profits others might make in depriving him of these. In this Disraeli joined vital issue with the Free Traders. For they were not concerned with the social consequences of the system of trade they advocated, believing that those consequences, through the unimpeded operation of economic law, would always look after themselves.

It was Disraeli's lot to see his counsel neglected and his country adopt the policy he deplored. Until the Corn Laws were repealed he was only a back-bencher. On the very day that the fatal measure finally passed the Lords, he became a leader of the Tory rump which Peel had betrayed. For twenty years, with two short breaks, he remained in the political wilderness—the derided mentor of "a fat cattle opposition" which had lost touch with the spirit of the age. Like a wise man who realised the strength of his countryman's infatuation, he accepted their decision and warned his bucolic followers that they must allow a fair chance to the experiment on which Parliament and the nation had resolved. "You are in the position of a man who has made an improvident marriage," he told them. "You have become united to Free Trade, and nothing can divorce you except you can prove the charmer to be false. Wait, then, till that period has arrived; when you find that you have been betrayed, then will be the time to seek a divorce from that pernicious union. You have become united to the false Duessa, and you must take the consequences; and the consequence, I venture to predict, will be that the House of Commons, after a fair, full and ample trial of this great measure, will be driven to repeal it from absolute necessity, though at the termination of much national suffering; but that that suffering will be compensated for by the bitterness and the profundity of national penitence."[1]

That the question of Protection was not dead but merely sleeping, was the recurring theme of Disraeli's argument. "Protection to native industry is a fundamental principle." "It may be vain now," he said in another speech, "in the midnight of their intoxication, to tell them that there will be an awakening

---

[1] *Monypenny & Buckle, I, 839.*

of bitterness; it may be idle now, in the springtide of their
economic frenzy, to warn them that there may be an ebb of
trouble. But the dark and inevitable hour will arrive. Then,
when their spirits are softened by misfortune, they will recur
to those principles that made England great and which, in our
belief, will only keep England great."[1] Punch, at a loss on whom
to bestow the dunce's cap for the year's most ridiculous member
of Parliament, hesitated between Disraeli who championed
Protection, and Smith O'Brien who advocated Irish self-
government.

. . . .

There was a final tableau to be played before the curtain fell
on the drama of the middle 'forties. It was one incidental to
the main theme, but of peculiar horror and tragedy. The scene
was Ireland. It turned on the mysterious sickness of the potato
root which in the wet autumn of 1845 had given Peel his chance
to insist on the opening of the ports.

The people of Ireland, as a result of the curiously irresponsible
policy which their English rulers—partly through fear and partly
from religious hatred—had adopted towards them for two
centuries, were ignorant, poor and degraded. To Disraeli, with his
conviction that the welfare of a nation depended on the social
happiness of its people, the Irish question was a plain one—
"a starving population, an absentee aristocracy and an alien
Church and . . . the weakest executive in the world."[2] It could
be solved by the application of certain unchanging political
principles. "The moment you have a strong executive, a just
administration and ecclesiastical equality, you will have order
in Ireland, and the improvement of the physical condition of the
people will follow—not very rapidly, perhaps . . . but what are
fifty years even, in the history of a nation?"

The story of the great Irish famine of 1846 revealed what
could happen to a people without either social cohesion or strong
government in an hour of crisis:

"The hungry sheep look up, and are not fed,
But swollen with wind and the rank mist they draw,
Rot inwardly and foul contagion spread."

[1] *Monypenny & Buckle, I, 785.*
[2] ". . . That is the Irish question." *Monypenny & Buckle, I, 590.*

It was the fitting climax of a history of neglect and oppression which went back into the mists of antiquity. Of late the English, grown kindlier and more tolerant, had endeavoured to make amends for the wrongs they had done to Ireland by removing the political disabilities of the Catholic majority and even by voting small sums of money to assist their education. But the brutish poverty of a people whom long deprival of property and opportunity had rendered idle and improvident, remained a standing reproach to British wealth and civilisation. Whenever in the early issues of *Punch* it was desired to depict an Irishman, there was drawn a poor, fierce, half-mad-looking savage with simian features, stunted nose, low brow and matted hair, wearing a tattered tail-coat and broken crowned hat, and squatting with his shillelagh beside a slatternly hovel or brute-like in the mire before the figure of a fat priest.

The English were not unacquainted with Irish misery and degradation in the slums of their own cities. But they never asked what had created them. The Irishman who fled into England from his own despoiled land carried vengeance in his person. Nothing did so much to impoverish and debase the English urban worker as the inrush of hungry Irish labour glad to accept the lowest wages and worst conditions offered by the greediest millowner. Engels reckoned that 50,000 arrived from Ireland annually, packed like cattle into filthy boats at 4*d.* a piece. By 1844 there were over a million of them in England.

The slums of Dublin, fouling its lovely bay, were among the most hideous and repulsive in the world. In the twenty-eight tiny rooms of Nicholson's Court, 151 human beings lived in the direst want with no other property or conveniences between them but two bedsteads and two blankets. These conditions and the habits they engendered the Catholic Irish brought with them into Protestant England and Scotland, thus unconsciously repaying an ancient debt. In the slums of Manchester a whole Irish family would sleep on a single bed of filthy straw. Many cellars housed up to sixteen human occupants as well as pigs. A few hundred yards from the heart of the Empire, in the Rookery of St. Giles, there were courtyards and alleys swarming with Irish barbarians, the walls crumbling, the doorposts and window-frames loose and without doors and glass, and with heaps of garbage and excrement lying on every floor. It was by their needs and standards that employers, buying in the cheapest market according to the gospel of *laissez-faire*, fixed the price of British unskilled labour.

The prophet Carlyle saw the truth of it—the writing on the wall of Britain's splendid imperial destiny:

"The wild Milesian features, looking false ingenuity, restlessness, unreason, misery and mockery, salute you on all highways and byways. The English coachman, as he whirls past, lashes the Milesian with his whip, curses him with his tongue; the Milesian is holding out his hat to beg. He is the sorest evil this country has to strive with. In his rags and laughing savagery, he is there to undertake all work that can be done by mere strength of hand and back—for wages that will purchase him potatoes. He needs only salt for condiment, he lodges to his mind in any pig-hutch or dog-hutch, roosts in outhouses, and wears a suit of tatters, the getting on and off of which is said to be a difficult operation, transacted only in festivals and the high tides of the calendar. The Saxon-man, if he cannot work on these terms, finds no work. The uncivilised Irishman, not by his strength but by the opposite of strength, drives the Saxon native out, takes possession in his room. There abides he, in his squalor and unreason, in his falsity and drunken violence, as the ready-made nucleus of degradation and disorder . . . . Thus the condition of the lower multitude of English labourers approximates more and more to that of the Irish, competing with them in all the markets."

The autumn of 1846 saw a climax to the suffering and misery that had begotten this Nemesis. The English harvest was bad, there was a world food shortage, and for the second season running the Irish potato crop, ravaged by disease, failed. Wheat and provision prices soared. The British Government, faced with the prospect of a whole nation starving, advanced ten million pounds to relieve distress and bought yellow maize from India to make broth.[1]

It was in vain. Through the neglected villages of the stony west and south famine stalked. The weak hand of Dublin Castle could not stay it. The wages of those in work fell to 8*d*. a day. The Unions were beseiged by applicants: by December over

[1] It was known in Ireland as Peel's brimstone. *Early Victorian England, I, 69.*

40,000 were totally dependent on poor relief in County Roscommon alone, while the streets of Cork were thronged with five thousand homeless wretches in the last stages of famine. By February the number had doubled. Men, women and children filled their stomachs with cabbage leaves and turnip tops: hundreds died weekly in every rural union. In the remoter villages beyond even the feeble reach of the Government, the dead lay in the roads and ditches unburied.

In a letter that Christmas to the Duke of Wellington, a local Justice of the Peace described a visit to the district of Skibbereen. On reaching the village of South Reen with supplies of bread, he was surprised to find the hamlet apparently deserted.

"I entered some of the hovels to ascertain the cause, and the scenes that presented themselves were such as no tongue or pen can convey the slightest idea of.

"In the first, six famished and ghastly skeletons, to all appearances dead, were huddled in a corner on some filthy straw, their sole covering what seemed a ragged horse-cloth, and their wretched legs hanging about naked above the knees. I approached with horror, and found by a low moaning they were alive. They were in fever—four children, a woman and what had once been a man.

"It is impossible to go through the details. . . . In a few minutes I was surrounded by at least 200 of such phantoms, such frightful spectres as no words can describe. By far the greater number were delirious, either from famine or from fever. Their demoniac yells are still ringing in my ears, and their horrible images are fixed upon my brain. My heart sickens at the recital, but I must go on. In another case my clothes were nearly torn off in my endeavours to escape from a throng of pestilence around, when my neck-cloth was seized from behind by a grip which compelled me to turn. I found myself grasped by a woman with an infant just born in her arms, and the remains of a filthy sack across her loins—the sole covering of herself and babe. The same morning the police opened a house on the adjoining lands which was observed shut for many days, and two frozen corpses were found lying upon the mud floor, half-devoured by the rats. . . .

"A mother, herself in fever, was seen the same day to

drag out the corpse of her child, a girl of about twelve perfectly naked, and leave it half covered with stones. In another house within 500 yards of the cavalry station at Skibbereen the dispensary doctor found seven wretches lying, unable to move, under the same cloak—one had been dead many hours, but the others were unable to move themselves or the corpse."[1]

The English, who since the days of Lillibullero had never been able to take the Irish seriously, did not see themselves as responsible for these sufferings, though with their habitual humanity they subscribed liberally to charities to relieve them. Greville in his gossiping pages reported that the state of Ireland was deplorable, but set it down to the people themselves, whom he described as "besotted with obstinacy and indolence, reckless and savage." He thought them secretly well off, stated that they had money in their pockets and used it to buy arms instead of food. *Punch*, then a humanitarian journal, depicted the ragged Irishman impudently begging John Bull to spare a trifle "for a poor lad to buy a bit of a blunderbuss with." And when Disraeli and his die-hard friends of the Fat Cattle Opposition put forward a project for a Treasury grant of sixteen million to build Irish railways, it asked with amusement:

"Who would ever travel on an Irish railway? . . . Who does not see that an Irish Great Western would run due east—a Midland counties along the coast? A passenger booked for Dublin would infallibly find himself at Cork. . . . The whistle would never be sounded till after the collision . . . the coals would be put in the boiler and the water underneath it, and when the train came to a standstill, the engineer would thrash the engine with his shillelagh. If the Irish could afford to travel by them, they would certainly reduce the population."

In the course of one terrible winter it was believed that over a quarter of a million Irish peasants died of starvation. The very repeal of the Corn Laws, which had been undertaken with the object of aiding Ireland, had the contrary effect, since by depriving her of her preferential position in the British corn

[1] *W. O. O'Brien, The Great Famine, 78.*

market, it necessitated her transformation from an agrarian into a more scantily inhabited pastoral country.[1] Within the next five years, during which the ravages of famine still continued in a milder form, her population declined by two and a half million or about a third. Of these more than a million perished of starvation and pestilence: the rest emigrated to America. Even of these a quarter are said to have died from their hardships within a year of landing. There are no statistics to measure the sum total of human misery represented by these figures. Their consequences, and those of the tragic history that preceded them, were writ large in the annals of Britain and Ireland for the next seventy-five years, and in those of the United States and of its relations with Britain.

[1]See *Lecky, Leaders of Public Opinion in Ireland, II, 92-3.*

CHAPTER FOUR

The Fighting Fifties

"Tennyson says that he and a party of Englishmen fought a cricket match with the crew of the *Bellerophon* on the *Parthenopoean hills*, and *sacked* the sailors by 90 runs. Is not this pleasant?—the notion of good English blood striving in worn-out Italy. I like that such men as Frederic should be abroad: so strong, haughty and passionate. They keep up the English character abroad."
Letters and Literary Remains of Edward Fitzgerald, I, 71.

THE REPEAL of the Corn Laws did not relieve Ireland, which continued to starve and fall in population. Nor for the time being did it ruin English agriculture. More than a quarter of a century was to elapse before far-seeing capital could enable the corn-growers of other lands to enter into the heritage reserved for them by British legislators. And the pillars which supported the island's supremacy were strong and to all appearance unaffected by the shifting of the foundations. To our father's fathers they seemed to be growing stronger.

For Cobden's triumph and Peel's betrayal of his Party were followed by a period of increasing prosperity. 1847 was a year of violent fluctuations: corn which touched 124/- a quarter in June had fallen to 49/6 by September; corn dealers and bill-brokers were ruined; there was a crash in the railway market and the Bank Act was suspended. But after that things began to look up, and gloomy prophets like Croker, who had predicted ruin at the first quarter-day after repeal, were proved wrong as ever. The "monopolists" were confounded; there was a sudden "awful appearance of plenty in Mark Lane," and from the pages of *Punch* a beaming Ceres with a full sack and a 7d. loaf brought consternation to a few tight-stocked old buffers in top-hats and at least a glimpse of prosperity to every one else.[1]

Thereafter for the disciples of *laissez-faire* everything seemed to prosper. Trade not only recovered but grew every day. Millions in Ireland, in the industrial towns and the London underworld lived in dirt and poverty. But millions more were thriving; demand was brisk and the capital laid down in

[1] *Punch, XII, 241.*

machines was yielding quicker returns. Though in reality
repeal of the Corn Laws made little difference to the price of
wheat, which averaged no less a quarter in the Free Trade 'fifties
than it had done in the protectionist 'forties, the new railways
cheapened the price of provisions, clothes and coal. Every one
seemed to have a little more to spend and there was ample room
for expansion. The hungry 'forties were over. The free-traders
to whom these blessings were attributed were felt to have earned
well of their country.[1] Protection, formally abandoned by the
repeal of the Navigation Laws in 1849, was a lost cause.

In the forefront of all this prosperity came in 1849 the rush
to the gold diggings in California. Two years later more gold
was found in Australia. Both America and Australia were able
to increase their imports of British goods with gold payments.
In 1852 there was more gold in the Bank of England than had ever
been there before. Money was plentiful and interest rates low.

With improved transport and increased purchasing power,
the capitalist organisation of industrial society entered on a
new and vaster phase. The unexploited markets of Asia and the
newer continents became accessible to the manufacturer. A golden
era dawned for south Lancashire, the West Riding, Tyneside,
Staffordshire, the Clyde and South Wales. Industrial Britain
was becoming the workshop of the world. The opportunity of
the greater capitalist was at hand.

As he grasped it, and trade began to boom, the lot of the
worker improved also. Employment expanded, and the larger
firms which wider markets created had no need with their larger
turnover to resort to such petty economies and merciless conduct
as their predecessors. Wages tended to rise, hours of labour to
fall, and the worst abuses of truck, sweating and child labour
to diminish. Lord Shaftesbury's Ten Hours' Bill and other
measures incompatible with the strictest letter of *laissez-faire*
found their way on to the statute book. The country, pleased
with its growing prosperity, felt at last that it could afford them.

An England, growing rich by increasing dependence on
other lands, naturally looked across the seas. She needed a
peaceful world that would afford her abundant raw materials
and expanding markets. John Bull could less afford than
before to ignore the antics of the foreigner. He might

---

[1] When Peel died in 1850 *Punch* depicted his memorial as a pyramid of cheap loaves
round which were grouped a workman's family eating plentiful bread. *Punch, XIX, 571.*

disapprove of them, but they concerned his pocket and future security.

His difficulty was to control them. Insular England could never fathom the cause of European events: it merely observed their consequences in its export orders. In 1848 they suddenly became exceedingly grave. On Monday, February 22nd, the people of France enjoyed to all appearance the rule of a powerful, peaceful and impregnable monarchy. Two days later her King was a fugitive in England and the flag of the terrible Republic again flew over barricaded streets. Before the summer she was drifting into mob rule and all Europe was following her blood-stained example. Italy and Germany, with their confused, divided petty kingdoms and principalities, were in a blaze from the Baltic to the Tyrrhenian Sea: even Vienna and the high priest of the *ancien regime*, Prince Metternich, did not escape. In Dresden, where the King of Saxony fled, the corpses were piled up six or seven high in the streets. In all Europe, only Britain seemed to ride out the storm. The fact gave Englishmen considerable satisfaction: "in the midst of the roar of revolutionary waters that are deluging the whole earth," wrote Greville, "it is grand to see how we stand erect and unscathed." *Punch* depicted the proprietor of Mivart's Hotel—forerunner of Claridge's—presenting his humble respects to the Crowned Heads of the Continent and begging to inform them that his hotel in Brook Street continued the favoured house of call for dethroned potentates.

Not that England in this year of revolutions wholly escaped a little revolution of its own. But though prefaced by a prodigious amount of noise and oratory, it was only a mock one and did no one any harm but the revolutionaries. It was staged by the Chartists who, relying on the general substratum of poverty, called a monster demonstration on Kennington Common for April 10th to present a petition to Parliament. But the government, remembering 1842, promptly fetched in the military, put the defences of London into the hands of the aged victor of Waterloo and swore in the city and the Whitehall clerks as special constables. Against such preparations the mob was helpless. The day, a fine one, ended in Fergus O'Connor, the Chartist leader, shaking hands effusively with the police inspector who forbade the procession and, after advancing on Westminster in a cab, thanking a rather astonished Home Secretary for his leniency. A rising in wretched Ireland later in the year fared even more ignominously: here the liberator, Smith O'Brien, was taken prisoner by a railway guard after a broil in the widow McCormack's cabbage patch.

.   .   .   .

It was not surprising, as the dust of the European arena settled down and a dishevelled continent tried to return to normal, that the English congratulated themselves. In Doyle's cartoons of 1849 one can see them doing so—a fat, good-humoured, smiling English working family sitting by its own fireside with a picture of Queen Victoria on the wall and a newspaper on father's knee describing the awful state of Europe; while round the border scowl and grimace a crew of mad, savage foreigners—Spanish peasants chasing priests with knives, licentious and brutal soldiers charging barricades, the artillery-men of tyrants bombarding defenceless capitals, and slavish Frenchmen worshipping a Napoleonic hat and jackboots on bended knees. The liberty enjoyed by a Briton was never so attractive as when contrasted with the slavery of his neighbours.

The truth was that the British working-class, which, though for a time capable of popular frenzy and exaggeration, always returns in the end to its normal state of phlegmatic good-humour, had tired of revolutionary politics. With the aid of the railways and the 7d. loaf it was learning to accept urbanisation as its lot. The improvement in trade and the growing attempts of the middle-class to ameliorate the factory towns assisted the change. The first effect of the repeal of the Corn Laws was largely psychological; it took the bitterness out of public life. The mob orator with flashing eyes, a brogue and a leaning to incendiarism was superseded by the earnest student reading in the public library and taking minutes at small meetings of the republican elect under a gas jet. It was the age in which Karl Marx, driven from the continent by the suppression of the German and French workers' revolutions, settled in furnished rooms at Camberwell and started in the fusty calm of the British Museum to evolve his universal but apparently harmless philosophy of hate.[1]

---

[1] Among his innumerable hates were the gods, the Christian religion, his parents, his wife's uncle—"the hound"—his German kinsfolk, his own race—"Ramsgate is full of fleas and Jews"—the Prussian reactionaries, his Liberal and utopian Socialist allies, the labouring population—"Lumpenproletariat" or riff-raff—democracy—"parliamentary cretinism"—and, of course, the British royal family, "the English mooncalf and her princely urchins," as he called them. His self-imposed task he defined as "the ruthless criticism of everything that exists."

Under this sober stimulus Chartism died and was buried, and its place taken by radicalism and academic republicanism. The latter was not so much a practical attempt to overthrow monarchy as a creed. It was not at all blood-thirsty; to cater for its high-tea tastes the title of Harney's "Red Republican" was changed to "The Friend of the People." It met at places like the Discussion Hall in Shoe Lane, the Temple Forum in Fleet Street, the Cogers tavern near St. Bride's and the John Street Institution, Blooms-bury, where the chairman sat in a canopied chair with pipe and brandy and water, and the famous Mrs. Dexter lectured on and in the "bloomer" costume. Its adherents were eager young artisans who had educated themselves. They were much enamoured of foreign revolutionaries whose doings they followed with intense and quite uncritical enthusiasm: for them they generously subscribed their scanty pennies and when, as destitute fugitives, the latter fled to England, they lionised them in a humble but fervent way. In the eyes of these English radicals Poles, Hungarians, Italians, Germans and other oppressed minorities were all heroes and pioneers of European freedom; had they been able to see the national tyrannies into which their faiths were to be transmuted, they would have been horrified. Incidentally their foreign friends with the ingratitude of their kind were apt to be a good deal less enthusiastic about them.

For as these interesting exiles found to their annoyance, England was not a revolutionary country at heart. Given a modicum of bread and beer and a little liberty and leisure to enjoy himself, the sweating toiler in the classic island home of the proletariat proved astonishingly good-humoured. In August, 1848, the year of revolutions, a middle-class writer in a popular journal noted in rhyming couplets how—

"Townward from Richmond, at the close of day,
　Two of us were on foot returning straight,
　We having dined—the fact 'tis meet to state—
　A pleasure van there passed us on the road,
　Which bore of honest folks a goodly load;
　Holiday makers of the class and rate
　Of working people, by our estimate.
　The party was obstreperously gay;
　Slightly elate, it may have been, with beer.
　Joining in chorus as they roll'd along,

' We won't go home till morning,' was their song.
We hailed those revellers with a gentle cheer;
And ' Ah! that that truly British strain,' said we,
' Is livelier than, Mourir pour la patrie.' "[1]

Despite the sufferings of the factory operative and the slum-dweller, there was something incorrigibly jolly about England. If it was given the chance to be, it was fundamentally healthy, kept its pores open and its heart kindly and merry. It did so when it could, even in the new towns. With the passing of the Factory Act in 1850 and the legal enforcement of a Saturday half-holiday, the week-end habit began and, as wages increased, the supply of cheap amusement arose to cater for the demand. It was often of a rather vulgar, garish, sodden kind: there was much drunkenness and often a good deal of brutality. But at its core was an invincible love of good fare and of sport. In Lancashire and the West Riding, gala days, wakes and feasts emptied the mine and stopped the wheels of the mill at customary times each year. Excursion trains, packed with pale-faced workers and their families with bands, banners and bottled beer, descended annually from the cotton towns on Rock Ferry and Blackpool: it was close by the cheap ferry for Liverpool to the Cheshire shore that Nathaniel Hawthorne in 1853 saw a working man pulling from his pockets oyster after oyster "in interminable succession" and opening them with his pocket-knife. There was whippet-racing and pigeon-flying for miners and scarlet-vested railway navvies, horse-racing of a rough kind on the Yorkshire and Lancashire moors, wrestling, boxing, quoits, bowls, and cricket and football of an order more democratic and vigorous than any that would be officially recognised to-day. In London the working-class population affected the open-air gardens where in the summer families could eat, drink and be merry at little expense. Vauxhall, sinking rapidly lower in the social scale, lingered on until 1859; Cremorne in Chelsea, founded by a uniformed Prussian baron in 1830, proffered fireworks, cascades, balloon ascents, bad music, rather indecorous dancing, alfresco theatrical entertainments and polar bears in white cotton trousers to very mixed company; and there were pleasure gardens at Chalk Farm, Hackney, Hoxton, the Eagle, Islington, the Red House, Battersea, and many another suburban resort. In all

[1] *Punch XV, 51.*

this, partaking of the village from which it had so lately sprung, the proletariat of urban England showed how little its heart was in ideological abstraction. It was difficult to make it class conscious. It just wanted to be comfortable and jolly and have a good time. Its class anthem was not the *Marseillaise* but the deathless song whose roaring refrain went:

> "Damn their eyes
> If ever they tries
> To rob a poor man of his beer!"

It was the teuton Prince Albert who demonstrated to the world how harmless and pacific the British proletariat really was. In 1849 he and a little group of serious and cultured persons of like mind began to prepare plans for a Royal Commission to organise a great Exhibition of industry in London. All the world was to be invited to contribute exhibits and to view in turn the triumphs of British art and manufacture. Nobody at first took the idea very seriously, but the Prince was persistent, and in the following winter, after five thousand guarantors had been reluctantly enlisted, the Royal Commission was set up. Sixteen acres of land on the southern side of Hyde Park, now used for football, were secured and a design for a monster palace of glass accepted from Joseph Paxton who had built the conservatories at Chatsworth.

For about a year the project was the joke of London. *Punch* depicted royal Albert begging from door to door in the guise of the industrious boy, crying "Pity the sorrows of a poor young Prince," or pulling at Dame Britannia's elbow with an, "Oh, Mum, here's a to-do! here's all the company come and the streets full of carriages and brooms . . . and the candles isn't lighted and the supper ready nor the man dressed who's to wait nor the music nor anything!" At first nobody thought either the money or the glass "ark as big as a warehouse" would ever be raised, but, as the giant iron columns, some of them over a hundred feet high, appeared in the Park, laughter changed to apprehension. With the vast concourse of visitors whom it would draw to the West End of London from abroad and from the dangerous working-class districts, almost anything might happen. The park—favourite haunt of beauty and fashion— would be filled with East End rowdies who with their tobacco smoke, Waterloo crackers and practical jokes, would turn it into another Greenwich Fair with lousy and potentially murderous foreigners; and, most ominous of all, with savage heathens from the northern industrial towns. The beds would be trampled on, the flowers picked and finally the great human tide, leaving its scum behind in the devastated park, would surge out by night to pillage Belgravia and Kensington.

The American press, even more alarmist than the English, prophesied general massacre and insurrection. Every gloomy prognostication was canvassed: one gentleman, possibly with his tongue in his cheek, went so far as to write to *The Times* pointing out that, though glass possessed certain advantages over other materials, it suffered the disability of being liable "to fracture from the reverberations of sound. It appears that upon the arrival of the Queen at the Crystal Palace a Royal Salute is to be fired, and, if as is probable the muzzles of the guns be presented towards the glass wall of the building . . . the result will be that the officiating gunner will carry off the honours of the day by creating a crash such as will render the loudest tones of the organ utterly insignificant."[1]

But the Prince was not to be turned from his purpose. Gradually, under the hands of two thousand workmen, the great building, over six hundred yards long, containing nearly a million square feet of glass and affording over eight miles of table space for the exhibitors, rose like a dazzling Aladdin's palace of crystal over the grass, the birds[2] and the trees. The old wooden railings were removed, and Anne Hicks and her white cottage, apples and gingerbread were ruthlessly ejected to make way. All over London shopkeepers, anticipating the great influx of foreigners, began to hang notices announcing their ability to speak French, German, Italian and Spanish and every other strange tongue.

On May Day, 1851, the Great Exhibition was formally opened by the Queen. The capital was prudently filled with troops: the Rifle Brigade was moved from Dover to Woolwich, the 1st Royal Dragoons from Nottingham and the 8th Hussars from Brighton to billets in Hampstead and Highgate, and the 4th Light Dragoons

[1] *Times, 30th April, 1851.*
[2] Some of the latter, clinging to their ancient haunts in the branches, were accidentally enclosed. Their droppings marking the valuable exhibits, and the use of shotguns being out of the question, the Queen sent for the Duke of Wellington The aged hero's advice was brief and to the point. "Try sparrow hawks, ma'm."

from Dublin to Hounslow, while a strong contingent of artillery
was quartered in the Tower. The park itself was protected by
three cavalry regiments and seven foot battalions of the Household troops and two regiments of Lancers. In addition over
6,000 police were on duty in the capital.

Even before it was light every road leading to the park was
thronged. After long rain the sun was shining. At seven o'clock
the gates were opened and the great multitude began to pour in.
All the world seemed to be wearing its Sunday best. An hour
later a reporter found a continuous traffic block from the City to
Hyde Park Corner on both sides of the river. Every kind of
vehicle had been requisitioned, many from the forgotten past;
old rickety post-chaises that had rotted for years in stable yards
blazed their faded glories for the last time in the sun. There
were spring vans, handsome phaetons and crested coaches,
donkey carts, cabs and even wagons and trucks all jumbled
together: "the proudest equipage of the peer was obliged to
fall in behind the humblest fly or the ugliest hansom."[1]   On
Westminster Bridge many buses stuck fast, unable to mount the
slope from their weight of passengers.

Near the gate of the park the crush of pedestrians moved
forward like a huge river: London had never known such
crowds. Many from the provinces had slept on the doorsteps
and were breakfasting in the scrum off sausages and enormous
hunks of bacon and feeding their children out of milk bottles.
Farmers, wearing unwonted tailcoats, bright-coloured waistcoats and wide beaver hats, were accompanied by rosy-cheeked
wives and daughters in bonnets and stiffly starched flowered
print frocks. In Mayfair the streets were packed with the coaches
and carriages of country gentlefolk who, determined not to
miss the sight, had slept overnight in their vehicles and were
now having breakfast, the girls' crinolines and ribbons shining
in the early sunshine while powdered footmen boiled kettles and
fried eggs and bacon on the pavement. Around them surged
the rough multitude all with a single goal:

> "That wondthrous thing,
> The palace made o' windows."

There was naturally a good deal of rough horse-play: a lady
overheard one mother exhorting her willing son to stamp on

[1] *Punch, XX, 190.*

the feet of those who opposed his passage, and noticed another systematically making his way through the crowd by butting with his bullet head.

Yet no one could deny that the crowd was astonishingly good-humoured and appreciative. On that lovely May Day it was out, not to stampede the police and sack London, but to enjoy itself. It accepted the rich in their carriages, the great ones driving to their allocated places in the crystal palace, the Queen and royal family as part of the splendid show provided for its entertainment.

At nine the doors of the Exhibition were opened for the 25,000 invited guests and season-ticket holders,[1] who alone were allowed to be inside for the opening ceremony. They were disposed throughout the great building among the exhibits, the ladies seated and the gentlemen standing like gallant knights behind. Opposite the principal door on Rotten Row the trees of the park seemed to have burst out into a crop of eager little boys whom no policeman could dislodge.

At twenty minutes to twelve the Queen, accompanied by her two eldest children—the future Edward VII wearing kilts and the Princess Royal—the Prince and Princess of Prussia and Prince Frederick William of Prussia, left Buckingham Palace with a cortege of nine carriages. Wearing pink and glowing with pride at her husband's achievement, she looked out on one continuous sea of cheering humanity all the way down Constitution Hill and Rotten Row. It was a wonderful lesson, *Punch* thought, to tyrants. A few drops of rain encountered at Hyde Park Corner made the ensuing sunlight seem only the more lovely. Presently the gigantic edifice swung into sight with the flags of all nations flying above its gleaming domes and pinnacles: there was a glimpse of the north transept through the iron gates in Rotten Row, of waving palms, flowers, statues and cheering spectators fluttering hats and handkerchiefs from every recess of that great crystal bow, and then to the flourish of trumpets the royal procession advanced on foot up the long nave towards the glittering fountain and the throne under its blue and silver canopy. Here the Prince Consort, the Officers of State and the Queen's Ministers, the Foreign Ambassadors and the Heralds and the Executive Committee and officials of the Exhibition were waiting to pay homage.

[1] Gentlemen subscribed three guineas and ladies two.

In this great national triumph, the dedication of the "grandest temple ever raised to the peaceful arts," there was a supreme moment. After Prince Albert, standing at the head of the Royal Commissioners, had read aloud the report that told of the completion of their labours, and the Queen had replied and the Archbishop prayed, the massed choirs of the Chapel Royal, Westminster Abbey, St. Paul's and Windsor Chapel, supported by the members of the Royal Academy of Music and the Sacred Harmonic Society, and accompanied by an organ with 4,700 pipes, broke into Handel's "Hallelujah Chorus." Outside, where the waiting crowd covered every available inch of the park, the artillery beyond the Serpentine sounded welcoming salvoes. Then the Queen with her husband and children about her, and at the head of a procession which included the aged Commander-in-Chief and the Master General of the Ordnance,[1] who thirty-six years before had respectively commanded the British army and cavalry on the field of Waterloo, swept down the west nave, threading their way between lines of statuary, objects of art and the products of industry. The sword wielded by the English brave had been melted into ploughshares: righteousness and peace had kissed each other. For that ecstatic moment in time the English were really happy.

So, in the words of the *Gentleman's Magazine*, "the delicate female whose tempered sway is owned by a hundred millions of men pursued her course among the contributions of all the civilised world." As she passed Godfrey de Bouillon's gigantic armoured equestrian figure, the very personification of physical strength, the same writer could not help reflecting "how far the prowess of the crusader is transcended by the power of well defined liberty and constitutional law."[2] The Queen herself seemed to realise it. That night she wrote in her diary that it had been a day to live for for ever. "God bless my dearest Albert! God bless my dearest country which has shown itself so great to-day! One felt so grateful to the great God who seemed to pervade all and bless all."

Afterwards "the visitors dispersed themselves through the building to gratify their curiosity without restraint." They were astonished at the wonders they saw. Here was the apotheosis

---

[1] Lord Anglesey had lost his leg on the field. "By God that was my leg!" cried that gallant officer. "By God it was!" remarked the Duke after a glance.

[2] *The Gentleman's Magazine*, Part I, Vol. XXXV, 653-6.

of free trade and the peaceful products of man's hand and ingenuity. Since the days of Noah's Ark nothing so compendious had ever been assembled. There were four Sections. In the first were Raw Materials and Produce. In the second were the various kinds of Machinery, arranged in six groups; machines for direct use such as railways and carriages, manufacturing machines and tools, mechanical, engineering, architectural and building contrivances, naval and military ordinance and accoutrements, agricultural and horticultural machines and implements, and philosophical and scientific instruments. In the third Section were the various Manufactures divided into nineteen groups, and in the fourth the Fine Arts. Some of the exhibits in the last being contributed by artists and foreigners caused a certain amount of misgiving: a marble statue of a "startled nymph," who from her lack of clothing seemed no better than she ought to be, caused at least one family—a motherly-looking woman and two apple-cheeked daughters in flounced skirts—to come to a sudden pause and then, blushing furiously, to vanish into the silk department.

In the weeks that followed the humblest in the land came to view the Great Exhibition. Throughout the summer the daily attendance at times exceeded 60,000. After the third week the admission fee to the building was reduced to a shilling on four days a week. The shilling days proved the wonder of the season. Instead of the brutal behaviour and rioting which many had expected, an endless stream of orderly, good-humoured working-class folk, gaping and admiring, passed under the crystal dome. No Communist broke the glass or seized the Koh-i-Nor. "There is a smock-faced rustic considering among other matters rural a Canadian plough," wrote *Punch*, "that quiet, self-instructing peasant is—one shilling. There is a fustian jacket with a quick critical eye examining machines: that jacket is one shilling."[1] The workman's square cap, the decent finery, the gaping ragged children, the humble picnic bag, the babies, the ginger beer gave an unexpected thrill to the well-to-do and respectable. The sight caused undemonstrative Englishmen to shake hands in the streets and even to shed tears in public. Here were the dreaded working-class people of England and they had come as friends. "The great event brought to London thousands who perhaps had never seen a train before, people speaking the strange

---

[1] *Punch*, XX, 2.

tongues of Lancashire and Durham, and the official reports of their behaviour as they flocked through museums and gardens are full of unconcealed pride. Not a flower was picked, a picture smashed. And ten years before, the Londoners who now welcomed them had stood silent in the streets to watch the guns going north to Lancashire."[1]

To the nation that fairy palace towering over the blossom and foliage of the park symbolised a great social reunion and the dawning of a new era of hope, based on enterprise, freedom of trade and cheapness of production and communication. To innocent eyes—and there were many that saw it—it seemed a palace of light glittering in the summer sun with its central crystal fountain reflecting all the jewels of the world, an Arabian nights' creation "so graceful, so delicate, so airy that its translucent beauty remains graven on memory as something which must defy all rivalry."[2] To the simple sons of toil from the industrial north who had saved up their pennies to make the first and only pilgrimage of their lives to visit it, its beauty seemed something that was scarcely of this earth. They saw it, not like a sophisticated posterity as something comic, but as a dream of fairyland and, in a world which contained the slums of Irkside and Little Ireland, and in which all things are comparative, it is not surprising.

.   .   .   .

The Great Exhibition, born of the hopes excited by Free Trade, was expected by its promoters to herald the dawn of perpetual peace. It was a hope shared by every Briton. In the past Britain had won many great prizes in war. But she had done so because she had emerged victorious from her wars and not because she had sought them. Her people, though redoubtable fighters, were deeply impregnated by a desire to live at peace and by a belief that wars were always caused by foreigners.

This had never seemed so true as in 1851. Increasingly dependent on imports, with a growing export trade, with a vast empire (in which they had almost lost interest), and with a glorious record of victories behind them, the islanders had nothing to gain by war and everything to lose. All that was now necessary was to persuade foreigners who were not in the same state of blessedness to think likewise. The light of reason,

[1] *Early Victorian England, I, 212-23.*
[2] *Lord Redesdale, Memoirs, I, 78-9.*

the healing gospel of Free Trade and the outward and visible sign afforded by the Crystal Palace would surely convert them. It was to their material advantage.

The weakness of the Englishman's attitude towards foreigners was that he expected them to think and behave exactly like himself. When, true to their own alien natures, they failed to do so, he either laughed at their folly or—if their behaviour outraged his moral code, as it frequently did—became justly indignant. And as, being a free-born Briton, he scorned to conceal his laughter or disapproval, misunderstanding between him and his continental neighbours was bound to arise.

The ruling principles of Britain's foreign policy were to preserve the balance of European power, protect the Low Countries and the Channel coasts, keep open her trade routes and strategic communications, and establish the rule of righteousness on earth. The last object—that of playing St. George to the dragon of foreign tyrants—generally coincided with the first, since any ambitious despot with a large army who threatened to overthrow the balance of power inevitably trampled in doing so on the liberties of his own subjects and weaker neighbours. In repelling such threats to her own interests, Britain was thus in the happy position of also fighting the battle of human freedom and morality. As her statesmen and people were always quick to emphasise this point, she was less liked by large nations than by small. And by making herself the unofficial patron of every liberal or subversive movement abroad, as well as by her generous policy of granting refuge to political exiles, she won the sometimes embarrassing goodwill of foreign rebels but the suspicion and resentment of their governments. This policy, alike unaggressive and provocative, was pursued by both political parties—the Whigs because they liked foreign Liberals on principle and the Tories because it was a cheap way of escaping the reproach of being reactionary.

During the long forty years of peace that followed the defeat of Napoleon, the Channel shores were secured by the international neutralisation of the Low Countries—divided after 1830 into the small pacific kingdoms of Holland and Belgium—and the temporary exhaustion of France. So long as the latter remained quiescent, Britain's jealousy of despots was spasmodically directed towards her three former allies of 1813-15—Russia, Austria and Prussia. But these states, though governed by despots under very illiberal constitutions and therefore a proper source of contempt to an English patriot, enjoyed the comparative advantage of being a long way away. Only one of them, Russia, which was the possessor of a fair-sized navy, offered any threat to British interests. For Russia was an Asiatic as well as a European power, and her steady expansion towards India and Persia caused constant uneasiness in Whitehall. Above all her tendency to intervene in the affairs of the decaying Ottoman empire on behalf of the Christian subjects of the Sultan was regarded with a suspicious eye by statesmen responsible for preserving British communications with India. If Antwerp was a pistol pointed at London, Constantinople was one levelled at India. Britain preferred to keep it in the palsied hand of the Turk.

All this, however, was of much more interest to the serious statesman and student of politics than to the ordinary Briton. Russia was a long way away. And though its Czars were unquestionably tyrants and the knout and Siberian prison camp were horrors that outraged every honest heart, it was hard to present the maintenance of the corrupt and cruel rule of Turkish pashas over Christian subject peoples as a campaign for moral righteousness. And even the protection of vital British interests —especially such distant ones—could not arouse the public without the stimulant of a great moral cause.

In the early years of Queen Victoria's reign the English therefore contented themselves with a good deal of genial abuse of tyrants in their parliamentary speeches and newspapers without taking any very active steps to oppose them. The Emperors of Russia and Austria and the King of Prussia were regularly caricatured as a trio of stupid, arrogant, absurd, epauletted, high-collared, tight-breeched, top-booted tyrants, and any act of high-handed dealing by their minions—of which there were plenty—that found its way into the British press was held up to moral obloquy. This national habit of lecturing, combined with so much good fortune and wealth, made the English extremely unpopular in the greater chancelleries of Europe and led to charges being brought against them of hypocrisy, meddling and Machiavellian warmongering. It was particularly resented when, as often happened, it took the form of holding out the British constitution as the model for every other country and intriguing, regardless of local circumstances, against the established authorities on behalf of discontented radical minorities. Behind the convenient cloak of parliamentary forms, British politicians in opposition, and sometimes in office, did a good deal of this.

. . . .

In his bold, confident and even dashing behaviour towards foreign rulers, one English statesman of the time above all others represented the moral feelings, prejudices and generous if narrow sympathies of his countrymen. Palmerston, who with one brief break was Whig Foreign Secretary from 1830 to 1841, and again from 1846 to 1852, was the pride of Britain and the *enfant terrible* of Europe. In all that he said and did, in which there was much shrewdness and an incontestable love of his country and her institutions, he was animated by a belief that he was exposing the powers of darkness. Except for a few over-travelled and superior persons, every Englishman shared his faith and most of them applauded the steps he took to give it effect. That these were as often as not tactless, impetuous and needlessly provocative did not trouble them. However much they pained the meticulous Prince Albert and Palmerston's own colleagues—it was his rollicking practice to act first and consult afterwards— they well suited the mood of England, rustic, middle-class or proletarian. When in 1850 the honest draymen of Barclay's Brewery chased an Austrian general, who was reputed to have flogged some rebel Hungarian ladies, down Bankside into good Mrs. Benfield's bedroom in the George public-house, and bombarded him with mud pies and cries of "Cut off his beard!" they were only enacting in their own rough way the familiar Palmerstonian technique. They meant no harm but they wished a foreign scoundrel to learn what an Englishman thought of him.

Rebukes and scrapes only enhanced Palmerston's popularity and stimulated him to new outrages on the authoritarian proprieties of Europe. Like a true Englishman he was irresistible in recoil. His famous *Civis Romanus sum* speech in the summer of 1850, after a vote of censure on his high-handed Don Pacifico policy, won the House round in spite of itself and made him, not for the last time, the hero of his country. When eighteen months later he was forced to resign after a further outrage on the royal prerogative and the rights of his colleagues, the London urchins, voicing the universal feeling of the common people, paraded the streets singing:

"Small Lord John has been and gone
And turned adrift Lord Palmerston,
Amongst the lot the only don
Who didn't take care of number one;
Out spoke Home Secretary Grey,
' I wish old Palmy was away.'
' Aye, turn him out,' they all did say,
' For he's the people's darling!'"

Whatever grave persons and a prosy German Prince Consort
might say, "the Viscount, full of vigour and hilarity and overflowing with diplomatic swagger," was the man for England.

"Let tyrants tremble!" might have been Palmerston's motto,
and it was certainly his country's. Yet, so long as tyrants kept
their distance, neither Palmerston nor England wished to go to
war. They merely claimed the right to speak out their mind
freely about them. But there was one species of tyrant whom
an Englishman not only hated but feared—a French tyrant.
Between the glorious Revolution of 1688 and the equally glorious
Battle of Waterloo in 1815, Britain had been at war with France
for more years than she had been at peace. Many of the Queen's
subjects could remember a period of twenty-two years almost
continuous conflict with the revolutionary French Republic and
the Napoleonic Empire: when all Europe had been a camp
armed against an island fortress and watchers on the Kentish
shore on clear days could see the would-be invaders drilling on
the heights above Boulogne and Wimereux.

So long as France remained weak, English fears that all this
might happen again slept. But after the revolution of 1830 and
the enthronement of the revolutionary dynasty of Orleans in
Paris, ancient suspicions revived. Louis Philippe—the old fox
pacing the Tuileries terrace in his grey greatcoat and huge stapel
hat—was scarcely in truth much of a menace to his neighbours.
Yet many sensible Englishmen watched his every move with
alarm, whether towards Spain or Belgium or the African shore,
feeling they could only be attributed to "the cravings of French
vanity and insolence" and still more to "that revolutionary
spirit which . . . seeks to become formidable by stimulating the
passions and allying itself with all the vanity, pride and restlessness, besides desire for plunder, which are largely scattered
throughout the country."[1] Palmerston was never more English

[1] Greville, *Reign of Queen Victoria I, 352-3 (13 Nov., 1840)*.

than in his sturdy resistance to French projects and disregard of French pride. A contemporary, who had returned from Paris shortly after his retirement in 1841, believed that, had Palmerston continued much longer at the Foreign Office, nothing could have prevented war between the two countries, seeing "that he intrigued against France in every part of the world and with a tenacity of purpose that was like insanity."[1] Neither he nor the public he so ably represented saw in this anything but a proper distrust of a dangerous and slippery customer.[2]

.   .   .   .

The Revolution of 1848 made France once more a republic. Before the year was out, worse had happened. In a violent revulsion of popular opinion against disorder and Socialist excesses, a nephew of the great Napoleon was elected President. The alarm aroused in England coincided with a period of misgiving about the nation's military and naval preparedness. As always after a long peace, the army seemed quite insufficient for any warlike task: its most serious preoccupations were sartorial such as the new shell jacket and the peculiar-looking shako recently designed for its use by Prince Albert. The aged Duke of Wellington could not sleep at night for thinking of the defenceless state of the coasts. Worse, the Navy itself was growing rusty. The greater part of the battle fleet was laid up in harbour, "dismantled aloft and disarmed below." And in the new inventions which had come to revolutionise maritime warfare like other human activities, the volatile and nimble-witted French had stolen a dangerous march. In 1837 they had adopted explosive shells in place of the solid shot that had won Trafalgar, and their pioneer efforts with steamers in the early 'forties had been more successful than those of the statelier and more conservative British Admiralty.

All this combined with the events in France to cause a good deal of surface alarm. Yet the sense of England's superiority was so innate and the general complacence and love of peace and comfort so deep-rooted that it quickly died away. *Punch*

---

[1] *Greville, Memoirs, Part II, Vol. II, 82.*

[2] Lord Holland, expressing the traditional Whig minority view of friendship to revolutionary France, remarked to Palmerston, "For God's sake, if you are so full of distrust of France, if you suspect all her acts and all her words, put the worst construction on all she does, and are resolved to be on bad terms with her, call Parliament together, ask for men and money, and fight it out with her manfully. Do this or meet her in a friendly and conciliatory spirit, and cast aside all those suspicions which make such bad blood between the two countries." *Greville, Memoirs, Part II, Vol. I, 325.*

depicted a number of seasick French colonels and poodles attempting to cross the Channel[1] while a very senile Duke of Wellington in a Field Marshall's cocked hat vainly tried with a quill pen to tickle up a sleeping British lion which only replied, "All right, old boy, I shall be ready when I'm wanted." Palmerston confessed to Russell in 1851 that it was "almost as difficult to persuade the people of this country to provide themselves with the means of defence as it would be for them to defend themselves without those means."[2]

At the end of that year there came a new alarm, Louis Napoleon, interpreting the will of the rising generation in France, established himself in permanent power as life President by a military coup d'etat. A year later he became Emperor of the French in fictitious succession to his famous uncle. This arbitrary act, though accompanied by remarkably little loss of life, aroused the utmost indignation among English radicals, who merely saw it as a brutal attack on their liberal and socialist brethren across the Channel. It outraged their English respectability and their most cherished democratic ideals. They pictured the "man of December" as throttling the nation he had sworn to serve. "The soldiery had already been corrupted by a feast of sausages and champagne. For the officers there was gold. . . . The gutters of the boulevards ran with blood . . . a disreputable adventurer was wading through blood to the throne."[3]

The relapse of France into imperial despotism seemed to complete the isolation of England: the three Eastern tyrants were now joined by a Western. *Punch* went so far as to address a salutation to the democrats of the United States, hitherto little liked in aristocratic England:

"Oh, Jonathan! dear Jonathan! a wretched world we see;
There's scarce a freeman in it now, excepting you and me.
In soldier-ridden Christendom the sceptre is the sword;
The statutes of the nation from the cannon's mouth are roared.

[1] "Ye broode of Gallic cocke,
　　Defying rolle and rocke,
　　Across ye Channele sailing
　　With retching and with railing."
　　　　　　　Punch, XIV, 33.
[2] *H. C. F. Bell, Palmerston, I, 403.*
[3] *W. E. Adams, Memoirs of a Social Atom, I, 342-51.*

Ordnance the subject multitude for ordinance obey;
The bullet and the bayonet debate at once allay:
The mouth is gagg'd, the Press is stopp'd, and we remain alone
With power our thoughts to utter, or to call our souls our
    own.

They hate us, brother Jonathan, those tyrants; they detest
The island sons of liberty and freemen of the West;
It angers them that we survive their savage will to stem,
A sign of hope unto their slaves—a sign of fear to them."[1]

Faced by such a situation, patriotic feeling revived.[2] Cobdenism
and Free Trade notwithstanding, the nation began to rearm. A
Militia Bill was brought in by a short-lived Conservative government in the summer of 1852, and a new note crept into national
journalism—of the first rifle clubs, of serious searchings of
heart about Navy victualling scandals and the boilers of the
new steam warships, of Admiral Napier, K.C.B. of "Little Billee"
fame, and of jolly tars in big straw hats, striped jerseys and bell-
bottom trousers getting ready to show the world that peaceful
England could still teach a presumptuous foreigner a lesson.

Yet, after all, it was not the French tyrant with whom an
awakening England was to test her strength. For it happened
that British interests, real or illusory, caused Britain to fight
beside the French tyrant instead of against him. The Eastern
question cropped up again, and the island victors of Trafalgar
and Waterloo, who had dedicated themselves at the shrine of the
Crystal Palace to perpetual peace, drifted into a war to safeguard
the overland route to India. And in challenging those who
threatened their vital communications they challenged tyranny
too. No one could deny that Nicholas of Russia was a despot.
Though a more remote one, he was both more autocratic and
more offensive than Louis Napoleon.

For being an upstart, far from certain of his position and
anxious to prevent any revival of the Waterloo coalition against
France, Napoleon III sedulously courted England and did his
best to soothe her fears and susceptibilities. The despot of all
the Russias cared nothing for the English or any other public.
In his own remote and barbarous country public opinion did

---

[1] *Punch, XXII,* 13.
[2] "A very laudable feeling is glowing in the hearts of thousands of the British
people—the feeling for rifle practice. . . . We hate martial instruments. Bayonets are
bad but . . . chains are worse than bayonets." *Punch, XXII,* 62.

not exist. He was accustomed to dealing only with despots like himself. In pursuit of his imperial interests he had for some time been proposing to British statesmen and diplomats that as the Turkish Empire was obviously dissolving through its own inertia and corruption, Russia and Britain should forestall competitors by anticipating the demise and dividing the carcase between them. Russia should have its long-sought outlet to the Mediterranean, and Britain should have Egypt and Candia.

In two momentous conversations in 1853 with the British Ambassador at St. Petersburg this impertinent tyrant outlined his plans for partitioning the possessions of "the sick man" of the Porte. Had he known anything of the mind and conscience of England, he would never have suggested making her a partner in anything so outrageous. Had he been able to foretell the future he would have known, too, that in another half-century Britain would be honourably installed in Egypt, while the land-bound Muscovite would still be as far as ever from his Mediterranean goal and his hope of exercising suzerainty over his fellow Christians of the Balkans. The British government returned no answer but made it clear that it was without territorial ambitions of any kind.

The Czar of all the Russias was not to be turned from his purpose by the nicety of British scruples. If Britain would not join in his designs, he would execute them by himself. Meanwhile he had become involved in a dispute with Louis Napoleon, whom he persisted in treating as a low upstart, over the protection of the Christian shrines in the Turkish dominions. Consequently when in pursuance of his great design he moved his troops into the principalities of Wallachia and Moldavia—now Romania—he was confronted with the opposition not only of Britain but of France.

The British government—a talented but uneasy coalition of Peelites, Whigs and Radicals bound together by no other principle but dislike of the Protectionists—was in a difficulty. It had no wish to involve the nation in a war over the ownership of remote Syrian shrines and Balkan villages. On the other hand, a principle of British diplomatic policy was at stake and a foreign despot was openly flouting her Majesty's government. A compromise was therefore sought which recognised both the independence of the Ottoman Porte and the Czar's right to protect the Orthodox Christians in Turkey.

But it was one thing to propose a compromise: another to get two despotic and cunning orientals to accept it. The Sultan was resolved to keep his Christian provinces and to yield nothing. The Czar was equally resolved to obtain the substance of his ends, though, being anxious to obtain them if possible without war, he was temporarily the more reasonable of the two. But the Turk, seeing an opportunity of fighting a war (which he regarded as sooner or later inevitable) with the backing of two great Christian Powers, and, judging that such a chance might never occur again, refused any compromise whatever.

Step by step the British Prime Minister, Lord Aberdeen, was driven into a war which he deplored and whose results he dreaded. Most of his Cabinet were men of peace like himself, but a small war group led by Palmerston and Russell and strongly aided by the British Ambassador to the Porte—Lord Stratford de Redcliffe—drove him ever further into a position from which there was no withdrawing. Public opinion, waking up to the fact that the country was being flouted by a notorious despot, suddenly became intensely bellicose. Aberdeen found it harder to retreat than ever. A guarantee to the Turk which had been intended as provisional was imperceptibly transformed by that wily oriental into a document whose execution lay in Turkish, not British hands.

Without having any clear idea of what the struggle was about except that it was against tyranny and without the government having made any adequate preparations to conduct it, the British people in the spring of 1854 found themselves, in alliance with France and Turkey, and at war with Russia. The country, apparently so pacific a few years before, had completely changed its outlook: John Morley in his free-trading, radical Lancashire home, remembered hearing at his parental fireside heartfelt wishes that Cobden and Bright—still bravely advocating peace—should be flung together into the insanitary waters of the Irwell. What was even more surprising was the alignment of England beside the French "usurper," whose "foul lips"—in contemporary radical parlance—actually kissed the cheeks of Queen Victoria during a royal war-time visit to France.[1] A few far-seeing observers predicted that the war would be hard to wage and impossible to bring to a successful conclusion, and that

[1] "When we read of this last indignity at Cherbourg, there was not an honest woman's face in Britain that did not burn with shame." *W. E. Adams, Memoirs of a Social Atom, II, 350-1.*

the British people would soon be as heartily sick of it as they were now hot in its favour. They were an insignificant minority and no one took the least notice of them.

The difficulty was to find a scene of operations. Despite universal hatred of the Russians and intense detestation of the Czar, the first six months of the war passed without any hostilities worth mentioning. An Anglo-French naval expedition to the Baltic accomplished next to nothing. A military force sent to aid the Turk in the Balkans saw more of cholera than the enemy, and it was not till the late autumn of 1854 that British and French troops landed in the Crimea peninsula and set siege to the naval fortress of Sevastopol.

The battles that followed—Alma, Balaclava, Inkerman—and the long siege in the trenches proved that the English had lost nothing of their ancient valour. They also revealed their curious inability to plan adequately ahead. The army command, which had neither learnt nor endeavoured to learn anything since 1815, might have been ready for the battle of Waterloo but was certainly not for a winter campaign in the trenches of Russia.[1] In the first few months of the campaign everything failed: transport, commissariat, supply and hospitals. The Government and public which had talked glibly of taking Sevastopol in a few weeks were faced by the prospect of a long and hazardous campaign thousands of miles from home against a superior and apparently inexhaustible enemy fighting on his own ground.

During that winter—even in England it was one of the coldest in human memory—the losses of the little professional army were appalling and the foolish boastings of the summer soon turned to mourning. Tales of men fighting in the frozen trenches without greatcoats, or packed, filthy with disentry and gangrenous wounds, into unequipped hospitals built over Scutari cesspits, aroused a wave of indignation which brought down the government and temporarily disgraced and even imperilled the aristocratic system of the country. But the story of their courage and endurance also thrilled England: the charge of the Light Brigade in the valley of death was like Thermopylæ. The national mood was reflected by Macaulay, who told a friend in a letter how anxious he was about the brave fellows in the Crimea, how proud for the country and

[1]The British Commander-in-Chief, Lord Raglan, an old Peninsula veteran, invariably referred to the enemy as "the French." *Greville Memoirs, Part III, I, 212.*

how glad to think that the national spirit was so high and unconquerable. The annals of the tough simple soldiery who stuck
to their hopeless task until the Muscovite, unable to endure
longer, abandoned Sevastopol, were remembered in after years
by one of them, a farm labourer who had enlisted at sixteen,
as cold and starvation, unremitting duty for days at a stretch,
and what to lesser men would have been almost indescribable
suffering.

The Crimean War continued till 1856. It ended in a nominal
gain for Britain and France, though there were no fruits of
victory. But it at least produced two results: it gave time for
the Balkan peoples to achieve independence from the Turk
before the Russian could absorb them, and it awoke in the English
a growing spirit of self-examination that led to a great series
of administrative reforms of which Florence Nightingale's
lifelong work for nursing and military hygiene was only one.
Incidentally the peace treaty that concluded hostilities—signed
at Paris with a quill plucked from the wing of an eagle in the
Garden des Plantes—involved a voluntary surrender by Britain
of her right to seize goods other than contraband in neutral
ships at sea.

. . . .

Within a year the country was fighting again. For several
months, until the tide turned in favour of the little handful of
red-coated columns moving under a burning sun across distant
jungle and plain, England waited in suspense at the end of the
electric cable for news of beleaguered Cawnpore, Delhi and
Lucknow. Of the causes and significance of the Mutiny the
English had no notion. A few among them who had spent a
working lifetime under the oriental sun among the "drums
and gaudy idols . . . the black faces, the long beards, the yellow
streaks of sect, the turbans and the flowing robes, the spears
and silver races" of an alien continent, knew something of their
country's Eastern destiny. But to the great mass of the respectable
middle-class electors of Victorian England, India was only a
name.

This philosophical indifference to, almost unawareness of,
the origins and nature of their own empire was a source of
recurring bewilderment to the English. An event like the Indian
Mutiny always took them by surprise. The Scots, a proud race
of hereditary paupers who had had to travel to live, and even

the Protestant Irish who had the instinct for garrisoning in their blood, knew more of the empire than the English commercial classes whose wealth and power sustained it. It had come into being almost accidentally, not as a result of conscious national or governmental effort but as the bye-product of the activity of innumerable private persons. The law of primogeniture, by creating in every generation a surplus of portionless younger sons educated in a standard of comfort which they could only maintain by going out into the world to seek their fortunes, had had the effect of changing the status and allegiance of a quarter of the globe. During the seventeenth century, while the mind of England was obsessed with questions of internal government and religion, the first British Empire had been founded by the private enterprise of individual Englishmen who had been unable to secure the kind of life they wanted in the home country. A hundred and fifty years later, owing to the inability of the British Parliament and people to comprehend it, it had been lost.

Yet even while the first empire was dissolving, a second had been growing up in the same haphazard way. The process, though it had reached gigantic and almost unmanageable dimensions, still continued during Victoria's pacific reign. A good example of the way in which it occurred was afforded by the life of James Brooke, the first British Rajah of Sarawak. After an adventurous youth in the service of the East India Company, Brooke, at the age of thirty-five invested the modest capital left him by his father in a schooner of 142 tons in which he sailed on a voyage of exploration for Borneo. Here he became beneficently involved in the unhappy internal politics of the head-hunting county of Sarawak, and, making himself by his tact, energy and great administrative talents indispensable both to its rulers and people to whom—to the embarrassment of an indifferent British government—he became enthusiastically attached, was within a few years appointed hereditary Rajah of Sarawak by the Malay Sultan of Borneo. He died in 1868, ruler of a country as large as Scotland, which his heirs in the fullness of time and in the teeth of Whitehall added to the British Empire.

The process of expansion went on, in short, without either the initiative or the conscious will of an imperial government which obstinately refused to recognise itself as imperial. Palmerston, himself the embodiment of the spirit that made the British Empire, pooh-poohed the idea that his country should annex Egypt in order to safeguard her communications with India: a gentleman with an estate in Scotland and another in southern England, he remarked, did not need to own the post-houses along the Great North Road. Initiative was left in this, as in all things else, to the individual: the state in its corporate capacity only existed to protect the individual in his just gains and lawful occasions. The continued growth of the Empire was forced on an ever reluctant government (which, having to consider the interests of taxpayers who were also voters, was always cautious) by the restless energy of its private citizens. For every Englishman, rich or poor, who had courage, a strong body, willing hands and capital enough to buy a passage there was boundless opportunity and elbow room waiting in lands beyond the oceans. Two brothers, aged nineteen and seventeen, belonging to a family of twelve, left for New Zealand with £2,000 capital between them and a superabundance of animal spirits prepared for any risks and any labour. To "build, fell trees, plough, reap, pasture cattle, shear sheep, all these with the hands!"[1] was the task they cheerfully set themselves. Within a dozen years each looked forward to returning with a capital of at least £20,000 to seek a wife and found a family. And the interests represented by that new capital and its future returns would demand in due course the protection of the imperial government, whether these interests lay in the British dominions or, as often happened, in more populous lands under some other flag.

. . . .

The unit of the national life was the family—the sacred nursery of the individual. The wealth and power of the empire grew in ratio to the size of this homely unit. The first half of the nineteenth century saw the population increasing more rapidly than ever before, not because more children were born but because, thanks to advances in hygiene and medical science, more survived. Between 1841 and 1861 the population of England, Scotland and Wales rose from seventeen to twenty-three millions. Not only in working-class homes but in those of the upper and middle-class large families were still the rule. The Queen herself had nine children: a Judge of the High Court twenty-four. Strangers admitted to the sacred circle of the home would usually

[1] Taine, *Notes on England*, 69-70.

find their hostess in the family way and be greeted by the spectacle of a flock of little boys running off to hide and little girls running out to peep. Often the children would mount in unbroken yearly steps from the baby at the breast to the grown youth of nineteen.

Around that holy of holies centred a life of the strictest regularity and order. Paterfamilias, for all the love he bore his family, was an awe-inspiring figure, infallible in his judgments and irreproachable in his whiskers and moral conduct: his wife—a few years before a slender and clear-complexioned girl— "a housekeeper, a nurse, a sitting hen," as a distinguished French critic saw her, "broad, stiff and destitute of ideas, with red face, eyes the colour of blue china . . . spreading dresses . . . stout masculine boots . . . long, projecting teeth."[1]

In the more prosperous families the boys would start work early with a tutor and at eight or nine leave home for the rough republic of one of the great boarding schools which were constantly expanding and multiplying to train new rulers for a growing commercial empire. Here sensitive children from rich and sheltered homes would rise in the small hours of the morning to light fires and boil water for their majestic seniors, sweep rooms, run errands and do the meanest chars, endure flogging and bullying without a murmur, and sleep at night in noisy, crowded dormitories subject to influences which would have made their mothers and sisters swoon.

In contrast, the lives of girls in well-to-do families were often sheltered to an extent that cut them off from the roots of life. The men were trained to make wealth: the women to transmit and form part of it. They were regarded as the chief measure of a husband's or father's opulence and social dignity: their elegant accomplishments, their delicacy and chastity were sources of male pride and satisfaction. As girls they were taught to play the piano, draw, dance, make wax flowers and bead-stands and do decorative gilding and crochet work. That a man's womenfolk should be able to devote themselves to occupations so materially useless was a tacit tribute to the labour and self-sacrifice that had gone to the making of the wealth that sustained it. "Oh, yes, mum," said the cook in *Punch* of the squire's bride, "she's a perfect lady, mum. Don't know one j'nt o' meat from another, mum."

[1] *Taine.*

Young ladies, artificially kept from all knowledge of the seamy or even normal side of life, grew up, in tight waists and voluminous skirts, like flies in amber. The pursuit of wealth to the exclusion of almost every other worldly object was affecting changes in every department of English life but in none more than its tendency to rob the English gentlewomen of useful occupation and of knowledge of the domestic arts and of the world in which she lived. The process was gradual and, so long as large families remained the fashion, tempered by the discipline and give-and-take of communal home life. With the growth of commercial wealth and of the mechanical means of multiplying comforts and luxuries, its effects became ever more insidious. For in the end it deprived many women of the upper and middle class of the natural sources of vitality and strength and the instinctive feeling for wise and balanced living which, as mothers, it should have been their lot to transmit to future generations. More of the ills of our present epoch of reckoning may be due to this cause than is yet realised.

The strong, imitative instinct and desire to excel of the English led to a constant approximation of the lower types of social life to the higher. On a simpler and more spartan scale the family life of the north-country manufacturer followed that of the lawyer in Kensington and the banker in Bayswater. Often he still lived on the premises of his own works in the shade of the smoke and within earshot of the hammering that created his wealth. In other cases he had moved out to one of the suburbs of gardened, gothic villas that were growing up on the outskirts of places like Manchester and Birmingham. His daily round and social habits were less leisured than those of the Londoner: he still went to the mill at six, dined in the middle of the day and went early to bed after a hot meat supper and family prayers. Sometimes his working day would last sixteen or more hours. He sent his sons into the works in their early teens instead of to public school and college which, he held, unsettled the mind for commercial pursuits.

Though many of those engaged in trade were men of cultivation—buyers of pictures and founders of Libraries and Colleges —the bulk of the provincial merchants tended, like their richer Forsyte brethren in London, to be Philistines, valuing all worldly things by the sterling standard, ignoring and despising art and having little truck with intellect which they left to the leisured and endowed landed gentry. The spiritual side of their natures would have been stifled but for their feeling for religion. This was like themselves: downright, undiscriminating and practical. Its dominant note was a militant Protestantism, which comprised a great readiness to criticise, a strong sense of self-righteousness, a very real respect for integrity and sound moral conduct and an unreasoning distrust of the Pope and of all foreign fal-lals. It found vigorous expression in the busy black-coated, white-tied unction of Exeter Hall—the League of Nations Union of the day—where middle-class opinion was ceaselessly mobilised in favour of missionary, pacifist and humanitarian ventures, all of a strongly Protestant trend. Its antithesis was the Puseyite movement which, spreading out from Oxford—still the home of lost causes—was filling long-neglected, sober Hanoverian parish churches with painted chancels, niches, candles, altars, Popish-looking rails to keep off the profane laity, and painted windows bearing the idolatrous image of the Virgin Mary.[1]

This drift to Rome, as it seemed to many of our great-grand parents, aroused all the Protestant pugnacity of the British people. In 1850 an attempt by the Pope to create English metropolitan titles for Catholic bishops all but brought down the government, who were suspected of being lukewarm in their opposition to this outrageous act of "invasion."[2] Mobs processed through the streets of quiet provincial towns, smashing Catholic shop windows, tearing up chapel railings and bearing effigies of the offending Pope and his Cardinals (previously exhibited in some local tailor's window) to the bonfire. In his public letter repudiating what *Punch* described as "an insolent papal brief," the Premier, Lord John Russell, assured an anxious nation that "no foreign prince or potentate will be permitted to fasten his fetters upon a nation which has so long and nobly vindicated its right to freedom of opinion, civil, political and religious. . . . I will not bate a jot of heart or life so long as the glorious principles and the immortal martyrs of the Reformation shall be held in reverence by the great mass of a nation which looks with contempt on the mummeries of superstition." This, and a great deal more like it, was the kind of language the serious

[1] "I wanted Oliver and his dragoons to march in and put an end to it all." *Letters and Literary Remains of Edward Fitzgerald*, I, *180*.
[2] *Some New Letters of Edward Fitzgerald* (ed. F. R. Barton) *148*.

middle class of the eighteen-fifties liked to hear. To still its honest fears the Government brought in an Ecclesiastical Titles Bill, as a "slap in the face"—it was little else—"to papal aggression." There was an eternal child in the English heart, and a little make-believe, so long as it was kept out of business hours, was necessary from time to time.

There was no make-believe in the genuine piety of the English middle-class home. Occasionally tyrannical and more than frequently oppressive—for the English seldom did things by halves —it was none the less the central core of life for a great body of men and women who represented between them the major portion of the wealth, power and activity of the world. It gave them regularity of habit, a rule of sober conduct that made them invincible in their narrow achievement and a certain intensity of purpose that lent dignity and even beauty to their otherwise monotonous and ugly lives. Over the frieze of one of the chief London banks were written the words, "Lord direct our labours": the very railway terminuses provided bibles chained to reading-desks for the waiting business man to consult.

The Frenchman, Taine, in his *Notes on England*, has left a picture of the head of an English family conducting prayers in the sheltered bosom of his household. "On Sunday evening he is their spiritual guide, their chaplain; they may be seen entering in a row, the women in front, the men behind, with seriousness, gravity, and taking their places in the drawing-room. The family and visitors are assembled. The master reads aloud a short sermon—next a prayer; then every one kneels or bends forward, the face turned towards the wall; lastly, he repeats the Lord's Prayer and, clause by clause, the worshippers respond. This done, the servants file off, returning in the same order, silently, meditatively . . . not a muscle of their countenances moved."[1]

One saw the full intensity of that spirit of worship on the Sabbath. The English kept this day holy and unspotted from the world: that is to say, they did no work on it, avoided travel, attended church or chapel and stayed at home. Here the family virtues were intensively cultivated. An old man who once taught the writer of this book has recalled his childhood's Sunday round in mid-Victorian days. At eight the elder children breakfasted as a Sabbath treat with their parents, and after breakfast

[1] *Taine, Notes on England, 111.*

and family prayers settled down quietly until it was time for
chapel over some special illustrated Sunday magazine: *Good
Words*, *The British Workman*, *The Band of Hope*, *The Sunday
Magazine*. These works were not quite as heavy reading as
their titles suggested, for, interspersed with moral sermons
and excerpts from the Scriptures, were serial stories by approved
writers which, published elsewhere, might have been set down
as frivolous and pernicious novels but which, between sacred
covers, took on an almost privileged guise. In the afternoon
the programme of devotional reading and instruction was
repeated: a missionary narrative read aloud by mother after
dinner, Sunday School in the nursery conducted by a nurse, a
Bible lesson from father at four, family tea followed by hymns,
evening chapel for the elder children and family prayers again
after supper.

Such was the kind of day of which Macaulay was thinking
when he appealed in the House for proper week-end leisure for the
factory worker. "We are not poorer but richer because we have,
through many ages, rested from our labour one day in seven. That
day is not lost. While industry is suspended, while the plough lies
in the furrow, while the Exchange is silent, while no smoke
ascends from the factory, a process is going on quite as important
to the wealth of nations as any process which is performed on
more busy days. Man, the machine of machines, the machine
compared with which all the contrivances of the Watts and the
Arkwrights are worthless, is repairing and winding up, so that
he returns to his labours on the Monday with clearer intellect,
with livelier spirits, with renewed corporal vigour."[1] He cre-
tainly needed it in that age of strenuous endeavour. Gaining so
much from the Sabbath rest itself, the respectable middle class,
whose votes now swayed the legislature, naturally wished to
assure the same blessings for the rest of the population. It was
prepared to use its political power to enforce them.

Sunday observance was one of the salient peaks of the mid-
Victorian scene. On that day over a busy nation there fell an
awful calm. Any attempt to relieve it was met by the full terrors
of the canalised English forces of moral righteousness. In 1856
an effort was made by certain scholarly aristocrats to open the
National Gallery and the British Museum on Sunday. The
storm this aroused in a House of Commons assailed by all the

[1] *Sir G. O. Trevelyan, Macaulay II, 176-7.*

propagandist powers of Exeter Hall caused them quickly to withdraw. A proposal in the same year to provide Sunday bands in the dreary Manchester and Salford parks met with a like repulse.

At midnight on Saturday—a noisy drunken evening in any working-class district—all movement and sound suddenly ceased. As Big Ben's new clock chimed its last stroke a solemn hush announced that the Sabbath had begun. Next morning the food shops opened for a few hours, but at eleven, the time for divine service, every shutter went up. For those with large houses and affectionate families, the quiet scene had a familiar and reassuring air: to those who lived in tiny tenement rooms and had no playground but the drab streets it was less pleasing. Taine, visiting England in 1860, found the prospect almost more than he could bear:

> "Sunday in London in the rain: the shops are shut, the streets almost deserted; the aspect is that of an immense and a well-ordered cemetery. The few passers-by under their umbrellas, in the desert of squares and streets, have the look of uneasy spirits who have risen from their graves; it is appalling.
>
> "I had no conception of such a spectacle which is said to be frequent in London. The rain is small, compact, pitiless; looking at it one can see no reason why it should not continue to the end of all things; one's feet churn water, there is water everywhere, filthy water impregnated with an odour of soot. A yellow, dense fog fills the air, sweeps down to the ground; at thirty paces a house, a steamboat appears as spots upon blotting-paper. After an hour's walk in the Strand especially, and in the rest of the City, one has the spleen, one meditates suicide."[1]

．　．　．　．　．　．　．　．

The virtuous middle class had the franchise: the working-class majority had not. It was the middle class, therefore, that enforced the new urban English Sabbath in conformity with its own frugal virtues. But there was one point on which the rough majority insisted: Jewish Sabbath or no, it would drink when it pleased. Beer and gin, and plenty of them, were the unspoken price with which the busy Gradgrinds and Bounderbys reconciled the proletariat to the social chaos and

---

[1] *Notes on England, 9.*

vacuum of *laissez-faire*. When, in 1856, an evangelical peer brought in a bill to close the pubs on the Lord's Day, the church parade of high society in Hyde Park was interrupted for three successive Sundays by an angry multitude who booed every rider and carriage on the first Sunday, pelted them with showers of turf and stones on the second, and on the third made the few daring survivors ride for their lives till the police, in long lines, raining blows on rioters and spectators alike, cleared the park. After that the bill was withdrawn and the pious aristocrat left the country.

At midnight on Sunday the Sabbath gloom lightened. The respectable classes, replete from their devotional exercises and anticipating an early start to the new week of labour and lawful gain, slept the sleep of the just. But the dancing saloons and the all-night haunts of vice in the metropolis turned on their lights and began to revel again openly.[1]

. . . .

This was of a piece with the national taste. England kept its more austere moments with great solemnity and decorum, but it liked to do itself well and knew how. The Forsytes carried their love of good living from the country to the town, and with their new wealth, were the better able to gratify it. They loved to take the summer steamer to Blackwall or Greenwich and dine in Lovegrove's great room or at the Ship or Trafalgar off piled plates of whitebait, salmon and India pickle, spitchcocked eels and stewed carp, followed by roast duck and haunch of mutton, tarts and custard, iced punch, hock, champagne and port, while the river shimmered in the rays of the setting sun and the white sails passed against the twilight. Toasts, pipes and good stories rounded off the feast, and singing in the train all the way home, and a draught of soda and a purge of pills before negotiating the stairs to join one's sleeping partner.[2]

They did themselves as well at home. The merchantry and the semi-commercial professional classes were making money hand over fist and they disposed of it, partly in ever growing investments but partly in comfortable living. They spent little on splendour, art and travel: they left these to the aristocracy and gentry. They concentrated on dinner parties. In this there was much competitive expenditure. A man and his wife

[1] *Francis Wey. A Frenchman sees England in the Fifties, 250-6.*
[2] *Punch, XVII, 102.*

measured their status by the weight of their table silver—vast épergnes, massive salvers, tureens and candlesticks—the fineness of their table damask, cut glass and china, above all on the quantity of dishes served. Vast saddles of mutton and sirloins of beef, whole salmons and turbots, interminable courses of potages, fishes, removes, entremets and removes of the roast, were helped out by vegetables boiled in water, pastries and enormous Stilton and Cheshire cheeses. The wines followed each other in equal profusion until the table was cleared for further orgies of dessert, preserved fruits, nuts, port, madeira and sherry. All this suggested to a foreigner that the race would soon eat itself to a standstill. Taine reckoned that to the one and a half sheep consumed in a year by a Frenchman, an Englishman ate four. In England, an American noticed, even the sparrows seemed fat.

The circumference took its standards from the centre. The larger industrial towns were beginning to evolve a social life for the well-to-do modelled on that of the metropolis, with their own clubs, fashionable places for promenade and recreation and assembly and ball-rooms. In Liverpool, the most aristocratic city of the industrial north, the merchant princes wore white cravats and evening dress coats on Change, and in Manchester's Athanæum and at its world-famous Hallé concerts, first established in 1848, well-to-do quakers could be seen soberly conversing in broad-brimmed hats, neat grey or mulberry-coloured coats, frilled shirts and knee breeches. The urban sporting world, familiar to the twentieth century, was beginning to take shape: the I. Zingari was instituted in 1845 and a regular All England cricket eleven began to play a few years later, travelling the country in billycock and checked shirt and arousing widespread enthusiasm for the game, soon to bear fruit in the first county matches. Rugby football was also evolving from a local into a national sport, with its own customs and rules: the famous Blackheath Club was founded by a little group of old Rugbeians and Blackheath boys in 1858.

For though England was turning urban and the old field sports could no longer suffice, the strong national love of pleasure reasserted itself as soon as the first rush for wealth was over. A new form of recreation, first tentatively essayed at Weymouth, Scarborough and Brighton in the days of George III., found especial favour with the well-to-do merchant and professional

classes. The annual seaside holiday had the supreme advantage
of catering for the whole family, and its healthful properties
gave a fillip to business. Many London families emigrated for the
summer to Margate, the breadwinner coming down the river
for the week-end on Saturday night on the "husbands' boat."
The place was already an institution before the middle of the
century, with its trim houses and spired church, its famous
pier and fishermen, arbours and seats, its old ladies in deck-chairs
and gentlemen in straw hats and its rows of horse-drawn
bathing-boxes and bottle-nosed bathing women wading through
the water in great bonnets.

Though newer resorts of quality like Folkestone and Hastings
were winning favour, Brighton was still the first seaside town
in England with many survivals of its Regency heyday, including
"old, wicked-looking gentlemen with thin faces, long noses and
quaint hats who had drunk Regent punch with King George
the Fourth at the Pavilion." These mingled, a little incongru-
ously but in the English mode, with demure young ladies in
curls and bonnets, armies of children in jackets and knicker-
bockers, and fanatic-looking preachers in tall hats and white
ties who attempted to hold prayer meetings on the beach. The
normal costume of the seaside holiday-maker was a loose-fitting
check suit and a bowler. It was fun, after days in counting-house
and office, to stroll along the windy pier (where the French were
periodically expected to land) and watch the gulls and fishing-
boats and the old salts in jerseys and straw hats, to dine off turtle
and strawberry ices at Mutton's, to drive in an open fly from
one cliff to the other, eyeing the "gals" as they passed to and
fro in their crinolines and parasols before the rows of dazzling
white houses with green blinds and sun-blistered verandas, to
hear the fisherwomen hawking their prawns with shrill "Yeo
Ho's!" and, in the cool of the evening, to listen to the negro
melodists singing "I would I were in Old Virginny" and the
band playing the Overture to Zampa or the March from Athalie.

Even Victorian decorum relaxed a little by the seaside.
Monsieur Wey, a Frenchman of delicacy, noted with astonish-
ment how bathing took place in full view of a front swarming
with idlers of both sexes: at Brighton men bathing alone went
into the water stark naked. Never, he wrote, would he forget
his bathe there in 1856. It was on a Sunday at the time at which
worshippers returned from church. He had been assigned a

cabin in which to undress. It was a wooden construction on wheels placed at the water's edge with its steps half-submerged. He committed himself to the waves. When he was ready to return a fearful thing happened. Three ladies, a mother with her daughters, settled themselves on camp stools in his direct line of approach. They seemed very respectable females, and the girls, he noted, were both pretty. There was no possibility of reaching his cabin without passing in front of them. They each held a prayer book and watched him swimming about with serene unconcern. The Frenchman's feelings can be imagined. To give them a hint without offending their modesty he advanced cautiously on all fours, raising himself by degrees as much as decency permitted.[1]

English notions of propriety were always hard for a foreigner to appreciate, for strict as they were, they seemed founded on no principle and were often a matter of words. A Frenchman noted that the more respectable islanders would sooner die than mention the human posterior by name, yet in mixed company would roar with laughter at the story of the lady who said she had plenty to sit on but nowhere to put it. Mr. Roget in his famous *Thesaurus* of English words and phrases, published in 1852, classified all concept and matter except the human body, which was discreetly scattered about the book, the stomach concealed under the general title of "receptacle," the genitals under that of production. Yet physical rough and tumble, often of the crudest kind, was the essence of the national humour.

For unlike the older territorial aristocracy to which in its power and wealth it was already beginning to give tone, the new English middle class was only half civilised, and its advance in manners, rapid as it was, could not keep pace with its fortunes. The moment it relaxed its puritanical decorum, the rude native Adam, so full of rustic nature and vitality, emerged. In its pleasures, urban England still smacked of the earth. When it went on the spree, it left its prudery at home. It sat top-hatted, eating devilled kidneys, drinking *aqua vitae* and joining in the roaring choruses of the smoky Cider Cellar in Maiden Lane: it kicked up its flounces and heels and stamped them on the ground in the rhythmic surge of the polka. All the vulgarity and vitality of the nation burst out in such annual institutions as the Christmas pantomime, when even the family

[1] *A Frenchman sees England in the Fifties*, 296.

split its sides in uninhibited and unashamed laughter at the gargantuan jests and antics of the Dame and goggled its eyes at the tight-laced, broad-bosomed, ample-flanked Principal Boy. The pantomime had full licence to be coarse, and respectable fathers and mothers who took their families to revel in its rich spectacle would have been gravely disappointed had it been otherwise. The crowded house rocked at the broad jests, gaped with delight at the tinsel scenes in which fairies and genii floated before ethereal landscapes of gold, crystal and diamonds, and uproariously applauded the brutal, noisy but good-humoured parody of the Harlequinade.[1]

To see Victorian England really enjoying itself, no spectacle compared with the Derby. With the growth of London it had become the chief sporting event of the year. On the way to Epsom all the world mingled, fours-in-hand with rakish young gentlemen smoking cigars and wearing check trousers and muslin shades on their top-hats; ladies with parasols in open carriages; crowded family brakes; pearl-buttoned costers in donkey carts; cabs, barouches, droskies. Every one was laughing, chaffing and shouting, with only a single thought and destination. The windows and balconies of the mellow, shaded Georgian houses along the road to the Downs were alive with smiling faces, the walls were crowned with cheering schoolboys and on every village green stood groups of pretty girls with new ribbons and finery fluttering under the tender, sun-kissed leaves of the chestnut trees. Every girl who acknowledged the waving hands and

[1]There is a description of one in Monsieur Wey's account of a visit to the Surrey Theatre in the closing year of the Crimea War :

"All the characters join in a rough-and-tumble, and the pantomime commences in real earnest. Blows are freely exchanged with any available instruments, the actors kick, laugh, yell, jest, roar and rollick in an indescribable pandemonium. Thereupon mock policemen intervene and are roughly handled by the actors. Meanwhile the background representing the different London districts moves slowly past. Then comes a scene of political satire. The General Staff of the British Army drag themselves in on crutches; Cobden and his adherents are flogged like schoolboys; food adulterers are belaboured by the people. Suddenly the scene changes to a market-place and is swarming with live chickens, turkeys, pigeons, ducks.

"Meanwhile Admiral Napier had appeared in full-dress uniform, ordered a few Cossacks to be put in irons, shaken the editor of the *Times* by the hand, been chaired, then discarding his uniform danced a frantic jig with Harlequin. It all ended by a scene in an enchanted island lit by multi-coloured Roman candles. From the centre rose an enormous spray of flowers, supporting the figures of Queen Victoria and Napoleon III. standing hand-in-hand. These parts were taken by small children in consideration of the demands of perspective. The Prince of Pearls and the Queen of Grapes crowned them with laurel wreaths, the young ladies of the ballet grouped themselves around with their legs in the air, Columbine and the clown fell on their knees, Richard III's soldiers presented arms, and the curtain fell to the majestic strains of ' God Save the Queen.'" *A Frenchman sees the English in the 'Fifties, 214-21.*

kisses blown to her was greeted with a cheer. Among the sweet-williams and Canterbury bells sat old gentlemen at their cottage doors smoking long pipes and giving as good as they took from the wags on the passing brakes. At each successive turnpike there was a jam, and here and at the roadside pubs the noise was like all England speaking at once.

On the course itself the colours of the rainbow, and many more crude, mingled. Round the carriages and coaches bare-footed, hungry-looking beggars, gipsies and children swarmed seeking food. The world of fashion and the workaday City rubbed shoulders with comic negro singers, hucksters selling trinkets and red-haired Scottish lassies dancing to the sound of bagpipes. On vehicles overlooking the course sat jolly old boys from Change or counter in top-hats with side whiskers, high stocks and massive gold chains suspended across monumental waistcoats, drinking champagne out of long glasses and eating game pie, sandwiches and melon. Behind them were painted booths and bookies' stands, and all the fun of the great day—boxers and banjos, thimble rigs and knock-em-downs, shooting and archery galleries, skittle alleys and dirty, bright-coloured, bawling vendors of every kind.

Towards evening, when the races were over and swarms of carrier pigeons had borne their news of triumph or disaster into every corner of England, the carnival entered on its final stage. Bacchus and the old Saxon gods of horn and mead seemed to have descended on to the packed, twilit downs. The astonished Frenchman, Taine, tried to describe the scene:

"Twenty-four gentlemen triumphantly range on their omnibus seventy-five bottles which they have emptied. Groups pelt each other with chicken bones, lobster-shells, pieces of turf. Two parties of gentlemen have descended from their omnibuses and engaged in a fight, ten against ten; one of them gets two teeth broken. There are humorous incidents: three men and a lady are standing erect in their carriage; the horses move on, they all tumble, the lady with her legs in the air; peals of laughter follow. Gradually the fumes of wine ascend to the heads; these people so proper, so delicate, indulge in strange conduct; gentlemen approach a carriage containing ladies and young girls, and stand shamefully against the wheels; the mother tries to drive them away with her parasol. One of our party who remained till midnight saw many horrors which I cannot describe; the animal nature had full vent."[1]

A drunken land at times the old fighting England of the urban 'fifties was: the right to empty his can of beer whenever he pleased was the first clause of Magna Carta which the Englishman took with him from the country to the town. In 1850 Manchester, with its 400,000 inhabitants, had 475 "publics" and 1,143 beer houses. Every night the eternal revelry would begin outside their flare-lit doors: the tip-tapping of the wooden clogs, the tangled hair and dirty, sodden faces swaying, swinging, and leaping to the music of fiddle or seraphine. In the casinos or music saloons, where a man might pay 2d. or 3d. for admission, eat apples and oranges and afterwards sup on tripe and trotters, drink and harmony went hand in hand, as, amid a strong flavour of gin, corduroy and tobacco smoke, the rough audience joined in the chorus of the last music-hall ditty. On Saturday night, after the workman's weekly pay had been taken, it was a revolting sight for a sensitive man to witness the ghastly scenes at the tavern doors. Drunken women by the hundred lay about higgledy-piggledy in the mud, hollow-eyed and purple-cheeked, their ragged clothing plastered with muck.[2] Occasionally one would stagger up to fight or to beat off some whimpering wife come with her bedraggled babes to seek a drunken husband before the coming week's housekeeping money was all spent.

. . . .

For though the worst days of hunger, destitution and low wages were over, and the industrious, frugal artisan, like the resourceful manufacturer, was enjoying better times, the more the nation became industralised, the more squalid became the background of the bulk of its people. The greater towns— several of them now nearing the half-million mark—were still organised on the parish model that had sufficed when they were half rural: that is to say they were without efficient local government, sanitation or communal amenity. Even the capital, the seat of Parliament and the centre of national culture and fashion, was by modern standards indescribably filthy. Here, as everywhere else, the rate of expansion had outgrown the civic institutions and organisation of the past, and the result was

[1]*Notes on England*, *43*.   [2]*F. Wey, A Frenchman sees the English in the 'Fifties*, *117·18*.

pandemonium. London was increasing at the rate of 2,000 houses a year. Efforts of public-spirited individuals to cleanse it were always defeated by the flow of fresh immigrants from Ireland and the country. Even the new fashionable districts of Belgravia and Pimlico were unpaved and almost without illumination. Footmen carried lanterns at night in front of their masters, and the highway down the centre of Eaton Square was a sea of ruts with islands, brickbats and rubbish.

For the new London as it grew outwards rose on the muck of the old. Its Medical Officer of Health, in a report issued in 1849, described the subsoil of the City as "17 million cubic feet of decaying residium." Belgrave Square and Hyde Park Gardens rested on sewers abounding in the foulest deposits which blocked the house drains and emitted disgusting smells, spreading purulent throats, typhus, febrile influenza, typhoid and cholera among the well-to-do and their servants. As late as the middle of the century a summer's evening walk by the waters of the Serpentine sometimes ended in fever and death brought on by the morbid stench of the stream-borne drainage of Paddington. Even the Queen's apartments at Buckingham Palace were ventilated through the common sewer: and a mysterious outbreak of fever in Westminster cloisters led to the discovery of a mass of old cesspools from which 500 cartloads of filth were subsequently removed. Many of the busier streets were ankle-deep in horse-dung.

If these were the sanitary conditions among which the prosperous lived, those of the workers can be imagined. Off Orchard Street, Portman Square, a single court 22 feet wide, with a common sewer down its middle, housed nearly a thousand human beings in 26 three-storied houses. And the passer-by, pursuing the course of Oxford Street towards Holborn, was favoured by the sight and whiff of a narrow, winding, evil-smelling lane lined with hovels, through the open doors of which could be seen earthen floors below the level of the streets swarming with pallid, verminous, crawling human animals. "Is it a street or kennel?" asked *Punch*.

> "foul sludge and fœtid stream
> That from a chain of mantling pools sends up a choky steam;
> Walls black with soot and bright with grease; low doorways,
>   entries dim;
> And out of every window, pale faces gaunt and grim."

In Wapping the courtyards were deep with filth, like pigsties, in which incredibly ragged and often naked children crawled seeking for vegetable parings and offal among the refuse. In Bethnal Green there were 80,000 inhabitants living under almost completely primitive conditions. Until the first parliamentary Sewer Commissioners in the middle 'fifties laid down over fifty miles of underground arterial drainage and pumped out millions of cubic feet of nauseating sludge, almost every street was barricaded against overflowing sewers. London that had become a city such as the world had never before seen was still governed like a village. *Punch* depicted the Court of Aldermen guzzling at one of the great traditional feasts, while King Death, with folded arms and socket eyes, gazed down on his henchmen, the spectres of Carbonic Acid Gas, Miasma, Cholera and Malaria, who took their toll of gaunt, ragged humans amid arched sewers and slime.

As for the state of the river into which all this unmastered nastiness drained, it beggared description. Its shores were rotten with "guano, stable dung, decaying sprats, and top dressings from the market gardens." In the hot summer of 1858 the stink became so foul that there was talk of removing Parliament. In a famous cartoon England's leading comic journal apostrophied Father Thames as a filthy old man dragging up dead rats from a liquid, gaseous mass of black mud and dying fish.

> "Filthy river, filthy river,
> Foul from London to the Nore,
> What art thou but one vast gutter,
> One tremendous common shore.
>
> All beside thy sludgy waters,
> All beside thy reeking ooze,
> Christian folks inhale memphitis
> Which thy bubbly bosom brews.
> · · · · · ·
> And from thee is brewed our porter,
> Thee, thou gully, puddle, sink!
> Thou vile cesspool art the liquor
> Whence is made the beer we drink."[1]

The water supply of three million people was polluted. Not till

[1] *Punch, XV, 151.*

the establishment in 1855 of the Metropolitan Board of Works
—forerunner of the London County Council—did the evil begin
to abate.

Not only inertia and a certain native spirit of muddle, un-
tamed by the discipline of established leadership, but the selfishness of vested interests operated to keep mid-Victorian London
dirty and unhealthy. Two scandalous examples were the
state of Smithfield—another Troy, reeking with the carcasses
of half a million beasts slaughtered annually in the heart
of the City, which stood a ten years' siege by the sanitary reformers—and the privilege of intra-mural burial still claimed
under ancient charters by private dynasties of citizens. These
suicidal rights, automatically repeopling the piled-up church-
yards, continued unabated until 1852. This was all part of the
intense and traditional individualism of England: up to 1851,
any one could open a slaughtering yard. Private citizens like
Mr. Boffin made fortunes out of suburban dust-heaps—stinking
fly-haunted abominations poisoning the atmosphere for miles
round—and the city bakehouses were little better than common
nuisances.

So too in the narrow crowded streets pandemonium was long
permitted in the sacred name of liberty. The drivers of the 2d.
buses, growing in numbers as well as in girth, raced each other
through the City while their stripe-trousered "cads" or conductors ran shouting beside them, sometimes almost dragging
unwilling passengers into their vehicles. The pavements were
blocked with long, rotating files of wretched men encased in
huge quadrilateral sandwich boards, and the narrow streets with
advertising carts towering ever higher like moving pagodas in
the attempt to overshadow one other. Vans stuck fast between
the stone posts that still served to mark the footways: vendors
of vegetables with wheel-barrows and ragged organ-grinders
paraded the cobbled gutters. In the national mania for turning
everything to money-making the very paving-stones were
scrawled with injunctions to buy so-and-so's wares. Bill-stickers
were allowed to cover every vacant wall and hoarding with
advertisements, beggars, their clothes caked with a layer of
phosphorescent grime, to exhibit their sores and destitution.
Within a stone's throw of the heart of London, Leicester Square,
formerly the home of great artists, was a "dreary abomination
of desolation." In its centre a headless statue, perpetually bom-

barded by ragged urchins with brickbats, stood in a wilderness of weeds frequented by starved and half-savage cats.

All this was founded on and excused by the national passion for independence. In the new towns order was lacking: custom which to the English is always the warrant of law had yet to arise. The right of a man to do what he liked with his property, labour and time—the triple-guarded heritage of every Englishman—had still to be tempered in the urban England that had taken the place of the rustic by a realisation that society depended on a general performance of social duty even when it clashed with the promptings of individual self-interest and love of liberty. *Punch* put the prickly English attitude in a parable of a fire that consumed a long street piecemeal because each occupier refused to subscribe to a fire-engine on the grounds that centralisation was inefficient and mischievous, crying "Let every man get his bucket and squirt and put out the fire himself. That is self-government!"[1] On the same principle a foreigner noticed that when an Englishman went skating and fell through the ice, it was not the business of authority to get him out of the water.[2] Instead, assistance was afforded him by professional life-savers who hovered perpetually round threatened points with the implements of their humanitarian trade. The efficiency and promptitude of such aid naturally bore some relation to the kind of fee likely to be paid by the beneficiary.

.   .   .   .

It was a good England for the healthy and successful: a fearful one for the weak and inefficient. Yet, for all the gloomy horrors of its growing towns, the nation still had enough of vigorous country blood in its veins to make light of its cancers. It stood four-square to the world with a confident smile on its good-humoured pugnacious face ready to take on all-comers. Its wealth was growing day by day, its ships sailed triumphant and unhindered on every sea, the beauty, order and peace of its countryside were the wonder and admiration of every foreigner who visited it. The loveliness of that Miltonian landscape, the prosperity of its rose and ivy-covered cottages, the strength and assurance of its thriving farms and lordly parks and mansions blinded the indulgent eye to the darker corners of the new cities.

[1] *Punch, XV, 78.*

[2] "In London, where every citizen is free of his actions so long as he does not interfere with his neighbour, the police look on placidly and respect the skaters' liberty to the extent of watching them drown." F. Wey, *A Frenchman sees the English in the 'Fifties, 232.*

There was so much to love in England—those wonderful oaks and green lawns, the sleek, lowing cattle, the smoke curling up from cottage chimneys in a mysterious and blended sea of tender verdure, the strong, kindly men and women who were so at home among its familiar scenes—that there was no room for criticism. One just took this strong-founded, dynamic island of contradictions for granted and accepted it as a whole.

It seemed fitting that the chosen leader of such a land should be Lord Palmerston. With his jaunty mien, his sturdy common sense, his straw between his lips and his *soubriquet* of Cupid, the game old man was the idol of mid-Victorian England and the embodiment of everything for which it stood. From 1855 until his death at the age of 81 in 1865 he was continuously Prime Minister, with one short break in 1858-9 when the discredited protectionists under Lord Derby and Disraeli had a brief spell of minority office.

The last of the aristocratic Whigs of the tradition of the "Glorious Revolution," he represented the Liberals in his contempt for obscurantist mysticism and the Tories in his hatred of doctrinaire reform. For ten years he kept a fast-changing Britain in a political back-water of time and ruled not by the magnetism of ideals nor by the machinery of party organisation —for he had neither—but by sheer personal popularity. Nothing could shake his hold on the British people. They loved him for his brisk contempt for foreign ways and threats, for his English balance, for his unshakable individualism, for his courage and assurance—"an old admiral cut out of oak, the figure-head of a 74-gun ship in a Biscay squall." They delighted in his sporting tastes, his little jokes—"it is impossible to give the Shah the garter: he deserves the halter!"—even his little scrapes: a rumoured affair at the age of 78 with a clergyman's wife on the eve of an election brought from the lips of his opponent, Disraeli, who had learnt to know his countrymen, a hollow, "For God's sake don't let the people of England know, or he'll sweep the country!" That familiar figure—the tilted white hat, tight-buttoned coat, cane, dyed whiskers—riding down Piccadilly before breakfast or rising to jest or bluff away an awkward situation in the House, gave the English confidence in themselves. It was just so that they liked to think of themselves, standing boldly before a world of which they had somehow become lords.

E.S.   L.

They saw him as their glorious prototype—both liberal and tory, jingo and crusader—the game old cock whom *Punch*, voicing the national sentiment, apostrophied on his 77th birthday:

> "An Irish Lord my John was born,
> Both dullness and dons he held in scorn,
> But he stood for Cambridge at twenty-one,
> My gallant, gay John Palmerston!
>
> With his hat o'er his eyes and his nose in the air,
> So jaunty and genial and debonair,
> Talk at him—to him—against him—none
> Can take a rise out of Palmerston.
>
> And suppose his parish registers say
> He's seventy-seven if he's a day;
> What's that, if you're still all fire and fun
> Like Methuselah or John Palmerston?"

The spirit and health of this old man sprang from the same sources as those of the nation for which he stood. Palmerston directed the course of a great commercial empire from his town house in Piccadilly. But when he needed recreation he rode in white trousers across the green fields to the wooded Harrow Hill of his schooldays or went down for the vacation to his native Broadlands in Hampshire. So it was with England. Since the 'forties John Bull had donned the sober civic wear of the towns, abjured horse for train, and settled down to work at lathe or ledger among the chimney pots. But his strength still derived from the countryside of his fathers in which, for all his new absorption in money-making, his heart lay. "Home, sweet home," the Englishman's favourite song, pictured not a tenement building but a country cottage. London was only an encampment from which all who could afford it fled so soon as the Season and parliamentary session were over, when the blinds were drawn, the hotels left empty and the clubs asleep.

"In France," a French traveller wrote, "we live in the towns and go to the country. The Englishman resides in the country, where his real home is. There he keeps his treasures, and pride of race and station is given full play."[1] Here the rural gentry,

[1] F. Wey, *A Frenchman sees the English in the 'Fifties*, 199-207.

still untouched by commerce and living on the cultivation of the classical and leisured past, had its strong roots, sending out its shoots into the professional and administrative life of the nation and Empire which it kept honest and sweet. At the back of the educated Englishman's consciousness in the 'fifties lay always the thought of the country house and the green shires: of slow talk of acres and timber, of bullocks and crops, of sport by covert-side and river, of sitting in the saddle among the blackthorn bushes, of the smell of the gun-room, meadow hay and hot leather, of dining out at the full moon, of archery parties and croquet on smooth lawns, of familiar names and faces and childhood's remembered scenes repeated in the churchyard on Sunday mornings after service, when countrymen met their neighbours among the mounds beneath which their fathers slept.

Somewhere in the 'fifties the urban population of England began to exceed the rural. But agriculture remained the great central productive industry of the country, employing more than two million skilled men. The competition of the new wheat-growing lands overseas had still to be developed: free trade spelt cheap and abundant raw materials for the manufacturer but not yet unlimited imports. Despite the ceaseless rise in population, not more than a quarter of the country's wheat was imported and very little of her oats and barley. The urban worker had more in his pocket, and he spent it on the products of the English farmer. During the Crimea War wheat prices rose, averaging 74/8s in 1855—a figure not to be equalled till 1917—and fluctuating for many years around 50/-, or 10/- a quarter more than they had been in 1850. The nemesis of Free Trade was not yet. The middle period of Victoria's reign constituted a golden age for British agriculture, when capital was cheap and plentiful, markets expanding and improvements profitable for landlord and tenant farmer.

The age of the small man was almost done. But there were still nearly 100,000 men farming holdings of less than fifty acres without hired labour. The agricultural worker was ill-paid and without a real stake in the country, but his wages, which averaged well under 10/- a week in the South in 1850, touched 11/- in the early 'sixties and 13/- in the next decade. He had his garden, a wife who could bake his bread, and many small perquisites —harvest money, beer or cider in the field, occasional firewood and gleanings. So long as he was healthy—and his life kept him so—he was happy. Old Jas Dagley of Gawcott, Bucks, who with his low forehead, eagle eyes, powerful nose and jaw, and stern trap mouth, looked like Gladstone, paid £2 a year rent for his cottage, never wanted for good wholesome food in all his long life of thrift and labour—"plenty a vegetables the whool yeeur round and a flitch a beeacon . . . . . alwiz hangin' up in the kitchen and plenty a rabbuts round the meddurs"[1]—worked on his allotment every night when his day's work was done and boasted that he had never missed a feast in any one of the villages about, and that he had once carried a nine-gallon cask of ale in a sack on his broad shoulders for three miles.

Strength and endurance were still the virtues that England, rustic or urban, prized above all others. In April, 1860, on a lovely spring morning, Tom Sayers, the English champion, met Heenan, the American, known to the fancy as the Benicia Boy, on the edge of a wood near Farnborough to fight for the championship of the world. For weeks in every town and village in the land men and women had canvassed the chances of the event, and the police, fearing a fatal casualty in those days of timeless contests and bare fists, had forbidden the fight and kept close watch on the would-be combatants. But where there was a will there was a way; old England was not to be disappointed. On the night before the great day every tavern and public-house in London remained open all night until the word went round where the trains to the secret ringside were to start.

Sayers was thirty-four, stood five foot eight, and weighed ten stone twelve. His American challenger was eight years younger, stood five inches taller and weighed thirteen stone. In the opening rounds the Englishman was knocked down repeatedly, only to rise smiling for more. The blood poured down his brown, tanned face which shone in the morning sun as though it had been carved of old oak. For two hours after his right arm was broken by a terrific blow of Heenan's he fought on, and, when the police broke through the exultant crowd into the ring, the English champion, giving as good as he took, was still undefeated.

[1] *H. Harman, Sketches of the Bucks Countryside, 17.*

CHAPTER FIVE

The March of the Caravan

"I wander thro' each charter'd street,
Near where the charter'd Thames does flow,
And mark in every face I meet
Marks of weakness, marks of woe.

In every cry of every man,
In every infant's cry of fear,
In every voice, in every ban,
The mind-forg'd mannacles I hear."

W. Blake.

To a foreigner visiting England for the first time in the 'sixties and 'seventies of the 19th century, there seemed something terrifying about its energy and power. "Every quarter of an hour," wrote Taine of the entry to the Thames, "the imprint and the presence of man, the power by which he has transformed nature, become more visible; dock, magazines, shipbuilding and caulking yards, stocks, habitable houses, prepared materials, accumulated merchandise . . . From Greenwich the river is nothing but a street a mile broad and upwards, where ships ascend and descend between two rows of buildings, interminable rows of a dull red, in brick or tiles bordered with great piles stuck in the mud for mooring vessels, which come here to unload or to load. Ever new magazines for copper, stone, coal, cordage, and the rest; bales are always being piled up, sacks being hoisted, barrels being rolled, cranes are creaking, capstans sounding.

". . . To the west, rises an inextricable forest of yards, of masts, of rigging: these are the vessels which arrive, depart or anchor, in the first place in groups, then in long rows, then in a continuous heap, crowded together, massed against the chimneys of houses and the pulleys of warehouses, with all the tackle of incessant, regular, gigantic labour. A foggy smoke penetrated with light envelopes them; the sun there sifts its golden rain, and the brackish, tawny, half-green, half violet water, balances in its undulations striking and strange reflections. It might be said this was the heavy and smoky air of a large hothouse. Nothing is natural here, everything is transformed, artificially wrought from the toil of man, up to the light and the air. But the hugeness of the conglomeration and of the human creation hinders us from thinking about this deformity and this artifice; for want of pure and healthy beauty, the swarming and grandiose life remains; the shimmering of embrowned waves, the scattering of the light imprisoned in vapour, the soft whitish or pink tints which cover these vastnesses, diffuse a sort of grace over the prodigious city, having the effect of a smile upon the face of a shaggy and blackened Cyclop."[1]

For over this vast city, in size, wealth and power the greatest communal achievement of man's sojourn on the planet, had fallen a perpetual pall. The classical pillars and ornaments of the churches and larger buildings were half hidden under soot: the naked Achilles in the park, tribute to the Iron Duke, was almost black. Even the dripping trees and foliage were grimy. It was like Homer's Hell—the land of the Cimmerians. "The vast space which in the South stretches between the earth and sky cannot be discovered . . . there is no air; there is nothing but liquid fog."[2]

For in the urban England that was taking the place of the rustic England of the past, a people who still loved virtue, freedom and justice and wished in their hearts to be generous and chivalrous, were unconsciously sacrificing everything in the last resort to the making of wealth. Over every city tall chimneys cast a pall of smoke between earth and sky: the Thames ran no longer blue and sparkling but rayless under the grimy bridges. The summer's trip to Greenwich—joy of so many generations of Londoners—was no longer a thing of delight; the trees on the Isle of Dogs had begun to give way to ugly factories and mean houses, and the yachts and pleasure boats to belching steamers and strings of coal barges. Even the time-honoured ministerial Whitebait Dinner was soon to be abandoned: men had less leisure than before for the graces and amenities of civilised life. For with the chance of growing rich, there were more important things.

The complete absorption of the English urban middle classes in this single pursuit was both impressive and rather terrifying. The

[1] *Notes on England, 6-8.* [2] *Notes on England, 10.*

old talkative, hail-fellow-well-met London was yielding place to one more sombre and self-contained. Men went silent and absorbed about their business: "faces do not laugh, lips are dumb; not a cry, not a voice is heard in the crowd; every individual seems alone; the workman does not sing; passengers travelling to and fro gaze about them without curiosity, without uttering a word."[1] They were on the make, each man pitting his strength and cunning against his neighbour and seeking not to make things for the joy of making or to win the applause of his fellows, but to amass sufficient wealth to keep himself and his family in time of need. Their perpetual nightmare was the fear of poverty. Unredeemed by the neighbouring field sports of the countryside and cut off by the factory smoke and the high walls of the houses from the cheerful sun, the life of the streets was not to be borne without wealth. Those who had won it by their sweat and struggle dreaded to lose it: "to have £20,000 in the funds or cut one's throat" was their unspoken thought. Those without it were driven back, as the fields receded, into a life ever more drab and uninviting. Taine noticed how many working-class faces wore a starved, thwarted look: hollow, blanched and spent with fatigue. In their patient inertia they reminded him of the old "screws" in the cabs standing in the rain.

In the world of the new city, property was the breath of life: without it men and women shrivelled and died. Save for murder, offences against property were more severely punished than those against the person. A barman and a glazier for stealing 5s. 4d. were sentenced to five years' penal servitude: a hideous assault on a woman with child was expiated with six weeks' imprisonment. The sanest people in the world, in their new city surroundings, were losing their sense of values. So long as a man kept the law, the right to buy at the cheapest price and sell at the highest over-rode all other considerations. Against the supreme right of commerce, even duty as it came to be regarded, nothing was held to weigh: social amenity, happiness, beauty. Whatever did not contribute to this one great commercial object was neglected. In the British Museum in grimy Bloomsbury the greatest masterpieces of human sculpture stood covered with dust on filthy floors in a neglected yellow hall that looked like a warehouse.

No one protested, for the English townsman had come to

[1] *Wey*, 5.

accept such a state of affairs as the natural order. On the railways, the second-class carriages were without upholstery; in the third the windows were unglazed and the floors never swept. Men had no rights but those they paid for after process of free bargain with their fellows. Not even, it seemed, the right of life for, though accidents were frequent, the railways directors kept the doors of the carriages locked while trains were in transit lest any passengers should escape without paying for their tickets.

Business was business: wherever English commerce reigned the phrase was sufficient to explain and justify almost every terrestrial happening. A man must abide by the law: he must keep his bond: he must deliver the goods he had promised or pay the forfeit. Beyond that, there could be no challenge: Shylock was entitled to his pound of flesh. He had earned it by his industry, skill and integrity. In the innumerable little grimy brick houses between the Tower and St. Paul's, whose modest brass plates bore names famous throughout the world, the sons of millionaires arrived each morning with the punctuality of their own clerks to transact business and later bought their mutton chops and threepenny loaves in a Cheapside tavern for their Spartan midday meal. Only when they went home in the evening to Portland Place or Grosvenor Square did they indulge the princely tastes to which their hard-earned wealth entitled them.

Such men were resolute in purpose: iron when any one crossed their strong intent. Taine on his visit observed their kind closely.

"When at eight o'clock in the morning, at the terminus of a railway, one sees people arriving from the country for their daily avocations, or when one walks in a business street, one is struck with the number of faces which exhibit this type of cold and determined will. They walk straight, with a geometrical movement, without looking on either hand; without distraction, wholly given up to their business, like automatons, each moved by a spring; the large, bony face, the pale complexion, often sallow or leaden-hued, the rigid look, all even to their tall, perpendicular, black hat, even to the strong and large foot-covering, even to the umbrella, rolled in its case and carried in a particular style, display the man insensitive, dead to ideas of pleasure and elegance, solely preoccupied in getting through much business well and rapidly. Sometimes one detects the physiognomy of Pitt—the slight face, impassive and imperious, the pale and ardent eyes, the look which shines like the fixed gleam of a sword; the man is then of finer mould, yet his will is only the more incisive and the stouter; it is iron transformed into steel."[1]

Under the pressure of the claims of money-making, the character of the English middle class was changing. It was growing sterner, narrower in sympathy since too much sensibility weakened the will. The new kind of public school which Arnold of Rugby had made the model for England catered for those who needed hardening: the virtues it bred were reticence, regularity and rectitude, above all self-reliance. An English boy of the mid-Victorian age if he was short-sighted was not expected to wear spectacles.[2] If he was cold he was not expected to wear a great coat. His heart and senses were put on ice: from the first day he was chucked into the lonely maelstrom of a great boarding school he was taught to keep a stiff upper lip. For the highly sensitive or affectionate child this stern schooling was hell: in self-defence boys learnt to keep their emotions to themselves, if possible to eliminate them. In France, Taine reflected, happiness depended on affection: in England on having none.

Boys brought up in this way were like young bull-dogs in their teens: tough and tenacious, sometimes ferocious, unconquerable. Being discouraged from excessive feeling, the average product of the public school could feel little sympathy for the classical authors whose works he laboriously and mechanically translated and parsed[3]: he preferred organised games. From this time dates the start of the decline in English upper-class culture and classical learning. Save at a few schools like Eton and Winchester, where much of the older and freer tradition lingered, the scholar of an earlier age was to become the despised public-school "swot," the solid lad of brawn and muscle the hero. This made

---

[1] *Notes on England, 79-80.*

[2] *Arthur James, Earl of Balfour, Chapters of Autobiography, 7-8.*

[3] "They do not appear to be really acquainted with history; they recount the legends of Curtius and of Regulus as authenticated facts."

"They have read many classical texts; but the explanation which is given to them is wholly grammatical and positive. Nothing is done to set forth the beauty of the passage, the delicacies of the style, the pathos of the situation; nor is the process of the writer indicated, the character of his talents, the turn of his mind; all that would seem vague." *H. Taine, Notes on England, 133-4.*

little difference to the object of the new public school, which was the training of character for a competitive world, and was as well effected by the harsh discipline of the dormitory and the football ground as by the Greek syntax. That the average boy responded more readily to the former than to the latter, made the task of the new school-master all the easier. But the loss in human sympathy and intellectual alertness in those who were to become the nation's rulers was to have serious consequences later.

At the Universities the tremendous early discipline of the public school was relaxed. Here the freer and more liberal model of the eighteenth century past was retained: a gentleman was encouraged to choose his own life and tastes and to be a scholar if he chose. But the harm as well as the good of the public school system was already done. The average lad of eighteen from Harrow or Rugby came up to Oxford or Cambridge what his school had made him. If, as still frequently happened, he came from a cultivated home or had an exceptionally brilliant teacher, he might have wide sympathies and genuine love for learning. But more normally he cared for nothing but sport which he pursued in the academic groves with the same zest as on the Sixth Form Ground or Old Big Side. He had character, integrity, energy—the qualities needed for worldly success. But his emotional and intellectual development were stunted. For that reason he fell the more readily into the unthinking worship of material attainment that was the fault of his age. The poor prize-man of the schools might still be the talk of the Upper Common Room; on the long benches of Hall the man acclaimed was the "Blue" and the "blood" with money to burn.

The commercial type created by the conditions of the urban middle-class homes and academies that had not yet attained public school status—the nursery of Matthew Arnold's "Philistines"—has been drawn for all time by John Galsworthy in the Forsyte Saga. It valued strength, order, above all things property: it despised weakness, subtlety, width of sympathy. It was redeemed by its native boyishness and by a certain inherent kindliness in the English soul that no pursuit of mammon could wholly eradicate. But to a foreigner its superficial appearance was not congenial: these English merchants with their stiff, big-boned frames and repressed, self-contained faces looked stupid, frigid and unfeeling, caring for nothing but money and the animal pleasures of the chase and table. There seemed to be too much roast-beef in them. Sometimes they were lean, gaunt and awkward; more often they ran to fullness of flesh, brick-red faces and apoplectic tempers; Taine met such a one in the train going to the Derby—"large ruddy features with flabby and pendant cheeks, large red whiskers, blue eyes without expression, an enormous trunk, noisy respiration."[1] Probably beneath that alarming exterior there beat a kindly and, if only its sympathies could be awakened, boyishly chivalrous heart. The difficulty was to awaken them.

For those with gentle blood, with family traditions and connections, and the status afforded by a University degree, there was employment in the civil and military services of the crown, in the empire and the learned professions. For the great majority commerce was the one sure road to the desired goal of private wealth, security and comfort. With the rapidly expanding population and with improved transport— supported by British sea-power and arms—opening ever new markets in lands overseas, the opportunities for growing rich were enormous. Between 1850 and 1872 the annual exports of Britain, almost doubling themselves every ten years, increased from £90,000,000 to £315,000,000.

A walk through the central districts of London bore eloquent testimony to that wealth. A wide circumference of nearly a mile round the country-like parks of the west end was being filled by large six or seven-story houses, mostly built in the Italianate style, for the residence of the upper middle merchant and professional classes. "Paris," Taine reported, "is mediocre compared with these squares, these crescents, these circles and rows of monumental buildings of massive stone, with porticos, with sculptured fronts, these spacious streets. . . . Sixty of them as vast as the Rue de la paix; assuredly Napoleon III. demolished and rebuilt Paris only because he had lived in London."[2] Such great houses needed establishments of seven or eight servants apiece and could not be supported by incomes of less than £2,000 or £3,000 a year: yet scarcely any were empty. They were the homes of "carriage-folk"—of families who kept private carriages, whose numbers by 1856 ran into five figures.

The great summer afternoon parade in Hyde Park between four and six revealed Victorian society in all its glory: the long unbroken stream of brilliant equipages and lovely horses between

[1] *Notes on England, 50.* [2] *Notes on England, 16.*

Cumberland and Albert gates, the fine ladies with their glaring coloured silks, crinolines and parasols gossiping and quizzing under the chestnuts, the Dundreary-whiskered gentlemen with their white top hats and silver-topped malacca canes, who leant over the iron railings of Rotten Row to chat with elegant, long-skirted, veiled equestrians or lolled on the fashionable grass slope by Lancaster Gate. To a poor man who had ventured into the park at such an hour amid all this splendour, the spectacle might well have seemed to represent the wealth of the entire world assembled in the persons of a few thousand fabulously favoured creatures in this little space of English earth.

Foreigners in that age never ceased to wonder at the wealth of England. Taine recorded that if one took a cab from Sydenham, where the re-created Crystal Palace stood, one could travel for five continuous miles past houses representing an annual outlay of £1,500. In this feast of property, the professional as well as the commercial classes had their share. While a professor at the Sorbonne had to content himself with the equivalent of £500 a year, the Head of an Oxford or Cambridge College could look for several thousands. The Headmasters of Eton and Harrow, the poet Tennyson and the novelist Thackeray all enjoyed incomes of £5000 or more. And successful lawyers and doctors made far more in days when income tax stood at 7d. in the pound. Yet even their comfortable emoluments paled into insignificance when set against the princely incomes of the great industrial manufacturing and engineering masters of the north. The Whitworths, Platts, Kitsons, Fairbairns, Hawthorns, Stephensons constituted a new millionaire aristocracy of effort whose title deeds of wealth and power were their own revolving wheels of iron.

.   .   .   .

This commercial aristocracy looked far beyond the boundaries of the little misty island which their works and warehouses enriched. There was scarcely any place on earth capable of trade where their representatives were not established. In distant Shanghai and Hong-Kong one met the English merchant princes of the China trade, men of almost fabulous wealth made out of tea, silk and opium. Every years the tea-clippers—the fastest sailing ships ever made by human hands—took part in the famous race from Foochow to London river to win the £600 bonus for the first cargo of the season to reach the English market. John

Masefield in his *Bird of Dawning* has drawn the picture of one of these beautiful ships coming up the Channel, her three months' voyage done, and of the rough, true, simple men who manned her.   Galsworthy's Jolyon Forsyte, the elder, is the counterpart of Captain Trewsbury: the City merchant of taste and flawless integrity with his great house in South Kensington and his fastidious ways, whose palate for tea was a byword. A supreme expression of what that sea-borne trade meant to England is to be found in the pages of Joseph Conrad's *Nigger of the Narcissus*.

"The *Narcissus* entered the chops of the Channel.   Under white wings she skimmed low over the blue sea like a great tired bird speeding to its nest.   The clouds raced with her mastheads; they rose astern enormous and white, soared to the zenith, flew past, and falling down the wide curve of the sky seemed to dash headlong into the sea—the clouds swifter than the ship, more free, but without a home.   The coast to welcome her stepped out of space into the sunshine. . . .

"At night the headlands retreated, the bays advanced into one unbroken line of gloom.   The lights of the earth mingled with the lights of heaven; and above the tossing lanterns of a trawling fleet a great lighthouse shone steadily, such as an enormous riding light burning above a vessel of fabulous dimensions. Below its steady glow, the coast, stretching away straight and black, resembling the high side of an indestructible craft riding motionless upon the immortal and unresting sea.   The dark land lay alone in the midst of waters, like a mighty ship bestarred with vigilant lights—a ship carrying the burden of millions of lives—a ship freighted with dross and with jewels, with gold and with steel.   She towered up immense and strong, guarding priceless traditions and untold suffering, sheltering glorious memories and base forgetfulness, ignoble virtues and splendid transgressions. A great ship! For ages had the ocean battered in vain her enduring sides; she was there when the world was vaster and darker, when the sea was great and mysterious, and ready to surrender the prize of fame to audacious men. A ship mother of fleets and nations! The great flagship of the race; stronger than the storms; and anchored in the open sea."

The lovely ships that carried the tribute of the world to the
cliffs of England sailed, since the repeal of the Navigation Act in
1849, under many flags. Yet most of them, including the best,
were owned and built by Britons, for free trade if it took privileges from the merchant marine with one hand gave with another since it stimulated interchange of sea-borne merchandise.
With the absorption of her chief shipping rival, the United
States, in a long and exhausting civil war during the early
'sixties, Britain had things very much her own way at sea for
three halcyon decades. The new iron ships, triumphs of the
marine engineering works of the Clyde and Tyne, of Birkenhead
and Belfast, were beginning to come into their own: the Great
Eastern, the famous iron leviathan, 700 feet in length and 80 in
beam, was launched at Millwall in 1858. Yet two years later not
more than a tenth of the merchant service of the United Kingdom
was steam driven.

In that year the country's sailing tonnage reached its zenith.
These proud masterpieces of timber and canvass, cleaving the
ocean "with mainyards backed and bows of cream and foam"
were the key to Britain's commercial and industrial supremacy.
They were recognised as the élite of the sea in every port of the
earth.[1]

This art and skill and the wealth that sprang from it rested

[1]Masefield, who once himself served before the mast, has hymned their vanished
glory:

> "These splendid ships, each with her grace, her glory,
> Her memory of old song and comrade's story,
> Still in my mind the image of life's need,
> Beauty in hardest action, beauty indeed.
> ' They built great ships and sailed them ' sounds most brave,
> Whatever arts we have or fail to have;
> I touch my country's mind, I come to grips
> With half her purpose thinking of these ships,
> That art untouched by softness, all that line,
> Drawn ringing hard to stand the test of brine;
> That nobleness and grandeur, all that beauty,
> Born of a manly life and bitter duty;
> That splendour of fine bows which yet could stand
> The shock of rollers never checked by land.
> That art of masts, sail crowded, fit to break,
> Yet stayed to strength, and back-stayed into rake,
> The life demanded by that art, the keen
> Eye-puckered, hard-case seamen, silent, lean,
> They are grander things than all the art of towns,
> Their tests are tempests and the sea that drowns.
> They are my country's line, her great art done,
> By strong brains labouring on the thought unwon,
> They mark our passage as a race of men,
> Earth will not see such ships as these agen."
>
> John Masefield, "Ships" (Collected Poems, 386.)

in the last resort on the British command of the seas. This was often forgotten. But during the later 'fifties and early 'sixties fear of the French Empire under Louis Napoleon had recalled an island race immersed in moneymaking to the necessity of looking to its moat. After the Crimean War a period of naval reorganisation began which, quickened by a panic over the new French strength in ironclads,[1] culminated in the launch of the 9000 ton iron frigate, *Warrior*, the fastest and most powerful ship in the world. It was the first of a new fleet of iron-hulled, armoured, screw-driven ships armed with muzzle-loaders, the latest product of Armstrong's, and capable of blowing the old three-decker navies of the past out of the water.[2] This mighty force—the strongest single unit of ordered power in the nineteenth-century world—was supported by a secondary fleet of unarmoured wooden frigates and corvettes and by naval bases in all the seven seas—a standing terror to the slaver and the pirate and to all lesser breeds without the law.

Out of all this sprang great comfort for the English possessing classes. Peasants toiled in distant China and Ceylon to fill the teapots of rich old ladies in Lancaster Gate, naked Malay boys laboured to draw up pearls from the bottom of shark-infested seas, and trappers fought with bears in the frozen snows of Hudson Bay to send home furs and hearthrugs. As they grew rich the hardy English surrounded themselves with costly comforts, the elder generation of the Forsytes because they valued the outward forms of the wealth for which they had laboured so hard, the younger because they were growing accustomed to them. Soft pile Brussels carpets, thick padded settees and ottomans, elaborately-carved tables of polished mahogany and rosewood with marble tops, enormous gilt mirrors flowed in a never-ceasing flood out of the factories and warehouses and fashionable furniture emporiums into the spacious houses of Kensington and Bayswater, Edgbaston, Stockport and Everton until even their great rooms seemed crowded out with these heavy symbols of tribute. A cultured foreigner staying in an English house in 1861

[1]"The war preparations of the French Marine are immense. Ours despicable! Our Ministers use fine phrases, but they do nothing; my blood boils within me." *Prince Albert.* "Heaven send Cherbourg may never be graven on Queen Victoria's heart." *United Service Magazine.*

[2]"There is not a mail-clad man of war on
  Ocean's breast that rides,
But this great gun will knock a hole
  slap through her ironsides."
Punch, XLIV, 134.

was amazed by the furniture of his bedroom—the entire floor carpeted, a strip of oilcloth in front of the wash-stand, matting along the walls; two dressing-tables, a swing looking-glass, a great bed covered with the whitest and softest of tissues, three pairs of candles, two of them in a writing-table, porcelain extinguishers, wax matches, paper spills in pretty holders, pin-cushions. The most intimate piece of furniture in the room was a miracle of elaborate ingenuity, made of the finest mahogany and marble: the washstand was furnished with a large and smaller jug for hot and cold water, two porcelain basins, a dish for toothbrushes, two soap-dishes, a water-bottle with a tumbler and a finger glass with another. In addition there was a large shallow zinc bath, and a towel-horse in the cupboard with several towels of different sizes. A servant visited the room four times a day to see that all was in order.

When an Englishman of the upper middle order travelled, the same observer noted, he carried so many glasses, opera-glasses and telescopes, umbrellas, canes and iron-tipped sticks, overcoats, comforters, waterproofs and wrappers, dressing-cases, flasks, books and newspapers that it seemed astonishing that he should ever have set out under such a burden at all. Every year the English with their all-conquering Midas touch sank deeper under the weight of their own possessions. From the Queen on her throne, who, in the course of her reign accumulated a vast museum of objects, each acquiring with usage attributes of an almost sacred kind and possessing its own hallowed and unalterable place in one or other of her palaces, to the thrifty and well-to-do artisan who filled every inch of wall space in his cottage with engravings, keepsakes, mementoes, grandfather clocks, samples and photographs, and kept apart a special airtight compartment named the parlour for the display of more treasured pieces of furniture and *vertu*, the nation seemed to have gone mad on property. As ever with the English and the object of their heart's desire, it became invested with a semi-religious and mystical quality. Since the pursuit or retention of wealth was for the time being the first end of their single-hearted lives, that which wealth bought was worthy of worship. The drawing-room furniture, the silver and best china in the safe, the contents of the maternal jewel case, were the sacred vessels on the altar, and a visit to the banker or solicitor was conducted with a solemnity like going to church.

Property, being sacred, and demanding decorum and reverence in its treatment, conferred respectability. The contrary was also true: the man without property was suspect. The "snob" who drove up to a gentleman's door in a public conveyance with cab straw on his trousers was despised as a low adventurer who could not afford a carriage. The third class passenger who could buy no better ticket was kept off the platform until the last moment lest he should offend his social superiors by his mean presence. The vagrant without visible means of support was an object of suspicion to be imprisoned and punished unless he could prove his *bona fides*.

From this arose tragic consequences. Poverty in other lands was regarded, as it had been in England in the past, as part of the eternal human lot: to be pitied, to be avoided if possible, to be relieved or ignored according to a man's nature or temperament, but not to be despised. It was a share of humanity's bitter heritage, like sickness, tempest and death. But in London and urban England in which the making of wealth had been elevated into a moral duty, poverty hung its head for shame. It crept out of sight into that new phenomenon of industrialisation—the working-class district in which no man of wealth or position lived. The new East End of London with its miles of mean, squalid streets covering an area greater in extent than any continental city, was something of a portent in the world. It was not for nothing that the scholar Marx was studying economic phenomena in the British capital.

Here lived the poor—not merely the respectable artisan but the countless broken outcasts of the industrial system. These were pallid and gin-sodden; their ragged reeking clothes, which had passed through many phases of society in their long, declining history, were so vile that they left a stain wherever they rested: they stank. They herded together in bug-ridden lodging houses and rotting tenements: they slept under railway arches and on iron seats on the new Victoria Embankment. They were the "submerged tenth," the skeleton at the rich Victorian feast, the squalid writing on the whitened wall.

They were not merely congregated in the "darkest London" of Charles Booth's later survey: they were to be found in every place where the untrammelled march for wealth had broken down the old world of status and social morality. They were living testimonies of that against which Coleridge had warned his country

M

—trespasses on "its own inalienable and untransferable property —the health, strength, honesty and filial love of its children." Across the lives of the rich and comfortable, of all who inherited or had acquired established property they passed like a remote shadow: to the remainder of their countrymen, especially to the lower middle-class and the skilled and respectable artisan, they were a terrible menace whose horrid existence it was almost impossible to shake from the mind. Their pale, degraded, beseeching faces and dripping rags were a reminder of what unemployment, sickness or any lapse from the straight and narrow path of social integrity might bring: like wraiths they rose out of a precipice into which every man without property might at any moment of his life fall. More than any other cause, they account for the almost fanatic desire of the Victorian of all classes to acquire and retain property.

"I recall," wrote Taine, "the alleys which run into Oxford Street, stifling lanes encrusted with human exhalations; troops of pale children nestling on the muddy stairs; the seats on London Bridge where families, huddled together with dropping heads, shiver through the night; particularly the Haymarket and the Strand in the evening. Every hundred steps one jostles twenty harlots; some of them ask for a glass of gin; others say, ' Sir, it is to pay my lodging.' This is not debauchery which flaunts itself but destitution—and such destitution! The deplorable procession in the shade of the monumental streets is sickening; it seems to me a march of the dead. That is a plague-spot, the real plage-spot of English society."[1] Once down in that mire there was no rising again. The sordid round of drink, debauchery, violence, punishment, incompetence and hideous destitution never ceased. "The great social mill crushes and grinds here . . . the lowest human stratum."

. . . .

For the great individualists who had made nineteenth-century Britain rich beyond the dreams of avarice had forgotten that man was part of an undying order. The price of a social crime — greed, slavery, the oppression of a subject people—is seldom paid by those immediately guilty of it. It is paid later—by their innocent descendants. The sins of the fathers are visited on the children and the children's children.

[1] *Notes on England, 36.*

"Thro' midnight streets I hear
How the youthful harlot's curse
Blasts the new-born infant's tear,
And blights with plagues the marriage hearse."

Victorian Britain, for all her wealth, power and empire was no exception. Her rulers, in their devotion to their creed of self-help and holding that through liberty good would grow naturally out of evil, allowed social injustice to be done on a vast and terrible scale. The progeny of those to whom that injustice was done were to become in the fullness of time sources of national weakness and division.

.   .   .   .

The individualists never admitted this. They believed that men, left to themselves, could look after themselves. Starting from the ancient English insistence on the liberty and dignity of the individual, they assumed that every man could be trusted to judge all things rightly for himself and follow the law of his own will. By registering and counting individual expressions of will, and giving legislative effect to those of the majority, universal human well-being could be ultimately attained. The will of the people was the will of God, and the statesman who wished to consult the oracle should study statistics. Since the dead and the unborn cannot record votes, the utilitarians were little concerned with the national past or future: the more logical of them could see no reason why there should be a nation at all.

From the teaching of Adam Smith, the utilitarians derived the further and contradictory assumption that the wealth of a nation was to be measured by the sum total of the riches of its individual members.[1] They held that if, as a result of any process that increased this aggregate—such as the preference of foreign to domestic trade—one million citizens were enriched but the other nine millions impoverished, that nation would not be poorer than it was before but richer. A Medieval or Tudor statesman would have taken the opposite view, on the grounds that in the next generation the bulk of its people would inherit less not more of the attributes that material well-being can create.

[1] ". . . The aggregate of the wealth of individual citizens makes up the wealth of the nation, and . . . if each is as free as possible to pursue his own gain the wealth of the nation will be sufficiently attended to and its power will follow as a matter of course." W. Cunningham, *The Growth of English Industry and Commerce*, Part I, 595.

The core of Victorian economics lay in the doctrine of un-limited contractual freedom. If, as the Benthamites contended, the exercise of liberty was the highest human function, every man had a right to bind himself in any way he chose, even to his own disadvantage. No authority ought to have any power to stop him.

"Ought a borrower to have the right to obtain a loan which he urgently requires," asked Dicey in his contemporary study of nineteenth-century legal trends, "by the promise to pay usurious interest? Ought a man . . . to be allowed to make a contract binding himself to be the servant of his neighbour for life? . . . Ought every person of full age, acting with his eyes open and not the victim of fraud, but who nevertheless is placed in a position in which from the pressure of his needs he can hardly make a fair bargain, to be capable of binding himself by a contract?"[1] The rigid individualist replied, yes. For within the limits of the minimum of law necessary to preserve order and enforce contracts every man ought to be his own master. He should be free even to sell his own freedom.

But the moment man is viewed, not as an insulated and self-contained being but as a member of a continuing society, the individualist's answer becomes inadequate. From his own point of view, it may be best that a man should have the right to bind himself as he pleases. But suppose that in doing so he damages the community? For as a member of a complicated organism, man binds more than himself. He binds his children and children's children. He binds them with his own status and reputation. He binds them with their upbringing, with the influences with which he surrounds their most impressionable years, with the transmitted traits of his blood. Every living man has an unfair advantage over posterity. So has every generation.

Unless the state acts as trustee for the helpless unborn, society can scarcely endure. For through the unthinking and un-restrained greed and selfishness of its life tenants, its heritage will be wasted, and its slowly accumulated and hard-won unity, prosperity and civilisation will be succeeded by disintegration, ruin and barbarism. Selfishness is the age-long dissolvent of ancient communities. No nation in the past had been more conscious of this than the England of the Normans, the Planta-genets and the Tudors. The English law of primogeniture and

---

[1] *A. V. Dicey, Law and Public Opinion in England, 151.*

entail was its peculiar expression in the purely material sphere. By denying the younger sons the enjoyment of inherited wealth and strictly limiting its use by the elder, the national property was preserved from dissipation while its educative influence in each generation was rendered as wide as possible.

It had been the attempt of the state to fulfil its ancient functions of trusteeship that had most irritated the early individualists. English Liberalism began as a protest against every legal restraint that prevented the citizen from exercising his full freedom of choice. That in an old country like England there were a great many such restraints and that most of them in the light of the sudden changes wrought by the industrial revolution were hopelessly out of date lent popular force to what might otherwise have been a purely academic and therefore ineffective rebellion against traditional paternalism. A poor man might not settle in a new parish lest he should become a burden to the ratepayers, skilled artisans were forbidden to leave the country or migrate to the colonies, machinery might not be exported. Usury and forestalling—the very life-blood of modern commercial practice—were still in theory proscribed by laws enacted in the Middle Ages. Because of the seventeenth century Navigation Acts, American ships calling for freight in this country had often to enter British ports empty while British ships fetching cotton from the United States were forced in retaliation to make their outward journey across the Atlantic without cargo. The consumer had thus to pay the cost of freight twice in his purchase price. A stubbornly conservative country continued to maintain laws and institutions which had done yeoman service in the past but which were little better than a mockery to the hungry generations of the new industrial towns. The demand for their abolition became irresistible with the increasing urbanisation of the country.

The Benthamite assault on the statutory interference of society with the freedom of the individual thus presented itself at first as the march of common sense and humanity against the ramparts of obscurantist corruption and privilege. From 1830 to 1874 Liberalism—the political expression of Benthamism—was the most dynamic force in Britain. It derived its strength from the urban and educated middle-classes who enjoyed electoral supremacy between the first and second Reform Bills, from the manufacturers who wanted nothing to stand between them and their search for wealth, and from the still unenfranchised masses of the industrial towns whose sufferings under a senile system made a strong appeal both to humanitarian and rational feelings. That these sufferings were far more due to the absence of protective social institutions than to the presence of antiquated and inefficient ones was not yet realised.

For fifty years British legislative annals mark the steady removal from the statute book of every law that offended against individualistic reasoning. Privileges and illogical anachronisms were ruthlessly swept aside with almost universal approval. No law or institution, however venerable, that could not withstand the cold test of utilitarian logic was safe from the iconoclasts. The constitution was "lawyer ridden" and "aristocracy-ridden," the administration controlled by "sinister influences," the King himself the "Corruptor-General." The reform of the electorate in 1832, of local government in 1834 and of the Poor Law in the following year were seen as the first steps in the triumphant advance to a pure and radical republic. Protective duties, religious tests, the Established Church, marriage as a sacrament instead of a contract, titles and dignities, the House of Lords and even the Throne would ultimately be swept away. Macaulay wrote in 1833 that should the Lords oppose a certain popular Whig measure, he "would not give 6d. for a coronet or a 1d. for a mitre."

Yet for all its temporary enthusiasm for reform, England was at heart a conservative country. It was also one in which vested interests were numerous and powerful. At the head of the party which espoused radical reform in Parliament were the historic Whig nobles, who, though sympathetic to popular ideals of an academic kind and always glad to dish the Tories, had no intention of doing away with their own privilege and power to please a few bourgeois doctrinaires. There was a pause—after the repeal of the Corn Laws and the turn of the economic tide in the late 'forties a very marked pause—in the advance towards the utilitarian republic. During the ten years in which Lord Palmerston was Prime Minister, the movement towards Utopia almost ceased.

But with the death of the old champion in 1865, and the succession of Gladstone to the Liberal leadership in the Commons, a new era set in. The son of a Liverpool merchant, William Ewart Gladstone was not, like his predecessors, a Whig aristocrat, but a member of the vigorous middle-class stock from which the disciples of Bentham were mainly recruited. He had begun life as a Conservative but had followed Peel over free trade. Since then he had moved steadily towards the left and to the advocacy of everything that extended the scope of abstract freedom. As Chancellor of the Exchequer from 1853 to 1855 and again from 1859 to 1865 he had applied the Benthamite principles to the realm of national finance. The annual Budget, which in his hands almost achieved the popularity of a sporting event, was framed to express "the greatest happiness of the greatest number": its object was to exempt as large a portion of the nation as possible from the unwelcome obligation to contribute to the national financial burdens. The last remaining tariffs were swept away and the poor man's breakfast table freed from imposts. The result, despite Gladstone's declared intention to abolish it, was to make the income tax the first potential source of national revenue. Nor could all his unsparing and brilliant efforts to achieve strict economy, even at the expense of paring the defence services to the bone, prevent the hated tax from creeping slowly upwards.

Disraeli, Gladstone's opposite number on the still unpopular Conservative benches, protested. If, he argued, as a result of free trade, direct taxation had to provide the national revenue, it should be made as general as indirect. To restrict it to a single class was to undermine the historic English principle of taxation which had secured the liberty of the subject by granting to the Estates of the Realm, representing the various types of property-holder, the sole right of allocating taxation. By adopting the principle that a majority might levy all taxes on a minority, the Radicals were unconsciously substituting the ideal of a forced for a voluntary contribution. At the moment this might matter little: later it might well prove the starting-point of a new despotism more arbitrary than any imposed by feudal baron or Stuart king. But the country, still in the first flush of a triumphant materialism and little troubled by a tax which, though irritating, was still very low, was not interested in historic principles. Disraeli's attempt, while Chancellor of the Exchequer in a minority administration, to extend direct taxation to lower incomes was easily defeated.

Between 1865 and 1874, the advance towards radical uniformity went forward with great rapidity. When in the former year Gladstone left the university constituency of High Church Oxford for radical South Lancashire, Pegasus was unloosed. Tests, oaths, bigotry and hereditary privilege were, it was understood, to be sent packing. Most of the reforms associated with the name of Gladstone, who became Prime Minister for the first time in 1868, were long overdue. Many of them were wholly beneficial. Purchase was abolished in the army, the ballot established and electoral bribery heavily penalised. The universities were thrown open to all irrespective of religion. Jews were admitted to the constitution, corporations reformed, ancient acts in restraint of trade repealed, the civil service opened to competitive examination the laws simplified and the venerable Courts of Law reformed and rationalised. The high towers of feudal privilege were sent toppling : henceforward there was to be no place where the industrious and resourceful man of intellect might not go. The principles of the French Revolution were peaceably applied to an England which seventy years before had withstood the siege of all Europe to destroy them. The career of the bourgeois was thrown open to the talents.

Yet all this was only a beginning. For there were more venerable fish to fry. England was still burdened with an established Church, an hereditary second Chamber and a Monarchy. On rational grounds there was no defending them. They were expensive, non-utilitarian and either potentially or in fact reactionary.

The difficulty was to remove them. The English were so conservative in their instincts that many of them still regarded these irrational institutions as sacred and so mentally lazy that many more, though indifferent to them, could see no sufficient cause for getting rid of them. The light of pure reason, as the reformers had long found to their cost, was not enough to awake them. To arouse the English to a great effort nothing but the irrational force of faith would suffice. And by a strange chance, which only a rationalist could refuse to regard as a miracle, that force was suddenly afforded.

For Mr. Gladstone, though the sword of the utilitarian and leader of the Liberals, was not a rationalist. He was a man of faith. And he was so constituted that whatever he undertook became invested with moral significance. He had only to embrace a task, for it to become a holy one. At such moments the blood of the old Covenanters from whom he was descended would course through his veins and his eyes would shine with prophetic fire. And such was the magnetism of the man that millions of lesser men who saw and heard him would, in their humbler way, believe, too.[1] In a land where in the last resort a sober people will only bestir themselves for a moral and religious cause, Mr. Gladstone unconciously transformed Benthamism into a crusade. What old Jeremy in his glass case in University College, Gower Street, would have thought of it all, had he still been alive, it is hard to say.

One of the irrational institutions in which Mr. Gladstone himself had been brought up to believe was the Established Church. His veneration for it even partook of the mystical: its decent, prosaic ceremonies and homely organisation became invested in his eyes with the fire on Sinai and the tongues of flame that spoke out of the whirlwind. This mental weakness of Mr. Gladstone's was a great trial to his Radical followers. On several occasions it all but caused an open breach between them.

Yet when the moment came to do so—the electoral moment —Mr. Gladstone proved ready to attack a vital outpost even of the Established Church, and to do so with a crusader's fervour. The scene of the miraculous conversion to reason was Ireland. The ecclesiastical establishment of that country was a peculiarly irrational institution. It was Protestant. At least three-quarters of the inhabitants were Catholics and regarded its ministrations —for which they paid—as heretical. Of the Protestant remainder, half were Presbyterian and never went near its doors. And as Ireland was in a state of permanent misery and unrest, with its peasants starving and its tenants unable or unwilling to pay their rents, it seemed obvious to a utilitarian mind that the existence of an irrational and useless Church must be a chief cause of all this suffering and disturbance. Nature could not tolerate so absurd an anachronism.

Yet it seemed on the face of it that it would be almost as hard to get Mr. Gladstone to lead an attack against an ecclesiastical establishment as it would be to persuade a Scottish minister to declaim against the Sabbath. And up to a year of his assault on it, nothing could well have been farther from his mind. But it happened that a task even more manifestly righteous than the

---

[1] An opponent testified: "That white-hot face, stern as a Covenanter's yet mobile as a comedian's, those restless, flashing eyes, that wondrous voice whose richness its northern burr enriched as the tang of the wood brings out the mellowness of a rare old wine; the masterly cadence of his elocution, the vivid energy of his attitudes, the fine animation of his gestures—when I am assailed through eye and ear by this compacted phalanx of assailants . . . what wonder . . . in defiance of my very will, I should exclaim: 'This is indeed the voice of truth and wisdom: this man is honest and sagacious beyond his fellows. He must be believed; he must be obeyed.'"

defence of established religion presented itself to Mr. Gladstone. And it presented itself as a sacred duty and one which it was impossible for him to refuse. It entailed the disestablishment of the Irish Church. It did more: it justified it.

For in 1868, on the retirement of Lord Derby, Mr. Disraeli had become Prime Minister. And if there was one thing more detestable to Mr. Gladstone than another, and more symptomatic of the existence of evil, it was that this man should become Prime Minister. For in Gladstone's eyes, his enigmatic rival was the embodiment of everything that was sinister. He was flashy, he was a Jew—not that Gladstone, the champion of tolerance, had the least objection to a Jew in his proper place—he was a writer of the lighter kind of fiction, he uttered cynical epigrams, he wore diamonds on his person and was known to have had recourse to moneylenders. All this might have been forgiven by a broadminded Christian, but there was worse. For Mr. D'Israeli —and that was what his father's name had been—had been guilty of the vilest political tergiversation. He was completely unscrupulous. He had changed his opinions, and not like Mr. Gladstone for the highest but for the basest motives. In order to advance himself he had brazenly championed stupid and harmful causes: such, for instance, as protection for which it was obviously impossible for any intelligent man—and no one could deny Disraeli's intelligence—to feel the least sympathy. And the fellow was diabolically clever. He had just, by a feat of cynical legerdermain unparalleled in parliamentary history, carried, in the face of a superior if divided opposition, a measure of electoral reform only slightly dissimilar to that which Gladstone himself had vainly endeavoured to carry when leading the Commons a few months before and which nothing but evil mesmeric powers could possibly have made acceptable to the stupid and reactionary Tories. Like the good Sir Robert Peel whom he had cynically attacked for doing so, Disraeli had caught the Liberals bathing and run away with their clothes. And as a result he had established himself in 10 Downing Street.

There was only one course open for a good man who loved the fair name of his country and its reputation for political purity: to get the trickster out with the least possible delay. And as God had given Mr. Gladstone, in a humble way, the power of leadership, it was plainly Mr. Gladstone's business. He did not shirk it. Reform of the franchise—hitherto the Liberal

party's strongest and most legitimate card—having been shamefully filched by the Tories, the disturbed state of Ireland offered
the surest means of discrediting a perjured government. And the
anachronism of the Irish Church Establishment, to which
Gladstone had been recently devoting much serious study, was
the obvious Achilles heel of the administration.

Here, indeed, was a question on which it would be almost
impossible for Disraeli to join issue without suffering defeat in
the House. Once made the question of the hour the absurdity of
the Irish Church could not be defended. Yet—and this was the
charm of the situation—as a result of his own former baseness,
Disraeli would be compelled to defend it. For this frivolous
Jewish adventurer had repeatedly made a pretence, both in and out
of the House, of his devotion to the Established Church. And his
own party, the "squire and parson" Tories, were trebly committed
to defence of the Church and its perquisites. A vigorous movement to disestablish and disendow its outwork in Ireland could
not fail to bring down the government. The Radicals and the
enemies of the Church of England had the additional satisfaction
of knowing that the measure would be the thin end of the wedge.
Once the principle of unalterable establishment had been
destroyed, the rest would follow automatically.

Everything happened at first according to plan. Disraeli was
caught in a cleft stick. Even his malign influence over the Queen
could not save him. The new working-class electorate he had so
cynically enfranchised proved itself honest and English and
turned against him. A dissolution to avoid an adverse vote in the
House cost the Tories more than fifty seats. A few weeks before
Christmas, 1868, Mr. Gladstone became Prime Minister.

.   .   .   .   .   .

But in the course of the debates on the disestablishment of the
Irish Church Disraeli put the case against the whole trend of
Liberal and Radical reform. He saw it as he saw every political
programme, not—like Gladstone and the normal, honest, unimaginative Englishman—as a complete step in itself but as an
inseparable part of a process. The utilitarian viewed the nation
as a collection of individuals to whose separate interests and rights
all other considerations were subordinate. In such a state privilege in whatever form was manifestly indefensible: every decent
instinct of man demanded equality.

But Disraeli did not see the state in this way. To him it was a continuing society in which the full value of each individual life could only be attained and measured by its contribution to the common weal.   Privilege, though it involved inequality was desirable, even necessary, if it evoked from selfish man a greater measure of service and sacrifice to the community.   For through the imagination it had the power to appeal to self-respect and civic conscience. What mattered was not that all men should be equal, as Radicals desired, but that all men should have an equal opportunity to the kind of privilege that made them readier to serve their country.

In this Disraeli based his argument on a profounder knowledge of human nature than that possessed by the middle-class utilitarians who were massed against him. He was an artist with an artist's insight into human motive: he was a member of the oldest civilised race in the world. Unlike the sanguine and innocent radicals he never believed in the perfectibility of human nature: he merely believed in the divine instinct in man that, given the right background, had power to raise him from the brute to the citizen, the martyr and the saint. It was his perpetual study as a statesman to make the institutions of the State afford that background.

In this Disraeli had the support of English history which he had studied far more closely than most Englishmen. Thirty years before while still a young man he had written:

"The basis of English society is Equality. But here let us distinguish: there are two kinds of equality; there is the equality that levels and destroys, and the equality that elevates and creates. It is this last, this sublime, this celestial equality, that animates the laws of England. The principle of the first equality, base, terrestrial, Gallic and grovelling, is that no one should be privileged: the principle of English equality is that every one should be privileged."[1]

In his maturer age he had improved on this. "Unlike the levelling equality of modern days the ancient equality of England elevates and creates. Learned in human nature the English constitution holds out privilege to every subject as the inducement to do his duty." Instead of wishing like the Radicals to level every ancient institution and human right that offended against the notion of mathematical uniformity, Disraeli sought consistently to main-

[1] *Vindication of the English Constitution (1835), Ch. XXXIV.*

tain and by reforming to extend them. In what seemed in that materialistic age a paradox he maintained that the greatness of England depended not on her numerical superiority to her neighbours but on the institutions which in the course of three centuries had enabled her people to create such a system of extended liberty, wealth and empire as the world had never seen. A community whose slow but mighty growth had yielded so much of permanent benefit to man would be betraying civilisation if it permitted unthinking zealots to destroy it by cutting away its roots. In a speech to the House of Commons during the reform debates of 1866 Disraeli recurred to a theme which he never ceased to repeat:

"You have an ancient, powerful, richly-endowed Church and perfect religious liberty. You have unbroken order and complete freedom. You have landed estates as large as the Romans, combined with commercial enterprise such as Carthage and Venice united never equalled. And you must remember that this peculiar country, with these strong contrasts, is not governed by force; it is not governed by standing armies, it is governed by a most singular series of traditionary influences, which generation after generation cherishes because it knows that they embalm custom and represent law. And, with this, what have you done? You have created the greatest Empire of modern time. . . . You have devised and sustained a system of credit still more marvellous. And, above all, you have established and maintained a scheme so vast and complicated of labour and industry, that the history of the world affords no parallel to it. And all these mighty creations are out of all proportion to the essential and indigenous elements and resources of the country. If you destroy that state of society, remember this—England cannot begin again."[1]

There lay the eternal thought of this strange and alien patriot who had learnt amid the Chiltern beechwoods to love the land of his adoption: that England could not begin again. If in pursuit of a theory or for a transient commercial opportunity she relinquished the great character-forming institutions that had made her what she was, she would find too late that she had

[1] *Monypenny & Buckle II, 144.*

exchanged "a first-rate monarchy for a second-rate republic." A uniformity which aimed at eradicating every influence that endowed the subject with a sense of duty and civic pride, could only end in transforming a nation into a mob.

Of such influences the greatest in Disraeli's eyes was the Church.[1] Proud in his membership of the race which had founded the religion of the western world, this Jew never forgot the lesson which he believed it to be the eternal lot of Israel to teach the forgetful and materially-minded sons of men. "The Church," he wrote, "is a sacred corporation for the promulgation and maintenance of certain Asian principles, which, although local in their birth, are of Divine origin, and of universal and external application."[2] Without moral justice, honesty, truth, mercy, charity and a humble belief in a divine purpose, England would not be England but a barbarous Teuton island on the outer fringe of civilisation. It was the recognition of the Church by the State that gave politics its significance and saved it from degenerating into a mechanical affair of police and statistics. It stood as a constant reminder to statesmen and electors—as it had stood to kings in the past—that the tenure by which they ruled was their acknowledgment of moral truth. Without this political institutions were "meat without salt, the crown a bauble, the Church an establishment, Parliaments debating clubs, and civilisation itself but a fitful and transient dream."

It was because their rulers had felt themselves bound to honour the Christian verities that Englishmen were free and that throughout the world the name of England was synonymous with freedom. Deny or ignore them, and arbitrary acts, arising from human passions and greeds whether of individuals or assemblies, would be committed with as much impunity in England as in other lands.[3] But its presence beside the temporal power was a

---

[1] "There are few great things left in England, and the Church is one." *Monypenny & Buckle, II, 83.*

[2] *Preface of the fifth edition of Coningsby, 1849.*

[3] "A wise Government allying itself with religion, would, as it were, consecrate society and sanctify the State. But how is this to be done? It is the problem of modern politics which has always most embarrassed statesmen. No solution of the difficulty can be found in salaried priesthoods and complicated concordates. But by the side of the State in England there has gradually arisen a majestic corporation—wealthy, powerful, independent—with the sanctity of a long tradition, yet sympathising with authority, and full of conciliation, even deference, to the civil power. Broadly and deeply planted in the land, mixed up with all our manners and customs, one of the main guarantees of our local government, and therefore one of the prime securities of our common liberties, the Church of England is part of our history, part of our life, part of England itself." *Monypenny & Buckle, II, 96.*

constant reminder of values, a check to the abuse of authority and an insurance against tyranny.[1]

For this reason Disraeli opposed the disendowment of the Irish Church. He did so not because he wished to save vested interests or to penalise those who did not conform with ecclesiastical authority but because he saw that an Established Church, however much in need of reform, was a bulwark against the moral decay that threatens earthly kingdoms. He knew English history too well to be under any illusion as to what happened when the floodgates of confiscation, for whatever reason, were once opened.[2] The wealth of the Church was in principle the people's patrimony. If it was not being used as such, the State should see that it was. But it had no right to appropriate it.

The Radicals with the highest intentions wished to destroy this safeguard to conscience and the liberty of the subject. It angered them as illogical and unegalitarian, and they could not see the need for it. In their reforming zeal they were constantly urging their Liberal allies to denounce the union between Church and State. But for Disraeli's determination to preserve it, they would probably have succeeded in abolishing it altogether.

For though it was not within his power to save the Irish Establishment—and, though its destruction did nothing to solve the Irish problem, it was scarcely worth saving—Disraeli did succeed in arousing popular support in defence of the Church of England. To him more than any other man is due the gradual reawakening of the English people before it was too late to a realisation that their ancient institutions were worth preserving. While their intellectual leaders were cheerfully bidding them cast them aside, Disraeli, during 35 years as the real leader of the Conservative party, fought a delaying action against the forces of reforming radicalism. At the time these seemed so strong that any further advance towards electoral democracy was expected to spell the certain doom of the privileges of the Established Church.

Yet Britain is to-day a democracy in the fullest sense. There is still an Established Church. There is still a Throne. There is even still a House of Lords. In the eighteen-sixties, for all the immense deference paid them by the older generation and in the semi-

---

[1] It was this, and not the denial of the individual right to worship, that inspired Pastor Niemoller's brave stand against Hitler.

[2] "I have never found that Churches are plundered except to establish or enrich oligarchies." When Disraeli spoke in these terms, the word plutocracy was not in general use.

feudal countryside, none of these institutions seemed safe to the student of politics. The more educated among the younger generation in the growing towns had no feeling for them but contempt or indifference. It was that new urban generation which was to govern the England of the future. The teaching of the rationalists had taken deep root: the spirit of the age was one of critical egalitarianism, of ceaseless questioning in matters secular, and in religion of honest doubt. The publication of Charles Darwin's *Origin of Species* in 1859 and of similar scientific works laid bare the absurdity of the popular theological history on which past generations had been brought up. The revelation of the laboratory confirmed the gospel of the utilitarian. Biological and chemical evolution—clear and mathematically demonstrable —was the explanation of everything.[1] To thinking men belief became harder with every year. Organised religion was nothing now but a convenient form by which morality and decency could be preserved until the ignorant masses were ready to do without it.

For the great revolutionary inventions and changes of the age of progress proved too much for those who had been taught to put their trust in reason. Outwardly Victorian life, with its unde-viating round, stolid respectability, growing physical comfort and strict religious observance, seemed stable and secure beyond anything conceived of in former ages. But beneath the surface, nothing was static and everything familiar was changing at a bewildering pace. Lack of faith means lack of vitality: nothing is more fatal to action than the divided and tortured mind. Apathy and inertia are its inevitable aftermath. As yet the disease of modern life only touched the few: the great majority, the workers and countryfolk, the vigorous merchants and manu-facturers, the sporting gentry and aristocracy never troubled their heads with doubts about the meaning of existence. But those who were to teach their children and set the intellectual and moral tone of the next age were falling into a ferment of philosophic scepticism. In the 'seventies it became intellectually demodé to believe: fashionable to doubt.

[1] "Everything that the illuminating explanation of all things on earth and in the heavens above the earth by evolution could be stretched to bring within its sphere, was pressed through our ordeal. Evolution was passed on from the laboratory and the study to the parlour, and the eternal riddles that a dozen years before had been proposed and answered, and then in their crudest form, in obscure debating societies and secularist clubs, now lay upon the table with the popular magazines."

                                                        J. Morley, Recollections, I, 88-9.

The Oxford Movement—the great ecclesiastical revival of the 'forties—had already spent its force or had lost itself in stagnant Roman backwaters. But Disraeli, with his enigmatic eye ever on some remote future, continued in a sceptical age to preach the necessity of faith. Man, he declared, was born to adore and obey. Without something to worship he would merely "fashion his own divinities and find a chieftain in his passions."[1] "If no Church comes forward with its title-deeds of truth, sustained by the tradition of sacred ages and by the conviction of countless generations, to guide him," he told the graduates of Oxford in the Sheldonian Theatre, "he will find altars and idols in his own heart and his own imagination."[2] The scientists might have exploded a few false scriptural glosses: but they had not touched the central rock of religion. "Science may prove the insignificance of this globe in the scale of creation, but it cannot prove the insignificance of man." Battle had been joined between those who labelled man an ape and those who believed him an angel: the cynic Disraeli, who like Charles II. knew men to a hair, amused his contemporaries by coming down on the side of the angels.[3]

Disraeli laughed at a society which, having mastered a few scientific principles, mistook comfort for civilisation. Material progress meant nothing for man—a spiritual being—if not accompanied by moral purpose and enlightenment. Otherwise the gifts with which science was enriching humanity would prove not instruments of life but of destruction. The tendency of the age was to emulate the scientists and measure all things by a material rule, forgetting that more than half of man's nature and existence could not be measured by any such rule. "The spiritual nature of man is stronger than codes or constitutions. No government can endure which does not recognise that for its foundation and no legislation can last which does not flow from that foundation. . . . Religion invigorates the intellect and expands the heart. He who has a sense of his relations to God is best qualified to fulfil his duties to man."[4]

For England to lose her sense of spiritual values seemed to

---

[1] *Coningsby.* A prophecy horribly fulfilled by the totalitarian Creeds which arose from the ruins of the age of reason.

[2] *Monypenny & Buckle, II, 105.*

[3] *Punch* depicted him dressing for a Bal Masque with wings and stars. *Vol. XLVII, 239 (25th Nov., 1864).*

[4] *Monypenny & Buckle, I, 606.*
   Monypenny & Buckle, II, 605.

Disraeli the greatest tragedy that could befall her. "A civilised community must rest on a large realised capital of thought and sentiment; there must be a reserve fund of public morality to draw upon in the exigencies of national life. Society has a soul as well as a body. The traditions of a nation are part of its existence. Its valour and its discipline, its venerable laws, its eloquence and its scholarship are as much portions of its life as its agriculture, its commerce and its engineering skill. . . . If it be true . . . that an aristorcacy distinguished merely by wealth must perish from satiety, so I hold it equally true that a people who recognise no higher aim than physical enjoyment must become selfish and enervated. Under such circumstances the supremacy of race which is the key to history will assert itself. Some human progeny, distinguished by their bodily vigour or their masculine intelligence . . . will assert their superiority and conquer a world which deserves to be enslaved. It will then be found that our boasted progress has only been an advancement in a circle, and that our new philosophy has brought us back to that old serfdom which it has taken ages to extirpate."[1] When these prophetic words were spoken sixteen years had still to elapse before Adolf Hitler was born in an obscure town in central Europe.

The real wealth of England was the character of her people. To impair it was national suicide. Neither profits nor utopian theories could ever justify a policy so short-sighted. "A domestic oligarchy under the guise of Liberalism, is denationalising England," Disraeli wrote in 1840, at the outset of his political career: "Hitherto we have been preserved from the effects of the folly of modern legislation by the wisdom of our ancient manners. The national character may yet save the Empire. The national character is more important than the Great Charter or trial by jury." On the dusty roads from Mons to Marne river, in the blood-stained agony of Somme and Passchendaele, on Dunkirk Beach and in the skies above the Channel, the truth of that century-old prediction became clear.

It was because her ancient institutions fostered that character that Disraeli guarded them so jealously. In an age when thinking Englishman were taught to regard them as anachronisms, a Jew made it his life's work to educate the British people in an understanding of the true tradition of their country. His success was

[1] *Monypenny & Buckle, I, 487.*

only partial. The spirit of the age, with its emphasis on the individual and its consequent mania for theoretical equality, was against him. The ancient truths he taught were harder to instil into half-educated minds than the surface logic of the rationalists: the superficial is always easier to grasp than the profound. And because of his disabilities he had to wait most of his life for other men's shoes. When his triumph at last came it was too late for him to do much more than restate from the highest forum in the land the lessons he had expounded throughout his long, half tragic career.

Yet it was sufficient to save the people he served from self-destruction. The very romance of his career—its persistence and courage—endeared him and the creed he preached to a great multitude. In the hearts of millions of his countrymen, including many of the new working-class voters whom he helped to bring within the pale of the constitution, a seed of thought was planted that enabled them to resist the over-simplified and destructive reasoning of the rationalists. Against the logic that sought to destroy Monarchy, Church, property and local independence in the name of abstract equality and to reduce the British parliament —the most delicate and intricate machine for reflecting the opinions of a free people mankind had ever evolved—to a single vote-counting assembly enforcing the edicts of despotic party caucuses and state officials, Disraeli reinforced the instinctive but inarticulate conservatism of the ordinary man with a reasoned body of principle capable of withstanding the iconoclast on his own ground. In place of the paper perfection of a dead and abstract uniformity he opposed the pride and glamour of a living patriotism, based not on official forms and figures but on the realities of human nature.

So also he defended the Crown and the hereditary Second Chamber, treating both with a deference that seemed to some snobbish or insincere but which arose from his detached realisation of their poetic qualities and their contribution in preserving the delicate balance on which English liberty depended. His opponents imagined that by concentrating all power in the hands of a single omnipotent assembly, elected by popular suffrage, the will of the people would be imposed automatically and the age-long tyranny of the few made impossible. Disraeli saw how easily such power could be perverted to the ends of the ambitious and unscrupulous: of demagogues, dictators, party wire-pullers and plutocrats. The House of Commons by itself could never preserve liberty. Without counter-availing forces securing popular rights it might easily itself become a weapon of despotism and one against which there would be no appeal.[1]

For the people by themselves could never be strong. Votes alone could not secure their rights if the use of the power entrusted by those votes to the ruling few was not kept in check by the existence of institutions strong enough to resist the abuse of executive power. "None are so interested," Disraeli wrote to a working-man's club, "in maintaining the institutions of the country as the working-classes. The rich and the powerful will not find much difficulty under any circumstances in maintaining their rights but the privileges of the people can only be defended and secured by popular institutions."[2] It was this which caused Disraeli to defend, for all its manifest absurdities and deficiencies, the House of Lords—"an intermediate body between the popular branch of the legislature and absolute legislation . . . supported by property, by tradition and by experience, ready to act with the critical faculty which is necessary when precipitate legislation is threatened and at least to obtain time, so that upon all questions of paramount importance the ultimate decision should be founded on the mature opinion of an enlightened nation."[3] Such an institution, as recent European experience showed, could not be created artificially: it had to grow gradually out of national needs and realities before it could rest firmly on instinctive popular support.

All this was true of a yet more venerable institution. Since the long insanity of George III., the English monarchy had been in jeopardy. The dignity and good sense of Queen Victoria had done something to redeem it from the odium into which it had fallen through the scandalous lives of her royal uncles. But in the 'sixties it was far from being a popular institution. The interminable and teutonically exaggerated retirement into which the royal widow had fallen after the death of the Prince Consort caused widespread criticism. The tone of radical youth increasingly tended towards a republic. To many thoughtful minds it

[1] In one of his earliest electoral addresses, Disraeli expressed such a fear. "I will allow for the freedom of the Press; I will allow for the spirit of the age; I will allow for the march of intellect; but I cannot force from my mind the conviction that a House of Commons, concentrating in itself the whole power of the State, might . . . establish in this country a despotism of the most formidable and dangerous character." *Monypenny & Buckle, I, 276.*

[2] *Monypenny & Buckle, II, 297.*   [3] *Monypenny & Buckle, II, 35.*

appeared inprobable that the young Prince of Wales, who in his pleasures seemed reverting to the less decorous traditions of his Hanoverian forebears, would ever succeed to the throne. The spirit of a progressive age demanded a republic.

In one of his early political works Disraeli defined his life-long attitude to the Crown. "The wisdom of your forefathers placed the prize of supreme power without the sphere of human passions . . . Whatever the struggle of parties, whatever the strife of factions . . . there has always been something in this country round which all classes and parties could rally, representing the majesty of the law, the administration of justice and involving . . . the security of every man's right and the fountain of honour." More than any other institution, the hereditary throne represented to Disraeli the continuing community as opposed to the government of the hour. For it embodied his conception of perpetual trusteeship. His wise and delicate conduct towards his sovereign whom he encouraged to resume her traditional functions in the pageantry of state was part of his political creed. His unfailing defence of the royal prerogative[1] in the Commons was another. It was not the least of his services to posterity that he laboured to revive popular sympathy and affection for the throne, and with the aid of his royal mistress to re-establish it on the firm foundation on which it had been the pride of the great Tudor monarchs to rest it—the hearts of the people.

In all that he did and advocated Disraeli strove to place the government of Britain and its empire on a broad basis of independence and privilege. He believed it to be his mission to close the breaches created by the Industrial Revolution and to blend the diverse elements of the nation, not by levelling them but by bringing them into sympathy with the spirit of a new age. "In a progressive country," he declared in 1867, "change is constant, and the great question is, not whether you should resist change which is inevitable, but whether that change should be carried out in deference to the manners, the customs, the laws, the traditions of the people, or in deference to abstract principles and arbitrary and general doctrines."[2] It was his aim therefore—pursued for more than thirty years in the face of constant

[1] "It is not difficult to conceive an occasion when, supported by the sympathies of a loyal people, its exercise might defeat an unconstitutional Ministry and a corrupt Parliament." Disraeli, *Lord George Bentinck, Ch. IV.*

[2] *Monypenny & Buckle, II, 291.*

detraction and disunderstanding—to make his Party the expression not of stupid and selfish reaction but of enduring national interests secured by popular principles and institutions. "What is the Tory party," he once asked, "unless it represents national feeling? Toryism is nothing . . . unless it represents and upholds the institutions of the country."[1]

His Liberal opponents, whose ranks included some of the noblest and most disinterested men of that time, did not see the the importance of preserving the national institutions. They had, as they conceived, a higher goal—the greatest good of the greatest number measured by the expression of the popular will in an equally elected and all powerful assembly. "I see before me," Disraeli declared in a famous speech, " a numerous and powerful party, animated by chiefs whose opinions in favour of all that can advance the cause of pure democracy have been openly proclaimed. All unite in the march of the caravan towards the heart of the desert, and if there be those who then discover that the fountain which allures them on is but the mirage it will be too late to return. . . . If England is to continue free, she must rest upon the intermediate institutions, which fence round monarchy as the symbol of the executive force from that suffrage of unalloyed democracy which represents the invading agencies of legislative change."

For a nation was "a work of art and a work of time." It was created gradually by a variety of influences. "If you destroy the political institutions which these influences have called into force . . . and which are the machinery by which they act, you destroy the nation." "The formation of a free government on an extensive scale," Disraeli had written on an earlier occasion, "while it is assuredly one of the most interesting problems of humanity is certainly the greatest achievement of human wit. Perhaps I should rather term it a superhuman achievement; for it requires such refined prudence, such comprehensive knowledge and such perspicacious sagacity, united with such almost illimitable powers of combination, that it is nearly in vain to hope for qualities so rare to be congregated in a solitary mind. . . . With us it has been the growth of ages, and brooding centuries have watched over and tended its perilous birth and feeble infancy."[2]

[1] *Monypenny & Buckle, II, 287.*
[2] *A Vindication of the English Constitution Ch. V.*

CHAPTER SIX

Shooting Niagara

> "Those who take 'leaps in the dark,' as we are doing, may find themselves in unexpected places before they recover the beaten tracks again."—*Froude, Oceana, 15.*
>
> "The life of a constitution is in the spirit and disposition of those who work it."—*Bagehot.*

IN 1864 while the Commons were perfunctorily debating a private member's motion for reform of the franchise—a question which in the view of most people had been dead since 1832[1]—Mr. Gladstone, then Chancellor of the Exchequer, electrified the House by declaring that every man who was not incapacitated by some consideration of personal unfitness or of political danger was morally entitled to come within the pale of the constitution. The declaration marked the beginning of a new phase in English history. Electoral power which thirty-two years before had passed from the aristocracy to the middle-class was now to shift by ordered but rapid stages to the masses. The workers by virtue of their numerical superiority were to become the dominating class of the future.

A few years before no one but a few fanatic reformers regarded such a development as within the sphere of practical politics. Pure democracy was an ultimate goal: an equal vote for every citizen a pious aspiration, widely honoured like the beatitudes and acceded to by none. The rough type produced by the factory and the housing conditions of the factory town was not one to which the wealth, safety and honour of a rich and ancient kingdom was likely to be entrusted, even by the most sanguine. Where in other European countries, like republican France, democracy had been tried, the result had been an orgy of blood, plunder and anarchy followed by a military despotism. A practical people like the British felt little drawn to such visionary courses.

Even in America where the experiment of eighty years back

---

[1] John Bright, attempting an agitation in favour of household suffrage in 1859, observed it was like "flogging a dead horse."

had so far escaped shipwreck—presumably through the smallness of the population and the immensity of the territory—democracy seemed in the 'sixties to be culminating in disaster. The educated classes in Britain believed that the war waged by the vulgar Yankees and their backwoodsman President against the aristocratic Southern cotton-planters could only end in one way. Even the liberal-minded *Punch*, until the final magnanimous apology over the great democrat's murdered corpse,[1] persistently depicted Lincoln as a crude demagogue, half clown and half dictator. His defeat by an army of gentlemen appeared inevitable.

The triumph of the North, after three years of disaster, surprised the English ruling classes. It did not surprise the British factory hands who grasped from the first the real significance of the "slaveowners' war." Their strong sympathy for Lincoln's cause helped to prevent the recognition of the South by the government of Palmerston and Gladstone. During the cotton famine caused by the blockade in 1862-3, the patient fortitude of the cotton operatives impressed and shamed their betters. Gladstone's pronouncement that such men were entitled to a place in the constitution awoke an answering chord in thousands.

The movement towards electoral reform, stagnant since the collapse of the People's Charter in the 'forties, took on a new complexion. It coincided with the end of the Palmerstonian era and the succession of Gladstone to the Liberal leadership in the Commons. In 1866 a Liberal government introduced a bill reducing the occupation franchise in the counties from £50 to £14 and in the boroughs from £10 to £7. By this it was hoped to add another 400,000 voters to the electorate.

The bill's promoters regarded it as a logical step in the process of advancing the happiness of the greatest number through the exercise of intelligent self-interest. It was now assumed that the better class of working man was a rational being. In making him master of his destiny and the nation's, he could be trusted like his bourgeois betters to follow the law of his own advantage and so automatically serve the common weal.

But though the Liberals were in a majority their whig sup-

[1] "Yes, he had lived to shame me from my sneer,
To lame my pencil and confute my pen,
To make me own this hind of princes peer,
This rail-splitter a true-born king of men."
—*Punch, XLVIII, 182.*

porters, led by Robert Lowe, regarded the measure as an uncalled-
for step towards the destruction of property and freedom. "With
our own rash and inconsiderate hands," he declared, "we are
about to pluck down on our heads the venerable temple of our
liberty and our glory."[1] Entering the lobbies with the reactionary
Tories, the "Adullamites," as the old reformer Bright called them,
defeated the bill in committee. The government resigned, and
the Conservatives, still in a minority, took office.

But Disraeli, their leader in the Commons, having nursed his
Party for twenty years in the wilderness without enjoying a
majority, had no intention of committing it in the hour of
recovery to the same policy of obstinate resistance to the popular
tide which had ruined it in 1830. The debates had reawoken the
country to an interest in reform. There were demonstrations
in its favour in Hyde Park that July when, the gates being locked
by the police, the mob tore up the railings of Park Lane.[2] The
government opened the session of 1867 by introducing a reform
measure of its own. *Punch* depicted the Prime Minister, Lord
Derby, in bonnet and petticoats making off with the infant
bill while its mother, Lord Russell, surveying the empty pram,
cried out, "Hi! help! ple'-ae-ce! She's a takin' away me cheild."

The new bill went farther than that of the Liberals. In the
counties the basis proposed was household suffrage qualified
by personal rating and two years' residence. In adopting what
seemed to many a Liberal policy Disraeli was honouring an ideal
which he had proclaimed at the outset of his career. For it had
always been his contention that the first Reform bill had
impaired the English principle of representation. He had
objected to it not, as many Tories had done, because it increased
the electorate but because it made the representation of opinion
less effective.[3] The object of a parliamentary system, he held,

---

[1] *Parliamentary Debates*, CLXXXII, 2118. A still stronger expression of the case
against unnecessary concessions was made by Bulwer Lytton in a speech of 1859. "Do
not give to-day what you regret to-morrow that you cannot restore. Democracy is
like the grave—it perpetually cries, ' Give! give!' and like the grave it never returns
what it has once taken. But you live under a constitutional monarchy which has all
the vigour of health, all the energy of movement. Do not surrender to democracy
that which is not yet ripe for the grave."

[2] Demonstrations occurred in other parts of the country, especially at Manchester,
Newcastle, Birmingham and Glasgow. Those in Hyde Park had one interesting
consequence in leading to the permanent policing of the west-end parks.

[3] "In a hasty and factious effort to get rid of representation without election, it
will be as well if eventually we do not discover that we have only obtained election
without representation."—*Disraeli, Vindication of Constitution* (*1835*), *Chapter
XVI*.

was not to count votes—a mere means to an end—but to weigh opinion. And if a nation was to pursue a responsible policy, it must be responsible opinion.

It was an English principle that the vote, like the exercise of any other form of authority, should only be entrusted to those fitted for responsibility. The Whigs in their remedy for the electoral anomalies of five conservative centuries had forgotten English history. It was right that the manufacturers and shop-keepers of the new industrial towns, wrongly excluded from the pre-1832 constitution, should have been enfranchised. But, in Disraeli's view, it had been wrong to allow a single class, hitherto without political experience, to outvote every other national interest merely because of its numerical superiority.

Disraeli had therefore always contended that the defence of the settlement of 1832 was no concern of a Party which claimed to represent national as opposed to sectional interests. During a brief spell of office in 1859, he had proposed an extension of the franchise to important interests overlooked by the whig re-formers, and had advocated an additional vote for university graduates, ministers of religion, lawyers, doctors, certificated schoolmasters, civil service pensioners, fundholders and Post Office Savings Bank depositors. Opinions were not merely to be counted but weighed. The House of Commons, reverting to its older tradition, was to become "a mirror of the mind as well as the material interests of England."

This conception, which received little support at the time either from Disraeli's own party or his opponents, was now revived in the proposals which he placed before Parliament. In addition to bringing the responsible artisan within the constitution by widening the borough qualification, he offered a dual vote to every direct taxpayer and extended the franchise to all with a certain standard of education or £50 in the Funds or Savings Bank.

In all this Disraeli challenged the whole utilitarian thesis of his age. If, as Bentham argued, the happiness of the greatest number was to be secured by giving every man the maximum power to pursue his own selfish good, the more electors admitted to the constitution the better. The Liberals accepted this in theory, but qualified it in practice by denying the vote to the majority. For their rough habits and lack of even the most rudimentary education unfitted the workers in middle-class eyes

for the suffrage. An electorate of respectable shopkeepers and
city merchants was poised uneasily on the horns of a dilemma.
It had either to refuse to honour its Benthamite ideals or subject
its security and property to the vote of a rude multitude of
unlettered toughs—of garrotters, wife-beaters, drunkards, foot-
pads, and ragged, lousy beggars.

Disraeli shared neither the practical fears nor the idealist
hopes of the bourgeois. He had no illusions about the consequences of further extension of the franchise on a numerical
basis. He was not less willing to trust his countrymen—he was
more so—but he knew that in any state which based power
purely on numbers the result must be "the tyranny of one class
and that in the least enlightened."[1] For against an unchanging
popular majority, the individual has no appeal. However mildly
exercised, such uniform despotism was bound to destroy
diversity of type and character.

> "I have no apprehension myself that, if you had man-
> hood suffrage to-morrow, the honest, brave, and good-
> natured people of England would resort to pillage, incendi-
> arism, and massacre. Who expects that? But though I
> would do as much justice to the qualities of our countrymen
> as any gentleman in this House, though I may not indulge in
> high-flown and far-fetched expressions with respect to them
> like those we have listened to—for the people may have
> their parasites as well as monarchs and aristocrats—yet I
> have no doubt that, whatever may be their high qualities,
> our countrymen are subject to the same political laws that
> affect the condition of all other communities and nations.
> If you establish a democracy, you must in due season reap
> the fruits of a democracy. You will in due season have
> great impatience of the public burdens combined in due
> season with great increase of the public expenditure. You
> will in due season reap the fruits of such united influence.
> You will in due season have wars entered into from passion,
> and not from reason; and you will in due season submit to
> peace ignominiously sought and ignominiously obtained,
> which will diminish your authority and perhaps endanger
> your independence. You will, in due season, with a demo-
> cracy find that your property is less valuable and that your

[1] *Monypenny and Buckle, II, 146.*

freedom is less complete. I doubt not, when there has been realised a sufficient quantity of disaffection and dismay, the good sense of this country will come to the rally, and that you will obtain some remedy for your grievances, and some redress for wrongs, by the process through which alone it can be obtained—by that process which may render your property more secure, but which will not render your liberty more eminent. . . ."[1]

In his Reform Bill of 1867 Disraeli tried to constitute the vote a privilege and not a right "to be gained by virtue, by intelligence, by industry, by integrity and to be exercised for the common good."[2] He wished to extend the franchise, not degrade it. As he had always done, he wanted to see the working man a partner in the constitution but not its dictator. But he held office on sufferance only, and his power to carry the bill was dependent on his acceptance of Liberal amendments.

The spirit of the age was still utilitarian, and the machinery for restoring an older and more English ideal of government was sabotaged in committee. The second Reform Bill passed its third reading on July 15, 1867, but without the provisions for the dual vote for education and property.

The bill added a million voters to the electoral roll, roughly doubling it. It created a democracy of heads of houses, that is of men with some stake, however small, in the country. Its weakness in its author's eyes was that it gave too much ultimate voting power to mere numbers. It was in Lord Derby's famous phrase "a leap in the dark."[3] And the direction it took suggested further leaps into still deeper darkness before long.

   .   .   .   .   .   .

The first general election fought on the new register gave the liberal party a six years' lease of power. But as Disraeli had prophesied, the interests of artisans and middle-class utilitarians

[1] *Monypenny and Buckle, I, 1608-9.*
[2] *Monypenny and Buckle, II, 144.*
[3] Carlyle stigmatised it as "shooting Niagara," and the poet Coventry Patmore wrote mournfully of—

> "The year of the great crime,
> When the false English nobles, and their Jew,
> By God demented, slew
> The trust they stood twice pleged to keep from wrong."

To the future Lord Salisbury, Disraeli's successor as conservative leader, it was "a political betrayal which has no parallel in our annals."

were not the same. The latter wanted to restrict the functions of government and leave the ring clear for the individual with talent and industry. The workers on the other hand, though the educated and therefore better-to-do minority among them tended to absorb liberal middle-class sympathies, needed state protection against the economic excesses of the individual. As soon as they realised the power which the vote had given them, they began to demand it. They leant not towards the classic liberalism of *laissez-faire* but towards that social reform which Disraeli had preached since his Young England days and which Shaftesbury and the factory reformers had fought for against the utilitarians.

Gladstone's programme of civic emancipation, Irish Church disestablishment and administrative reform therefore made little appeal to the working-class electorate. After a few years of Liberal rule the country became surfeited with organic change. The sun of "the People's William" waned: that of "Dizzi," the inspired Jew boy who had "climbed to the top of the greasy pole," rose flamboyant. In 1874 for the first time in 33 years the Conservatives obtained a majority.

The date marks the dividing line between the utilitarian legislation of the middle half of the nineteenth century and the collectivist or socialist legislation which has since taken its place. The change was in some degree due to Disraeli, who at the age of seventy was able to apply an instalment of the social policy which he had advocated in his thirties. It was far more due to the crying needs of the working classes and to the preponderating influence in legislation which the extension of the franchise had given them. With every expansion of the industrial population, that preponderance increased.

During the quarter of a century that followed the collapse of the Chartists the working-class movement had silently gathered momentum. In every town where skilled workers were assembled, the Trade Unions made their appearance. The quiet years of widening trade and employment helped their growth, giving them cohesion, tradition and financial reserves to meet the stormier years ahead. Local consolidation was usually followed by amalgamation on a national scale. The first great national Union, the Amalgamated Society of Engineers, was founded in 1851 with the fusion of over a hundred local trade societies. In the next fifteen years its membership of 12,000 more than doubled

With its many imitators it fought against piece-work, overtime, victimisation and the employment of unapprenticed men, survived early attempts of impatient employers to destroy it by lock-outs and taught a hostile bourgeois world to tolerate and fear, if not to respect it.

To the middle-class citizen in his top-hat and castellated home, the Trade Union was long something of a bogey—a secret and treasonable society threatening mob violence and plotting confiscation and revolution. In popular repute its shady path was attended by a succession of outrages: explosions, stones and broken glass, striking mobs intimidating honest Britons out of their property and right to work as they pleased. None felt this more strongly than the progressive radicals of the north. "Depend upon it," wrote Cobden, "nothing can be got by fraternising with Trade Unions. They are founded upon principles of brutal tyranny and monopoly. I would rather live under a Dey of Algiers than a trades committee."[1]

The law, reflecting middle-class opinion, treated the Unions with suspicion. Judges, who still regarded them as combinations in restraint of trade, refused to protect their funds from the defalcations of dishonest officials. A Trade Union was an association to coerce individuals and limit their profits. It was therefore viewed by a generation educated in *laissez-faire* principles as injurious. It was only tolerated because it was impossible to prevent it. That by improving conditions, removing the workers' sense of injustice and substituting orderly for chaotic terms of employment, collective working-class action might stabilise and so improve trade was still beyond the ken of mid-Victorian philosophy.

Yet, though those brought up in the principles of Bentham tried not to see it, everything that was happening in the crowded urban world which individual enterprise had created was minimising the importance of the individual and raising the power of the herd. The sturdy pupil of self-help, who by his devotion to his individual interests had created a thriving industrial unit employing 5000 workers where only fifty had existed before, had unconsciously called into being a community whose common hopes and interests must presently clash with his own. For though the more he prospered the more they multiplied, the more they did so the more certain became their ultimate triumph over

[1] *Morley Cobden, I, 299.*

himself. So soon as they realised that their opportunity of happiness lay not in their action as individuals, in which being poor and ill-educated they were powerless, but in their collective strength, their final victory was certain.

In his great work, *Capital*, first obscurely published "amid carbuncles and the constant dunning of creditors" in 1867, Karl Marx demonstrated the course events were taking. He saw that with its ever-increasing scale of operations capitalism was digging its own grave. The evolution of a society which put its faith in figures was predestined. "While there is thus a progressive diminution in the number of capitalist magnates . . . there occurs a corresponding increase in the mass of poverty, oppression, enslavement, degeneration and exploitation; but at the same time there is a steady intensification of the wrath of the working class—a class which grows ever more numerous and is disciplined, unified and organised by the very mechanism of the capitalist method of production. Capitalist monopoly becomes a fetter upon the method of production which has flourished with it and under it. The centralisation of the means of production and the socialisation of labour reach a point where they prove incompatible with their capitalist husk. This bursts asunder. The knell of capitalist private property sounds. The expropriators are expropriated."

To Marx's logical, academic but violence-loving mind, the inevitable end was revolution. Divorced by his circumstances and temperament from the contacts of normal life and society,[1] this morose prophet never grasped the nature of the people whose commercial institutions he studied with such brilliant and prophetic insight. He failed to see that in an ancient country like England, with its strong social character and representative institutions, revolution would be deflected into smoother channels. There would be no explosion, only a gradual process.

The great change that Marx predicted happened. But it took place in so unexpected a way that nobody, not even Marx, realised that it was happening at all. The utilitarians thesis, which supported *laissez-faire*, involved the extension of the vote to the poor man. He used it to obtain legislation to offset his disability in contracting power. In England the passage

[1] His mother, Martha-like, reflected the spirit of her age in wishing that her Karl has made some capital instead of writing about it.

of the second Reform Bill, and not the shouting proletarian crowds and the blood-bath of the exploiters, marked the end of unlimited freedom of contract and therefore of *laissez-faire*.

The application of the democratic thesis advanced not utilitarian ideals but those diametrically opposed to them. Mathematical democracy belied the hopes of those who had sought its triumph. Instead of peace and retrenchment—the central pillars of the Benthamite structure and the prerequisites of unrestricted individual liberty—democracy within a span of little more than two generations was to bring about wars and state expenditure on a scale never previously imagined. Instead of freedom of contract, opinion and speech, it was to create a mass paternalism and regimentation of thought and expression beyond the dreams of Strafford and Laud. The island home of liberty that had fought against ship-money and forced billeting was to give its suffrage for penal taxation and conscription. Within seventy-three years of the passing of the second Reform Bill, it was to become possible for any newspaper to be suppressed by bare order of a state department for advocating a policy opposed to that of the government and for an Englishman to be arrested and kept in prison without trial or right of appeal for an expression of past opinion. To argue that such powers, greater than any sought by Pitt in his struggle against Napoleon, were solely the result of a threat to national existence is to ignore the historical trend of nearly a century.

The scene being England, the transition from individualism to collectivism was scarcely perceptible. At first nothing appeared to have happened at all. Even after a quarter of a century, when a respected liberal statesman made his cheerful admission "we are all socialists now," the process was cloaked by so many English, and therefore conservative phrases and fictions, that most people were unaware that it was taking place. For, as always in England, the continuity of outward forms remained and the great individualists rode to the guillotine at Westminster in their own private coaches attended by the Benthamite livery. Most of the socialist legislation under which modern Britain is governed was passed by a Liberal government of Manchester individualists between 1906 and the last European War and the remainder by equally individualistic Conservative administrations between 1922 and 1940.

The new direction was first set by Disraeli's aristocratic

government in the latter 'seventies. In the course of five years this administration of rich hereditary peers and landowners passed legislation which, though little noticed at the time, struck at the roots of the Benthamite thesis that the individual should be left free to enrich himself as he chose. Factory acts were extended and consolidated and the hours[1] and conditions of labour codified. The process of private enclosure was reversed—though too late to save more than a fragment of what once had been public property — and the conversion of common land forbidden unless it conferred a public as well as a private benefit. By the Public Health Act of 1876 the interests of the individual were first subordinated to the requirements of public sanitation. It was only a beginning. Defending a policy which he described as "Sanitas sanitatum, omnia sanitas," Disraeli replied to the contemptuous attacks of those who felt he was reducing statecraft to a mere affair of sewerage:

"It must be obvious to all who consider the condition of the multitude with a desire to improve and elevate it, that no important step can be gained unless your effect some reduction of their hours of labour and humanise their toil. . . . I ventured to say a short time ago that the health of the people was the most important subject for a statesman. It is a large subject. It has many branches. It involves the state of the dwellings of the people, the moral consequences of which are not less considerable than the physical. It involves their enjoyment of some of the chief elements of nature—air, light, and water. It involves the regulation of their industry, the inspection of their toil. It involves the purity of their provisions, and it touches upon all the means by which you may wean them from habits of excess and brutality. . . . Well it may be the policy of sewerage to a Liberal Member of Parliament. But to one of the labouring multitude of England, who has found fever always to be one of the inmates of his household—who has, year after year, seen stricken down the children of his loins on whose sympathy and support he has looked with hope and confidence, it is not a policy of sewerage but a question of life and death."

[1] Limited by an Act of 1874 to 56 hours a week, 10 on five weekdays and not more than 6 on Saturdays.

The same government introduced an Artisans' Dwelling Bill, empowering local authorities to demolish insanitary dwellings and replace them by houses built expressly for working men. The measure was not compulsory but only permissive.[1] It was no more than a tentative beginning: a mere drop in the still rising ocean of slum. Yet its ultimate effect was revolutionary. For it revived, in however dim a form, the ancient ideal of the state as the guardian of the people's homes.

Behind all this legislation lay the silent voting power of the workers. In 1874 there were returned to the House of Commons two men who were to be the pioneers of a mighty army. Even at the time Alexander Macdonald and Thomas Burt, the first two working-class M.P.'s, were something of a portent among the landed squires and thriving manufacturers at Westminster. Burt was Secretary of the Northumberland Miners' Association, which, by helping to establish that the occupants of colliery houses, though not paying rates direct, were entitled to voting rights like the compound householders in the towns, had secured a majority of pitmen in the constituency of Morpeth. These representatives of the sons of toil tended at first to vote with Disraeli's "gentlemen of England" rather than with his opponents. Macdonald told his constituents in 1879 that the Conservative party had "done more for the working classes in five years than the Liberals in fifty."

For the old Jew, now nearing his end, for all his absorption in duchesses and oriental splendour, believed in a tory democracy and saw in the working man, with his native prejudices and conservative instincts, an ally against the levelling utilitarian forces he had fought all his life. He did not believe that the simple, pleasure-loving Englishman in the craftsman's square cap and apron wanted the drab uniformity so dear to Benthamite pedants. In his own phrase he made it his task to " soften the feelings of the working multitude."[2] By redressing injustices he sought to end the fatal gulf between the "two Englands" which more clearly than any other public man he had perceived in his

[1] "Permissive legislation," Disraeli explained, "is the character of a free people. It is easy to adopt compulsory legislation when you have to deal with those who only exist to obey, but in a free country and especially a country like England, you must trust to persuasion and example as the two great elements if you wish to effect any considerable changes in the manners of the people."—*Monypenny and Buckle, II, 731.*

[2] *Monypenny and Buckle, II, 712.*

youth and still hoped—though it was almost thirty years too late—to bridge.

His administration's labour laws were an attempt to further that hope. The common law, dating from an age when status was fixed and the workman given security of tenure by the state, treated breach of contract by an employer as a civil offence and that of his workman as criminal. The application of *laissez-faire* to commercial relationships had long made this distinction grossly unjust. By an act of 1875 Disraeli ended it by placing the workman on the same legal footing as his employer. In the same year he righted a still greater grievance of industrial labour against the law. Though the ancient doctrine of "conspiracy" had been modified by an Act of 1825, the Courts still refused to accord Trade Unions full legal status. Their funds were unprotected against breaches of trust by their own employees and their officers criminally liable for certain actions carried out in the course of their duties. By a new Act of 1875 Trade Unions were given the protection of the law. The mere fact of association to defeat an employer was freed from criminal taint. It could only be indicted as a conspiracy when it constituted what done by a single person would have been a crime.

By this change in the law "peaceful" picketing became permissible if unaccompanied by violence or threat of violence—though, as the upshot proved, it still remained open to judges to take such a view of "intimidation" as to constitute all picketing "unpeaceful." Not until the Trade Disputes Act of 1906, passed by a Liberal government which had repudiated *laissez-faire* for full-blooded collectivism to win working-class support, did the Trade Unions establish the privileged position they sought.[1] To a believer in great national institutions, preserving by their trusteeship undying liberties and rights, it was a position to which a Trade Union was entitled. To a middle-class lawyer, nursed in the tenets of Benthamism, it was not. For several decades after the second Reform Bill the struggle between *laissez-faire* and the new socialism of the great towns *laissez-faire* had created continued.

.   .   .   .

It was often for the early leaders of labour a cruelly hard one. They had to do their public work in their spare time and

---

[1] It reversed the decision of the judges in the Taff Vale case and freed Trade Unions funds from liability for damages committed by its members in the course of strikes.

finance it out of their wages. The pioneers of the Dockers' Union met "like conspirators hatching a second Guy Fawkes plot in a gloomy cellar with only the flickering half-lights given by tallow candles thrust into the necks of pop bottles." In the 'eighties the members of even the executive council of so famous a union as the Amalgamated Society of Engineers—at least two of whom in after years became cabinet ministers—used to receive one shilling and sixpence a night for their direction of the leading Union of the time and think themselves lucky to get it. Trades Union leadership in those days was less a career than a vocation. It was sometimes a martyrdom.

For this reason, and because of the wrongs from which their class had suffered and was still suffering, these pioneers of a still inconceivable future were often politically embittered. The good-humoured rank and file in pub and music hall, on the beach at Blackpool or the racecourse at Aintree, troubled their heads little about past history or future proletarian aspirations. But their leaders, and the earnest young men studying under immense difficulties in public libraries and Mechanics' Institutes[1] who were to be their leaders in the next generation, were painfully aware of the fact that they and their class had not had a square deal.

Yet with the vote in the workman's wallet, time was on their side. They felt that they had only to open the eyes of the wage slaves, teach them to combine and to use their latent strength with discipline and loyalty to obtain their share of the kingdom. The prejudices against them—the malice and victimisation of employers, the biased use of the civil arm and even the military in time of strikes, the snobbery and class treachery of the workers themselves—were not so strong as the social impulse of the exploited to combine or perish. Whenever times were hard the men the Unions battled for, who were oblivious of their efforts when employment was regular and beer and bread plentiful, were reminded of how much still remained to be won before there could be any security for themselves and their dear ones. Without the Trade Union there could be only loss of hearth and home and starvation for the workman who lost his job, and worse for

[1] The Working Men's College in London was founded by the Rev. Frederick Denison Maurice, in 1854, with a voluntary staff of middle-class "Christian Socialist" sympathisers who included Ruskin, Tom Hughes—author of *Tom Brown's School Days* —Lowes Dickinson, Vernon Lushington, Ford Madox Brown, Dante Gabriel Rossetti and Edward Burne Jones.

the family of the man crippled or killed by accident in the course
of his employment.[1]

Neither the error and human frailty of leaders nor the folly
and shortsightedness of the rank and file could halt the steady
march of organised labour. In 1880 the Trade Union Congress
only represented 600,000 members: by 1892 the figure had
doubled. It was not only for advances in wages that the older
Unions now fought, but for recognition as the sole representatives of the workers in all negotiations with employers. They
demanded a share in the direction of their labour. To the fury
of the old-fashioned capitalist, to whom freedom of contract
meant freedom of choice for the master and obedience for the
man, the new Trade Unionism sought to abolish overtime and
regulate piecework. It went further. It used the threat of the
worker's vote to appeal over the head of the employer to a Parliament now dependent on that vote, for legislation to enforce its
demands. At its annual Congresses, begun in 1866, the T.U.C.
instructed its members to press parliamentary candidates for
such reforms as an eight-hour day, compulsory compensation for
injured workers, the limitation of shop hours, new factory
regulations, further amendment of the law of conspiracy and the
abolition of child labour. It also demanded free elementary
education, land for allotments in country districts and the
appointment of working men to the Bench.

Organised labour in these years sought more than the protection of the skilled worker. As Cobden had prophesied in the
hungry 'forties, the triumph of *laissez-faire* had brought enhanced
prosperity to many workers. The skilled artisan had taken his
share, however small, in the increased prosperity of his country.
He had enjoyed good wages, untaxed and plentiful food, long
continued employment, cheap transport and amenities—municipal parks, libraries, galleries and concerts—such as his father
in a grimmer age had never known. In many cases he had been
able to put away money, insure against old age and sickness, even

---

[1] "Life was cheap in those days. It was by no means an uncommon thing to see
the maimed and sometimes the dead being brought up from the dock bottom. . . . I
remember two cases in our gang, George Washington, a smith's striker, fell into the
dry dock one foggy night on his way home and was found at the bottom half dead
in the morning. Jim Platt, a machinist, had his back nearly broken by the fall of a
loose plank from the workshop roof. The result was the same in both cases—patched
up in the hospital and then death after a year or two of lingering pain at
work. But compensation was never thought of."—*G. N. Barnes, From Workshop to
Cabinet, 34.*

to buy his own home. The utilitarian state had given him opportunity and he had taken it.

But the skilled artisan in employment was only a part of
labour. For if *laissez-faire* postulated the successful workman
growing rich like his master through his own thrift and industry,
it also necessitated a residue of unskilled labour to meet the
fluctuating demands of a competitive world. This the capitalist
used in good time and discarded in bad. Such a system multiplied
the wastrel, the diseased and the ne'er-do-well. It multiplied
their inefficient and unhappy posterity. The statistics of the
economist showed the profits of unrestricted competition. The
slums of the industrial cities revealed its wastage.

It was no part of *laissez-faire* that the successful should burden
themselves by helping the failures. The only economic place for
the weak was the rubbish heap. It was at this point that *laissez-
faire* always clashed with the English temperament. The middle-
class employer in the rarified privacy of his sanctum might—in
the interests of a higher wisdom—suppress his inherited feelings
of charity and kindness. But the working man who had never
heard of *laissez-faire* could not. He never even tried. For he was
nothing if not sentimental, and under his corduroys beat a heart
full of English instincts and prejudices. One of them was an
incorrigible desire to help the underdog.

It was from such a motive, unreasoning and unscientific, that
English socialism first sprang. Abroad socialism followed more
logical channels: the brand that Karl Marx was preaching to his
fellow Germans and to embittered and excitable French and
Russian comrades was of a severely practical kind. There was
nothing that Marx[1] despised and disliked so much as an underdog.
He merely wished to use him and his misery to destroy the capitalist system. What would happen to the wretched, snivelling,
inefficient creature in the bloody process never troubled him.
For the underdog like the bourgeois was himself a product of the
capitalist system. Only when he was swept away would the brave
new world of the revolutionary logicians' vision become possible.
To waste tears on him, let alone effort, was a crime against the
classless society of the future.

But English Socialists, even when they paid polite lip service

---

[1] Marx despaired of the English. "England," he wrote, "possesses all the necessary
conditions for social revolution; what she lacks is a universal outlook and revolutionary passion."—*E. H. Carr, Karl Marx, 79.*

to the theses of their continental comrades, seemed curiously
unaware of all this. It was precisely because they wished to help
the underdog, that they were Socialists at all. Men like William
Morris and Arnold Toynbee devoted their lives to the working-
class movement because their English sense of justice and kindliness was affronted by the sickening misery and cruelty of a great
reserve of unskilled labour like the East End of London. They did
not wish merely to use the underdog but to tend and cherish him,
just as they wished not to exterminate the bourgeois but to
convert him. The University Settlement, then first taking shape,
was a characteristic product of both these wishes. And in their
dreams for the future the early English Socialists sought nothing
but a gentle Christian paradise after their own kindly middle-
class hearts. Morris's *News from Nowhere* published in 1890 is
as far removed from Marx's *Capital* as the Gospel of St. John
from the Book of Judges. "I know," said its author of a working-
men's procession, "what these men want: employment which
would foster their self-respect and win the praise and sympathy
of their fellows, and dwellings which they would come to with
pleasure, surroundings which would soothe and elevate them;
reasonable labour, reasonable rest. There is only one thing that
can give them this—Art."[1]

To modern middle-class revolutionaries, with their armoury
of Marxian dialectic and their pessimist's despair of the living,
there must seem something incurably futile about this lovable
old man, haranguing in his gentle voice on Eelbrook Common
and looking in his blue serge reefer jacket like a cross between a
farmer and a sea captain. At that time he and his proletarian
prototype, John Burns, were the life and soul of militant English
Socialism. Their object was to save the underdog from the shameless sweating and exploitation which he suffered by organising
him like his comrades, the prosperous artisans of the skilled
Trade Unions. During the recurrent trade depressions of the
'eighties they organised vast processions of unemployed—of the
unwanted and starving army of *laissez-faire* capital. One of these,
on "Bloody Sunday," November, 1887, became part of English
history. Long drab companies of pallid ragged men, marching
behind red banners and bands of antiquated instruments, con-
verged in defiance of the police from the outer slums on Trafalgar

[1] Speech delivered at Burslem, 13th Oct., 1881, *cit. R. H. Gretton, A Modern History
of the English People,* 64.

Square: here they were repeatedly charged by massed constables with drawn batons until hundreds of skulls were cracked and bleeding. It was the first glimmer of the red light that threatened social explosion. "No one who saw it will ever forget the strange and indeed terrible sight of that grey winter day, the vast, sombre-coloured crowd, the brief but fierce struggle at the corner of the Strand, and the river of steel and scarlet that moved slowly through the dusky swaying masses, when two squadrons of the Life Guards were summoned up from Whitehall."[1] Afterwards two of the leaders, John Burns and the chivalrous Cunninghame Graham were taken into custody.

The red light was not unheeded. The conscience of England is sometimes hard to awake but it never fails in the end to respond to a great wrong. Two years later the selfless pioneers of the British Socialist movement won a great triumph. In August, 1889, several thousand labourers in the London Docks struck work. Such men were the poorest of the poor—the floatsam and jetsam of the water-side. They were unorganised, despised even by their fellow workers, without hope or craft. They slept in the fo'c'sles of empty ships and subsisted on scraps of mouldy biscuits left over by their hard-bitten crews, were subjected by sub-contractors—often more brutes than men—to work with rotten plant and defective machinery and left to perish in crippled destitution and misery when their limbs had been mangled in some squalid accident on the dock-side.[2] In the frantic competition for freights, they could scarcely ever look for more then two days' continuous employment. But stirred by the new spirit among their downtrodden kind, they now made the unheard of demand that their labour should be hired at not less than four hours at a time and at a uniform rate of 6d. an hour. It was rejected by dockowners who relied on the poverty and stupidity of the poor derelicts they exploited to ensure their defeat. But the sullen resolve of the men, fanned to anger by the fiery eloquence of one of their number, Ben Tillett, and sustained by the growing

---

[1] *J. W. Mackail, Life of William Morris, II, 191.*

[2] Sir James Sexton, earning a precarious living as a dock-walloper, was hurled into a barge by a sling of bags of grain which broke loose through a defective hook at the end of the rope-fall and an untrained incompetent at the winch. His right cheekbone was smashed, his eye forced out of the socket, and his skull fractured. For two hours he lay unattended on the wintry dockside, for such accidents were too common to be allowed to interfere with work. Owing to a defect in the Employers' Liability Act, then recently passed, no compensation was paid him.
                                        —*Sir James Sexton, Agitator, 74-5.*

sympathy of the public, proved stronger than the familiar weapon of starvation. For two months the docks remained closed. Then the dockowners gave way. Not only was "the docker's tanner" won but a great Union of "unskilled" labour—the Dock, Wharf and Riverside Labourers' Union—had been founded.

Yet by itself Trade Unionism was not enough. In a society seeking profits through world trade and based on economic fluctuation, an army of surplus labour was inescapable. Under the existing system its periodic unemployment was attended by the extreme of destitution and degradation. This hard rock of unorganised and soulless poverty was a constant threat to the Trade Union movement. In the highly-skilled trades, the aristocrat of labour could present a solid front to the capitalist aggressor. But elsewhere the employer could always count on the amorphous mass of starving poverty from which to draft non-Union or "free" labour into his factories and so break a strike. The bitterness of Union feeling against the "blackleg"—generally some poor down-and-out in need of a meal—and the sullen insistence on the rightfulness of peaceful picketing sprang from this.

Before labour could secure its full rights, the working class as a whole needed to be redeemed from extreme poverty and given self-respect, knowledge and *esprit de corps* through better housing, education and above all some sort of living wage. Organised Labour could not stand erect so long as it rested on the social morass of the submerged tenth. State action was necessary to give the workers' organisations—Trades Unions and co-operative societies—a secure field of operation. Otherwise the capitalist, with his constant recourse to new machinery displacing skilled men by unskilled, might beat them in the end.

It was the recognition of this that inspired the foundation in 1885 of the Fabian Society. It began as a little group of youthful radicals—drawn mostly from the middle-class—who had repudiated the *laissez-faire* tenets of utilitarianism but who retained the utilitarian's contempt for the inefficient and illogical. One of the members was a young, red-haired Irishman named Bernard Shaw who about this time electrified a conference of intellectuals and highbrow politicians by reading a paper to prove that the landlord, the capitalist and the burglar were equally the enemies of society. The Fabian thesis was that before social revolution could be achieved, the educated leaders of society must themselves be brought to see the necessity of revolution. In a law-abiding country like England mob oratory and emotional appeals to mass violence could never succeed. The capitalist state was not to be stormed but gradually occupied by a process of infiltration.

This was the policy of "permeation." It aimed at permeating the political organisations and institutions of the country with Socialist ideas without any open avowal of socialism. The Fabians were encouraged to seek membership of every society— Liberal, Tory or Labour, Christian or atheist—that would admit them and there secure by the arts of persuasion and lobbying the adoption of socialist measures. Especially were they to seek to permeate the Opposition, since by its very nature parliamentary Opposition is inclined to be revolutionary and always seeking to overturn the government.

The Fabians pinned their faith to an extension of legislative action. They announced that "the era of administration had come." The state was to be socialised through its own machinery. Instead of concerning themselves with such questions as free trade, retrenchment, Church disestablishment and the abolition of the House of Lords, the Fabians were to concentrate on free education, municipal trading, the provision of state-aided houses and small holdings and the graduated taxation of incomes and estates. They were not to dictate but to throw out suggestions. Nothing could have been better adapted to the spirit of the time or the character of England.

Fabianism went with the tide of contemporary thought. The Benthamites had long emphasised the sanatory qualities of reforming legislation supported by an incorruptible and centralised bureaucracy and inspectorate. As a result of their teaching, Liberals had purged the civil service of corruption in the name of utility and reason. An efficient administration, subject to a Parliament increasingly taught to regard itself as legislative rather than a debating assembly, was now to be applied for a purpose which its utilitarian sponsors would have viewed with horror—"the practical extension of the activity of the state."[1] The weapon the utilitarians had forged was to destroy economic utilitarianism.

For only the state's intervention could now redress the state's neglect. The only remedy for the evil of *laissez-faire* seemed to

[1] A. V. Dicey, *Law and Opinion in England*, 309.

be to repudiate *laissez-faire*. For many years past great teachers like Ruskin and T. H. Green at Oxford had impressed on younger consciences the ideal of social responsibility. A new generation of educated men and women was now growing up whose minds were contemplating the necessity of solving the problems created by a century of industrialism

But it was too late to undo what *laissez-faire* had done. In fifty years its hold on English thought had transformed the face of society. By 1881 seventeen and a half of out twenty-six millions were living in towns: by 1891 twenty-one millions out of twenty-nine millions. Eager Americans visiting Britain in the 'eighties and 'nineties looked in vain in the city streets for the hordes of rosy, golden-haired, blue-eyed children whom they had been led to expect in the Anglo-Saxon island. The national type, already affected in London by the constant influx of cheap foreign labour, was growing smaller and paler. Bad teeth, pasty complexions and weak chests were becoming British traits.

For the great mass of the population the traditionary, religious and rural England of the past had already passed out of memory. In its place had risen a new Britain of, "male employment, boy labour at relatively high wages, early marriages, over-worked mothers, high birth and death rates, high infant mortality, bad housing, a landscape scarred and smudged."[1] In the interests of capital the majority of the British people had assumed lives that bore little resemblance to those of their country forebears. The age-long birthright of man—pure air, fresh food, the sight and touch of growing nature, space for reflection—had ceased to be theirs. In its place they had been given the atmosphere of the smoke-stack and the pea-souper fog, the herd society of the streets, the gin palace and the halfpenny newspaper. After a generation they scarcely any longer missed what they had lost.

It was therefore idle to hope to return, with William Morris and the socialists, to the days of peasant communities and hand-craftsmanship. Capitalism had created the proletariat, and the proletariat was not a theory but a fact. It could not be destroyed or ignored: it could only be transformed by education and improved urban conditions. It was in this that the problem of the reformers lay.

[1] *Fifty Years, 1882-1932, Thomas Jones, The Life of the People, 177.*

Education and municipal reform were the intellectual themes of the hour. The need for the first impressed even reactionaries. "We must educate our masters," Robert Lowe had declared before the passing of Disraeli's Reform Bill. The older ideal of education based on religion and the teaching of hereditary crafts in the home had vanished with the migration into the towns. Only the most rudimentary instruction in reading, writing and arithmetic had as yet taken its place. The great mass of the nation was illiterate.[1] In 1869 only one British child in two was receiving any education at all. Of those, more than half were being taught in schools maintained by the Church of England, which together with other denominational and voluntary schools had for some time been in receipt of small government grants-in-aid.

In 1870 William Edward Forster, the Quaker Vice-President of Gladstone's first liberal administration, introduced an Education Act, setting up compulsory Local School Boards to provide secular elementary education for all children between the ages of five and thirteen[2] not already provided for by denominational schools. The cost was met partly out of state grants and rates and partly out of parents' fees. Owing to jealousy between the churches, the principle was laid down that all grant-aided education should be unsectarian. By this means religious teaching inspired by conviction was virtually ruled out. It thus came about—though no one seems to have realised it at the time—that the idealism of future generations, founded on a secular state education, differed from that of the old, which still derived from the Christian ethic. Between the two was to arise an almost unbridgeable gulf of misunderstanding.

Forster's Act affected little more than half the children in the country. It was unpopular with working-class parents who resented the limitation put on the family earning capacity by

---

[1] The ignorance of the young factory operatives in the 'forties—the forerunners of the new urban nation—is illustrated by the Report of the Childrens' Employment Commission, cited by Engels in his *Condition of the Working Class in England, 112-13.*

"Several had never heard the name of the Queen nor other names, such as Nelson, Wellington, Bonaparte; but it was noteworthy that those who had never heard even of St. Paul, Moses, or Solomon, were very well instructed as to the life, deeds, and character of Dick Turpin, and especially of Jack Sheppard. . . ."

"To the question who Christ was, Horne received the following answers among others: 'He was Adam '; 'He was an Apostle'; 'He was the Saviour's Lord's Son '; and from a youth of sixteen, 'He was a king of London long ago.' "

[2] The school leaving age was raised to 14 in 1900 by a Conservative Government which in the previous year established a national Board of Education.

school attendance.[1] Yet its underlying principle served the ends of organised Labour, not only by bringing cheap education within reach of the workers but by its indirect check on the competition of juvenile labour and its tendency to raise adult wages. A strong demand arose, therefore, to extend its scope. In 1876 a Conservative government tightened the obligations of parents and in 1880 a Liberal government made them universally compulsory. In 1891 another Conservative administration dispensed with fees and made elementary education free for all. Thus both parties acknowledged the collectivist principle that the rich should be compelled to contribute to the education of the poor.

The insignificance of the contribution could not alter the significance of the principle. Once established, the pressure of electoral numbers was sure in the end to do more. Because of the normal Anglo-Saxon indifference to the claims of intellect, the advance of state education was at first deliberate rather than rapid. But the figures speak for themselves. In 1870 the total grant out of revenue towards national education was £912,000. By 1888 it had risen to £4,168,000. By 1905 it was nearly £11,000,000 and the contribution from local rates another £7,000,000. At the turn of the century London alone was paying a million a year or £28 per child—almost the equivalent of a contemporary farm labourer's wage. After the liberal triumph in 1906 school medical services were established and public funds afforded for feeding necessitous children. To an old Chartist, who fifty years before had paid 6d. a week for his fees at a night school, the new policy appeared one of "coddling." "It is well to educate the people," he wrote, "but the tendency of much of the School Board policy of the day is to pauperise the people. Yet School Boards ought, above all things, to beware of undermining the independence of the individual."[2]

In municipal administration the collectivist advance was even more striking. Within a generation a vast new vested interest, officially subordinated to the general will as expressed in local

---

[1] A few years after the Act a visit by two antiquarians to the dingy neighbourhood of Tuthill Stairs, Newcastle, caused a panic among the mothers of the place who, mistaking the learned gentlemen for school inspectors, made a rush to hide their children.—*W. E. Adams, Memoirs of a Social Atom, II, 373.*

[2] *W. E. Adams, Memoirs of a Social Atom, II, 109-10.* Young Reginald Brett, afterwards Lord Esher, was wiser. "It is pleasant to see small and dirty boys reading the labels in the shop windows," he wrote in 1874. "It is one of the signs of the happier future. Shall I live to see education of children forced upon parents? Why can it not be done? That great good which must come, but for which we have to linger and wait?"—*Journals and Letters of Viscount Esher, I, 21.*

and parliamentary elections and controlled by salaried public servants, had sprung into existence in the island dedicated to the sanctity of private wealth. Parliamentary powers of collective control and ownership, and sometimes of monopoly, were sought and obtained, at first by the greater cities, later by the counties and smaller urban areas. The Local Government Act of 1888 established elective County Councils with control of local affairs and taxation. In that year London achieved its County Council—presently to revolutionise the life of its poorer inhabitants. The services of communal life which individual effort had failed to give to the vast urban agglomerations it had created, were supplied step by step by local authorities. They were paid for out of rates and loans charged on rates. The first successful flotation of municipal stock was made in 1880 by the Liverpool Corporation. By 1896 the local government debt of the country was already 200 million pounds. Only fourteen years later it was three times greater.

The first services performed by the new local authorities were lighting, paving, and cheap transport. By far the most important were education and housing. In nothing had *laissez-faire* achieved so much and so badly as in housing. It had built homes for millions of new factory workers, and not to endure but to perish. The vital attribute of a home is that it should be permanent. The principle of the jerry builder was to make as quick a profit as possible on as large a turnover for as little expenditure of labour and money. The houses went up fast enough but they did not last. They were not meant to.

They were built in rows and usually back to back—poky, hideous, uncomfortable and insanitary. The last thing that was thought of in making them was the convenience of the occupant.[1] Except in the granite towns and villages of East Lancashire and the West Riding they were so flimsy that they swayed with the wind and their walls so thin that their inmates were traditionally reputed to be able to hear their neighbours making up their minds.

Frequently such houses were erected by the companies that employed their occupants This was particularly so in iron and coal districts where there was little alternative employment. A man who lost his job lost his home. The rents were "kept back" from

---

[1] Jack Jones, the Labour M.P., said of one of them in the House of Commons that when a man got up in the morning he had to put his legs through the window to get his trousers on.

the weekly wages. The feeling of security and the pride of owner-ship which home should foster in a free man were lacking.

It was due to the slowly-growing realisation of at least some of this by the comfortable classes, many of whom were now encount-ering slum conditions at first hand in their "settlement" work, as well as to the galloping deterioration that had by now begun in the earlier industrial dwellings, that a Royal Commission on the Housing of the Poor was set up by Gladstone in 1884. It was, most significantly presided over by the Prince of Wales. Its interim report published a year later proposed a preliminary purchase at a statutory price of three old prison sites for housing estates. This, in itself, was a most important modification of utilitarian principle since it recurred—in however tentative a form—to the old medieval ideal not of a market but of a "fair" price. It was the first sign of recognition of a new, or rather a very old, ideal of government.

The Housing of the Working Classes Act of 1890 which embodied the main part of the recommendations of the Royal Commission stemmed if it did not reverse the rising tide of slum-dwelling. It created new powers of buying and demolish-ing insanitary houses, opening out congested alleys and *culs de sac* and building new dwellings on their sites. In practice, until tightened up by increased powers of government inspection and the growing force of organised working-class opinion, the Act was frequently evaded or perverted. Representation on local councils was usually confined to the smaller capitalists who alone had both the time and the inclination to give to municipal work: all too often they were prompted by the opportunities afforded of serving their own interests. Jerry builders were apt to pack Health and General Purposes Committees in order to frame—and what was worse supervise—the bye-laws about building and sanitation which Parliament had intended to control them. And the purchase of land for building purposes was often proceeded by elaborate and shady manœuvres by those who were—according to democratic notions—supposed to represent and protect the people but who in practice used the machinery of democracy to exploit them further. For it was for-gotten by reformers that every reform is dependent in the last resort on the men who carry it out, and national leadership, whether aristocratic or democratic, on the fitness, spiritual as well as intellectual, of those who govern.

Yet, as the theory of social responsibility increasingly haunted the minds of the educated minority, a process characteristically English took place. The larger and better-established capitalists—and above all their sons—began to devote themselves to the service of the public they or their forebears had fleeced. They did so without hope of further profit and out of a sense of *noblesse oblige*, gained more often than not at the new public schools which since Arnold of Rugby's days had opened their gates and their ideology to the commercial classes. A new type of public man arose—provincial, aggressive and democratic in method and appeal—whose interest lay neither in foreign policy nor parliamentary debate but in the extension of municipal services. Living on the private wealth acquired or inherited under *laissez-faire*, they were able to throw their entire energies into the work of mitigating the evils wrought by *laissez-faire*. These new, and to their individualist fathers' way of thinking, heretical radicals were still iconoclastic towards the older notions of privilege and decorum. But though they resented the power of the landed aristocracy and lost no opportunity of humbling it, they were no enemies to the capitalist and manufacturer. The very inroads they made on *laissez-faire* practice helped to maintain the prestige and opportunities of their class by appeasing the social unrest of the masses. The most famous of these local radical reformers was Joseph Chamberlain, the dapper young hardware merchant with the orchid, the monocle and the terrible republican sentiments who became Mayor of Birmingham in 1873 at 37, and President of the Board of Trade in Mr. Gladstone's second Administration in 1880.

In all this the domestic history of Britain during the last two decades of the nineteenth and the first of the twentieth century constituted the first act of a great revolution. During these years a vigorous capitalist and less vigorous but still powerful aristocratic England were converted to an elementary socialism whose basis was that the weak and inefficient should constitute a first charge on the strong and able. The pioneer activities of a humane and intelligent minority of their own members contributed to that conversion. But the real driving force came from the superior votes of the urban workers, which by a third Reform Act in 1884 had been reinforced by those of the county householders.

The ruling classes did not consciously admit their conversion, for they were unaware of it.[1] And their struggle against it, like all English struggles, was grudging and tenacious. But, while denouncing the name of Socialism which they believed to be synonymous with mob plunder and the bloody destruction of their homes and altars, they allowed socialist principles to inspire their laws and, in an illogical, piecemeal and incomplete way they increasingly applied socialist practice. For the void in the great industrial towns that their fathers' search for wealth had created left them no alternative. The more the towns grew the more it clamoured to be filled.

. . . .

The triumphs of science hastened the triumph of the collectivist. Gas and electric lighting and fuel, steam and electric transport, the telegraph and the telephone made for a communal rather than an individualist organisation of life. So did the course of capitalism itself. For the new collectivism that was imperceptibly destroying *laissez-faire* did not only spring from working-class discontent at *laissez-faire* conditions.

It arose out of the very core of Benthamism. For the Benthamite, in his exaggerated tenderness for the individual, proclaimed his right to make any contract he liked in the pursuit of his own interests. It followed that two or more individuals were free to associate in any way they chose and in pursuit of their aggregate interests to agree to act as a single person.

With the extension of machinery and transport, industry perpetually tended to increase its scale of operations. For this it needed ever more capital. The individual trader was thus increasingly impelled to bind himself in association with others. The

[1] Mr. Sidney Webb, now Lord Passfield, spoke of this unconscious conversion of the capitalist middle classes to Socialism in a conversation recorded by Mr. George Eastgate in *The Times* of 23rd August, 1902.

"The practical man, oblivious or contemptuous of any theory of the social organism or general principals of social organisation, has been forced, by the necessities of the time, into an ever deepening collectivist channel. Socialism, of course, he still rejects and despises. The individualist town councillor will walk along the municipal pavement, lit by municipal gas, and cleansed by municipal brooms with municipal water, and seeing by the municipal clock in the municipal market that he is too early to meet his children coming from the municipal school, hard by the county lunatic asylum and municipal hospital, will use the national telegraph system to tell them not to walk through the municipal park, but to come by the municipal tramway to meet him in the municipal reading-room by the municipal art gallery, museum and library where he intends to consult some of the national publications in order to prepare his next speech in the municipal town hall in favour of the nationalisation of canals and the increase of Government control over the railway system. ' Socialism, Sir,' he will say, ' don't waste the time of a practical man by your fantastic absurdities. Self-help, Sir, individual self-help, that's what's made our city what it is.' "

fictitious trading personages so created enjoyed the legal rights of the individual of *laissez-faire* society. But the powers created by their joint wealth far exceeded those of a single person. Just as organised labour acquired rights against the individual, so organised capital assumed powers that left the private merchant a pigmy in a realm of giants.

Though the ordinary man was slow to perceive what was happening, his vaunted liberty and significance were dwindling every year. Even by the 'seventies a handful of railway companies owned wealth equal in the aggregate to three-quarters of the National Debt. In the course of their business such corporations sought vast powers. Where these were denied them by the common law, recourse for legislation could be had to a House of Commons in which the successful business man and financier was beginning to succeed the country gentleman as the predominant type. Through new forms of investment the entire propertied class of the country was learning to delegate its wealth and responsibilities to corporate bodies. The historic justification of private property had been that it fostered responsibility and acted as a bulwark against tyranny. It was now being used by the individual to purchase freedom from responsibility. It was accumulating despotic powers in the hands of mechanical corporations without conscience or sense of obligation.

A generation which had been taught to believe that the pursuit of profits was the one road to national prosperity made no attempt to secure the threatened birthright of their race. The freedom of the subject inherited from the great English patriots and martyrs was unconsciously bartered away for increased dividends. The later Victorians, for all the probity of their private and domestic lives, cheerfully surrendered the liberties of their unborn children to the soulless corporations that gave them wealth. They never paused to reflect what they were doing.

Yet in all that they did as individuals the Victorians were guided by conscience: in this they were the inheritors of the English past. No generation ever had a higher record in this. The honesty and integrity of the Victorian merchant and manufacturer was a byword throughout the world. Again and again private charity, pity and a sense of duty and public service redeemed the consequences of a false economic philosophy.

Yet the conscience of the individual was also betrayed in the end to the theory of the overriding sanctity of profit-making.

In the late 'fifties and early 'sixties Liberal governments to suit the convenience of the commercial community passed legislation conferring on joint-stock companies the privilege of limited liability. Henceforward fictitious bodies, enjoying the legal rights of individuals, could incur unlimited financial obligations without their individual shareholders becoming fully responsible for them.

Up to this time a man's power to make money by transferring his credit and freedom of commercial action to others was restrained by his liability for the obligations they might incur. This check on irresponsible delegation was now removed. A man could grow rich in security and even innocence from business practices which would have outraged his conscience as an individual. He could avoid both the risks and stigma of transactions done by others in pursuit of profits in which he shared.

At first the investing public was slow to avail itself of the opportunities afforded by the Companies Act of 1862.[1] For a generation the use of limited liability was chiefly confined to the professional commercial community. But after the failure of the City of Glasgow Bank in 1879, when many private share-holders were called upon to meet obligations hundreds of times greater than the value of their shares, private investors increasingly entrusted their money to concerns carrying only limited liability. During the last eight years of the century more than thirty thousand limited companies were floated and ten thousand wound up. In 1899 there were 27,969 registered companies in the United Kingdom with a paid-up capital of £1,512,098,098: by 1914, 64,692 with £2,531,947,661. Ownership of the nation's wealth was thus increasingly separated from its control. And the conscience of the individual ceased to regulate its use.

The consequences of the Companies Act of 1862 were perhaps greater than that of any single measure in English parliamentary history. They completed the divorce between the Christian conscience and the economic practice of everyday life. They paganised the commercial community. Henceforward an astute man by adherence to legal rules which had nothing to do with morality could grow immensely rich by virtue of shuffling off

---

[1] By the Companies Act of 1862, it became possible for any one to found a limited liability company by obtaining signatures to a memorandum of registration and adding the word "Limited" to its nomenclature.

his most elementary obligations to his fellows. He could not only grow rich by such means. He could grow immensely powerful.

The break-up of the medieval church had transferred power from the Christian state, with its theoretic moral control over all human economic activities, to the landowner, who though he may have begun as an avaricious courtier and a plunderer of monastic lands, was gradually transmuted by the magic of the English countryside and the personal responsibility attaching to his rustic form of wealth into the country gentleman. In less than two centuries the hard, grasping usurer of Tudor times had grown into Sir Roger de Coverley. But by that time the pursuit of wealth was already taking new forms. The great fortunes of the eighteenth century were made by overseas trade. The Turkey merchant and the East India nabob were the pioneers of the new national economy. They also were absorbed by marriage and purchase into the ranks of the landed gentry until in the early nineteenth century their place was taken by still newer leaders— the industrialists and shipowners, the capitalists of coal, cotton and iron.

The principle of limited liability now set up another arbiter of economic society. The company promoter—Sir Georgius Midas of du Maurier's drawings and uncle Ponderevo of Wells's romance —was the social wonder of the last years of the old and the first of the new century. Before his glittering if nebulous throne all who had money to invest prostrated themselves, lured by his promise of quick and easy profits. His craft consisted in raising money on loan to float or purchase commercial concerns on favourable terms and in subsequently disposing of them at a profit, not necessarily by developing their productive capacity but by enhancing their market value. He raised the latter by the arts of display and suggestion as a stock breeder raises a fat pig. His journeymen were advertisers, publicity agents, stockbrokers and share pushers. If in the course of his over sanguine efforts to boost them, his concerns collapsed before they were ripe for selling—and in his early days they frequently did— he could escape under cover of limited liability, wind up the company and with the full blessing of the law start again. The burden was borne by the company's creditors and by such credulous investors as, allured by his arts, had bought their shares at an exaggerated price.

But the effects of these operations did not stop there. For by directing money into enterprises designed not so much for stable long-term production as for quick capital appreciation the new financier tended to make industrial employment even more precarious than it had been before. Mushroom companies sprang up in all directions to initiate or develop industrial processes which could have little or no enduring future. This directly affected the working man and his social background. More than ever his job and home became dependent on circumstances beyond his control. As an individual he became more and more helpless.

The stimulus to joint stock manufacturing and trading afforded by the principle of limited liability had another fatal consequence on the life of the working man. Under *laissez-faire* individualism it at least paid to be efficient. The workman who by his skill and industry furthered the interests of his employer had a reasonable chance of promotion, for he was too valuabe to lose. But when the control of business passed out of the hands of the private employer using his own capital into that of the financial company representing an intangible mass of absentee shareholders without active knowledge of its affairs, the industrious workman found it increasingly difficult to better himself. His efficiency and steadfastness had no value to directors whose only aim was to sell the concern that employed him at an inflated value. In any case he was less likely to be noticed by managers whose stake in the business was confined to salaries paid them by the shareholders and who were not personally interested in its success. Thus the conscientious workman was increasingly discouraged. The man with ambition and intelligence, instead of identifying himself with the industrial system of which he was part, was driven to rebel against it. Instead of becoming a small capitalist, he became a socialist.

Adam Smith had always maintained that manufacturing by joint-stock companies must prove injurious to the public interest. He argued that efficiency and consequently wealth resulted from every man attending scrupulously to his own self-interest. Such attention could not be successfully delegated. A large joint-stock company, financed by distant and "amateur" shareholders and managed by salaried nominees, was bound to be less efficient than a small concern directed by the man who would be the sole beneficiary if it succeeded and the chief loser if it failed.

With the growth of this kind of business, the control of commerce passed into less vigorous hands. The financial speculator with the talent for exploiting the shareholder and the man of routine who gave no trouble to the speculator took the place of the man of initiative and drive. Genius was discouraged: mediocrity preferred.

Had the world been governed by the purely mechanical and mathematical processes that so fascinated the pedants of *laissez-faire*, this would have mattered little, for it could not have endured. The joint-stock company would have cut its own throat and so perished. Its inefficiency would have promptly limited its capacity for harm. But what Adam Smith failed to see was that manufacturing by joint-stock companies might be successful though injurious to the public. For, as has been pointed out in a brilliant analysis of contemporary commercial practise,[1] "success for limited liability companies does not depend upon efficiency but upon an ability to corner the market." With the enormous concentration of capital secured through successful company promotion, monopoly of this kind became increasingly easy. The public, and not the joint-stock shareholders, paid for the inefficiency of the men who managed their concern. For though the latter might be, and generally were, less efficient as producers, they were not necessarily so as advertisers, manipulators of credit and political log-rollers.

The growth of collectivism in finance widened the gulf between the man of property and the proletarian. The latter, unless he had a gamin genius for financial manipulation, found it increasingly hard to rise out of his class. The former, if he invested his capital wisely, found it increasingly easy to live on its fruits without contact with the industrial processes in which it was employed. He became a *rentier*; a mere enjoyer of automatic wealth to whose making he contributed nothing in thought or effort. His responsibility towards those who did so became negligible.

.   .   .   .

All this strengthened the case for the state control of private wealth. The justification of privilege and power is the fulfilment of social duty. Possessions divorced from any personal sense of obligation seem a kind of theft on all who do not share them. They outrage the moral sense of mankind. Once the

[1] A. J. Penty, *A Guildsman's Interpretation of History*, 264.

sanctity of *laissez-faire* itself was repudiated, the riches of the Forsytes and still more of their *rentier* children were impossible to justify. They seemed to serve no other purpose but the private enjoyment of their owners. Even where, as often happened in kindly England, their possessors spent their fortunes in charitable deeds, their philanthropy had no visible connection with the processes, harsh and inhuman, by which they obtained their wealth.

The socialist attack that developed as the nineteenth century drew to its close was therefore levelled at the whole principle of private property. Because individual wealth was abused, it was argued that it should be abolished altogether. As a reaction against the maldistribution and inhuman conditions of capitalist production, the old demand was made—long unheard in Christian England—that production should be directly for use and not for profit. But those who voiced it, being either men without property or *rentiers* whose ownership was divorced from personal use, demanded not that the producer and craftsmen should resume their lost control over their own industry, but that the state should assume the functions of the capitalist. They were so accustomed to the despotism of absentee capital that their only remedy for its ill effects was to transfer its ownership from the individual to the community, and its control from the capitalist director to the state bureaucrat. They made no attempt to restore it to those who could make the best use of it—not the people in the abstract but the people as individual producers. The scale of modern machinery and the gargantuan organisation of life to which it had given rise seemed to them to render such an attempt impracticable.

The intellectual Socialist, who superseded the more sentimental Christian Socialist of the past, appeared as the champion of an omnipotent state. He argued that the state should restrict the power of the rich and powerful by taxing and ultimately confiscating the wealth that was the source of their power. In 1893 the Fabian Society issued its famous manifesto demanding the ownership by the community of the means of production, distribution and exchange. In the same year the Independent Labour Party was founded, dedicated to the same end and seeking it by direct socialist representation in Parliament and on local authorities.

From this development arose a curious contradiction in the

character of the British working-class movement. Its intellectual leaders set up the state as the *deus ex machina* which was to rescue society from the abuses of individualism. But the state is an abstraction and its supremacy can only be exercised through individuals. If the state is to be all powerful, the individuals who exercise its authority must be all powerful, too. To a Latin, German or Russian socialist, accustomed from birth to the ideal of an overriding centralised despotism, there was nothing repugnant in such a claim. But in England, the traditional home of individual liberty, a proposition that restored to a state official the power of the Stuart kings was disquieting. To argue that this omnipotent Whitehall would in turn be controlled by the elected representatives of the people was merely to say that uncontrolled power should rest in the hands of whoever could persuade or hoax the electorate into entrusting it to them. It might be a party caucus, it might be a popular dictator. It might even be the very capitalist whom the new state power was designed to suppress.

The early socialists in their enthusiasm for their thesis did not detect the weakness in their remedy. Their emotional appeal to the masses, and even more to their middle-class sympathisers, was to that love of liberty which the capitalist monopoly over the work and daily life of millions had outraged. Yet by attacking the private ownership of property they struck unconsciously at the foundation on which in the historic polity of England's individual liberty had always rested. Because the privilege of ownership had ceased to be widespread as in the past and had become restricted to the few, they supposed that its destruction would extend the freedom of the many.

They forgot that, apart from economic liberty, political liberty has little meaning. Only so long as a man knows that he can defy superior power and still support himself and his loved ones is he a free man. Without that knowledge, whatever his standard of living or theoretical status, he is a kind of slave. And when all power is vested in the state and the state is the owner both of the workers' homes and the means of production, private liberty becomes a rather nebulous thing. There was little enough liberty for the workers under the rule of the nineteenth-century joint-stock capitalist, except, of course, the liberty to starve. But in the Fabian paradise which was to take its place, though there might be a great deal more comfort, there was to

be no liberty at all. The State, or rather the state official, was
to rule all things.

Such a paradise, at first sight, seemed to offer so many things
of which the English worker stood in need. It offered better
wages and conditions of labour, cleaner and more commodious
homes, social services and public amenities in place of the drab
negation of the utilitarian city, above all the end of the shameless
exploitation of poverty by wealth which robbed men and women
of their self-respect. Yet when the promised land was examined
more closely, it was seen to contain a presence which was not
acceptable to an Englishman. For there in the midst of the
garden stood Nosey Parker with the sword of the all-seeing
State. And of all men none was more temperamentally likely
to resent that presence than the rough and liberty-loving
workman of England.

The socialist thinkers could see no problem in this. The
dictatorship of the state would be exercised, they argued, on
behalf of the working classes. Being for the most part men
of the study, they failed to see how their republic would work
out in practice. They never realised how heavily in an overcrowded country, in which the productive work and home life
of the million had been centred in great towns, the tyranny of
the official, if vested with absolute power, would press on the
working man. It is inevitably the poor not the rich who most
feel the humiliating effects of jack-in-office despotism, for as
individualists they have so much less power of appeal against it.
The Socialists in their passion for statistics—the instrument they
inherited from the utilitarians—forgot that the liberty of the
workers in the aggregate may bear little relation to the liberty of
the worker as an individual. They did not see how pathetically
helpless he might be against the pricks of petty tyranny.

The English working man, even after a century of factory
labour, did not take readily to aggregate conceptions of himself.
For all his exploitation he was the heir to the English ages: to
Simon de Montfort, John Hampden and old Kelly of Silverstone
who wanted nails over his coffin to stop his neighbours trampling
on him. He did not want liberty as a member of a class: he
wanted it as a man. An official bossing him about was no less a
tyrant in his eyes because he was vested with popular authority.
The English proletarian was a contradiction in terms: economically a wage slave, he was still spiritually and in his own eyes a

freeman. He was easily "put upon" but did not readily brook
interference. His fists and his tongue were always quick to assert
his independence.

The love of liberty came out in his phrases, in his jokes, in his
invincible, half-blasphemous, ironical commentary on the ups
and downs of his harsh life. His " 'Ere, who d'yre think yre a'getting at?" his "Tell us anuvor, guvnor," like his jokes about
mother-in-laws and old gentlemen slipping on banana skins,
were part of his protests against interference and pompous power.
He refused to part with his humour, his right to grumble, his
right to what little liberty the wage struggle left him to go
about his private business in his own way. Not clearly understanding how he had been swindled out of his birthright—home,
status and privilege—he was yet aware of the dignity of his
descent. He knew himself to be as good as any man, and better.

Robbed by the machine of pride and pleasure in his work, he
still kept inviolate his right to take pleasure in his liberty. His
most precious possession was his right to enjoy himself in his
own way. On Hampstead Heath or Hackney Marshes on a bank
holiday one saw him at his most uproarious: expressing himself
in cockney carnival: costers in all their pride of pearls and
feathers, frolicsome young women with tambourines singing
and making unblushing advances to jolly strangers, old parties
with bottles of stout and jests for every passer-by, and young and
old pressing into the side-shows and booths where giants and
dwarfs, nigger minstrels and performing dogs and every
variety of freak and novelty made merry for the delight of the
disinherited son, returned for a glorious hour to his father's
kingdom of freedom. So in more normal times in the trains from
Stepney to Highbury one might in the course of half an hour's
journey encounter a lad playing airs on a fiddle, an old man
beguiling his journey with an accordion and a chorus of young
workmen singing in unison. By being jolly and having a good
time when the occasion offered the English poor reminded themselves and the rich men they served that Jack was as good as his
master and that freedom was his birthright.

One saw industrial England at its roughest and freest in any
town where seamen congregated. In the Ratcliff Highway in the
'eighties and 'nineties almost every house was a tavern with a
dance hall at the back where a steam organ kept up perpetual
revelry. The whole place resounded with music, the shouting of

drunken sailors and their bright scarved girls, the clatter of the
steam organs and the strumming of nigger minstrels. But any
poor street on frequent occasion presented the same scene in
miniature: a German band, a dancing polar bear, a visit from
the Salvation Army or a band of morris dancers could bring the
population of every crowded house into the street. Most poor
districts had their quota of barrel-organs, whose owners, having
finished their day's work in wealthier parts, could generally be
prevailed upon to oblige with a tune to which the whole street
stepped it on the flags. A wedding was always the occasion for the
hire of a barrel organ for the day and for continuous music from
the time of the bridal couple's return to the adjournment of the
company to the nearest "boozer." Only a fight—a common
occurrence—could bring the harmony to a stop.

The supreme embodiment of the surviving character of the
English working people was the music hall. Here art held up
the mirror to nature. It was, as Mr. J. B. Booth of *Pink 'Un* fame
has written, "a purely native product, cheery, unregenerate,
optimistic." Springing spontaneously out of the sing-song of the
upper tavern room and the old out-of-door gardens of the artisan
of the pastoral past it became for a space of time a British institution. Its morality was to make the best of a bad job: its purpose
to make every one free and easy. Performers and audience, under
the genial and bacchanalian presidency of the chairman, with his
buttonhole, his mesmeric eye and his town crier's voice, combined
in expressing their own individuality. At the old South London,
whenever there was a hitch in the programme, the chairman,
"Bob" Courtney, glittering with false diamonds and laying aside
his glass and cigar, would rise to sing his traditional song,
"Britannia's Voice of Thunder," while the whole audience kept
time, drowning singing and even big drum with an equally
traditional refrain of "good old Bob! Bob! Bob! Bob!" Its songs,
circulating in succession among the entire population—
"Champagne Charlie," "Lardi-da," "It's all done by kindness,"
"How are your poor feet," "What ho! she bumps," "Pretty Polly
Perkins of Paddington Green," "Ask a policeman," and "Knock
'em in the old Kent Road"—were vernacular, irreverent, democratic, yet intensely individualistic, as of a nation of disinherited,
cheery aristocrats, and arose from deeply felt experience: they
were the English answer to the lot which had befallen the
English worker. They told a man (in rousing chorus) to "paddle

his own canoe," "to cling to his love like the ivy," and to fill himself up with "beer, beer, glorious beer," bade Tommy make room for uncle, and the nation put the foreigner in his place:

> "I'd wake men from their torpor, and every foreign pauper
>   That helps to make the sweater rich, and wages always low,
> I'd send aboard a ship, Sir, for an everlasting trip, Sir,
>   And a chance give to the English if I only bossed the show."

Such rough songs spoke of unchanging English virtues: of courage and cheerfulness in adversity, of loyalty to old "pals," of constancy to home and wife. There is scarcely a more beautiful, there is certainly no more English ballad in the whole range of song than that which Albert Chevalier wrote for his cockney impersonation of the old London workman philosophising over his pipe on the faithful wife of his youth:

> "We've been together now for forty years,
>   And it don't seem a day too much,
> Oh, there ain't a lidy living in the land
>   As I'd swop for my dear ole ' Dutch.'"

But above all the music hall expressed the English passion for liberty: the English desire, so hard to translate into the life of the factory, to follow the current of one's own nature and be true to it by being free. What was, however bad it seemed, had to be and was therefore in a humorous way good, since man being free could turn his necessity to glorious gain. So the fat woman, the grace and opportunity of youth gone for ever as it was for most of her audience, would stand up, mountainous and un-deterred, and, announced by the leering chairman as "your old favourite, So-and-So," send her steam-roundabout voice pulsat-ing through the thick pipe and cigar smoke:

> "I weigh sixteen stoney O!
> I'm not all skin and boney O!"

So, in a more studied and perfect expression of the inner soul of a great people who had lost everything but its cheerfulness and courage, Marie Lloyd in a later age, when the old music hall was dying, would sing her song "Dilly Dally": a vinous old female, moist-eyed, wandering but invincible:

"My old man said, Follow the van
And don't dilly dally on the way!
Off went the cart with the home packed in it,
I walked behind with my old cock linnet.
But I dillied and dallied, dallied and dillied,
Lost the van and don't know where to roam.
I stopped on the way to have the old half-quartern,
And I can't find my way home."

. . . .

It was to the people whose life this vulgar, proud and humane
art represented that the Socialist offered his collectivist remedy.
He assumed, not without the justification of logic, that the
English working man was already a proletarian slave and that
he would be only too willing to band himself as a nameless
comrade in the great army of his class against the rich and
privileged. But this was not so. The downtrodden wage-slave
did not think of himself as such but as the rightful inheritor—
as by ancestry he was—of a free tradition of transmitted privilege.
He only wanted to get back his own: to be the great gentleman
he knew himself to be, enjoying, generous and carefree. All the
while that the socialist propagandist was telling him of the proletarian heaven, he was dreaming of the day when a rich unknown
cousin would die in Australia or the horses he so hopefully and
religiously backed each week would bring him a fortune and he
would be able to have a house and a garden of his own and go to
race meetings and cricket matches every day instead of working
with his fellow proletarians in the factory.

Thus it came about that the first missionaries of the new
socialist religion were treated with derision by the rough, un-
believing multitude. They were denounced as atheists, anarchists
and republicans, as liars and quacks who offered " sum'at for nothing." Their meetings were frequently broken up amid rude
noises. In those days it was the Socialists who were heckled by
the local toughs and practical jokers, not the Tories. England
was so accustomed to being governed by well-spoken gentlemen
in top hats that the spectacle of an avowed Socialist going down
to the House of Commons in a check cap with a brass band
blaring at his side profoundly shocked many humble men and
women. Working men were at first exceedingly suspicious of
members of their own class who sought to enter Parliament as
if they were toffs and were always ready to listen to any

malicious charge, however wild, of peculation or self-seeking brought against them. Their creed was regarded, in pubs and other places, where sound men congregated, as laughable if not lunatic. In the 1895 election—a Conservative triumph—only one working man held his seat and every one of the twenty-seven candidates put up by the virgin independent Labour Party suffered defeat at the polls.[1] It was not till the great Conservative rout of January, 1906, when the rising tide of collectivism swept an almost revolutionary Liberal government into power that a Parliamentary Labour Party took its place as a permanent force in politics with a solid bloc of 51 seats and a strength sufficient to sway the course of legislation.

Even many of the Trade Union and Co-operative Society leaders—often stalwarts of the local Tory working mens' club—regarded the new socialism with disfavour. It was too highbrow and foreign for their shrewd liking[2]: too far removed from the familiar tastes and prejudices of the simple men they represented. Had those who represented the larger forces of organised capital been a little more sympathetic towards their Labour *vis-à-vis* instead of treating them, as they too often did, as impertinent inferiors who had forgotten their place, the intellectual socialist movement might well had died still-born.

Yet a new spirit was abroad in the land. A reconciliation between Capital and Labour that might have been possible a few years earlier, became harder with the coming of a new generation. For just as the first translation of the scriptures spelt out by unlettered zealots lent wings to an earlier English revolution, so the education of the board school helped to carry a new conception of life into the homes of the people. To cater for the needs of this new class of reader, a halfpenny press made its appearance, jejune, snappy, sensational. The first in the field was the radical *Star*—the "twinkle, twinkle little star" of the late 'eighties and 'nineties. It had many imitators. Those who controlled this revolutionary power might differ in politics and educational purpose, but the circulation of their papers and the

[1] The Party Chest for the Election totalled only £400. Ardent supporters pawned their watches, Sunday suits, accordions and fiddles.—*Sir James Sexton, Agitator, 145.*

[2] "Much daring, I went one night to speak at the Battersea Branch of the Social-Democratic Federation where I was so belaboured with words about exploitation, proletariat, bourgeois and others of learned length and thundering sound just then imported from Germany that I believe I retired sore all over and determined to go no more to Social-Democratic Federation Branches. And I never have."
—*G. N. Barnes, From Workshop to War Cabinet, 42.*

advertisements from which their profits came depended on their giving to the million what the million wanted.[1] Being obscure it wanted flattery and being poor a share of the pleasures of the rich. The cheap newspaper gave it the one and fed its appetite for the other. It promised that a time was coming when the hungry should be filled with good things.

For the intelligent young worker, to whom state education had given the key to the world of books and new ideas, and to whom the pub and the humorous philosophy of his class were insufficient solace, the background of life — even though it was already vastly improved — was dreary and uninspiring. As Joe Toole remembered, it was that of the street corner, the smell of the tripe-works, the clatter of clogs, the street brawls, short commons, the pawnshop and the cries of women giving birth to new citizens.[2] The usual lot was to start selling papers after school hours at eleven, borrowing 4½d. to purchase thirteen with a hope of making 2d. profit for each bundle sold. Three years later the scholar left school to plunge into a battle for life which took the form of constantly changing casual labour—sweeping floors or streets, holding horses' heads for commercial travellers, laying tram tracks, storekeeping, running errands and monotonous machine-minding sometimes for ten hours at a stretch. All these occupations were "blind alley": the weaker brethren never climbed beyond them out of the ruck of the unskilled. Between jobs one stood at the corner of the street or scoured the shop windows for a notice of "Boy Wanted." In such a start to life there were constant temptations: the skylarking, chi'oiking gang of boon companions who slipped imperceptibly from practical joking into petty larceny on sweet shops and battles with sticks and broken glass; the pubs to which a boy became accustomed from his earliest years, the racecourse and the bookie at the street corner. Later came the long losing battle with poverty, undernourishment and insecurity, the home with the verminous walls and broken window-sashes in the crowded dirty street, the risk of accident and maiming, and the certainty sooner or later of "slack times" and unemployment with the sickening tramp from factory gate to gate, the days of

---

[1] During a strike, a delegation of employers called on the editor of a popular newspaper to remonstrate with him for upholding the strikers' cause. "Well, gentlemen," he replied, "the working man's penny is as good as yours, and there's a damned sight more of 'em!"—W. E. Adams, Memoirs of a Social Atom, II., 615.

[2] Fighting Through Life, 20-21.

idle, hopeless hunger, the rot of body and soul and the dread of the workhouse at the end of that bitter road.

It was to those whom this dreary heritage inspired to bitter anger that the new socialism made its initial appeal. Behind the solid structure of Trade Unionism and the brittle façade of the intelligentsia fermented the spirit and fervour of a new religion. During the quarter of a century that preceded the first world war, Socialism was preached through the crowded cities of Britain as Methodism had been preached in the eighteenth century and Puritanism in the seventeenth—as a salvationist crusade. Into the drab lives and starved minds of the industrial masses came a new message of hope and righteousness, uttered on evangelist platforms by ardent believers with red ties and flashing eyes: that poverty and injustice could be abolished by state action. The little handful of the elect who gathered in the north-country market square after some crushing electoral defeat to sing Carpenter's Labour Hymn, "England, arise! the long, long night is over," was like the grain of seed which grew into a great tree.

Among the younger generation of the workers there were many who read more seriously. Henry George's *Progress and Poverty* sold in thousands, and Blatchford's *Merrie England*, published at 6d. in 1894, in tens of thousands. The latter's humble *Clarion*, issued under many difficulties, made proselytes wherever the factory chimneys and slated roofs marked the abode of the toiling masses. For humbler minds the new gospel was preached in its simplest and most appealing form. The bloated capitalist with his white top-hat, his gold watch-chain and his money-bags, was the Devil who sucked the blood of the workers. The upright young Socialist with his Union ticket and his Fabian pamphlet in his pocket was the pioneer of a new and better world, ready for martyrdom if need be but never for compromise with the evil spirit of greed which kept the virtuous proletariat in chains. In a more sophisticated way this point of view was broadly adopted by a whole generation of middle-class writers and artists who, appalled by the accumulating evils of *laissez-faire* industrialism, carried the message of Socialism into their art. Generous youth at Oxford and Cambridge and newer centres of learning thrilled at the gospel of apocalyptic hope: the school-masters, journalists, clergymen and civil servants of the future went out to their labour consciously or unconsciously imbued with the teaching of Socialists of genius like Shaw and Wells.

Yet the advance of Socialism was nearly always anticipated by the premature retreat of the individualist. Before the vanguard of the red revolutionaries reached each successive barricade the capitalists were already receding. Many of the demands of organised Labour were granted by Liberal and Tory politicians— quick to sense the changing wind of electoral favour—long before its Socialist representatives were in a position to enforce them. Successive Employers' Liability Acts limited and finally abrogated the old legal doctrine of common employment. Under pressure from the Unions the scope of the Factory Acts was steadily extended.[1] The Workmen's Compensation Act of 1897 made an employer theoretically liable for all the risks of his workers' employment. Charity, now invested with the prim pince-nez of the statistical bureaucrat, was restored to its former place as a civic obligation. The stigma of pauperism was removed and those in receipt of poor law relief were admitted to the franchise. Labour Exchanges were established at the expense of the taxpayer to help find work for the unemployed. Small holdings were provided for agricultural labourers.

The Socialist principle that the State as the ultimate owner of all property had the right to tax capital as well as income was admitted by the imposition of Death Duties in Sir William Harcourt's Liberal budget of 1893. Fourteen years later Mr. Asquith introduced the distinction between earned and unearned incomes and a new impost on very rich men called super-tax. In order to finance a nation-wide scheme of old-age pensions and other "rare and refreshing fruit for the parched lips of the multitude," the new levy was extended to all incomes of more than £5000 a year, by the Liberal Chancellor, David Lloyd George. To a modern reformer, saddened by the omnipresent spectacle of human greed, injustice and muddle, such modest measures of working-class amelioration, now taken for granted, may appear trifling. To a Liberal of the 'sixties they would have seemed a revolutionary interference with the laws of supply and demand and a half-way step to wholesale confiscation and Communism. To many old-fashioned persons like the Conservative die-hard peers, who sacrificed the powers of their own House in a last desperate attempt to stay the new electoral will, they seemed so even in 1910.

[1] Within a few years of bringing the dockers within the scope of the Acts, the number of dock accidents was halved.

E.S.   Q

For in the bewildering pace of modern evolution men have forgotten how short a period divides our age from that of the *laissez-faire* 'sixties, how vast are the ameliorating changes in the conditions of the industrial worker which have been achieved in the course of a single life-time. Because the world is still imperfect and the evil curse of the past not wholly expiated, it is often assumed that nothing has been won. Old men who grew up in the Victorian industrial scene tell a different tale.

For the underdog it was a far cry from the socialised industrial England of Lloyd George's budgets, still more from that of Baldwin and Ramsay MacDonald, to the grim commonwealth of liberty to survive or perish of the mid-nineteenth century: from the omniscient government inspector, the statutorily enforced closing hours and half holidays, the working-class housing estate with its bathrooms and gardens to the "young ladies" of Madame Elise's dressmaking establishment with their fifteen hours' working day and airless, fever-stricken dormitory, the filthy, ragged child crossing-sweepers sleeping under the Adelphi arches, and the days when W. E. Adams, tramping through Salford in search of work, found at Peel Park with its Museum and Free Library an almost solitary example of municipal enlightenment.

Looking back in 1923, one whose whole life had been passed in the service of the Labour movement which had raised him from a poor apprentice's bench to a Privy Councillorship and a seat in the Cabinet, made an attempt to sum it all up. "I have seen many lands," he wrote, "but none as good as my own. I have mixed with many peoples but found none with so large measure of fellow feeling or sense of fair play.

"And, finally, I have seen freedom broadening down to the class in which I was born and bred and which I have tried to serve. When I was young, working folk were uneducated and unenfranchised. They were poor and dependent and their working days were bounded by age and want without concern by the State which their labour had enriched. Now they have at least a modicum of education, they are politically as well as industrially organised, and although there is still unemployment and, in too many instances, fear of want, yet these grim problems are being tackled with greater knowledge and more humane feeling than ever before. I take the present signs and tokens as indications of better things to be."[1]

[1] G. N. Barnes, *From Workshop to War Cabinet*, 295.

All this was true. The good man, looking back on his life of struggle and seemingly miraculous achievement, knew how much greater were the opportunities of the young workers of the new age than were those of the old. But the young who had never experienced the full fury of the storm of *laissez-faire* merely knew that they were born into a world of mean streets, monotonous labour, cramping poverty and narrowing uncertainty. They inherited from the past, not only elementary and secondary schools, labour exchanges, and Council houses, but bad digestions, uninspiring surroundings and the instability of a commercial system based not on human welfare but on profits. They were better off than their parents, but they were not satisfied with their lot. For their instincts, as well as the professional preachers of discontent, told them that something was still lacking.

CHAPTER SEVEN

"Lest We Forget!"

"If you're planning for one year plant grain; if you're planning for ten years plant trees; if you're planning for a hundred years plant men."
—*Old Chinese Proverb.*

THE summer of 1879 was the worst recorded in modern times. It rained continuously. Everywhere the harvest blackened in the fields, and farmers were faced with ruin, landlords with depleted rentals. In England and Wales alone three million sheep died of rot. Meanwhile industry struggled against one of those periodic slumps which seemed inseparable from the capitalist system. It was a universal tale of woe : of cataclysmic falls in prices and streets full of unemployed. The fog which lay over London that winter—yellow, choking and foreboding—seemed to symbolise something out of joint in the times. The pursuit of wealth for its own sake was resulting in what? For a moment the British vision seemed to have grown too narrow: the basis of a community which lived on an uncertain and uncontrollable export trade too small.

Yet for industry the trade depression of the early 'eighties was only a passing phase: a pause in the progress of expansion. It was followed in due course by recovery and renewed prosperity. Demand for industrial products was still expanding faster than supply: rich veins of unexploited markets remained to be developed by the capitalist. But for English agriculture the blackened crops of 1879 and the years of continued rain and cold that followed marked the end of an era. It never recovered.

It had enjoyed a glorious evening. The three decades between the repeal of the Corn Laws and the fall of Disraeli's last administration were the golden age of farming. The bumper harvests of the 'fifties and 'sixties had been accompanied by expanding home markets, plentiful capital and cheap transport and labour. The landed estates of Britain, employing more than a million skilled workers and supporting the richest aristocracy the world had seen, gave bread to 17,000,000 and meat to the whole population.

Those were the days when the Earl of Ladythorne sat at the covert side like a gentleman at his opera stall, thinking what a good thing it was to be a lord with a sound digestion and plenty of cash, when tenant farmers built conservatories and planted ornamental trees, and young ladies in flowing skirts and jackets and little feathered caps played croquet on ancient lawns or gossiped over "hair brushings" in rooms once habited by Elizabethan statesmen and Carolean divines. The great parks with their noble trees slumbered in the sunlight of those distant summers: children born heirs to the securest and happiest lot humankind had ever known, rode and played in their shade never guessing that in their old age they would see the classic groves felled by the estate breaker and the stately halls pulled down or sold to make convalescent homes for miners or county asylums.

Yet all the while behind the dark curtain of time, harvests were ripening on the virgin plains of other continents which were to put an end to all this prosperity. Year by year the railways crept farther into the prairies, while the freight of the iron ships increased and man's ingenuity found new ways to preserve meat and foodstuffs from decay.

When the trumpet sounded the walls of Jericho that had seemed so strong fell. They could not stand against the inrush of cheap foreign food. They lacked defenders. The urban voters had lost interest in the countryside. The rural workers were without votes and, since the enclosures of the past century, without a stake in the land. The social basis of British agriculture was too narrow: its ownership concentrated in too few hands. Some four thousand squires owned more than half the land of England and Wales. Seven hundred thousand cottagers between them only possessed 150,000 out of 39,000,000 cultivated acres. They could not defend an interest they did not enjoy.

Henceforward the foreigner was to feed Britain. Corn in bulk came from America: frozen mutton from Australia[1] and

---

[1] Australian frozen beef was appearing on British dinner tables as early as 1872 when *Punch* published a new version of "The Roast Beef of Old England" entitled "The Sirloin Suspended" :

> "Once mighty roast beef was the Englishman's food,
> It has now grown so dear that 'tis nearly tabooed;
> But Australian beef potted is cheap and is good,
> O the boiled beef of Australia, and O the Australian boiled beef!

beef from the Argentine made the work of the English farmer superfluous. In the next two decades more than four million acres of arable land went out of cultivation, and more than half a million workers left the country for the town. Against the competition of the new lands the farmer was powerless: a bad season spelt ruin, for a diminished turnover could no longer be offset by a rise in price. Falling rents, mortgages and bank overdrafts broke the back of the smaller squires before death duties and rising taxes drove them in the next generation from their ancient homes and lands. Only the very rich who had urban estates to offset rural and the farm labourer, helped after 1884 by the vote and the rising tide of social conscience, prospered a little in the general tide of decay. But the heart was going out of British farming. Henceforward the old conception of home as a place permanently associated with man's life and labour to be inherited from his forebears and transmitted to his children was for most Englishmen a thing of the past. The utilitarians thought of home only as a shelter from the weather. They could not see the need for beauty and continuity in human life. Under their guidance and that of the manufacturers and changers of money to whose keeping they trustfully committed England more factory workers could be supported with cheap food than ever before. But from the plain man, on whose character, integrity and valour England in the last resort rested, something precious had been taken away. The home smoke rising from the valley, the call of the hours from the belfry, the field of rooks and elms, had given place to a tenement in the land of the coal truck and the slag heap. Here his life was cast and the earliest memories of his children formed.

.　　.　　.　　.　　.　　.　　.

Yet the dream remained in pathetic attempts to keep curtains white in grimy back rooms above East London railway yards or to grow flowers in window-boxes in Bolton and Oldham. And English history suggested that whenever for any reason Englishmen failed to find the elements of home, as they conceived them, in their own land, they tended to seek them overseas. Such had been the history of the colonisation of the transatlantic virgin

It is capital cold, it is excellent hot;
And, if a large number of children you've got,
'Twill greatly assist you in boiling the pot. . . ."

forests and deserts that had grown into the United States of America. Denied opportunity in their own country, a race of invincible romanticists had made new homes in the wilderness to meet their heart's desire.

The new English nations so formed had rebelled against the home government's claim to control them and had formed an independent polity of their own. Yet even in the hour of the English schism, the age-long process continued. As the first Empire fell away, a second grew in its place. The united Empire Loyalists, unable to fit their own conception of home into that of a rebel federation, tramped across the Canadian border to seek a new habitation in the wilderness. Here they mingled with conquered French settlers and British emigrants to form in the fullness of time the Dominion of Canada. During the next century others crossed the oceans to make homes under the British flag in Newfoundland, Cape Colony, in the islands of New Zealand and the virgin continent of Australia. Most of these emigrants were poor men who sought on a distant soil the happiness and freedom they had failed to find in their own country.[1] Few amid the hardship of their lot found the promised land for themselves. They left it for their children to create after them.

In this process the pioneers received small help from the imperial government. The ruling classes at home were not interested in British settlers overseas. Their thoughts of them were coloured by the memories of the War of Independence and of the humiliations which had then befallen English statesmen. They wished to have nothing further to do with colonials. They regarded the Empire, apart from India, as a strategic network of trading factories, spice islands and naval bases in which squatters' settlements had no part. At the end of the eighteenth century they found a temporary use for New South Wales as a dumping ground for convicts. But when this practice was stopped in the 'sixties, the interest of the English official classes in the colonies sank to zero.

The utilitarians had even less use for such troublesome appendages. For to their way of thinking their only function was to embroil the country in expensive foreign entanglements.

---

[1] The graveyards of Quebec and Montreal were piled high with British immigrants who died in the crowded holds of the immigrant ships in the terrible [transatlantic passage against westerly gales.

The old view of the Empire as a profitable monopoly for native traders was outmoded, since it was a canon of free trade that a monopoly defeated its own ends. Even the preferential treatment of Empire producers, granted by Huskisson in 1823 in the course of a general reduction of tariffs to obtain reciprocal concessions in foreign markets, had since been discarded without regard to the interests of colonial traders. For the Benthamites held that the latter, like every one else in the utilitarian paradise, were best left to look after themselves.

This view of Colonial possessions accorded with that held in official circles. "I suppose I must take the thing myself," Palmerston remarked when he had some difficulty in filling the Colonial Office. "Come upstairs with me, Helps, when the Council is over. We will look at the maps, and you shall show me where these places are."[1] Gladstone's opinion was that the Empire was too heavy a burden to be borne. Even Disraeli at one moment of his career so far fell into the fashion of the day as to refer to the Colonies as millstones. They were an expense to the taxpayer, and, with their tiresome local politics, a constant source of annoyance to the official mind. For the exporter their under-inhabited markets were valueless compared with those of Europe, South America and the United States. Nor were they of any use to the politician. For the colonists had no votes at home. They even objected to the use of their chief official and magisterial appointments for uses of domestic patronage. The general view of the upper classes was that the colonists were rough and uneducated provincials unfit for refined company.[2]

All that the rulers of England were prepared to do for them was to give them their freedom. After the painful lesson of the American War of Independence no obstacle was placed in the way of their political development. They were given such constitutions as they desired and quietly encouraged to go their own way. Whenever opportunity arose they were reminded in frigid official language that the time of parting was at hand. "Colonies," Turgot had written, "are like fruits

[1] Communicated to J. A. Froude by *Sir Arthur Helps, Oceana* 11.
[2] " Scene: Five o'clock tea. Lady (to relative from Australia): 'Will you take any refreshment, Cousin George?'
George: 'Thanks, Bella. Don't mind if I do. Give us a handful o' tea and a billy o' water, and I'll boil it while you make me a damper.' "

that cling to the tree only till they ripen." This was the view
of Whitehall. A policy of veiled but deliberate disintegration
was adopted. "It is no use to speak about it any longer,"
a Colonial Office official said to the historian Froude. "The
thing is done. The great Colonies are gone. It is but a question
of a year or two."[1]

But the colonists themselves, though they had no love for
Whitehall and resented interference, wished to remain British.
They wanted to enjoy their lands of promise under the flag
their fathers had known. In other words, they were sentimental
about patriotism. They refused to view it like superior folk in
England as an old-fashioned thing to smile at. Few in numbers
and without electoral influence, their protest would have availed
nothing but for one of those inexplicable movements that occur
in the lives of great nations.

It came not from the ruling classes but from the common
people. For those who thousands of miles away were building
new and freer Englands were their own kith and kin. They had
left home in poverty and obscurity: years later their success
had gladdened the humble kinsmen they had left behind. Fresh
settlers were always following the old. There was formed
a link of sentiment and hope between working-class homes in
Britain and thriving townships and farms in Canada and
Australia. The rich and powerful might have no use for the
self-governing colonies. To the poor they seemed the promise
of a happier future: an appeal from the black chimneys, the herd
life of the slum, the selfishness of the lords of rustic England
with their closed parks and game preserves.

It was only after 1867, when the artisan householder received
the vote, that this feeling became a political factor. Yet it was
already a rallying point for all not content to subscribe to the
utilitarian thesis. The British middle-class were not all bagmen
and cotton-spinners: there was Norse blood in their veins and
an ineradicable love of adventure which kept cropping up under
their maxims of shopkeeping prudence. Buying in the cheapest
market and selling in the dearest was not everything. And as
foreign tariffs rose against British manufacturers and the employment of the crowded city population became ever less secure,
more and more questioned whether the utilitarian basis of the
economists was not too narrow and whether the time had not

[1] *J. A. Froude, Oceana, 7.*

come to call in a new world to redress the balance of the old.

One of the first to do so was Disraeli. At the moment when a new Europe was being born out of the national wars and uprisings of 1859, he predicted a course for his country diametrically opposed to that held in contemporary official circles:

"The day is coming, if it has not already come, when the question of the balance of power cannot be confined to Europe alone. . . . England, though she is bound to Europe by tradition, by affection, by great similarity of habits, and all those ties which time alone can create and consecrate, is not a mere Power of the Old World. Her geographical position, her laws, her language and religion, connect her as much with the New World as with the Old. And although she has occupied an emminent . . . position among European nations for ages, still, if ever Europe by her shortsightedness falls into an inferior and exhausted state, for England there will remain an illustrious future. We are bound to communities of the New World, and those great States which our own planting and colonising energies have created, by ties and interests which will sustain our power and enable us to play as great a part in the times yet to come as we do in these days and we have done in the past. And therefore now that Europe is on the eve of war, I say it is for Europe not for England, that my heart sinks."[1]

Many people thought Disraeli's growing interest in the Empire an affectation. It was certainly politically prescient. Just as he was able to associate his party with the growing demand for social reform, so he was able to associate it with that other popular longing—for a new world of opportunity overseas. He understood the nature of the attempt the utilitarians were making on the unity of the Empire, and realised that working men could have little sympathy with it. Almost alone at this time—though his foresight was later equalled from the Liberal benches by that of Charles Dilke, Disraeli realised that in a fast expanding Europe, an England that insisted for the sake of profit on remaining a small manufacturing island in

[1] *Monypenny and Buckle, I, 1631.*

the North Sea would presently find herself in danger from other and more despotic empires jealous of her wealth and resentful of the libertarian ideals she so light-heartedly and provocatively championed. It was this that made him the critic of those who, "viewing everything in a financial aspect and totally passing by those moral and political considerations which make nations great," granted self-government to the English-speaking colonies not "as part of a great policy of imperial consolidation" but merely in order to get rid of them. His instinct of coming danger made him alive to the necessity of responding to their craving for unity before it was too late.

The old Jew saw that the world which Cobden and the great Liberals had known was yielding to a new and sterner. He knew how nearly it threatened England. In 1860, with the help of a French assault on Austria, Italy achieved unity and a place, however at first precarious, among the European Powers. In 1864, Prussia under the inspiration of a Junker squire of genius, defied the protests of a disarmed England and seized the southern provinces of Denmark with the ultimate object of building an ocean fleet. Two years later Bismarck struck at his ally, Austria, and in the course of a six weeks' *blitzkrieg* won the leadership of Germany. The formal union of a new Empire under the Prussian dynasty was completed on New Year's Day, 1871, in the Hall of Mirrors at Versailles while Moltke's shells burst on the ramparts of a besieged and starving Paris.

Of these dynamic events liberal England, dedicated to the rule of reason and the peaceful making of wealth, remained a spectator. The Europe she had helped to reshape after Waterloo crumbled before her eyes. The principle of militant nationality which she had defied so successfully in the first years of the century was triumphing in every country. With a little voluntary army of 200,000 she was left to face a continent of great conscript armies running up into millions of men and actuated by motives far removed from Manchester's reckoning. Even the industrialisation in which the continental nations now feverishly began to copy Britain was made to serve the ends of armed power, conceived in terms of strategic railways and gun foundries and protected by bristling tariffs. Essen was Middlesborough in a nightmare.

Disraeli was sensitive to these mighty forces: his countrymen were not. He realised that England's present place in the world depended on the abandonment of the policy of "meddle and muddle" so dear to liberal and humanitarian sentiment, and its replacement by her historic doctrine of balancing Power against Power. Still more clearly he realised that her future depended on her capacity to find an outlet for her swelling population beyond her own dangerously congested shores. Because of this he was the first statesman to grasp the significance of the great canal which French engineers built in the 'sixties across the eastern Egyptian desert to link the Red Sea with the Mediterranean. By securing for his country the bankrupt Khedive of Egypt's controllling shares in the Suez Canal Company, Disraeli, during his final tenure of power, placed the most vital artery in the British Empire beyond the control of an international financial power. By simultaneously opposing a renewed Russian advance on Constantinople and the Mediterranean he defended the same artery from the threat of what seemed at that time—though as many believe wrongly—the dominant European power of the future

In doing so Disraeli was solicitous for interests still beyond the narrow ken of the average British voter and statesman. The tired imperial statesman who brought back "peace with honour" from the Berlin Conference unwittingly offended the humanitarian conscience of his country. It was his misfortune—many enthusiastic opponents regarded it as his fault—to have to maintain the independence of a Mohammedan despotism against an uprising of Christian peoples. To the kindly middle classes the inviolability of treaties, the balance of European power and England's strategic communications with India meant little or nothing. But the stories of the atrocities committed by Turkish irregulars in the Bulgarian provinces did. They aroused the country.

In the hands of Gladstone, the very incarnation of the English conscience, all this became a weapon to scourge a cynic in office. The north-country working man was swept off his feet by his appeal for moral righteousness. To humble minds the great Liberal's electoral campaign of 1880[1] seemed a crusade for

---

[1] A Conservative speaker who told his audience that Gladstone was only an ambitious politician with his eyes on the Treasury Bench was answered with a "Yes and he'll have his bottom on it soon if you don't look out."—*Esher, Memoirs.*

the rights of small nations trampled under by the imperial aggressor, whether Turkish or English : for the sanctity of life in the hill villages of Afghanistan and in the veldt farms of the Transvaal. "Amidst the din of preparation for warfare in the time of peace," Gladstone declared in his final speech at Edinburgh, "there is going on a profound mysterious movement that, whether we will or not, is bringing the nations of the civilised world, as well as the uncivilised, morally as well as physically nearer to one another ; and making them more and more responsible before God for one another's welfare."

The truth of this could not be resolved by statesmen. Its force lay in the fact that in his heart the ordinary Englishman believed it. The defeated and now dying Disraeli, whom the harsh experience of his race and a long life of struggle had made a realist, might have replied that there was no such instrument for bringing it about as the united and consistent policy of a world-wide commonwealth of peace-loving British nations.

. . . .

Because Englishmen wished to exercise power not for its own sake but to further moral causes, Gladstone, on assuming office in 1880, found himself involved in remote imperial adventures. Having no imperial policy, he was at a loss in meeting them. Among the charges brought against Disraeli by his opponents had been that of scheming to occupy Egypt. Yet it was Gladstone who actually and most reluctantly did so.

Egypt was an independent tributary province of the Turkish Empire. In 1876, being unable to wring any more out of his over-taxed people or to raise further capital to pay the interest on his debts, its ruler, the spendthrift Khedive Ismail, agreed to the appointment of a British and a French Controller-General of Finance to safeguard the hundred million pounds he had borrowed from French and British capitalists. Three years later as Ismail, unable to break with his prodigal habits, intrigued against his financial advisers, Britain and France induced his over-lord, the Sultan of Turkey, to depose him in favour of his son.

This measure of foreign financial control was enough to provoke the resentment of the Egyptian aristocracy and army. In 1882 a military adventurer named Arabi Pasha established a military dictatorship, and the Alexandria mob beat up and murdered foreigners. Save for remote outbreaks in China, the world was still unused to such popular jackboot reactions to the operations of international capital. The first "Fascist dictator" was dealt with by Gladstone's pacific government in the old vigorous John Bull manner. British tars bombarded Alexandria, and an expeditionary force under Sir Garnet Wolseley routed Arabi at Tel-el-Kebir. The French, fearful of another attack from Germany, preserved their freedom of action and left their British partners to act alone.

Having entered Egypt to restore order the latter were forced to stay to maintain it. For the only alternative was mob rule. The Khedive was restored to a nominal authority. Vague suzerainty continued to be vested in the Sultan of Turkey. But for the next quarter of a century the real ruler of Egypt was the British Agent and Consul General, Sir Evelyn Baring, later Lord Cromer. He was supported by British officials and soldiers.

Up to this point the Egyptian adventure had been prompted by financial interests. Capital, being free to operate where its owners chose, strayed outside the imperial field in its pursuit of profits. Its interest payments taking the form of imports on which the employment of British voters depended, any government which valued its existence was forced to use its diplomatic influence to maintain them. Where such influence provoked national reactions, military intervention became necessary to avert anarchy and punish outrages against British subjects.

Finance had led Britain into Egypt. Love of humanity and liberty impelled her next step. Almost immediately Gladstone was forced into further expansionist action by the moral forces from which he derived his authority. They sent Gordon to a martyr's death at Khartoum and Kitchener in the fullness of time to establish a new equatorial dominion in the heart of Africa.

The Sudan, stretching nearly 2000 miles south from Egypt along the Upper Nile, was an Egyptian province. The misrule of corrupt officials and the depredations of savage warriors and slave-traders had long been its lot. Shortly before the British occupation of Cairo the unhappy country was seized by a religious fanatic, the Mahdi. An Egyptian army, sent to restore order, was cut to pieces in the desert.

For this hell on earth Gladstone's government now found itself responsible. Feeling not unnaturally that a liberal

Britain had no business there, it resolved on a policy of immediate evacuation. But, though nine out of ten Englishmen had never heard of the Sudan, many of the government's most valued supporters were deeply interested in it. To the humanitarians of Exeter Hall it was a stronghold of the slave trade, a field for missionaries and the home of certain poor Christian converts.

In deference to their wishes Gladstone sent to the Sudan one who, while formerly its Governor General under Khedive Ismail, had won merit in their eyes by his Christian vigour in repressing the slave trade. General Gordon was a strange soldier—half-crusader, half-adventurer—but he was also a genius. His instructions were to withdraw the Christians and all remaining British and Egyptian subjects. But he deliberately interpreted them in such a fashion as to secure his own martyrdom in the Sudanese capital and the tardy dispatch of an eleventh-hour expeditionary force to relieve him and the country to which he had given his heart. Gladstone's natural reluctance to rescue this unjust but heroic steward aroused a wave of moral and patriotic indignation. After the fall of Khartoum he found himself regarded almost as a murderer. He had tried to refrain from action in the Sudan because he wished to avoid extending the already vast empire of Britain. But the very humanitarians who applauded his dislike of imperialism could not refrain from using the national might to suppress wrong-doing and cruelty. They hated force. But when it came to the point they hated slavery more. They did the hating and the soldiers they deplored did the fighting. And the end of it was a still larger empire than before.

This contradiction lay at the root of Britain's imperial difficulties. It was not practicable for a democracy which both indulged strong moral feelings and allowed its wealth to be used in large-scale operations outside its own borders, to govern an empire without an imperial policy. The only result was to provoke confused and angry situations in which the pressure of popular opinion compelled more violent imperial action than any originally contemplated. The bounds of empire continued to expand because its energies, moral and commercial, were never canalised in any clearly defined channel. Sometimes the force that made for expansion was God, sometimes Mammon. But it was nearly always a confused force.

Nothing illustrated this so well as the history of South Africa.

Britain had first appeared at the Cape during the war with the French Directory when her ally Holland, being overrun by the enemy, the Prince of Orange asked her to take the Dutch colony under her protection. Restored to Holland by the Treaty of Amiens, the Cape—the chief port of call on the ocean route to India—was reoccupied by British troops on the renewal of hostilities. This time the Dutch colonists resisted, but in vain. After the war the Cape was retained by Britain as her almost only territorial reward for her long struggle against Napoleon.

The Cape Dutch would probably have accepted the situation and have become loyal British citizens like the French Canadians but for one circumstance. They incurred the enmity of those very elements in England who might have been expected to defend their rights against over-zealous imperial administrators. For unhappily the Dutch attitude towards the South African native was different to that of the English humanitarian. The latter viewed him as a defenceless black brother whose welfare was a sacred trust. The Dutch farmer thought of him as a dangerous savage who could only be kept from vice and idleness by strong paternal discipline and a liberal use of the whip. Of the two views that of the Dutch was perhaps founded on the closer knowledge of the Cape Hottentot. But if the Dutch farmer was the man on the spot, the English middle-class humanitarian was the man who had the vote. The British government inevitably interpreted the views of the latter.

Sooner than suffer interference with their ancient rights and ways of life many Dutch left the Cape and trekked into the interior wilderness. Here they made new homes and founded two independent republics. But they were not allowed to enjoy peace, for they were represented by Exeter Hall as carrying fire and sword into the hereditary lands of the Kaffir, Basuto and Zulu. There was truth in both points of view. But interpreted by the strong if reluctant arm of the imperial government, that of the evangels of human equality and brotherhood usually prevailed in the end. The pity was that it did not always correspond with the facts as known to those on the spot. The British liberal voter genuinely cared for the welfare of the South African native. But he knew little of South Africa. Having no imperial principle or interest in the Empire he did not trouble to learn.

In this he and his rulers were to blame. For no aversion to imperial responsibility could alter the fact that they were morally responsible for the peace of South Africa. To interfere on behalf of their own ideological convictions and simultaneously to refuse to take any long view of imperial policy on the ground that imperialism was expensive and morally wrong was to light a fire on the veldt and leave it. Yet this was the habit of the English humanitarian Left for more than a century.

This hiatus in the application of moral principle to the government of an Empire again and again vitiated the history of British South Africa. In 1852 an attempt was made by a treaty with the Boers to stabilise the situation. Britain agreed to "meddle no more beyond the Orange River and to leave the Dutch and the natives to settle their differences among themselves." Yet seventeen years later Gladstone's first administration, yielding to the pressure of humanitarian supporters, intervened in breach of treaty to protect the Basutos against the Boers of the Orange Free State. Two years later it broke faith with the Dutch again, annexing Griqualand to satisfy not missionaries but prospectors. The diamond diggings—the richest in the world—which had been discovered on a Dutch farm beside the Vaal river, were named after the Liberal Colonial Secretary, Lord Kimberley. But, despite the production of a highly dubious treaty with a native chief, the annexation was repudiated by the Dutch electors of the Cape. To complete the circle of ill-will, the natives in the new occupied territory were armed by the British against the local farmers.

Almost as imperfectly informed about the internal situation of South Africa as Gladstone's government,[1] but animated by a different ideal, Disraeli's administration of 1874-80 applied imperial instead of humanitarian principles. The Colonial Secretary, Lord Carnarvon, satisfied that the union of Dutch and English was the only solution of the African problem, paid compensation to the Orange Free State for the loss of Griqualand and admitted the wrong done. But ill-advised as to the local facts and impatient to effect a federation of South Africa before the swing of the political pendulum should put a term to his office, he sent Sir Bartle Frere to the Cape with a premature mandate to unite the two races. Ignoring the accumulated animosities of generations and without waiting to allow the reviving trust of the Dutch to mature, Frere used its peril from

[1]According to Froude, Lord Cardwell, who had been a former Liberal Colonial Secretary, thought in 1875 that Cape Colony was purely British in population and that all the Dutch had migrated to the Orange Free State.—*Oceana*, *38*.

Zulu tribes as an opportunity to annex the bankrupt Boer republic of the Transvaal. Simultaneously he involved Britain in a costly war with the Zulus.

In the general election of 1880 the Liberals for the first time professed sympathy with the Dutch and promised to reverse the Transvaal annexation. This, however, they subsequently felt themselves unable to do.[1] The Boers, freed by British arms from the fear of Zulu massacre, rose in defence of their freedom. The government, torn between its aversion to imperial conquest and its desire to pursue its own native policy in the former Boer territories, failed to give its commander-in-chief sufficient support. On February 27th, 1881, Sir George Colley with a small force was cut to pieces by the Boer farmers at Majuba. Gladstone, with great moral courage but at a serious sacrifice of prestige, thereupon agreed to grant virtual independence to the Transvaal. The British at the Cape were left smarting under a sense of humiliation and injured patriotism. The Dutch both in the Boer republic and the Cape Colony and Natal were left with an even more dangerous contempt for the courage and tenacity of the British.

. . . .

The difficulty of ruling an empire while disbelieving in the virtues of imperial rule involved the Liberals in difficulties nearer home and for which they were not to blame. Ireland was the *damnosa hereditas* of British politics. Deep in the Irish heart, whether in Ireland itself or in England, America or the Colonies, survived the memory of ancient and terrible wrongs.[2] No kindly intentions or benevolent acts of English Liberals could wipe out this all too persistent past. The pig-nosed paddies in their high hats, tight breeches and ragged tail-coats who ambushed evicting landlords and chased their agents with shillelaghs and shot-guns across the stony fields of Kerry and

[1] "If Cyprus and the Transvaal," Gladstone had declared during the election, "were as valuable as they are valueless, I would repudiate them because they are obtained by means dishonourable to the character of the country." After the election, he explained that he meant the word "repudiate" in the sense of dislike.

[2] Sir James Sexton, whose father was evicted from the Vale of Avoca in the 'forties by an absentee landlord and whose maternal grandparents had been driven out of Ireland into industrial Lancashire by the religious and political persecutions that followed the Rebellion of 1798 wrote in his autobiography (17-18): "The story of those days of terror was handed on to the children of all who endured their agony; it spread all over the world, and engendered in the mind of every Irishman and Irishwoman who heard it hatred—bitter and boundless hatred—of everything connected with Britain and the British. That, so far as my mind was concerned, was my principal political and spiritual inheritance."

Clare; the Fenians or Republican Brothers who took fearful oaths and plotted in every part of the world and even invaded Canada from the United States; the invisible dynamiters and "Manchester martyrs" who swung from the English gallows tree for murder and arson were the terror and bugbear of the respectable English in the prosperous middle years of Queen Victoria's reign.

In vain did a just Gladstone sternly and righteously offer up the Irish Church to an ungrateful Irish priest and peasant. In vain did successive governments vote grants to Catholic colleges and pass land reform acts to protect the Irish tenant. Between the English humanitarian and the credulous, priest-led Paddy whom he wished to befriend and civilise a great gulf was fixed. The former did his best to believe in the existence of a body of loyal, respectable and peace-loving Irish ready to enrol as special constables against the Fenians, whose bloody and senseless doings outraged the peace and fair name of their country. Such Irishmen did exist, but they were Orangemen: black, Protestant Ulstermen from the grim North—an object of detestation to every southern Irish patriot.

The Irish wished to avenge themselves on the English. The English wished to let bygones be bygones and, though they would never admit they were in the wrong, to make amends for the past by making the Irish comfortable. The Irish did not want to be comfortable. They wanted to make the English uncomfortable. Above all they wanted to be rid of the English and their benevolent, insulting ministrations: they wanted to be free. The English could not afford to let the Irish be free. Ireland lay across England's lifeline. An Ireland in the hands of a stranger might one day mean death for England.

All through the middle years of the century a new Ireland was waking. Among a little minority in Dublin it was an Ireland of poets and scholars fired by a passionate dream of their country's future. Celtic Ireland, the Poland of the Western world, would be a nation once more. For the great majority, the motive power was a dull and sullen hatred: an angry resolve that spread in aimless trickles of murder and outrage over a dark, haunted land. They could do nothing without a leader. And a nation born of a long line of degraded, landless, persecuted peasants— feckless, cynically jesting and despairing—bred rebels more readily than leaders.

Yet the leader was forthcoming. He was a Protestant, an aristocrat and a landowner: the last man in the world any one would have predicted as a lawgiver to poor, squalid, rebel Ireland. He despised the arts of the demagogue: loathed crowds and politicians, and had an icy pride and reserve which few even of his closest lieutenants could penetrate. But he had three supreme assets: brilliant intellectual power, unshakable resolve and a cold burning passion which nothing could quench. That icy flame Charles Stewart Parnell applied for twenty years to a single task: the breaking of the link that bound Ireland to England.

His work began in the 'seventies when he first entered the House of Commons as member for County Meath. Until that time the Irish members had been an ineffective body, regarded by the desperate men who rode the stormy anarchy of Irish assassination and land agitation as helpless prisoners of England. Parnell realised from the first that the key to the Irish future lay at Westminster. If he could weld the four score or more members whom Catholic Ireland returned to the imperial parliament into a single disciplined body, he might use the balanced rivalry of the English parties to wring legal concessions that would open the road to Irish independence.

In the new Parliament of 1880 Parnell began to make his power felt. He discovered that by taking advantage of the intricate rules of parliamentary procedure which had grown up in the course of centuries, he could trapan the conservative English with their own love of legality. His quick penetrating mind made him master of these, and he taught his followers how to use them. There ensued an extraordinary situation. Night after night the most dignified and orderly parliamentary assembly in the world was held up by an interminable succession of unnecessary speeches, questions and interruptions as Irish member after member rose to delay business. The administration of a great Empire was hamstrung because, through an irony of fate, a handful of resolute and alien obstructionists happened to be members of its sovereign assembly.

By his success Parnell achieved two things. He became the most hated man in England. He united the Irish nationalists. It became realised that the battle of wits that the Irish members were waging nightly at Westminster was a struggle for the rebirth of a nation. It was more. It was a gauntlet flung down to England and her age-long dominion. The eyes of the entire world turned towards that little, mighty arena.

The Nationalist Party in Parliament had its counterpart in Ireland. The Land League, though not founded by him, also marched at Parnell's orders. The one aimed at destroying the rule of Ireland by the English Parliament: the other her exploitation by the English landlord. The League was an association of Catholic tenant farmers and peasants against the Protestant landowning garrison which had given local rule to Ireland since the seventeenth century. It prescribed rents, banned or "boycotted" all who paid more and made the taking of a farm from which a member had been evicted a social crime.[1] It was accompanied inevitably, though this was contrary to Parnell's wishes, by gang intimidation, cattle-maiming, rick-burning and murder.

The Liberal rulers of Britain were in a quandary. They wished well to Ireland. They hated coercion. But they were also men of peace and lovers of parliamentary government. They could not see law and order flouted and the democratic machinery of parliament sabotaged. They were forced against their will to act. They tried suspending the Habeas Corpus Act and putting Parnell in Kilmainham Gaol. By doing so they made him a martyr and themselves tyrants. As soon as they released him he continued the struggle. They were driven to limit the freedom of parliamentary debate and to abandon part of the democratic practice of centuries.[2] They only heightened Parnell's prestige. Ireland thrilled at the tale of his triumphs in the very temple of the Saxon tyrant. To aid his campaign thousands of pounds poured in from Irish sympathisers in America.

But the greatest of Parnell's conquests was Gladstone's conscience. Gladstone was a devout churchman and a man of

[1] "When a man takes a farm from which another has been ejected," Parnell told his followers in September, 1880, "you must show him on the roadside, you must show him in the streets, you must show him at the shop counter, you must show him in the fair and in the market place, and even in the house of worship, by leaving him severely alone, by isolating him from his kind as if he were a leper of old—you must show him your detestation of the crime he has committed, and you may depend on it that there will be no man so full of avarice, so lost to shame, as to dare the public opinion of all right-thinking men, and to transgress your unwritten code of laws."

[2] In the view of a great living authority on parliamentary practice, Sir Bryan Fell, the protective measures then introduced have since been used by the Executive to deprive the private Member of Parliament of his traditional position as the link between the Government and the Public.

splendid probity of life. Parnell was a concealed adulterer. Yet
Parnell made Gladstone ashamed. And what Gladstone's
conscience felt to-day, England's conscience would feel
to-morrow. In 1882 the 73-year-old Prime Minister, appalled
by the difficulty of governing Ireland and controlling the
Irish members, wrote to his Irish Secretary that so long as
there were no responsible bodies in Ireland with which a British
Government could deal, every plan framed to help them came
to Irishmen as an English plan. It was therefore probably condemned: at best regarded as a one-sided bargain which bound
the English but not the Irish. Because of the miserable and
almost total want of responsibility for public welfare and peace
in Ireland, reform was impossible. Such a sense of responsibility
could only be created through local self-government. "If we
say we must postpone the question till the state of the country
is more fit for it, I should answer that the least danger is in
going forward at once. It is liberty alone which fits men for
liberty." The faith of a Liberal was never more nobly expressed.

For Gladstone's mind, more sincerely wed to the conception
of freedom than that of any of his followers, had grasped the
logic of the Irish situation. Either England must rule the subject
peoples of her Empire according to her own moral standards
and through strong and consistent imperial policy, or she must
make no attempt to impose her ways of life, however noble, on
others and trust to liberty to teach its own lesson. Gladstone
believed in liberty and was prepared to rely on it. He was even
prepared to give it to the Irish.

To initiate a new departure in Irish policy, he therefore released
Parnell from Kilmainham Gaol, and appointed Lord Frederick
Cavendish, his beloved niece's husband and the most sympathetic
figure among the younger members of the House, as Chief
Secretary for Ireland. Four days after Parnell's release Lord
Frederick was murdered by Fenian assassins as he walked home
across Phoenix Park.

It was a mark of Gladstone's growing greatness that he
allowed neither this terrible crime nor the crop of Irish dynamite
outrages in England in the following year, to deflect him from
his purpose. Others, including Liberal elements in the Tory
Party, who were influenced by the example of the self-governing
colonies, were moving in the same direction. In 1885, when the
balance between the major parties was sufficiently even to give

the eighty-six Irish members under Parnell's leadership a deciding voice in a new parliament, he let it be known that he proposed to introduce a scheme of Home Rule for Ireland.

Had the question only been political, Gladstone would probably have carried his measure. The religious issue split the Liberal majority. Though religion as a political factor was a dying force in England, there were many of Gladstone's followers who could not look unmoved on the subjection of a Protestant minority to a Catholic majority. In such a case the democratic formula was somehow inadequate. The little handful of Whig aristocrats who still provided leaders for the Liberal Party derived their lands and honours from the glorious day when a Protestant Prince delivered England from a Catholic King. From the conquests of that Prince the Orange patriots of Ulster still boasted their claim to be the ruling faction in Ireland.

If the Right wing of the Liberal Party could not conscientiously drive Ulster out of a Protestant union into a Papist province, nor could the Left. Nonconformity, with its strong local organisation, was still a mighty power in the land. Though fast mellowing into humanitarianism, its historic inspiration had always been hatred of Popery. Its political leader was the uncrowned king of Birmingham, radical Joe Chamberlain. Though a man of wide sympathies who had looked with a lenient eye on Irish rebel aspirations—perhaps because he had so many himself—he now showed himself a true mirror of provincial middle-class England. Sooner than endorse Home Rule, he resigned from the Cabinet and joined hands with the Whig leader, Lord Hartington, to raise the fiery cross of Protestant and imperial unity.

When the Home Rule bill came up for its second reading, more than a hundred Liberals voted against the government or absented themselves. Defeated by thirty votes, Gladstone appealed to the country. Protestant scruples, patriotic pride and the fear and hatred engendered by the long Irish campaign of violence and intimidation were stronger even than his courage and magnetism. Three hundred and sixteen Conservatives and 78 Liberal "Unionists" were returned, but only 191 Gladstonian Liberals.

The decision was vital. The English democracy had refused to allow the Irish the right to govern themselves. Though for a further nine years Gladstone laboured to reverse that decision, giving all his immense powers to this single task, fate was against him. In 1890 Parnell's divorce case shattered the unity of the Irish Nationalist Party. "For five years I have rolled this stone patiently uphill," Gladstone complained, "and it is now rolled to the bottom again, and I am 81 years old." Yet even then the old man would not give in. His venerable courage almost won over England in spite of itself. In the autumn of 1892 an election brought him back to office with a chance of carrying Home Rule with the help of Irish votes. But as the dreaded hour of separation drew near opposition in the country became intense. *Punch* depicted an aged and sworded pilgrim advancing along a narrow ridge called Home Rule with the bog of Irish Nationalism on one side and the last ditch of Orange resistance on the other. After scraping through the Commons, the Bill was rejected by an overwhelming majority in the Lords. An appeal to the country would certainly have endorsed their decision. Soon afterwards Gladstone, 84 years of age and almost blind, laid down his burden.

With him died the last hope of self-government for Ireland for a generation. In its place she received a course of strong Conservative "repression" and of enlightened agrarian reform which, applied half a century earlier, might have made her a contented province like Wales. But the hopes aroused by Parnell's fire and Gladstone's intensity were not to be stilled by Balfour's elegant firmness or George Wyndham's squire archical benevolence. The resolve of the Irish to be free persisted and grew acid for the waiting. Their hour came in 1910 when English internal divisions and an even electoral balance between the parties once more made the Irish Nationalist members arbiters at Westminster. Making Home Rule the price of their support, they assisted one English faction to make a fundamental change in the constitution to spite another. They then demanded their price. The guttering candle of English Protestantism was by that time too dim to light another religious crusade to save the Irish Protestants. Though Ulster swore to fight, Home Rule was granted. But it was too late. The Irish ulcer had become too inflamed to be cured by any minor operation. In 1916 the Irish took up arms against the age-long oppressor. In 1922, still fighting, they achieved their independence.

Until the first rejection of Home Rule in the 'eighties, the

British people had shown no consciousness of the necessity for an imperial policy. But during the two decades of Conservative supremacy that followed Gladstone's defeat, they had become increasingly aware of the Empire. For the big steamer, the electric telegraph, the inventions of Marconi, were making the world a smaller place. They even made a united commonwealth scattered haphazard over its surface seem a practical possibility.

A few scholars and dreamers began the fashion that made men think in a new way. In 1883, John Seeley, Regius Professor of Modern History at Cambridge, published his lectures on the Expansion of England. His theme was that the outward spread of the English race had been the main human trend of the past three centuries. If England was wise enough to recognise her chance, her future could be more glorious even than her past. If she neglected it she would decline like Rome and Spain and see her commercial wealth pass to younger rivals. For the potamic and thalassic ages had been succeeded by an oceanic, and the future of the world lay, not with the small nation states of the past, but with composite world states like the U.S.A. and Russia linked by the new forces of steam and electricity.

It was a question not of lust for power or empire, but of common sense and civic responsibility. If the race were to survive in a changing world, its leaders must secure the conditions necessary for it to do so. Already hundreds of thousands in Britain were hungry and in need of work and living space. Yet they could have both for the asking: their heritage was already made. " It may be true that the mother country of this great Empire is crowded, but in order to relieve the pressure it is not necessary for us, as if we were Goths or Turcomans, to seize upon the territory of our neighbours. . . . it is only necessary to take possession of boundless territories in Canada, South Africa and Australia where already our language is spoken, our religion professed, and our laws established. If there is pauperism in Wiltshire and Dorsetshire, this is but complementary to unowned wealth in Australia. On the one side there are men without property, on the other there is property waiting for men."[1]

Three years later Seeley's work, which ran through many editions, was followed by one even more widely read. The historian Froude's *Oceana* was named after the seventeenth-

[1] *J. R. Seeley, Expansion of England, 70-1.*

century Harrington's dream of an English "commonwealth for increase . . . embraced in the arms of ocean." It described a voyage to the Cape, Australia and New Zealand, and compared the freedon and opportunity of a young country like Australia —an England set free from limitations of space where he never met a hungry man or saw a discontented face—with the slums which every year were engulfing a larger part of the English race—"miles upon miles of squalid lanes, each house the duplicate of its neighbour; the dirty street in front, the dirty yard behind, the fetid smell from the ill-made sewers, the public-house at the street corner." Posing the age-long question that the utilitarians had ignored, he asked what sort of men and women urban England was breeding to succeed the generations who had made her great?

The English could not survive only as factory drudges forced by hunger to be eternally manufacturing shirts and coats, tools and engines for the happier part of mankind. Like a tree a a nation had to breathe through its extremities. "A mere manufacturing England, standing stripped and bare in the world's market-place and caring only to make wares for the world to buy," was a pollard tree. The life was going out of it.

The colonists were already Britain's best customers, buying from her in proportion to their tiny population three times more than any stranger. They would not always be a mere ten and a half millions, weak and scattered. The Prime Minister of Victoria predicted in 1885 that in half a century at its present rate of development Australia alone would have a population of fifty millions.[1] Should danger ever come to England, the colonists' response would be unquestioning and automatic.

Froude did not advocate imperial federation. The time was not ripe for it. Nor was it needed. What mattered was that the patriotism of the colonies should be reciprocated. It was because they valued the imperial tie so much that they felt the sting in the suggestion of parting. Their attachment might not always be proof against contemptuous hints from frigid aristocrats and civil servants to take themselves away. Indifference might produce indifference.

England was refusing her destiny. There might be no second chance. "Were Canada and South Africa and Australia

[1] Because that development was not maintained, it is to-day only 7 millions, out of which Australia is sending Britain in her need the finest soldiers and pilots in the world.

and New Zealand members of one body with us," Froude wrote, "we might sit secure against shifts and changes." Without them a little overcrowded island would not be able to support its people or assure them the kind of life that made free men. Already in her squalid mushroom cities multitudes were growing up pale and stunted or were leaving her shores in despair. For lack of an imperial policy four-fifths of those who emigrated went to the United States, frequently in association with British capital invested there. Other nations—Russia, Germany and United States—were seeking new territories to provide for their people's future. England alone, in her materialist absorption with the present, seemed indifferent to hers.

Yet in her splendid past she had unconsciously made provision for it, "in the fairest spots upon the globe where there was still soil and sunshine; where the race might for ages renew its mighty youth, bring forth as many millions as it would and still have means to breed and rear them strong as the best which she produced in her early prime. The colonists might be paying no revenue but they were opening up the face of the earth. By and by, like the spreading branches of a forest tree, they would return the sap which they were gathering into the heart. England could pour out among them, in return, year after year, those poor children of hers now choking in fetid alleys, and, relieved of the strain, breathe again fresh air into her own smoke-encrusted lungs. With her colonies part of herself, she would be, as Harrington had foreshadowed, a commonwealth resting on the mightiest foundations which the world had ever seen. Queen among the nations, from without invulnerable, and at peace and at health within—this was the alternative future before Oceana."[1]

Froude was an old man with his historian's heart rooted in the past. He was no friend to democracy: he feared its destructive influences. But he ended his book with an appeal to the masses with whom future power lay to be wiser than the calico and hardware merchants they were supplanting. The other great Anglo-Saxon democracy sooner than forfeit its future had shed the blood of half a million of its sons to preserve the union. The continuance of a commonwealth of freemen was worth some sacrifice.

That was in 1886. Four years later came the biggest literary sensation since the appearance of *Pickwick*. A young man of

[1] *Oceana*, 10.

genius born in Bombay "between the palms and the sea" and bred
half in India, half in England, painted the life of the Anglo-
Indian community for his countrymen: the colour, scent and sound
of the East, the crowded bazaar opening for the sahib's horse,
the contrast with the grey, suburban, northern island from
which the characters of his witty, glittering, malicious stories
hailed. Since the day when Lord Craven drew his interminable
cocoa trees for Harriette Wilson, the English had been bored
by tales of their own Empire. And here was a young journalist,
still in his early twenties, who could cause a run on them in
every circulating library in London.

But Rudyard Kipling did more than tell stories. He told his
readers to think imperially. His message was not of opportunity
but of duty and destiny. From its hallowed centre at Westminster—"where the Abbey makes us we"—to the fringed palm and
the snow-capped fort at the outer circumference, the Empire was
a vast trust for humanity. "The white man's burden" constituted
the peculiar contribution to human progress of the Anglo-Saxon
race. Despite its strident energy, Kipling's work was as moral
in its purpose as Milton's or Bunyan's.[1] Its aim was to remind
Englishmen of their duty, by relating the vigour, courage and
pathos of those who dedicated undemonstrative lives to a great
ruling tradition. "As to my notions of imperialism, I learned
them from men who mostly cursed their work, but always
carried it through to the end, under difficult surroundings,
without help or acknowledgment."

With Kipling as with all the great English moralists, duty
was no mere negative virtue—a prudent, middle-class insurance
against Hell. It was a mighty force, giving life, poetry and fire
as it did to the Hebrew poets of old. His vision of the English
was of a race finding its destiny in free surrender, self-training
and self-dedication to a divine purpose. In his hymn of the old
Scots engineer M'Andrew, published in 1896, he epitomised it as:

"Law, Order, Duty and Restraint, Obedience, Discipline."
.　　.　　.　　.　　.　　.　　.　　.

But the man who above all others turned the thoughts of

---

[1] A French critic realised this more clearly than Kipling's own countrymen.
"Kipling, of all the great living writers of his country, stands alone for the absolute
in ethics, with a militant faith. A Wells, a Shaw, a Bennett, a Galsworthy, serve other
gods, the gods of reason or sentiment. Kipling's work appeals to our will . . .; he
is the teacher of conduct."—*Andre Chevrillon, Three Studies in English Literature*, 67.

his countrymen to the empire they had neglected or taken for granted was not a writer. Cecil Rhodes was born on the 5th July, 1853, the fifth son of a Hertfordshire vicarage. He was one of a line of small gentry and yeomen farmers: his forbears, he loved to boast, kept cows at Islington.

Though his elder brothers went to Eton and Winchester, the family resources restricted Cecil to the local grammar school. When he was sixteen, having developed a tendency to consumption, he was sent to join an elder brother on a Natal cotton farm. On a summer's day in 1870 he landed at Durban—a shy, tall, fair-headed lad, as lonely as Robert Clive at his first coming to Madras.

After a year of unsuccessful farming he followed his brother across the high veld to the new diamond diggings at Kimberley. Here he spent the next two years in a crazy community of rough diggers from every corner of the earth, Jewish speculators and native labourers; mud holes, mud slides, refuse dumps and tin roofs. In this school he learnt to know mankind.

As the youthful Kipling was impressed by the alternate scenes of England and India—the little, crowded, fog-bound island and the vast glittering empire it ruled by force of character—so Rhodes responded to the mining camp of Dutoitspan. He came back to England to complete his education with a profound sense of the honesty, kindliness and courage of the ordinary Englishman. While at Oxford, paying his fees by periodic visits to the diggings, he conceived a burning desire to further the expansion of his race. It was at the time that Ruskin, as Slade Professor, was firing the imagination of a new generation of undergraduates by lectures on their country's destiny, telling them that they were still undegenerate in race and blood, not yet dissolute in temper, with the firmness to govern and the grace to obey. "Will you youths of England," he asked, "make your country again a royal throne of kings, a sceptred isle, for all the world a source of light, a centre of peace; mistress of learning and of the Arts, faithful guardian of time-tried principles, under temptation from fond experiments and licentious desires; and amidst the cruel and clamorous jealousies of the nations, worshipped in her strange valour of goodwill towards men? ... This is what England must either do or perish. She must find colonies as fast and as far as she is able, formed of her most energetic and worthiest men; seizing any piece of fruitful waste ground she can set her foot on, and there teaching her colonists that their chief virtue is to be fidelity to their country. . . . If we can get men, for little pay, to cast themselves against cannon mouths for love of England, we may find men also who will plough and sow for her, who will behave kindly and righteously for her, and who will bring up their children to love her. . . ."

Rhodes did not doubt Ruskin's message. He linked it to his own experience, and to the healthy, empty uplands of the South African hinterland which he had seen on his travels—lands where Englishmen could live, labour and multiply without injury to others. To win those lands for England and to awaken the imagination of his countrymen to their possibilities was to be his life's work. He went further Since the English at their best almost alone possessed the three attributes which seemed to him to express most nearly the divine will—a sense of justice, a respect for liberty and a love of peace—the next stage in human evolution could best be accomplished through the peaceful expansion of the Anglo Saxon race. Like Milton, Rhodes held that if God wanted a thing done He sent for his Englishman.

With the crazy arrogance of youth he began to preach his creed while still at Oxford. With debts pouring in and the pump on his claim in the flooded diggings at Kimberley breaking down, he drew up a will—the first of many—in which he left a still non-existent fortune to found a secret society to spread the British rule into every unclaimed part of the earth where white men could live by their own labour. The whole Anglo-Saxon race was comprised in his grandiose dream; there was to be an end to the eighteenth-century "schism," a reunion, if necessary under the Stars and Stripes, complete freedom and self-government for every part of the vast commonwealth so formed, an imperial parliament and internal free trade. This great achievement in human co-operation would guarantee the permanent peace of the world. "I contend," he wrote, "that we are the first race in the world, and that the more of the world we inhabit, the better it is for the human race. I contend that every acre added to our territory provides for the birth of more of the English race who otherwise would not be brought into existence. Added to which the absorption of the greater portion of the world under our rule simply means the end of all wars."

There was nothing unusual in a young man dreaming dreams.

What was extraordinary was the speed and consistency with which Rhodes put them into practice. In an age when money had become power, he decided that nothing could be achieved without cash—"the needful," as he called it. He proceeded to make himself the richest man in the Empire. At 27 he founded the De Beers Mining Company with a capital of £200,000. Within eight years he was dictator of the South African diamond industry. Six years later, at the age of 41, he had achieved a similar position in the new gold-mining industry of the Johannesburg Rand.

His enormous wealth, and the power it gave him, Rhodes did not devote to personal or vulgar ends. Seeking, as he expressed it, to combine the commercial and the imaginative, he still pursued his dream. To his contemporaries there was something staggering, and to many even incredible, in the spectacle of a nineteenth-century speculator "spending the profits of a mining company on the development of an empire." Yet this was precisely what Rhodes did. "And the fun is," he loved to say, "we make Beit pay!" But his friend Alfred Beit, hard-headed Hebrew and shrewd financier as he was, never grudged a penny. He knew Rhodes, honoured his vision and loved him; and his devoted service to Rhodes's ideal continued after death.

> "The friend he loved he served through good and ill,
>   The man struck down, he served his memory still,
>   Nor toiling asked more recompense of fame
>   Than to be coupled with another's name."

As part of the task he had set himself Rhodes entered Cape politics. His success was as dazzling as in business: there seemed no resisting his energy and charm. At 36 he became Prime Minister of the Cape Colony. He had two objects: the expansion of British rule into the northern hinterland, and the union of British and Dutch in a federal South Africa.

To gain the first he had to fight against time. The early 'eighties saw the last scramble of the European Powers, all fast industrialising themselves, for unclaimed lands of settlement which might afford them raw materials and new markets. The African interior, recently opened by the missionary explorations of men like Livingstone, offered the last unoccupied territories of size in the world. To the north-western deserts of South

Africa came in 1884 the armed and bustling pioneers of Bismarck's Germany. Their annexation of Damara and Namaqua struck a blow at Rhodes's dream. For between the new German South-West Africa and the two straggling, ever-expanding Boer republics lay only a narrow corridor of disputed land linking Cape Colony with the uplands of the African hinterland which Rhodes coveted for the settlement of his race. If England did not speedily secure the missionaries' road through Bechuanaland to the empty north, the intriuging, ambitious German and the stubborn, jealous Boer would join hands and shut out the English for ever from their lands of promise.

It was the same situation that had confronted the American colonists in the eighteenth century when the French in Canada and Florida had sought to join hands along the Ohio valley and so cut off the Anglo-Saxon community from the interior. Had the French succeeded the future of the world would have been changed. Rhodes, a young man of 31 in the very thick of his struggle with fortune, saw himself at such a juncture of history. Neither his countrymen at the Cape nor in England shared his vision. He had to act before he could awaken them. With every ounce of his tremendous energy and will, he flung himself into the task of keeping the gateway open to the north. He got himself sent into Bechuanaland as Deputy Commissioner and played a leading part in the events that led to the establishment of a British Protectorate over the country. Here he made friends with his beaten opponents as was his way. "I have never," he said, "met any one in my life whom it was not as easy to deal with as to fight." In a letter he described how he came to terms with one Boer farmer, an angry giant who greeted him as he rode up to his door with the words, "blood must flow." "'No,' said I, ' give me my breakfast and then we can talk about blood.' Well, I stayed with him a week, I became godfather of his children and we made a settlement."

Having gained the corridor, Rhodes prepared to take the North." By devious ways he obtained concessions from the savage Matabele tribes who fought and hunted the vast empty hinterland. Then he turned to the imperial government. By badgering all parties and politicians,[1] and using his wealth and powers of persuasion to win over opposition, he secured a Royal Charter for the company which was to create a

---

[1] He used to say that the story of the importunate widow was the best in the Bible.

new dominion. In 1890 he launched his pioneers along the
northern road into the wilderness. In the next year, when he
could escape from his official duties at the Cape, he followed
them on a visit along the fifteen hundred mile trek to their
primitive capital at Fort Salisbury.

In all that he had done Rhodes was animated by a single and
unchanging ambition—to found homes—"more homes"—for
the race. His imagination never ceased to dwell on the future
shade of the trees he planted. He loved to think that the road
he made up Table Mountain would be used by men and women
of his race in a hundred years' time. It was not chance that
made him seek the friendship of General Booth and spend days
with him in the crowded London slums: the contrast between
the England of the utilitarians and the wider, freer England
of Rhodes's dream was his constant spur. The province which
he added to the Empire, and which later bore his name, was
equal in extent to Germany, France and Spain together: a
country where free men could work and breed and make a new
English nation.

When Rhodes came back to England to seek for his projects
the support of Conservative, Liberal and Irish politicians, of
royal Dukes and journalists, of speculators and social reformers,
it was always with the same idea. Somehow he had got to save
the English future from the blindness of the English—"the
greatest people the world has seen whose fault is that they do
not know their strength, their greatness and their destiny."
"Mr. Gladstone," he is reported to have said, "the practical
reason for the further acquisition of territory is that every
power in the world, including our kinsmen the Americans, as
soon as they take new territory, place hostile tariffs against
British goods." In his speeches to the shareholders of his Chartered
Company, essays in imperial planning, he reverted again and
again to the nightmare that haunted him: that the prohibitive
tariffs of a hostile world would one day pauperise and perhaps
starve an island people who could not feed themselves:

"The classes can spend their money under any flag, but the poor
masses . . . can only look to other countries in connection with
what they produce. Instead of the world going all right it
is all wrong for them. Cobden had his idea of Free Trade
for all the world, but that idea has not been realised. The

E.S.   s whole world can see that we can make the best goods in this country, and the countries of the world therefore establish against us, not protective tariffs, but prohibitive tariffs. . . .

"The question of the day is the tariff question and no one tells the people anything about it . . . These islands can only support six millions out of their thirty-six millions. . . . We cannot afford to part with one inch of the world's surface which affords a free and open market to the manufactures of our countrymen."[1]

"When I came back to England the first time, I went up the Thames, and what did I find they were doing? . . . for whom were they making? They were making for the world. Of course, Cobdenism was a most beautiful theory, and it is right that you should look to the world; but the human beings in the world will not have that. They will want to make their own things; and if they find that England can make them best they will put on their protective duties; and if they keep on doing that they will beat you in the end."

For a short while Rhodes made empire a fashion. It became the craze of society ladies and the theme of music-hall choruses. When Gladstone wished to evacuate Uganda in 1893 he was warned by his chief election agent that the price for doing so would be his own evacuation of Downing Street. The speeches which Rhodes made to his shareholders were listened to by breathless thousands and read by millions. Yet even he could not stir the sound, prosperous men who controlled the nation's trade and financial policy into constructive action or arouse the Westminster politicians from their dream of the parish pump and their eternal talk of municipal trams and three acres and a cow.

While Rhodes strove to expand South Africa he sought to unite her. His dream was of a single nation from the Block House at Table Mountain to the Great Lakes. He did not share the vulgar hope of the Cape patriots of subordinating the Dutch to the English. He liked the sturdy Dutch farmers and honoured the old Dutch culture of the Cape. "The Dutch," he said, "are the coming race in South Africa and they must have their share in running the country." He made friends with them, studied

[1] S. G. Millin, Rhodes, 174.

their interests and sought to find a solution of the native problem which had been the chief stumbling block between the two European races. His aim was their equal status in a South African union freed from the centralising trammels of Whitehall[1] but linked with the rest of the Empire by the Crown, the flag and imperial preference.

Rhodes wanted that union, like the wider world commonwealth of self-governing nations he envisaged, to follow the English tradition of freedom, fair play and opportunity for all. He once said in a speech in the Cape Parliament that England had two cardinal and historic principles: that its word, once pledged, was never broken, and that when a man accepted citizenship of the British Empire there was no further distinction of races. He did not want the South Africa of his dream to be exclusive but open "to all men who loved truth, freedom and the welfare of mankind."

After a time Rhodes won the trust of the Dutch. Those in the British colonies of the Cape and Natal came to look on him as their leader—an unheard-of position for an Englishman. In the independent Orange Free State also he made friends. But he had one serious obstacle—the character of the primitive Dutch Transvaal and, above all, of its leader, Kruger. For the little republic of Boer farmers that lay in the centre of the new South Africa, bestriding its internal communications, had no sympathy with Rhodes's ideals. Its leader had no dream of the future nor belief in human progress: only a stubborn resolve to live the life of bygone generations and preserve their simple pastoral ways. To the old Dutch President, with his spittoon and his Bible, Rhodes's ideal of "equal rights for all civilised men, irrespective of race, south of the Zambesi," made no appeal. His ideal was exclusion of all foreigners from the veldt and if possible from South Africa. He excluded their goods by clapping on a 33 per cent. tariff against all imports. He even tried to exclude their railways and telegraphs.

But mammon is a powerful dissolvent of conservative communities. The discovery of gold on the Witwatersrand in the 'eighties put President Kruger and his farmers in a dilemma. They could only secure the profit of that lucky find by admitting foreigners with capital and mining skill. And when they did so foreigners entered the country in such numbers that in a few

---

[1] He supported Irish Home Rule as part of his policy of imperial self-government.

years they not only paid the bulk of the country's taxation but outnumbered the Dutch burghers. Kruger could only maintain Dutch independence by denying them the franchise. If he granted them the rights of democratic citizenship, they would deliver his country and its ancient, primitive civilisation to the enemy. For the uitlanders, most of whom were British, naturally preferred Rhodes's conception of South Africa to Kruger's.

Rhodes had only to be patient. Kruger was trying for the impossible: he was fighting against a majority and against time. But, though no one knew it but himself, so was Rhodes. In his early forties he learned that he was a dying man. He had accomplished only a tithe of his great dream. If he was to see it achieved, it must be achieved quickly. He could not trust others to complete it. Already the power that had come to him was impairing his character: he was growing arrogant and impatient of opposition. Discarding the virtues— tact, patience and conciliation—by which he had climbed, he staked all on a gamble. The gamble failed.

The armed Jameson Raid from Rhodesia into the Transvaal put a term to Rhodes's power as a politician. The Dutch felt he had betrayed them: the English liberals and humanitarians, who had been growing increasingly suspicious of his wealth, his dubious companions and his attitude to the native problem, felt their worst fears confirmed. Rhodes had shown the cloven hoof. His failure discredited his vision and made Little Englandism a permanent mood among idealists and progressives. It was even assumed that he had engineered the raid to improve the value of the Chartered Companys' properties and shares. Henceforward he was a man tainted and cut off from the people he had sought to serve. Though there was much that was great in the final years of his life, the future of South Africa and the Empire passed into other hands. His legacy to his country was Rhodesia, the Rhodes Scholarships' Trust, and, when his mistake had been expiated by the Boer War, the Union of South Africa.

A few months before his death at the age of 49, at the bitterest moment of the war, when victory had become certain and foolish men were talking of revenge, Rhodes addressed the South African League at Cape Town. "You think," he said, "you have beaten the Dutch! But it is not so. The Dutch are not beaten; what is beaten is Krugerism, a corrupt and evil government, no more

Dutch in essence than English. No! The Dutch are as vigorous and unconquered to-day as they have ever been; the country is still as much theirs as it is yours, and you will have to live and work with them hereafter as in the past. Remember that when you go back to your homes in the towns or in the up-country farms and villages. Let there be no vaunting words, no vulgar triumph over your Dutch neighbours; make them feel that bitterness is past and that the need of co-operation is greater than ever. Teach your children to remember when they go to their village school that the little Dutch boys and girls they find sitting on the same benches with them are as much part of the South African nation as they are themselves, and that as they learn the same lessons together now, so hereafter they must work together as comrades for a common object—the good of South Africa."

Rhodes's last recorded words were, "So little done: so much to do." He was only 49 when he died. Had he lived another twelve years, he might conceivably, by his strength and commanding influence in the Anglo-Saxon world, have made it clear in the summer of 1914 that the Empire would intervene against an aggressor and so have averted the Great War and all its incalculable consequences. Had he lived till now, like his contemporary, Bernard Shaw, it is even possible that his full dream might have been realised, the "Anglo-Saxon schism" be ended and the peace and economic unity of mankind permanently secured by the establishment of a pacific world power as omnipotent as Rome. The Fates willed it otherwise.

. . . .

It was an English politician who took up Rhodes's work where he had left it half shattered at the end of 1895. In that year Joseph Chamberlain became Colonial Secretary. It was an office about which no one had troubled much before. For eight years Chamberlain made it the most important in the Empire. He reconquered the Sudan,[1] which during the Mahdi's rule had lost three-quarters of its population, and established a British province twenty times the size of England in the heart of equatorial Africa. He transferred the rule of the vast country which is to-day called Nigeria from the Royal Niger Company to the imperial crown. He secured, by a war in which Australians, Canadians and New Zealanders fought side by side with English-

[1] General Kitchener the Sirdar, annihilated the Mahdi at Omdurman in 1898.

men, British sovereignty over the whole of South Africa from the Cape to Lake Tanganyika. His policy of appeasement in the hour of victory laid the foundations of a new and free South Africa without racial predominance. He helped to bring about the long-delayed federation of the Australian colonies.

These achievements were only part of Chamberlain's service to the Empire. This dapper ex-radical and Brumagen hardware merchant with the frock coat, monocle and orchid, the art of a demagogue and the vision of a Roman Emperor, infused a new spirit into imperial administration. A business man of initiative and energy, in days when business still required both, he sought to make the Empire pay by making it efficient. But he took the long view of efficiency, looking to the interests not merely of the living but of the unborn. He regarded the Crown Colonies as undeveloped estates which could only be developed with imperial assistance. Some of them, after a hundred years of British rule, were still in the same state as when they had been annexed. Britain's stewardship could only be justified if it conferred active benefits on their peoples and the greater populations comprised in the imperial union.

Chamberlain set up a Royal Commission to report on the West Indian sugar islands, derelict and half-ruined after half a century of *laissez-faire*, founded an Imperial Department of Agriculture in the islands to investigate the causes of insect pests and stimulate the planting of alternative crops, and granted loans for colonial transport development at low rates of interest. His Colonial Office fostered the study of tropical medicine and hygiene, established native colleges and trained a new school of scientific imperial administrators versed in the laborious arts of making the wilderness flower. In Africa in particular his policy produced remarkable results: provinces which for centuries had been savage areas of vice, fetishism, slavery, filth and pestilence became in the course of a single generation orderly and well-governed communities with schools, railways and hospitals and a most unfamiliar atmosphere of hope.

Hope was, indeed, the dominant imperial note while Joe Chamberlain remained at the Colonial Office. His forceful optimism brushed aside difficulties: distance, provincial jealousies, lack of population, non-existent markets, want of capital to develop and of trade to repay development. There was talk of imperial federation and of some grand, nebulous scheme

of centralised government for the whole empire, for Chamberlain's mind ran on more bureaucratic lines than Rhodes's. A
succession of Colonial Conferences discussed questions of imperial
defence and federation and recommended the adoption of preferential trade within the Empire if ever Great Britain should
feel able to modify her sacrosanct commercial policy of unrestricted imports. In the third Conference, in 1897, the Prime
Ministers of the eleven self-governing colonies passed a resolution
in favour of federation should it become geographically feasible.
It was the year of the Diamond Jubilee: Empire and the pride
of Empire were in the air. The aged Queen drove in an open
carriage to St. Paul's through streets lined by British troops from
every continent, and Kipling, as the tumult and the shouting
died away, recalled his countrymen to the age-long truth that
sets a term to all empires:

> "If, drunk with sight of power, we loose
> Wild tongues that have not Thee in awe—
> Such boastings as the Gentiles use
> Or lesser breeds without the Law—
> Lord God of Hosts, be with us yet,
> Lest we forget, lest we forget!"

That was the climax of the new imperialism. There was an
inevitable reaction. For one thing there was the price of Empire.
During the Boer War it was at times a heavy one. And to
many people the new imperialism bore too much an air of
swashbuckling and bullying: it was overloud and protested too
much. Worse: it aroused too many financial hopes and offered
too many opportunities for the speculator masking his sly
operations under the folds of the Union Jack. For the new fashion
of Empire attracted a rather miscellaneous crew of patriots:
Jewish financiers, gold and diamond magnates of doubtful
antecedents, shady adventurers from foreign capitals peddling
concessions in African swamps and Australian mines to a public
which, at first swept off its feet by the mingled appeal to
patriotism and cupidity, became later increasingly suspicious
of both.

In these ventures, some of which were animated by a genuine
belief in the imperial future and some merely by a shrewd business
desire to make hay while the imperial sun shone, much speculative

capital was sunk in the Empire without any continuing return.
A great deal of it was lost in inflated share values which could
only have been justified by years of patient development.[1] Such
losses aroused deep-seated and subconscious distrusts. The
imperial financial bubble of the 'nineties left a nasty taste in
the mouths of men who might otherwise have wished well
to a broad plan of social development for the ill-distributed
populations who shared their allegiance.

But there was a deeper cause for the failure of the first attempt
to use British capital to develop the imperial heritage. Backward
and scantily populated territories can only be turned to profit
by a far-sighted use of credit. Under a system of private enterprise such credit can not be afforded unless there is a reasonable
certainty of an expanding and stable trade sufficient to repay
initial expenditure. Except as a quick gamble in share values,
investment in the British Empire seldom offered such certainty.
For so long as Great Britain stuck to Free Trade, its government
could not with the best will in the world afford sheltered markets
to young Empire industries. Other nations, wishing to foster
the growth of national industries, were able to grant protective
tariffs and bonuses. The economic faith of the British forbade
their doing so.

In 1897 Joseph Chamberlain, trying to develop a long-
neglected empire by parliamentary grants to agricultural institutes and schools of tropical medicine, received an offer from
Canada of a tariff in favour of British goods. This was followed
by a resolution of the Colonial Conference in favour of imperial
preference. But without reciprocity in the home market to
increase the colonial capacity to purchase British goods, such
one-sided preference, however generous, could be no more than
a gesture. All that the Colonial Secretary and his chief, Lord
Salisbury, could do was to exempt the British nations overseas
from the operations of the "most favoured" nation clause by
which free-trading Britain regulated her commercial treaties.
This ensured that if ever the British people should abandon
the policy of free imports and be ready to offer tariff preferences
to their imperial kinsfolk, they would not be forced to pass on
such preferences to every other nation with which they had
made a treaty.

---

[1] "In 1920 the chartered shareholders received, after thirty years, their first dividend.
It was sixpence."—S. G. Millin, *Rhodes*, *163*.

This concession meant little at the time. There were no British duties to reduce in favour of the colonies. Least of all could Britain offer the colonies the sheltered markets they needed for their two most important articles of export—food and raw material. Absolute freedom from restriction in both was an article of faith of the Liberal Party. Since the day when Disraeli had taught his followers in the early 'fifties to seek electoral merit by discarding the *damnosa hereditas* of protection, it was scarcely less so with the Tory.

It said much, therefore, for Chamberlain's courage that, at the age of 67, with a reasonable chance of the reversion of the Conservative leadership and the Premiership, he should have resigned his office in order to convince his countrymen of the necessity of an imperial tariff union. In 1903 this ambitious and vigorous man on his return from a tour in South Africa electrified England by going on the stump in a nation-wide campaign of economic education.

The outcry was tremendous. The Liberals, now long out of favour, were jubilant. They raised the most popular of all electoral cries—the People's Food in Danger. The Conservative Party was terrified, and for a while split from top to bottom. Its leader, the aristocratic Arthur Balfour, saved its unity by temporising. But when in 1905, refusing to follow his lieutenant's lead, he went to the country on a note of half-hearted interrogation, he was routed. Imperial preference was marked down for a generation.

It could hardly have been otherwise. For almost inevitably Chamberlain, in his Empire crusade, fell into a fatal error. He began by appealing to patriotism. He asked for tariffs against foreign imports in order to consolidate the imperial heritage of the unborn and to help the primary producers of the Empire who had fought for Britain in the Boer War and who were now voluntarily offering her traders preference. But having to win votes in a commercial age, he and his more worldly followers soon transferred the appeal to material self-interest. Ingenious and elaborately supported economic arguments were advanced to show that the British manufacturer and consumer would reap immediate rewards from a general tariff on foreign goods. The issue of imperial preference as a long-term patriotic investment became obscured by that of protection as an opportunity for quick profits. Great empire and little minds, as Burke saw, go ill together. The generous note first struck by Chamberlain became lost in a cacophony of log-rolling and auctioneering of rival figures.

Though the official Conservative Party refused to join open issue with them over protection—the general election of 1905 was won by the Liberals—largely on the cry of "Hands Off the People's Bread." Actually the addition to the price of the loaf involved in Chamberlain's original proposal of giving preference in the home market to imperial corn-growers would have been negligible. Owing to revolutionary changes in popular feeding habits, caused by new methods of ocean storage, bread was no longer the staple dietary of the masses. But in a conservative country the old parrot-cry sufficed.

The real strength of Free Trade lay not in its power to provision England cheaply but in the vested interests that in sixty years of commercial expansion had grown round its practice. A considered policy of imperial development might in the course of comparatively few years have afforded the British consumer and manufacturer adequate alternatives to most of the cheap food and raw materials bought from the foreigner. By guiding credit into the new area of preferential trade, and by adequately-financed facilities for migration, stable markets for British industrial exports could have been created in an expanding Empire. They would have involved some immediate sacrifice. But it would have been amply justified in, say, 1940.

But such a policy, however wise as a form of national insurance, would have involved a transfer of trade and investment from old-established into unproved channels. It scared cautious minds and threatened vested interests. In an old and rich country both were immensely powerful. With the extension of the franchise and the ever-growing cost of electoral organisation, both the main political parties were becoming dependent on the financial support of the City. And the City, as opposed to the provincial manufacturers, was opposed to any change in the country's trade and financial policy.

Behind the City was the ordinary investor. Since the general adoption of the limited liability principle an ever-growing number of citizens had obtained a shareholder's interest in commerce. Their money was invested in British companies trading with foreign countries in every part of the world. Their dividends were paid by the imports with which those countries purchased British goods. A policy which transferred part of the British home market to Empire producers endangered their interests. They argued that Britain could not increase, say, its sugar imports from Jamaica without taking less from Cuba. And they had more money invested in Cuba than in Jamaica.

Such forces preserving the *status quo* in commerce and finance were cumulative. Every year, while its virtual monopoly of manufactures lasted, a free-trading Britain, after paying for its foreign food and raw materials with manufactured exports, had a favourable balance. This balance, which for many years averaged a hundred million pounds, was allowed to remain in the form of accumulating loans to the debtor countries. The interest could only be paid by still more of their goods. The richer British investors grew, the greater became the foreign debtors' share of the British market. A creditor inevitably tries to keep his debtor in employment. The young empire countries, not being so heavily indebted, could not look for such help from money-lending Britain. For, having been long under-developed and under-populated, they had only recently appeared as large-scale borrowers on the London money market.

Thus all attempts to unite the Empire economically were still-born, because the mother country had prior and more paying financial affiliations with the foreigner. The Dominions and Colonies, it was felt, must be left to develop as best they could by forming similar affiliations with other nations who were not so deeply committed to established channels of finance and trade. For though in political matters Britain had become conscious of her empire, in those of finance and investment she still followed the teachings of *laissez-faire*. Scarcely any one seemed to see the contradiction in her doing so. The most ardent patriots, who glowed with pride at the thought of Australian bushrangers fighting in a British cause in South Africa, invested their savings in Latin America and bought their beef from the Argentine without a qualm.

Such men could not foresee the future. They were ordinary, honest, unimaginative Englishmen who were enjoying a prosperity which had no parallel in human history but which they assumed to be eternal and took for granted. Their right to do as they pleased with their own wealth, now mainly drawn from dividends, was something they never questioned: it had nothing to do with country or empire but was entirely their own affair. That if called on to do so, they would die for their King and Country was not to be doubted. They sat, red-cheeked and clear-eyed, in Pall Mall clubs or the Pavilion at Lord's, shot, hunted and fished in the appropriate seasons and transacted business in board-room or on 'change according to the unalterable laws of the Medes and Persians in which they had been trained. They paid their way with golden sovereigns and ruled the earth beneath tall silk hats in an aroma of lavender water and cigar smoke.

After the Boer War, with its early disasters and its long expensive litany of careless inefficiency, there were some mis-givings. "Let us admit it fairly," wrote Kipling,

> "as a business people should,
> We have had no end of a lesson: it will do us no end of good."

But such frank admissions were only temporary. The poet's conclusion—"we have had an imperial lesson; it may make us an Empire yet"—was not borne out by the course of events. A few months later he was writing savagely of "the flannelled fools at the wicket and the muddied oafs at the goal"—of a people who in their wealth and ease grudged even the slightest sacrifice to arm against the coming day of reckoning:

> "Ancient, effortless, ordered, cycle on cycle set,
>   Life so long untroubled, that ye who inherit forget . . .
>   But ye say ' It will mar our comfort.' Ye say ' It will minish
>   our trade.'
>   Do ye wait for the spattered shrapnel 'ere ye learn how a gun
>   is laid?
>   For the low, red glare to southward when the raided coast-
>   towns burn?"

But the only result of the poet's jeremaid was some loss of his own immense popularity. Everybody read him but nobody paid the least heed to his preaching.

For the English rich could not see what all the world but they could see: that their wealth created envy and jealousy, their empty empire greedy yearnings, their all pervading never-resting usury anger and resentment. They could not see that other nations, impatiently seeking outlets for their rising manufactures and populations, and armed to the teeth, were watching amid their jealousies a rich, obese and luxury-loving Britain as jackals watch a dying lion. Night after night as the London seasons of the young century sped by, amid the decorous revelry of the great saloons of Mayfair and the new hotels—Ritz, Savoy and Claridges—the lords of the earth in their starched linen, pearls and diamonds enjoyed their goodly heritage unquestioning. To watchers there seemed to be something reckless in the feverish speculation and worship of wealth that had invaded the formerly exclusive society of the Imperial capital.

The little Englanders and the Radicals and Socialists who accepted their kindly but narrow ideology, were no more aware of the dangers to their existence. To them the Empire seemed only a financiers' ramp for exploiting the backward races, or at best an invention of the Tories.[1] That the cheap meat and bread that fed them came by grace of the foreigner, that others were toasting the day when the age-long security and empire of the English should end, and that their own ways of life in the crowded cities might unfit them to stand in battle against the armies of young and jealous nations never troubled them for a moment. They went to their labours in the morning, perused their Sunday chronicle of murders and sensations, watched the gladiators of the football League battle in the arena for their favour, and cheered the cheapjack politicians of the hour who offered to plunder the rich and distribute the next year's seed-corn. And a despairing poet, feeling in his heart the imminence of doom, wrote:

"Now we can only wait till the day, wait and apportion our shame.
These are the dykes our fathers left, but we would not look to the same.
Time and again were we warned of the dykes, time and again we delayed:
Now it may fall we have slain our sons as our fathers we have betrayed."

[1] See *Punch CXLIV, 182.*

CHAPTER VIII

Battle in the Mud

By all borne and left unsaid
By the soldier. By the mire
Closing o'er a comrade's head,
By the faces stripped by fire,
By daylight's dumb and crowded wire
By moonlight's lonely loathsome dead,
By the slow, the final dread
Slaying very heart's desire:
Englishman, whoe'er thou art,
That is theirs, and this thy part—
Constant hold the English heart!
                              R. Nichols.

THE immediate cause of the Great War which burst on an apprehensive and excited Europe in 1914 was the arrogance of imperial Germany. Its people had been taught that war was the peculiar national instrument of the Teuton. Their philosophers had told them that in a German cause the end always justified the means. Nursed in the Prussian tradition and debauched by gross and ill-digested wealth, their statesmen had alternatively alarmed and angered every neighbour. In the summer of 1914 they threatened and blustered once too often and then found themselves unable to stop what they had started.

The real causes of the war were deeper. Since her union in 1871 Germany, with all the thoroughness and vehemence native to her people, had embraced the industrial revolution. In forty years her population had increased by one half and her wealth, measured by industrial assets and profits, many times over. Her government, embodying the national passion to excel—which in the first flush of her new-found unity amounted almost to a mania—had extended unlimited credit to her manufacturers and traders. She was thus committed to a policy of unceasing industrial expansion, since without it her capitalists could not pay the interest on the loans advanced them by the community.

The pace set by this system of state usury was too furious to last. In the first fourteen years of the century Germany quad-

rupled her industrial output. Her whole economic structure—
strong and flourishing to outward appearance—depended on her
ability to secure rapidly expanding markets. The liabilities of
her producers, ever accelerating their pace, pursued her : she
could only keep ahead of bankruptcy by moving still faster.
The nemesis of capitalism came to her more quickly. than to
any of her neighbours. It did so because she was more eager,
impatient and efficient. She positively flung herself at the
Gaderene precipice.

All the world was heading in the same direction. For following England's example and hoping to equal her success, the
merchants of every larger nation in Europe had taken to manufacturing. Fostering their infant industries with state subsidies
and artificial systems of credit, they struggled feverishly to
undercut their rivals in foreign markets. The whole earth
became a vast field of exploitation ranged by the agents of the
more civilised peoples competing with one another for customers
and raw materials to feed the wheels of their growing factories
and the mouths of their fast-breeding factory populations. And
after their agents came consuls, warships and expeditionary
forces to establish spheres of influence. Envying England's vast
empire, the industrial Powers hastened to found empires of their
own in still unexploited territories whence they could procure
cheap raw materials and force their manufactures on natives
subject to their exclusive control. During the latter half of the
nineteenth century Germany, France, Italy and Belgium all
pounced on large areas of unclaimed land in Africa and the
Far East. Holland and Portugal already possessed colonial
empires founded in an earlier age. Meanwhile the United States
and Russia each pursued a policy of unceasing continental expansion. Austria, backed by Germany, turned towards the
Balkans and the Middle East, and a new oriental manufacturing
Power, modelled on the most approved Western lines and sustained by modern fleets and armies, fought two victorious wars
against China and Russia to establish a Japanese commercial
sphere of influence in Manchuria.

But the unclaimed areas of the earth available were not enough
to satisfy the cumulative and inexhaustible needs of the capitalist.
The faster the usurer—state or private—supplied the more
intelligent races with machinery, the vaster the territories and
populations needed to pay the interest on his capital and the

more important to him their political control became. The forces of diplomacy and those grimmer forces that give weight to diplomacy, were inevitably marshalled in defence of the economic interests he created. There were successive crises which marked the clash of such forces, when one great Power in search of markets for goods or loans encountered another in the same field: Fashoda, Venezuela, Agadir. At each of these there was ominous talk of war, and an unloosing of popular national and racial feelings which had nothing to do with economics but which, deep-rooted in human hearts, could only too easily be aroused by the instruments of mass-suggestion. And these, unconsciously but inevitably, tended to fall under the control of the contending financial interests.

For when there was no more unoccupied land to seize or spheres of financial interest to penetrate, the great Powers began to covet each other's colonial possessions and economic fields. It was inevitable that those late starters in the twin race of colonial expansion and loan-mongering who had acquired the least should feel aggrieved. They thought of themselves as "have-not" Powers denied a "proper place in the sun." Germany, who, though second to none either in commercial or military pushfulness, had on account of her comparative newness obtained a rather bleak share of colonial plunder, made a special point of this.

The more ambitious of her people particularly resented the size of the British Empire. A young Englishman of education lacking an outlet in his overcrowded country could look for honourable and remunerative employment under his own flag and laws in one or other of his country's colonies. Germany, with half again Britain's population and apparently twice her energy and ambition, was less happily circumstanced: her hastily acquired colonies were confined mainly to tropical or semi-tropical deserts and forests in Africa and a few islands in the Pacific. She had nothing to offer the eager and pushing *alumni* of her overcrowded universities comparable in opportunity to the career afforded by the I.C.S. or the Sudan Civil. And, as Germany was finding, one of the inevitable concomitants of capitalist enterprise is the creation of large numbers of bourgeois youth demanding university education and some outlet for their talents more remunerative than handiwork and more honourable than trade. They found it inevitably in a bureaucracy, and, in the nature of things, in an expanding bureaucracy.

For these and other reasons the Germans and the English were rivals. The English did not consciously think of the Germans as such: but the Germans did so think of the English. They envied them, they admired them and they hated them. For the Germans were seeking what the English had long had and would not use for themselves—the hegemony of the world. Germany had her army. It was larger than any other army: it was better organised It had the repute of being invincible. But the English, though they refused to concern themselves in Europe's untidy affairs, would not allow the German army to rule Europe. They would not let it march through Belgium in 1870: they refused to let it attack defeated France in 1875. The stronger it became, the more the English, true to the most unchanging point in their foreign policy, tended to tilt the scales against Germany. Though contempt for France and fear of Russia had long been second nature to them, their states-men did not hesitate to lend their support to what the ingenuous Teuton regarded as a decadent France and a barbarous Russia in order to thwart the just and rightful ambitions of a virile central Europe. After the turn of the century and still more after Russia's defeat in the Far East, the English tendency was increasingly in this direction. Such spiteful interference in the affairs of the continent could only be explained, Germans con-tended, by jealousy; the English, fearing their success, wished to encircle them.

There were psychological differences too. When the Germans, seeking the omnipotence they could never quite reach, gave themselves airs, the English laughed at them. They thought of them as conceited, slightly comical "sausages" and enjoyed the name the discomforted but invincibly gay Viennese had invented for Berlin of "Parvenuopopolis." Their polite but occasionally ill-concealed contempt and their more normal indifference touched German vanity on the raw. There were always plenty of German statesmen, diplomats and merchants with a grudge against England which, fanned during war into a furnace of national hatred, was to astonish the English in 1914. In German regiments and in the ships of the High Seas Fleet toasts were drunk to *Der Tag*—the day that should not only be France's reckoning but England's.

E.S.   T

But the most serious difference, apart from the invisible rivalry of commerce, was the blue ribbon of sea power. With an expansionist Russia preaching nationality to every Slav minority on one side of her and a France with no more ground to yield on the other, Germany had to look like England to the younger continents for her *lebensraum*. Her industrialists looked overseas also for their markets and raw materials and, accustomed to military victories at home, confidently demanded the protection of the imperial government. A deep sea fleet came to be regarded as a national necessity. Even as early as 1864 Bismarck's campaign against Denmark revealed the new trend of German policy.[1] So did the purchase of Heligoland—unwisely sold by Lord Salisbury's government in 1890. After the succession of the young Emperor William II—Queen Victoria's grandson and in his own eyes heir-elect to Neptune's trident— the resolve to create a High Seas Fleet became a mania. The first German Navy Act of 1898 set a pace which within ten years had developed into a galloping race between Germany and a fast-awakening England for the command of the sea.

At first the English had treated Teuton naval ambitions as an immense joke.[2] To Englishmen there was something incongruous in the idea of fat Hans even trying to be a sailor. They had forgotten that in the Middle Ages the seamen of the Hanseatic League had sometimes given sea law to England and that in the seventeenth century the fleets, which under Tromp and de Ruyter had afforded her toughest naval encounters, had been largely recruited from the north German ports. But after the Boer War they began to wake up to the fact that a European Power was challenging Trafalgar. In the closing years of King Edward's brief reign and the first of King George's, the attention of England was torn from internecine disputes about wages, national health insurance, votes for women and Home Rule for Ireland, by the disquieting spectacle of German dreadnought after dreadnought gliding down the slips of Kiel and Wilhelmshaven into the waters of the Baltic and North Sea. It was all very well for the Kaiser to assure an English statesman that it

---

[1] Palmerston, answering a question in the House in July, 1863, stated: "There is no use in disguising the fact that what is at the bottom of the whole German design . . . is the dream of a German fleet and the wish to get Kiel as a German sea-port."

[2] At the time of the Danish War *Punch* depicted two bearded British seamen pointing at a fat, long-haired, shaggy-moustached, bespectacled Teuton and saying to one another: "Blow it, Bill, we can't be expected to fight a lot of lubberly swabs like him. We'll *kick* 'em, if that'll do!"—*Punch*, xlvii, 5.

was "*nonsensical* and *untrue*" that the German Navy Bill was meant as a challenge to British naval supremacy and to state that "the German Navy was built *against* nobody at all." For what, then, was it built?

It was this challenge which made England's participation by France's side in a European War inevitable. The sea was England's lifeline. Though her people did not know it, her rulers—almost without realising that they did so—were forced to commit her in advance. By an agreement to entrust the policing of the Mediterranean to France so as to concentrate the entire battle fleet in the North Sea, they made themselves morally responsible for the defence of the French Channel and the Atlantic coasts. Henceforward France and Britain had a common interest—resistance to Germany. For Germany threatened the existence of both.

Even then it was the educated minority rather than the majority who grasped the significance of what was happening. The unthinking multitude was still absorbed with its sports and its struggles for a happier existence. But in London *An Englishman's Home* played to packed houses, and young Winston Churchill, unconsciously turning towards the task that was his life's work, suddenly ceased to be the bitter opponent of army and navy estimates to become the Liberal First Lord who, defying Little Englanders and the Treasury, boldly laid down two keels to Germany's one and in a turning-point of history gave the order that kept the Grand Fleet at sea in the hour of Armageddon.

It only remained to set a spark to all this explosive material. For this simple task the rulers of imperial Germany were more than equal. They were neurotic, they were voluble and they were vain. They were also intensely arrogant. They were so obsessed with their own point of view that they were constitutionally incapable of listening quietly to, let alone seeing any one else's. At their head, though far from controlling them or the ruthless military machine they wielded, was the Kaiser—a clever, talkative, undisciplined, excitable egotist. His indiscretions were the terror of the European chancelleries. Add to this the fact that no German in authority, though quick enough to blunder and bluster, seemed able to apologise or withdraw, and that the jingo Press in all countries magnified every incident and hasty word, and it was obvious that an explosion could not be long delayed.

Everybody knew this except the islanders. Germany, in blind pursuit of new and urgently needed markets, and honouring a morality that placed her national *ego* above the law of nations, was resolved on expansion at all costs. On August 4th, 1914, the British people knew too. Throwing themselves at the eleventh hour on the side of an outnumbered France and an incalculable and distant Russia, they stood fair and square in the way. An irresistible force had encountered an immovable body.

Thus it came about that the British people for the first time in sixty years found themselves involved in a European war. It was clear that Germany had made a brutal and unprovoked attack on Belgium and that Britain had long plighted her word —as Germany had also—to maintain Belgian integrity and neutrality. Beyond that only a small minority had any clear idea of what the war was about. Scarcely any one realised that it threatened the very existence of the country. Invasion had been a press bugbear for some years before the outbreak of war, and invasion scares continued to alarm the public mind until 1916. But the very fact indicated how little the English understood the real nature of their peril. For should the naval situation deteriorate sufficiently to make sustained invasion possible, no invasion would be needed to bring England to her knees. For three almost out of every four mouthfuls that sustained her, Britain was dependent on sea-borne food. And her rulers, in conformity with a national economy which left such matters to private capital, had omitted to lay in any reserves. An overcrowded and unprepared island that could not feed itself for more than a few weeks or escape bankruptcy without the maintenance of a vast and complex export trade had challenged the first military and the second greatest naval power in the world.

. . . .

But the people of England only knew that the gauntlet had been thrown down and that their proud country was in the lists. After a century of security and of being taught by their rulers that the needs of the living were all that mattered, they were called upon to sacrifice themselves for the sake of the continuing community. Four generations of *laissez-faire* thinking and living had not robbed them of their patriotism. As one man they flung themselves into the fray.

"Comfort, content, delight—
The ages slow-bought gain—
They shrivelled in a night,
Only ourselves remain
To face the naked days
In silent fortitude,
Through perils and dismays
Renewed and re-renewed.

No easy hopes or lies
Shall bring us to our goal,
But iron sacrifice
Of body, will and soul.
There is but one task for all—
One life for each to give.
Who stands if Freedom fall?
Who dies if England live?

It was an astonishing spectacle. On the continent of Europe patriotism was the peculiar concern of the State. It was taught in the schools: it was officially stamped on the mind and body of the individual citizen in his conscript years. There was not a Frenchman, a German, a Russian or even an Italian between the ages of 18 and 60 who was not trained and liable at a moment's notice to serve in his country's army. When war came, his place in a mobilised nation was awaiting him.

In England it was different. The State did not teach the citizen patriotism: it scrupulously ignored the subject. It did not teach him nor expect him to serve his country. The State existed to serve the individual, not the individual the State. It provided him with legal and police protection, street lighting and paving and, under recent socialist legislation, with—for those who wanted them—free education, municipal baths and health insurance. It asked nothing in return except obedience to the law and the payment of taxes. If the individual chose to be patriotic, that was his own affair—a kind of hobby like collecting stamps or big-game shooting. Thus there was a voluntary Navy League, supported by private subscriptions, for awakening public interest in the Navy, and quite a number of rival Empire Societies for persuading people to think imperially. But the State itself had nothing to do with them except to assess them

for their shares of taxation. It treated them in exactly the same
way as it treated atheist or revolutionary societies. Even professional sailors and soldiers were only ordinary citizens without
special privileges. Outside the close corporation of their ships
and regiments they made no demonstration of their relation to
the State: in England an officer when off duty did not swagger
down the street in uniform, but punctiliously donned mufti
and went about like an ordinary private citizen. It was what,
in the eyes of the law, he was.

Continental observers—particularly German ones who loved
to contrast their own strident patriotism with English casualness
—assumed from this that English people had ceased to love
their country and under the influence of commerce and luxury
had become degenerate. They supposed them lacking in the
fighting virtues of self-sacrifice, discipline and *esprit de corps*.
They even thought them cravens. In the trenches before Ypres
and Le Bassée they received a rude awakening. For though in
England the State had long disinterested itself in the private
citizen's patriotism or capacity for war, the English with their
long history retained a stronger national consciousness and
underlying unity than probably any other people in the world.
They took their love of country and their willingness to die for
her for granted. For modern war they were out of date and out
of practice. But, as the event proved, when once they set their
minds to it, they caught up with the martial accomplishments
of their militarist neighbours at an astonishing rate.

It was perhaps just because the State left the Englishman so
free to serve the nation in his own way that he came to its aid
in the hour of need with such enthusiasm. He valued the virtues
of self-sacrifice, civic pride and comradeship the more because he
had had to foster them himself. For doing so the English had
unconsciously evolved a vast network of private organisations
and associations which, though legally divorced from the State,
kept alive the attributes on which the State depended. Theirs
was a capacity for creating loved institutions which amounted
to the highest political genius. Round these they wove a kind
of affectionate mystery. The more venerable they were the more
they loved them and the more sacred became every familiar and
hallowed accompaniment. Nothing short of a life-work of close
and loving scholarship could do justice to the love that grew
up in the course of a few decades round an institution like county

cricket or foxhunting or an Oxford Common Room. Englishmen were almost ready to die sooner than pass the port to the right or omit a phrase of the customary chaff and larking that attended the August Bank Holiday on Hampstead Heath or Ilkeley Moor.

This curious and apparently unconscious capacity for attaching individual effort to a corporate ideal embodied in group ritual informed almost every activity of the nation's life. Hospitals and charitable trusts like the City Companies transmitted traditions as unchanging and proud as those of the Brigade of Guards. Money-making abstractions like the Stock Exchange and Lloyds and far humbler commercial concerns had their sacred laws of the Medes and Persians unenforced by law yet which no member would dream of breaking and which good men loved to honour. The very newspapers evolved their own individual pride and code of honour: *The Times* was as much a national institution as Convocation or the House of Lords, and its staff regarded it with the same affection as a Pomeranian grenadier his regiment.

Even schoolboys shared the national aptitude. The ritual, increasingly hallowed by tradition, of a great public school was as intricate and finely woven as a Beethoven sonata and aroused in those who were subjected to it an affection which nothing but death could eradicate. When the school songs were sung in the Speech Room at Harrow grown and undemonstrative men —immersed in commerce or other individualistic pursuits— would let their eyes fill with tears in a surge of emotion which reason could not explain but which was an unconscious expression of their capacity for devotion to an undying ideal. In a humbler social sphere Workmens' Colleges and Council Schools began to gather traditions, and the ragged urchins of the street evolved their own rough loyalties and rules of honour. Playing for one's side was in the English blood. It only needed the alchemy of war and national peril to harness these diverse enthusiasms and loyalties to the service of the community. For when the Kaiser with his mailed fist threatened England, he did not threaten England alone. He threatened the Fourth of June, and the May Day choir on Magdalen Tower, and the village bonfire on Guy Fawkes Night; the M.C.C. and the Reform Club; the Amalgamated Society of Engineers and the Ancient Order of Buffaloes. Behind the easy façade of England there was something mightier than England: there was Hayward and Hobbs going in to bat, the Oddfellows' dinner and the Old Kent Road.

It was a people subject to such influences who created in the next few years, as though by a miracle, a military machine as vast and as efficient as Germany's. In the first eighteen months of the war Great Britain without compulsion raised two and three-quarter million men for the Services, and the self-governing Dominions close on another million. The miracle was achieved merely by asking for volunteers. They were told that their King and Country needed them, and it was enough. It was in the nature of things that the best went first and were the first killed. In the democracy of Britain there was no equality of sacrifice. The war graves of Gallipoli and the Somme are the memorials of a national aristocracy nobler than any Herald's College could have conceived. That spontaneous and inspired loss—of her very finest—was the price Britain paid both for her voluntary system and her past neglect. It won her the war but it cost her the peace. For by their elected sacrifice she lost the leaders she was to need when the war was over.

A nation of amateur patriots was absorbed into the little professional peace-time army, which itself suffered virtual annihilation while England buckled on her long-neglected armour. The traditions of that army were perfectly adapted to the subconscious nature of Englishmen. Men who a few weeks before had never seen a rifle handled or thought of soldiering with anything but contempt found themselves swelling with pride at regimental annals and titles won by remote forerunners, and boasted to their womenfolk that they were "Pontius Pilate's Bodyguard," or the "Devil's Own" or the "Diehards" or the "Fighting Fifth." For every unit in the army had its own pride and its own privileges, won for it on the battlefield. To many Englishmen, long robbed by factory life of status and privilege, that return to the army—for all its harshness—was like a recall home.

There was little of ease or comfort about it, much of hardship; and men came to realise that the certain end of the road they trod was death and wounds. But nobody who lived in England in that first winter of the first Great War will ever forget the training battalions of "Kitchener's Army," marching in their ill-fitting blue tunics down muddy country lanes and singing as they marched:

"Why did we join the Army, boys?
Why did we join the Army?
Why did we come to Salisbury Plain?
We must have been ruddy well balmy!"

One young officer, himself soon to fall in action, who shared
the comradeship and common purpose of that great and gallant
company, left behind him the picture of those wintry marches
across the English countryside:

"All the hills and vales along
Earth is bursting into song,
And the singers are the chaps
Who are going to die perhaps.
O sing, marching men,
Till the valleys ring again.
Give your gladness to earth's keeping,
So be glad, when you are sleeping.

Cast away regret and rue,
Think what you are marching to.
Little live, great pass.
Jesus Christ and Barabbas
Were found the same day.
This died, that went his way.
So sing with joyful breath.
For why, you are going to death.
Teeming earth will surely store
All the gladness that you pour."[1]

Among those who in those early months of the war chose
death for their bride were thousands of young men who had
seemingly been born to the happiest lot ever enjoyed by man.
Nursed in a traditional culture that had not yet quite lost its
hold on the well-to-do classes, yet admitted to the greater freedom
of a wider and more liberal educational ideal than the past had
known, they inherited the best of both worlds.

Of this generation one man in particular became identified in
the public mind. Rupert Brooke was in reality only one of

[1] C. H. Sorley, Marlborough, and other Poems.

many: he was not even wholly typical of those he came to embody. But the direct appeal of his poetry, the beauty of his appearance and the romance of his brief life caught the imagination of a wider circle than those who ordinarily read poetry. Even before the tempest burst and the publication of his 1914 sonnets took reading England by storm, he was known to many as the personification of a new kind of youth, careless of appearances, generous, out-spoken, almost Elizabethan in its uncalculating love of adventure, spiritual and physical. The dedication to death of one so much in love with life became momentarily the symbol of a whole generation's sacrifice. In the mood of 1914 he was youth going down with touched lips into the shadows as an earnest of a nobler and a happier life for all men in the years to come.

A greater poet than Brooke and a greater Englishman was Julian Grenfell. A fine scholar and a brilliant athlete, born to all the worldly gifts that any man could inherit, his sympathies —at a time when such sympathies were still unusual and regarded with disfavour—were always with the revolutionary, the crank and the under-dog. It was not that he rebelled against order but that he instinctively comprehended the causes of his age's discontent. A professional soldier before the war, he embraced the call to arms as a crusade—not so much against the German people or even their tiresome rulers as against the inertia and death that seemed to have fallen on the world. After enduring with astonishing happiness and cheerfulness the first harsh winter in the trenches, he fell in the spring of 1915. A few weeks before he died, looking over the April Flemish plain, he wrote one of the greatest lyrical poems in the language and which, so long as English is read, will remain the epitaph of himself and his generation:

> "The naked earth is warm with spring,
>   And with green grass and bursting trees
> Leans to the sun's gaze glorying
>   And quivers in the sunny breeze;
> And Life is Colour and Warmth and Light,
>   And a striving evermore for these;
> And he is dead who will not fight;
>   And who dies fighting has increase.

The fighting man shall from the sun
Take warmth, and life from the glowing earth;
Speed with the light-foot winds to run,
And with the trees to newer birth;
And find, when fighting shall be done,
Great rest, and fullness after dearth.

All the bright company of Heaven
Hold him in their high comradeship,
The Dog-Star and the Sisters Seven,
Orion's Belt and sworded hip.

. . . .

The blackbird sings to him, ' Brother, brother,
If this be the last song you shall sing,
Sing well, for you may not sing another:
Brother, sing 'l "

. . . .

The changing mood of England at war can be traced in the work of its poets. Almost at once there was a division between the professional poets at home and the combatant poets— amateurs in verse as in soldiering and astonishingly great in both. This division widened until in the end it became an unbridgeable gulf. It typified the greater gulf between the two Englands—the young living England that died and the old petrified England that lived. A quarter of a century later, when a second world war broke out, that gulf was still unbridged.

The early war poets were like the England that took up the challenge of the German War Lords: passionate in their sacrifice, confident, uncalculating. They never doubted their victory or the rightness of their dedication. Theirs was an almost mystical exaltation: the war had been sent as guerdon of their manhood, to test them and by their testing to purify a world "grown old and stale and weary." They positively rejoiced in their unlooked-for, elected lot: it was for this, they felt, that they had been born.

"Better far to pass away
While the limbs are strong and young,
Ere the ending of the day,
Ere youth's lusty song be sung.

Hot blood pulsing through the veins,
Youth's high hope a burning fire,
Young men needs must break the chains
That hold them from their hearts' desire."[1]

But by 1916 the note had changed. With the commencement
of the great slaughter on the Somme it could scarcely have
done otherwise. On the first day of the battle alone, 60,000
casualties were sustained—the very flower of England. And week
by week, as the brazen fury continued and a whole countryside was
churned into a slimy mire of death, victory was realised to be an
infinitely distant goal, far beyond the reach of most of those
striving for it. Courage grew commonplace, strength faltered,
vision faded. The poetry of fighting England became grimmer,
often bitterly ironic, yet none the less, with the extraordinary
capacity of the English for rejecting by ignoring calamity,
soaring in moments of ecstasy above "the smoke and stir of this
dim spot which men call earth," and seeing beauty above the
horror of carnage.

"Music of whispering trees
Hushed by the broad-winged breeze
Where shaken water gleams;
And evening radiance falling
With reedy bird-notes calling.
O bear me safe through dark, you low-voiced streams.

I have no need to pray
That fear may pass away;
I scorn the growl and rumble of the fight
That summons me from cool
Silence of marsh and pool,
And yellow lilies islanded in light.
O river of stars and shadows, lead me through the night!"[2]

In the last two years of the war, as poet after poet passed into
the ghostly company of the mouthless dead, the lyrical note was
drowned in the angry, unpitying clamour of a universe gone

[1]The Muse in Arms 32—*Poem by R. M. Dennys.*
[2]The War Poems of *Siegfried Sassoon, Before the Battle.*

mad: the last snatches of a lost world of colour going down into a welter of mud and desolation:

"What passing bells for those who die as cattle?
Only the monstrous anger of the guns,
Only the stuttering rifles' rapid rattle
Can patter out their hasty orisons.
No mockeries for them from prayers or bells,
Nor any voice of mourning save the choirs—
The shrill, demented choirs of wailing shells;
And bugles calling for them from sad shires."[1]

It was a subconscious protest of the human spirit which common unlettered fighting men also echoed, but in blasphemies and grim jests which no one has recorded.

Yet this people, out of whose finest minds such poetry was rung, could not be deterred from its purpose. Their will was equal to their task. "How to pull the English off?" wrote Walter Page, the American Ambassador in London, "that's a hard thing to say, as it is a hard thing to say how to pull a bull-dog off." Watching day by day the never-ceasing procession of inquirers seeking news at the Embassy of missing sons and husbands, the Ambassador was struck by their stoicism. "Not a tear have I seen yet," he wrote. "They take it as part of the price of greatness and of empire. You guess at their grief only by their reticence. They use as few words as possible and then courteously take themselves away. It isn't an accident that these people own a fifth of the world. Utterly un-warlike, they out-last everybody else when war comes. You don't get a sense of fighting here—only of endurance and of high resolve." In another letter Page painted the same picture, set against the awful background of battle—of a nation "sad, dead-earnest, resolute, united: not a dissenting voice—silent. It will spend all its treasure and give all its men, if need be. I have never seen such grim resolution."[2]

It was needed before the English came to their journey's end. There were disasters in distant places of the earth; allies— broken by the storm—fell away, and, as offensive after offensive with all their high delusive hopes failed, the angel of death beat

[1] *Wilfred Owen, Anthem for Doomed Youth.*
[2] B. J. Hendrick, *Life & Letters of Walter Page.*

his wings against the panes of innumerable homes. In the spring of 1917 the German submarine campaign, before it was brought under control, was sinking half a million tons of shipping a month. For a few weeks—though the hideous truth was hidden from the multitude—it seemed as though the price of uncultivated farms and a neglected empire would be famine and defeat. New methods, long obstinately rejected by leaders nursed in old ways, and the aid of American destroyers turned the tide at the eleventh hour.

The full magnitude of what Englishmen were called upon to endure was reached in the great offensive in the Flemish mud, sometimes called the third battle of Ypres and sometimes Passchendaele, which went on without a break for two drenching months in the autumn of 1917. The battle, long planned by the General Staff, was partly undertaken in the hope of driving the German submarine bases from the Belgian coast. But it was also fought in pursuance of a definite philosophy of war which, after the failure of successive attempts to break the ugly deadlock of trench warfare, had taken firm hold of the British military mind. It had already been pursued, it was argued, with considerable success, though at the price of half a million British casualties, in the four months' battle of the Somme. The dominating idea was that as the total population of the Allied Powers was higher than that of their foes, the process of scaling down both fighting populations, man for man, as rapidly as possible must end in the ultimate survival of the larger. The quicker the rate of mutual destruction, the military statisticians argued, the sooner the war would be over.

For many weeks the Passchendaele offensive, begun on July 31st, was regarded as the prelude to victory. Every day brought its black lettering of triumph in the popular press: that autumn, as in the *annum mirabilis*, 1759, gentlemen abed in England woke to ask what new victory had been won. An advance of a thousand yards over Flemish mud so churned up and battered that even the oldest denizen could not have recognised it, and won with a loss of British life heavier than which it had cost a century and half earlier to conquer India and Canada together, was hailed in *The Times* with headlines of "German Defence Broken!" "We have broken," the Special Correspondent of that paper wrote, "and broken at a single blow in the course of some three or four hours, the German system of defence." Next day it was broken again, and the next and the next.

Night after night watchers of the bombardment that preceded each day's attack saw "the flame of shell-fire ... stretching away round a great horizon," and heard "from near and far the ceaseless hammer-stroke of great guns making the sky red and restless with tongues of leaping fire and bringing unseen, unimaginable destruction to the masses of men hidden in the dark woods and trenches." Over such a landscape, if landscape it can be called, denuded by tornadoes of shells of all vestiges of vegetation or human habitation, men heavily laden with arms and military equipment were expected to advance against a pitiless rain of machine-gun fire. Whichever way they turned in pursuit of their orders, they floundered in oceans of knee-deep mud: even on the rare dry days of that ghastly autumn the solidest-looking earth proved as thin as half-cooked porridge into which a fully-equipped man sank until face, hands and tunic were soaked with black mire, fœtid with the obscene and decomposing remains of dead comrades. "Cold and paddling through sea of slime" to reach objectives whose value seemed as worthless as their own water-logged shell-holes and whose cost must be probably their own lives or mutilation, men yet endured and kept their pride and manhood. Many were drowned as they went forward or dragged their mangled bodies towards the rear.

Looking down from a slight eminence on that vast battlefield in the swamps between Ypres and the Passchendaele ridge, "the long bare slope down to St. Julien, the valley of the Steenbeek, choked with wreckage, churned into swamp and dotted with derelict tanks; the rising ground to Poelcapelle, and in the far distance fields and pastures new, green trees and a church spire,"[1] a young officer—no weakling but a hardened veteran—was reminded of a child's picture of *The Pilgrim's Progress*, unread since nursery days. "Here was Christian descending into the Valley of Humiliation and seeing in the distance the Delectable Mountains 'beautified with woods, vineyards, fruits of all sorts, flowers, also with springs and fountains' very delectable to behold, but in the path there lay 'a wilderness, a land of deserts and pits; a land of drought and of the shadow of death!' There was 'also in that valley a continual howling and yelling, as of people under unutterable misery who there sat bound in afflictions and irons;

---

[1] C. Edmonds, *A Subaltern's War*, 131-2.

over that valley hang the discouraging clouds of confusion; death also doth always spread his wings over it. In a word it is every whit dreadful, being utterly without order; . . . at the other end of this valley lay blood, bones, ashes and mangled bodies of men, even of pilgrims that had gone this way formerly'." In that place, though only the strongest and most faithful were gathered there, even the strongest and most faithful were near breaking-point.

Far from the blood-stained swamp, in the Olympian calm of G.H.Q., Haig, with his handsome head thrown back and his quiet, confident smile, would make a dramatic sweep with his hands over his maps to show visiting politicians how he was driving the Germans back to their frontiers. Mr. F. S. Oliver, the historian, contemplating the deluge that poured continually from the skies, admired the serene way the commander-in-chief ignored the elements and persisted in his attacks. Presently the distant ridge would be captured and the plain of Belgium would open up before his victorious troops. Or so it seemed, looking out through the tall, rain-spattered windows of the chateau of Montreuil. The German generals pursued similar visions of early victory; that autumn Russia, rent by revolution and anarchy, collapsed before their advancing armies, and in October the Austrians, believed to be at the last gasp, struck back with German aid at their Italian assailants and sent them in headlong rout with a loss of more than half a million men towards the Piave. These disasters, like those which had befallen Belgium, Servia and Romania in the earlier years of the war, were attended by a mass flight of non-combatants—of whole nations on the trek leaving behind a vast, untidy trail of dying women, old men and children and the skeletons of starved animals. The sum total of human misery was past calculation. Men, crueler than the beasts, grew indifferent to it. German civilians sang specially composed hymns of hate against England and, in the most civilised country in the world, quiet, inoffensive English gentlemen and ladies who had never seen a blow struck in anger scouted the very mention of peace and spoke of the whole German race as they would of a pack of wild beasts. Only in the battle-line itself was there no hatred: only suffering and endurance: death and infinite waste.

Through the autumn months the "triumphal crawl through the mud proceeded." Flemish villages, whose names had never been heard of before in England, fell amid national jubilations and at the cost of nearly 400,000 casualties—a loss equal to the entire population of Bristol. On the German side another 250,000 fell. For each of these casualties, somebody in some town or village far from the fighting line suffered anxiety, heart-ache indescribable, or irretrievable loss. It was a time when women all over the world wore set faces, knowing that their dear ones were in danger in a noble cause in defence of which no sacrifice could be too great.

When nearly half a million men had fallen, the battle was called off. For the time being there were no more men to send to the slaughter, and there was nothing for it for those who remained but to dig themselves into the mud and wait until the still undrained man-power of the new world beyond the Atlantic should arise to redress the exhaustion of the old. Then "the bovine and brutal game of attrition could begin again." Amid the stench of thousands of unburied corpses the victorious survivors consolidated their watery gains. These unfortunately were nearly all lost in the next German offensive.

Yet there was no surrender, for on both sides of the line congregated all that was most heroic and constant in the manhood of the most virile nations of the old world. These fighters, hidden from one another in the slime, subjected day and night to a ceaseless tornado of screeching death out of the darkened sky, tortured by every foul breath and sight that can appal the sensitive mind, were in that place and hour because they had chosen to be there. There were many roads out of the battle-line; they were necessary since none but the strong could stand the test. No unit wished to keep the weak. Behind the lines were all those fulfilling a thousand lesser tasks, who could or would not fight it out. The stalwarts remained. Along either rim of the rat-haunted, corpse-strewn limbo of no-man's land the philosopher seeking virtue in 1917 would have found the elect of the earth.

The men who formed the rank and file of the army of Britain did not only retain their courage. Under a cloak of ironical and often blasphemous jargon they preserved their native good humour. Even cheerfulness was constantly breaking through—in a world of thunder and screeching, mangled bodies, foul miasmas and ceaseless terror they laughed and joked. Bruce Bairnsfather's cartoon of the old veteran with his grim, ugly,

resolute face and his walrus moustache, telling the grumbling
youngsters in his mud-bath of a shell-hole—"If yer know of a
better 'ole, go to it"—was the epitome of an invincible army.
Whenever the nerves of the strongest were at breaking-point the
English soldier fell back on an inner fortress of his soul. It was
buttressed with a kind of stubborn laughter. He jested at fate
because he did not wholly believe in it. For he knew it was too
bad to be true.

Sometimes that defiant cheerfulness arose above the mire
and squalor in some communal expression like the great shout
that would spring from masses of men at the most unlikely
moments of "*Are we downhearted—No!*" or the impossible songs
with which troops beguiled the march, few of them printable.

> "Send for the boys of the Old Brigade
> To keep old England free!
> Send for me' father and me' mother and me' brother,
> But for Gawd's sake don't send me!"

More often in the latter stages of the war the regiments marched
in silence under their medieval steel-rimmed helmets with a
certain monotonous, almost brute-like grimness. But the humour
and cheerfulness found expression in an undertone of individual
facetiousness: the "'Ave a 'eart, Fritz, we broke our bloody
gun!" which accompanied an intensive German bombardment
unreplied to; the time-honoured, "There goes the —— receipt!"
when the British response came at last.

Sergeant Tozer, Little Martlow, Shem, Weeper Smart,
Madeley—the common soldiers of that great and forgotten epic
of England in trial, *Her Privates We*—were drawn from life
against a background of unimaginable nightmare which their
incorrigible valour alone kept from being more than nightmare.
"These apparently rude and brutal natures comforted, encouraged
and reconciled each other to fate, with a tenderness and tact
which was more moving than anything in life. They had
nothing, not even their own bodies, which had become mere
implements of warfare. They turned from the wreckage and
misery of life to an empty heaven, and from an empty heaven
to the silence of their own hearts. They had been brought to the
last extremity of hope, and yet they put their hands on each
other's shoulders and said with a passionate conviction that it

would be all right, though they had faith in nothing but in
themselves and each other." They never broke, never gave way,
never despaired; they only jested, stuck it out and died.

"What's the use of worrying?" ran the refrain of a music-hall
song much used for marching and barn-concerts at the end of
the war. "Eh, corporal, w'a's this?" asked the soldier of his
exiguous bread ration. "That, m'lad, is your bread ration."
"Blimey! A thowt it were 'Oly Communion!" An army which
could face hell in such a spirit was one which might be
annihilated. It could not be defeated.

It was not numbers nor efficiency nor even courage that did
England's business, though in all these, learning the art of
modern war by harsh experience, she came to excel. In the last
resort victory went to the nation with the greatest capacity for
endurance. During the final terrible year of the war Germany,
released from all danger on her long eastern front by the collapse
of Russia and temporarily relieved of any fear of Italian action,
concentrated her entire armament for a decisive blow in the
west. On a misty morning of March 21st, 1918, 62 German
divisions, attacking on a front of 25 miles, broke through the
fifth British Army. For the next four months the German
attacks scarcely ever ceased; at one moment, driving a wedge
between the British and French, they almost reached the vital
junction of Amiens: at another there seemed to be nothing but
one shattered, invincible battalion of Grenadiers between the
grey-coated hordes and the Channel coast. The gains of the
Somme, Cambrai, Passchendaele, the Aisne, even the Marne
melted away in a few days.

But somehow Britain and her failing ally, France, stuck fast.
The line held. American reinforcements were beginning to cross
the Atlantic in large numbers; in Palestine, Allenby of Jerusalem
and Lawrence of Arabia with shrewd hard blows brought down
the Turkish Empire, leaving an open door in the German rear.
By the beginning of August the army of Britain, decimated and
tired as it was, gathered its strength for a new spring. When
it came on August 8th it proved, contrary to all expectations,
the beginning of the end. The German Army had met its match.
It struggled bravely, wavered and finally broke. On November
11th, still falling back across the French and Belgian soil it had
conquered, it surrendered unconditionally.

·   ·   ·   ·   ·   ·   ·   ·

Behind the army lay another force without which its efforts would have availed nothing. During the four and a quarter years of the war the army absorbed nearly six million Britons, the navy only half a million. But those five hundred thousand men and their Admiral could have lost the war in a single hour. By their mere existence hundreds of miles away from the struggling armies and smoking towns that fed the battlefield, the strength of Germany was slowly sapped. The terrible purpose of England beset by foes was expressed in its final form in remote silence: among the islands of the North the Fleet was in being. It was enough. The only half-hearted attempt to challenge it ended in the thunder of Jutland; but when the mists and smoke of that confused cannonade lifted, the seas remained as they were— England's forbidden waterway. The people of central Europe tried every way to avert and postpone the hungry negation of that invisible siege. Even while their armies, out-gunned, out-manœuvred and out-fought, were falling back before the advancing surge of victorious khaki and blue, hunger was gnawing at the vitals of the German workers and housewives at home. Revolution and surrender went hand in hand. And at the end of all, the Kaiser's tall ships of war, manned by hungry and mutinous men, tailed in mournful submission to Scapa Flow.

Victory, eagerly hoped for in 1914, struggled for in vain and in the face of repeated disappointments and defeats in the long middle years, almost despaired of in the spring and summer of 1918, had come at last. Never a military nation, England, when it came to testing the martial virtues, had outlasted all others. That was why she won. In after years successful men of peace were to argue that her financial resources had given her victory just as the defeated Germans, forgetting their sores, were to contend that there had been no victory at all. But in the grim days of March, 1918, and during the fierce, terrible advance against the struggling German lines of that September and October, the fate of the world rested on the stubborn shoulders of the British soldier. He and the superb fighters that the British nations overseas sent from their lands of snow and sun to stand by England's side, were the ultimate arbiters of that iron time. Had they failed the world would have failed, and the German ideal of rule by power would have triumphed while Adolf Hitler was still a corporal. Not Britain's wealth but her character was the deciding factor in that hour of destiny.

Though the exhausted French and the broken Russians and the still untried legions of the United States all contributed to victory, the dominating force in the world on November 11th, 1918, were the five million fighting men—the greater part of them volunteers and amateur soldiers—drawn from a scattered community of thirty-five million English, four and a half million Scots, two million Welsh, a million or so of Ulstermen, eight million Canadians, six and a half million Australians and New Zealanders, and one and a half million South Africans—in all rather less than sixty million free people, of whom more than three-quarters were English or of English descent. Contrary to all expectation, they had given the German army the thrashing it needed and taught a would-be despot the lesson that, though imperial Britain herself would not give rule to Europe, no one else should.[1]

[1] A page of drawings by Fougasse in *Punch* in the year of the victory celebrations, showed how the process had been accomplished. " Well, I'm blowed," says the English civilian of 1914, first in his shirt-sleeves by the fire and then in his ill-fitting blue training suit. "What good can I be, turning out to fight them blooming Germans with all their guns and millions of men!" And thereafter one sees him with increasing efficiency, learning amid hardships and great difficulties to do the job in hand, until in the end, it is the professional and military German who is out-gunned, out-tanked and out-manœuvred. "It's not as if we were a military nation," adds the victor once more by his fireside, "or took kindly to it at all. I don't wonder it's taken us four years to finish the job !"—*Punch CLVII, 28.*

CHAPTER NINE

Crumbling Heritage

If England was what England seems,
An' not the England of our dreams,
But only putty, brass an' paint,
'Ow quick we'd chuck 'Er! *But she ain't!*
Kipling.

WHEN the war ended the simple fighting men who had
won it thought that a new world was about to be built
on the ruins of the old. They looked across a desolate
landscape of charred ruins and ghostly tree trunks—the very
field of Golgotha and dead men's skulls. Between them and the
life they had known before the war was an unbridgeable gulf of
scalding tears and the blood of dead comrades and of incommuni-
cable agony.

They had no clear idea of the exact form the world they felt
they had earned should take. It was a romantic rather than a
concrete conception, and one that, unspoken, had sometimes
floated through the smoky air of battalion concerts when some
prosaic enough looking singer regaled his comrades with "A
Long Long Trail" or "Roses are blooming in Picardy," homely
tunes which no one who heard them in that setting ever heard
again without a forewarning of tears. But being an English
dream, it was curious how it reverted to ideas of roses round the
door and nightingales singing and the sound of the rooster

"——the one that used 'ter
Wake me up at four a.m."

For most of the rough, hard-tried men who listened approv-
ingly and in the choruses sent their very souls humming into the
rafters, hailed from scenes far removed from the rustic para-
phernalia of their imaginary heaven. In the remote days of 1914
before they joined up, they would certainly not have thanked
any utopian visionary who had shifted them from the crowded,
noisy life of the street corner and planted them down in a country
cottage or woodland glade. But somehow after four years of

war they were far nearer, though they did not know it, to the vanished England of 1840 or even 1740 than to the *laissez-faire* industrial society of 1914. The encrustations of a hundred years of urban development had fallen from them, shed on the dusty, bullet-swept downs above Contalmaison or in the blood and mud of the Salient, leaving their souls naked as they had inherited them from their remote forebears. Bereft by the pitiless tempest of war of almost everything they had known in their brief, stunted city lives, their desires and needs were unconsciously dictated by their country's forgotten tradition. Put to the test the slum boy, made man by ordeal of battle, had acquired an atavistic memory of the things he had lost.

He wanted a home he could call his own, with perhaps a garden for vegetables and flowers, a regular job of work in which he could take pleasure and pride, security in his livelihood and the self-respect that comes from status and a fixed place in society. It was not a very exacting ambition, and by the universal acclamation of the nation he had deserved it. He had even been promised it by the politicians. There was nobody who wanted to deny it him.

Amid a wild delirium of hooters, squeakers, and flag-wagging men and girls on car-roofs, the nation shut off steam. No more digging potatoes for victory in dreary allotments beside the gasworks, no more going out on Special Constable's duty on cold winter nights: good-bye, reflected business England, to all that. The hour had come for every man to help himself and in his leisure to enjoy the good time to which his patriotic efforts had entitled him. For the British were not merely a profit-seeking people: they were an enjoying people. Golf, cricket, seaside holidays, sunny June afternoons on the river or at the wheel were the prizes which those able to awarded themselves.

Even in the armies overseas, after a slight pause, the same thing happened. The war was over: the goal was reached. There was no point in men who were not professional soldiers remaining soldiers any longer. The only thing to do was to get absorbed in civilian employment as quickly as possible. Self-sacrifice, devotion to the corporate ideal, *esprit de corps*, were no longer needed: dreams must wait. Within a few weeks the amateur soldier had only one thought: to get "demobbed" and back to clean sheets—if he had them—warm wife and the familiar sights of Blighty. A few old soldiers, cynical about politicians' promises and reckoning that they were in a tolerably snug hole and in a harsh world would find no better, made no hurry to doff their khaki and stayed where they were—so long as an indulgent Treasury would let them. The remainder evaporated. For four years they had placed duty and fidelity to comrades above self: now, the bugles having sounded armistice, there was a not unnatural reaction. Number One came first.

So the fighting man received the thanks of his country, a suit of civilian clothes, a pair of medals and a small cash gratuity. In the case of a private soldier it amounted to the equivalent of a few weeks' wages. In the case of an officer it was more liberal and was often sufficient to purchase a small chicken farm or a wayside garage and car.

Unless he had a disability pension—which carried with it the inconvenience of a disability—that was all. Like the Pied Piper, the man who, a little while before, had been acclaimed the saviour of his country, was given a matter of something to put in his poke and told by the Mayor and Corporation that any more was out of the question. The sacrifice of the past belonged to the past. It was already history.

Another history had begun—the history, as we now know, of the twenty years between two wars. It started in exhaustion and hope; it was to end in disillusion and disaster. The nineteen twenties and thirties are too near to be seen as history, and all narrative of them is still only conjecture. Surveying them from 1940 the historian is like a man looking back on a mountain range which he has just left. The peaks which are nearest still dominate the others: he cannot see the range in perspective nor perhaps even glimpse at all the highest peaks of all. He must travel farther before their true outline, so simple when viewed from far horizons, can be comprehended.

The soldiers who came back to the land they had defended greeted the peace in the mood of their dream. They supposed that they were going to devote the lives so miraculously spared them to the rebuilding of a better England, worthy of the men who had died for it. But they and the civilian majority to whom they returned—who, lacking their revolutionary spiritual experience, had never shared their vision—were almost at once overwhelmed by the necessity of forcing a living out of the economic system in which they found themselves. Few of them had any time or opportunity for political or philosophical reflection, let alone action. They had more than enough to do to earn their daily bread and, so far as they were able, a decent life for themselves and their dear ones. Beyond voting in masses at set intervals for two or more organised groups of politicians offering stereotyped legislative programmes of a general kind, whose practical purport was never very clear, they could not shape the course of events. They merely lived through them, reacting to them as their native feelings and their limited knowledge—mostly acquired through the newspapers—dictated. For the rest, they looked for jobs, worked hard to hold them when they had them—though seldom for the joy of working since few available jobs offered any scope for this—and, Englishwise, took whatever pleasure their confined lives afforded: in the bosom of their families, listening to the wireless, watching League football or the flickers, and holiday-making in cheap cars or charabancs.

What followed in the world of public affairs bore small relation to their desire. The emphasis at first was almost wholly domestic. It seemed attended by a great deal of bitterness and strife. There were constant strikes and lock-outs, and violent speeches in which Britons in the public eye called each other tyrants, bloodsuckers, murderers, firebrands, and red revolutionaries. These industrial upheavals involved much recurrent inconvenience to the ordinary man: clerks had to make their way to the office without trains or trams, housewives to cook without coal or gas, shareholders to forgo their wonted dividends, and strikers their wages, and often, as a result of prolonged economic dislocation and the loss of foreign customers, their employment. There was a general atmosphere of uncertainty and among the industrial masses who, though the ostensible beneficiaries, were the worst sufferers from these acrimonious efforts to better conditions, a great deal of very real bitterness against the social system in general and their more fortunate countrymen in particular. The paradise of "Blighty" as seen in wistful anticipation from the trenches proved, on closer acquaintance, to be somewhat precarious, even for those who had had the luck of the economic roulette. For the less fortunate there were times when it seemed, what with slum housing, tightened belts, hungry, querulous womenfolk and pinched children, almost as grim as the trenches and far less friendly.

Seen through the medium of the daily papers the first years of

the great Peace that succeeded the war to end war were disconcert-
ingly unrestful. Anger and strife were not confined to the
factory and soapbox. Ireland, India and Egypt were all in more
or less open rebellion. At Amritsar General Dyer gave the order
to fire on an Indian Nationalist crowd: in a few minutes 400 were
killed and nearly 1000 wounded. Some said that the general had
averted a second Mutiny, others that he had disgraced his uniform
and behaved like a Prussian. In Ireland British officers were
dragged from their beds by masked assassins and butchered in
front of their wives, an imprisoned Lord Mayor starved himself
to death to shame the Saxon despot, and Sinn Fein gunmen
maintained a rival and forbidden administration with their own
parliament, army, police and courts of justice defying those of the
imperial government with whom they waged ceaseless, secret,
and bloody war. The campaign was even carried into England,
where a Field-Marshal of Orange views was shot by Sinn Feiners
on the steps of his house in Eaton Place.

But when the Coalition government responded in kind to
lawlessness by abandoning law and recruiting a force of dare-
devil, ex-service misfits—nicknamed "black and tans"—to "raise
hell" in Irish villages, the tired English dream for a moment
reasserted itself. The English did not like the Irish, who, as
represented by the newspapers and their own actions, were a
manifest nuisance, but they had a sense of justice and an invincible love of decent and legalised dealing. "Authorised reprisals"
against innocent householders and women and children were too
much for them. Public opinion, for once rendered articulate by
unanimity, made itself felt, and the government, with an election
before it in the not distant future, changed its policy. In the
latter part of 1921, assisted by a timely speech from the King, the
more imaginative members of the Coalition made contact with
the less intransigeant of the Irish leaders. In the strained negotiations that preceded the Treaty which gave Dominion Status to
Ireland, one great Englishman, Lord Birkenhead, long lost in the
post-war moral confusion and welter, took his solitary chance to
prove his own wasted genius for statesmanship and the enduring
tolerance, common sense and humanity of British policy.

After 1921 imperial, like foreign problems, faded into the
background. In that year the full force of the economic anarchy
which scourged the post-war world struck commercial Britain.
The orders for urgent reconstruction after the devastation of the

war dried up: instead the European nations, struggling back into the industrial battle-line, began to manufacture for themselves. Their very ruin helped them: with their prior charges wiped out by inflation and their workers rendered servile by long famine, they were easily able to undercut British rivals. Prices, and with them wages, came tumbling down. So did employment. In June 1920 there were 67,000 unemployed in Britain. By July 1921 there were two and a half million.

The shock of this new adversity sobered the nation. It brought a temporary end to strikes and lock-outs and a drastic reduction in unnecessary spending. It also brought Lloyd George's grandiose Coalition to a slightly premature end. An unknown Worcestershire ironmaster named Stanley Baldwin, with an honest face and a penchant for pipes and pigs, led an unexpected Tory backbench rebellion against the Welsh wizard, and enthroned a Conservative government dedicated to tranquillity. The country, feeling by this time that tranquillity was about the best it could hope for, gave it a comfortable mandate; and its modest leader, Bonar Law, quickly falling mortally ill, the Premiership passed unexpectedly to the unknown Baldwin. The new dispensation proved a success, certainly with the business community. "Why all this fuss about the servant problem?" asked Mrs. Britannia in *Punch.* "There's my Baldwin—can turn her hand to anything, keeps the House in order, checks the accounts, doesn't want any evenings off, very tactful with visitors, especially foreigners, in fact a perfect treasure." In the circumstances of the time it was an advantage that the new government seemed rather humdrum.

. . . .

But if the business world was contented, the industrial workers were not. The terrible figures of unemployment were a cancer at the country's heart, retarding all recovery and embittering relations between Englishmen. For the commercial predominance of the past had vanished. The competition of younger rivals, most of them with inferior standards of living, was increasing. So was the urban population which Britain had built up behind her former manufacturing ascendancy and which could only be employed and fed by the sale of manufactured goods abroad. And the accumulated investments of the Victorian era which had helped to bridge the gulf between what Britain bought with her exports and what she was able to produce in foodstuffs and raw materials, were dwindling. More than half her pre-war capital invested in foreign countries outside the Empire had already been lost or was soon to vanish in default and depreciation.

The uncertainty of an anarchical Europe increased her difficulties. Though her own social fabric remained unbroken, Britain was dependent on the custom of foreign nations whose ability or readiness to pay for their purchases was constantly in doubt. She had to trade to live. Trading with uncertain customers in uncertain currencies, she could only live uncertainly. Fluctuation in foreign prices and markets meant fluctuation in domestic employment and social standards. A revolutionary situation abroad threatened a revolutionary situation at home.

The City, Englishwise refusing to admit reverse, put a brave face on things. It still continued to base the economic life of the country on the time-honoured assumption that every man who was industrious and prudent could make profits. The absence of prosperity was explained away by the assurance that a good time was sure to arrive as soon as the depression was over. The unemployed man standing in the rain outside the labour exchange, and the small manufacturer vainly waiting for the return of lost orders, were told that their sufferings would be compensated for by the magnitude of the coming recovery.

It never came. True, there were ups and downs, periods of slump and boom. But the booms were mostly confined to the fluctuating values of Stock Exchange shares and a few new luxury trades due to redistribution of national wealth and changes of social habit. At no time was there any steady expansion of British exports: throughout the greater part of the period there was steady decline. In little more than a decade those to foreign countries fell by nearly a third.

Because of these things unemployment remained a millstone round the neck of every post-war government. In the twenty years between the two wars every third working-class family in the land suffered at some time the despair and indignity of the dole. Every statesman promised or tried to find a remedy. Within six months of taking office Baldwin, himself a manufacturer, seeing Britain's manufacturers undercut by foreign rivals with lower social standards and wage costs, sought a mandate for a modification of her policy of free imports to enable him to bargain for reciprocal advantages for her traders abroad. But a conservative people, brought up to regard free trade and prosperity as synonymous and to suspect all would-be protectionists of log-rolling, was still not ready for the hour of economic retrogression and repentance which Disraeli had foreseen as inevitable. The Conservatives, themselves far from unanimous about their untried chief's impetuous lead, were defeated at the polls, and the Socialists, now the second largest Party, took office for the first time in December, 1923.

The newcomers, still in a minority, did not remain in power for long. Their foreign policy was unpopular, and their domestic reforms did nothing to solve the problem of unemployment. After nine months their Liberal allies withdrew their hesitant support. An appeal to the country did not help the Socialists. Despite their hold on the distressed areas and mining districts, they went down heavily. In November, 1924, Baldwin again took office.

During the next four years there was a slight improvement in trade, unemployment fell by nearly half a million and there was a reduction of 6d. in the £ in income tax. An attempt at a general strike, which for a dramatic week in the spring of 1926 created a revolutionary situation, was defeated by the refusal of ordinary Englishmen—most of whom sympathised with the miners on whose behalf the strike was ordered—to permit an outside body to dictate to an elected and lawful government. The coal strike was subsequently allowed to drag on for six miserable months to its dismal, inevitable end; thereafter industrial conditions became temporarily more normal. There was a good deal of slum clearance carried out by the joint efforts of private enterprise and local authorities with the aid of government grants: in the four and a half years of the administration 8,000,000 houses were built. Workmen's savings increased by £170,000,000, and there was a steady, if unspectacular, improvement in the extent and quality of the Social Services, whose cost, only £63,000,000 in 1911, rose by 1929 to £341,000,000. The general achievement was not inspiring and fell far short of the soldiers' dream. Yet it was the nearest post-war Britain ever came to prosperity.

But there still remained over 1,000,000 unemployed. There were still millions of English men and women living ugly, undernourished, uncertain lives, in cramped, mean, verminous dwellings, and bringing up their children in dirt and degradation. When the Baldwin government, in the summer of 1929, relying on the unimaginative slogan of Safety First, asked for a renewal of its mandate, it was found it had forfeited the confidence of the country. The change of rulers was not based on reason so much as on the human feeling that there was more suffering in Britain than flesh and blood should be asked to bear.

Yet the Socialists, who again took office with unofficial Liberal support, could do no more than the Conservatives to alleviate that suffering. In fact, through no fault of their own, they were able to do far less. In the autumn of 1929 a series of crashes on the New York Stock Exchange were followed by a failure of credit from one end of Europe to the other. The great world economic crisis or trade blizzard began. It was grimmer and bigger than any that had ever happened. By the autumn of 1931, unemployment in Britain was approaching 3,000,000. In the same month, the government's unbalanced borrowings to meet the deficit on the Unemployment Insurance Fund precipitated a panic among foreign depositors and an incipient flight from the pound. Amid much confused bandying of figures and waving of depreciated pound notes, and a wholly irrational but rather moving recrudescence of patriotic feeling, a hastily-formed coalition government appealed to the country for a "doctor's mandate" to solve the economic ills under which its people were suffering. It received it with a majority unprecedented in British electoral history. The Socialist and former pacifist Prime Minister, who had abandoned his Party at the dictates of his conscience and the Bank of England, was returned to power with a following of 556 members, 472 of whom were Tories.

The new government made little impression on the unemployment figures at first, which, true to the uncontrollable laws which seemed to govern world trade, continued to rise gently until 1933. Thereafter they fell substantially for three years, and then with the "National" government still in power, showed unmistakable signs of rising again. Yet it would be unfair to say that the administration's efforts, which were painstaking if uninspired, had no effect on them at all. Comprised in the doctor's mandate, though the purer and less accommodating Liberal free traders who supported the coalition subsequently denied it, was a *carte blanche* to adopt some form of protection for native and imperial industry. In the cumulative distress and anxiety of 1931, Britain, after close on a century, was ready at last to repudiate free trade. For men had cried to their totem, and their totem had failed them.

Not that any very vigorous protective policy was adopted. The worst abuses of dumping by State subsidised foreign importers, who had long regarded the unprotected British urban market as a happy hunting ground, were checked. And in 1932 a British Delegation, led by the Lord Privy Seal, Baldwin, agreed at the Imperial Conference at Ottawa to afford to the Dominions, in return for reciprocal advantages for British exporters, that preferential treatment which had been refused by Lord Salisbury's government at the Diamond Jubilee thirty-five years before. But the extent of such preference was strictly limited because the National Government felt itself unable to reserve more than a moderate fraction of the home market in foodstuffs for imperial producers. Its reluctance was dictated not so much by the old fear of raising the price of food to the British consumer as by its deference to the vested financial, commercial and shipping interests which had grown up round the imports of foreign agricultural products. For it was plainly impossible for Britain to take her beef simultaneously from British farms and from the Argentine: if she sacrificed the latter for the former, it would become difficult and perhaps impossible to transmit the interest on the British capital invested in that country. And as the vast and costly party machines necessary to a country with a democratic franchise inevitably received more support from bankers and shipowners than farmers, it was only natural that the former's interests should prevail.

So imperial preference, though popularly approved, was but tentatively encouraged instead of boldly applied. It was not possible to create a new economic order for the British Empire as the public wished without breaking financial eggs. In 1938, the Anglo-American Trade Agreement, without any mandate from the electorate, actually whittled down the modest concessions granted to Dominion producers in 1932. As for protection, this was virtually never possible without the repudiation of a complicated system of foreign commercial treaties which had been built up during the Free Trade years, and of which the public knew nothing. The whole economic structure raised in a century of titanic capitalist enterprise was too intricate and interdependent for any one to be able to produce, let alone execute, a plan capable for mending any one of its defective parts without injuring, perhaps irreparably, some other. However delicately one stepped, the floor of the commercial edifice was alive with vested interests, every one of which was apparently sacred and defended by a whole chorus of jealous hierophants. The utter fiasco of the much advertised World Economic Conference in London, in the summer of 1933, was an illustration, if any was needed, of the omnipresence of the disintegrating forces in contemporary human society. It was poor Ramsay Macdonald's last attempt to view the world as a unified whole. Despite his oratory and good intentions the task was beyond his or apparently any other man's comprehension.

.   .   .   .   .   .

Before the Conference broke up in cynical despair the emphasis was already passing from internal ills, still uncured, to still graver external ones. Adolf Hitler, rising to stormy political victory on a surge of angry oratory and the bitter despair of six million unemployed and thirty million underfed, became the ruler of Germany. His aims, shrilly enunciated for fourteen passionate years, were the repudiation of the Peace Treaties and the establishment of a greater Reich that should dominate the Europe which had humiliated her. He was a man of hate, who hated the French, hated the Jews, hated his own rivals and predecessors in hatred, the Bolshevists. He hated everything which opposed the interests and destiny of Germany and, as he always identified himself with Germany, by implication every one who barred his path.

Apart from an instinctive dislike for the man's manners and methods, the British people were not at first interested in Hitler. That they might themselves be among the causes, though as yet not amongst the immediate objects, of his vituperative fury never struck them. At the time of the Armistice, when almost every family in the land was mourning some relative and when many harsh and bitter things had long been said and done, they had not unnaturally responded to a hasty request from their politicians for a mandate to rebuild Europe by telling them to hang the Kaiser and squeeze the German lemon till the pips squeaked. After that, being heartily tired of foreigners and their problems, they had turned their backs on the Continent and, immersing themselves in their own affairs, left their politicians and publicists to reshape Europe as they chose.

Their brief spasm of ill-humour had soon passed. With tem-

peramental British inability to nurse a grudge, they wished
Germany nothing but well. The anxious efforts of the French
to keep their ancient and terrible enemy prostrate, only increased
British sympathies for her. Moreover, an island state dependent
on foreign trade found that she could ill afford so disturbing an
economic factor as a ruined central Europe. When the French
Premier pointed to his country's devastated areas as a reason for
tightening the screw, Lloyd George retorted by pointing to the
export districts of industrial South Wales and northern England
with an unanswerable "These are *our* devastated areas."

But of the Treaties still standing in their name—their content,
the extent of their enforcement, their effects on the conquered—
the British people, except for a small minority of intellectual
Socialists and Liberals who had always opposed the Peace Treaties
as politically inexpedient and economically suicidal, were almost
totally ignorant. They were unaware that Germany had been
ruined economically before a single mark of reparations had
been paid or even demanded. They did not know—or had forgotten if they had ever known—that for several years the peoples
of central Europe had starved, that the entire middle class of
Germany had lost its savings in the inflation, that hundreds of
thousands of German civilians had been driven at a few hours'
notice from their homes by French soldiers. Because in the
latter 'twenties Germany thrived for a while on the reckless loans with which British and American financiers tried to
resuscitate and exploit her industries, they never realised that
millions of Germans were secretly nursing bitter grievances and
irrational hatreds. They knew nothing of the dry timber which
the orator Hitler was seeking to ignite.

According to their lights such grievances as existed had been
allayed. The Locarno Pact, concluded in 1925 between Austen
Chamberlain, Stresemann, and Briand, which, in effect, merely
congealed the *status quo*, they enthusiastically acclaimed in the
belief that it consecrated the policy of let bygones be bygones,
and restored equality between victors and vanquished. That it
had not done so they learned with perplexity when, in their
successive attempts to achieve disarmament—their historic
practice after all wars—the Germans insisted on parity with the
French and the French on an overwhelming superiority in every
weapon as their only security against Germany. Wanting
nothing but peace—the one positive gain from the wastage,

cruelty and misery of the war—the British people assumed in their insular, hopeful way that every one else felt the same. Through their voluntary associations and parliamentary institutions they affirmed over and over again their sense of its necessity and their faith in the League of Nations and the machinery of international law. They even succeeded with the help of their Anglo-Saxon kinsmen in the United States in persuading the statesmen of the world to affix their signatures to a document called the Kellog Pact, repudiating war as an instrument of policy. For, having suffered so much from the tidal flood of war, they supposed, like King Canute, that an edict against tides would protect them from further inundation. Their courtiers, the democratic newspapers and politicians, loudly assured them that it would.

Yet, everywhere, the old national jealousies and fears barred the way to that rule of perpetual peace and international law that was the Englishman's ideal. Italy wanted naval parity with France, and the U.S.A. with Britain, who in turn depended for her very existence on the freedom of her sea routes. Japan wanted hegemony in Eastern waters; Soviet Russia, in order to secure and further the proletarian revolutionary experiment, wanted the largest air-force in the world; Poland wanted a big army, preferably mounted, to defend herself against Russia; and Czechoslovakia and Belgium wanted the continued profits from the sale of the armaments they so industriously manufactured. Every disarmament conference failed. For no formula could resolve these eternal discordancies.

Into this imbroglio of rival expedients, figures and formulas, like a bull entering a china shop, burst Hitler. Even before the easy-going, preoccupied British public had become conscious of his strident rancour, their pacific hopes had been dashed. In 1931, Japan, seeking preferential markets for the expanding industrial population of her overcrowded island, marched into an anarchic China to seize Manchuria. British peace-lovers protested, the more logical of them even clamouring to go to war to vindicate the decencies of international law and the rules of the League of Nations. But neither their fellow members of the League, nor Japan's great rival, the United States, was prepared to go to such an extreme and desperate course. Nor were the British—then in the throes of a financial crisis—in any position, after ten years of disarmament, to impose single-handed the rule of righteousness on a great naval Power at the far end of the world. The only result of Anglo-Saxon disapproval of aggression was Japan's exit from the League, taking her conquest with her.

Two years after Hitler's irruption on the European scene, a still more brazen aggression occurred. A noisy Fascist Italy, seeking preferential markets, raw materials and an outlet for her expanding population—now shut out from the Americas by restrictive emigration acts—revived a long dormant claim on Abyssinia.[1]

At the instance of Italy herself, Abyssinia had been admitted to the League, and was therefore recognised by the British public as an equal and sovereign fellow nation. What complicated the outrage was that Italy was still a kind of tacit ally of Britain and France. Mussolini, who, as western Europe's first dictator, was believed to have no love for his upstart Teuton imitator, had only recently declared from the stronghold of the Brenner Pass that Fascist Italy would not allow Austria to be absorbed in the Reich. With Germany rearming in open violation of the Peace Treaties, the loyal alignment of the three victor Powers against the reviving barbarian seemed vital to the safety of them all.

The French, always more sensitive than the British to the peril beyond the Rhine, were painfully aware of this. When Italy, true to her boasts and warlike preparations, marched into Abyssinia in the autumn of 1935, they did their best to restrain the pacific enthusiasm of the British for vindicating the violated principles of international law. But the British were not to be restrained. Their politicians had repeatedly told them that the Great War had been fought to end war for ever. The heroic and loved dead had died and the millions had suffered for the sake of that great consummation. And the League of Nations, honoured in Britain as nowhere else, was the guarantee that peace should endure. Its Covenant was the British people's war gain. They would not allow it to be flouted.

But their dilemma was tragic. For they could not protect the integrity of League principles without waging another war—that which they had hoped above all things to avert—and so

---

[1] In *The Times* Atlas of 1896 the whole of Abyssinia was coloured green as an Italian possession. Only the defeat of the Italians by the Abyssinian warriors at Adowa prevented Abyssinia from becoming Italian, as the Sudan, at that time, became British.

destroying the one achievement of the war to end war. Reluctant to ignore the Italian challenge, equally reluctant to embark on hostilities in which, as it became painfully clear, they could not count on the help of the nations associated with them in the Covenant, they tried the expedient of commercial sanctions. Even to these the associated nations, loath to dislocate their trade, gave only tepid support. Ineffectual for any purpose save to irritate Italy against what seemed British sanctimony—for who were the British to cavil at imperial conquest?—sanctions not only failed to stop her triumphal march into Addis Ababa but drove her out of the League into the arms of her hereditary enemy. Henceforward the two Dictators marched together on one brazen axis, with the other aggressor of the Far East in uneasy co-operation. Their declared aim was a New Order constructed on falsehood, menace and violence.

Hitler snatched at his opportunity. While the Italo-Abyssinian war was still waging, he reoccupied the demilitarised Rhineland, relying on pacifist opinion in a disarmed Britain to prevent more than verbal protests at this breach of the Peace Treaties and Locarno. France, suffering from internal dissension and industrial unrest, dared not act alone. The door of Europe was slammed in her face. Henceforward she could only come to the assistance of her eastern allies by breaking through a fortified German frontier. It was the end of Versailles. It was virtually, though scarcely any one yet knew it, the end of peace.

.   .   .   .

Such was the fate of the dream which the soldiers brought back from the trenches. On September 3rd, 1939, it seemed as if the dead had died in vain. The veterans of the Great War had seen their homely ideals of a decent life constantly frustrated by economic factors beyond their control or even that of their politicians. The home of their own with a garden, the job in which they could take pride, the security for themselves and their dear ones, had had to wait. In their patient English way they had accepted the fact, hoping that gradual amelioration of social conditions might one day ensure the promised land for their children and children's children. In that hope they had passively adopted the Baldwinian thesis, put aside bitterness, and worked for the slow realisation of a more just and happier society in the days after their death. But even for this limited realisation, peace was essential. A repetition of the terrible struggle of 1914-18 would put the clock of progress back fifty, a hundred, perhaps a thousand years. War marked the end of all their dreams, and war had come.

Yet there was nothing left for an Englishman but to fight and beat the enemy, cost him what it might. He had at least done his best to keep the peace. His cause, however tragic, was a noble one: he was fighting against evil things and a cruel, unappeasable aggressor who tortured racial minorities, who tore up treaties, who ranted and shouted and bullied and, when he was thwarted, rained death and desolation on peaceful millions.

Yet, even when the war had begun and the need for strong united action became obvious to the most obtuse, the national driving force still faltered. The fatal indecision and divisions that had weakened British purpose for twenty years persisted. For more than six months, while the Germans completed their preparations behind the Siegfried Line, the British effort at rearmament, begun leisurely in the old days of tranquillity and pacificism when Baldwin took office for the third time in 1935, and speeded up by Chamberlain since Munich, proceeded at what seemed little more than pre-war pace. The leaders of Labour were second to none in their resolve to destroy Hitler and the hated Nazis. But they did not mean to allow the almost equally hated Chamberlain to do so. And the Prime Minister, who had identified himself with appeasement and then, with palpable integrity, led the nation to war, was honestly resolved, like Sir Robert Peel, to be the chief executant of the policy he had formerly opposed.

It was not till the Germans, after their lightning conquest of Norway, had struck with their full force at the Netherlands and sent France reeling that Britain awoke to the magnitude of her task. The politicians and financiers who had assured her that her economic resources would alone enable her to beat the "have not" Powers were seen to be liars, the elderly Civil Servants who had complacently assumed their ability to crush the young revolutionaries of the Nazi Reich by rule of thumb were proved bunglers. Not to these but only to the enduring character of her people, made manifest on the Dunkirk beaches and in the skies above the Channel and Kentish Weald, could Britain look for deliverance. She was where she had stood in March, 1918.

Once more she was face to face with reality. For the *status quo* which the men of business had told her was the only feasible reality for a practical people had proved insubstantial as the kingdom of Cloud Cuckoodom. The sanctity of profits and dividends was a mere shadow. It had vanished before for the soldiers of the Great War in the smoke and flame of Somme and Paschendaele. As the German tanks thundered over the same battlefields it vanished again. Men were back with their own souls because the realities of the world of commerce and profit-seeking had failed them. Twenty years before they had been persuaded that their vision was an illusion. But as a tired England girded on again the invincible armour of her tireless valour, the vision was all that remained.

CHAPTER X

Way of Redemption

"In the city set upon slime and loam
They cry in their parliament 'Who goes home?'
And there comes no answer in arch or dome.
For none in the city of graves goes home.
Yet these shall perish and understand,
For God has pity on this great land.

Men that are men again; who goes home?
Tocsin and trumpeter! Who goes home?
For there's blood on the field and blood on the foam
And blood on the body when Man goes home.
And a voice valedictory . . . Who is for Victory?
Who is for Liberty? Who goes home?
                              G. K. Chesterton.

BUT what, puzzled men with long but hazy memories
asked, had happened? Why had the soldier who had over-
come so much failed after the peace to achieve those simple
and elementary hopes for which the dead had died? The things
he wanted in those far days in the trenches had seemed so reasonable, and for a rich country so easy. A tithe of the effort and
cost which Britain had expended in defeating Germany could
have made her a different land, offering good homes for all,
ample pleasant places unsullied by the wastage of competitive
industry, an assurance to every man of work in which he could
take pleasure and pride and by which he could earn a modest
but secure livelihood.

All over tortured Europe other men who had suffered and
bled had asked the same things. They also had had their dream,
conceived in an hour of blinding and agonising revelation—
Frenchmen and Italians; vanquished Russians, Germans and
Austrians, Hungarians, Bulgarians and Turks; Serbs, Belgians,
Romanians, Greeks, Jews, Poles and Czechs. They too had
wanted, each in the form dictated by their racial and national
pasts, the same elemental human satisfaction: the home of their
own, the craft of their choice, the bit of land—status, security,
creation and continuity. God who had made man in His own

image had meant him to have these things, and out of the whirlwind of Verdun and Caporetto had spoken of them.

It was not to these that the returning soldiers, marching with set faces to demobilisation across a broken Europe, returned. It was to frustration and disillusion: to hunger and enforced idleness, to untilled fields and empty factories. All they had suffered for their loved ones and country ended only in more suffering: not in a Christian and compassionate commonwealth but in a pigsty. The politicians in all countries had promised a land fit for heroes. But when the soldiers came home they found a world designed for stockbrokers and *rentiers* and civil servants. It was built not in the image of their apocalyptic dream but in that of the utilitarian labyrinth of the money-changers from which they had gone forth in 1914.

For industrial society as it had grown up in the past century, first in island Britain and then everywhere else, did not admit the fulfilment of the soldiers' need. *Laissez-faire* capitalism postulated a fluctuating reserve of labour and therefore unemployment, the power of the man with capital to hire and dismiss his workers as he chose and therefore insecurity; and the legal priority of usurious over equitable rights and therefore the accumulation of property in the hands of the few and its denial to every one else. The men who had gone to battle to defend such a society were divided from it by a great chasm which they had crossed in agony, sweat and blood. But those who had to reconstruct a broken Europe—the political leaders, the industrialists, the clever thinkers and capitalists who had stayed at home—were still on the other side.

The only remedy these men of an older generation could see for the ruin around them was to rebuild the world they knew before the war. It never occurred to them that they were restoring the situation that had caused the war. The basis of their world was the overriding necessity of earning expanding profits. The test of every human enterprise in every country had increasingly come to be: will it make enough to meet the contractual demands of the initiating lender? The universal search of the profit-maker was a fruitful field for exploitation in some other country. The *desideratum* of every national policy was not whether it increased the actual wealth of a country— the crops, homes, amenities, health, happiness and character of its inhabitants—but whether it multiplied the returns of the men of money and of those to whom their money, seeking multiplication by usury, was advanced.

The success of the great British capitalists of the nineteenth century had blinded civilisation to the essential difference between profits and real wealth. A rare combination of native character, vigour and inventiveness, geographical good fortune and historical opportunity had caused their experiment to succeed in its early stages beyond their wildest expectations. Britain became richer than any other nation had ever been before. But she also became poorer. Her soaring exports and accumulating investments were the products of the new economic individualism. So were the conditions of the early factory towns.

It was the paradox of the nineteenth century—an epoch in which Britain led the world—that the practice of a sturdy and often heroic individualism, which increased the potentialities of human wealth out of measure, unwittingly created social injustice and inhumanity on a scale formerly unknown to Christians. The economists were proved right in their contention that enlightened self-interest, unfettered by State control, could enrich men more quickly than any other means. Yet the human misery caused by its pursuit justified the prophets of a more ordered society who warned unheeding generations that profits created at the price of social health and contentment were illusory. In the long run they were not profits at all. For they had still to be paid for in the cumulative loss of working power sustained through inhuman conditions of life and labour and inferior breeding capacity. The flaw in *laissez-faire*, and in the entire system of accountancy to which it gave birth, was that it regarded man as a self-sufficient unit like a machine. It forgot that he grew. It failed to recognise that the human economic unit was the continuing society— nation, group or family—from which the individual derived his habits and instincts. It failed to perceive that the effect of under-nourishment, bad housing, unemployment and social injustice was not confined to the immediate victims but was transmitted to his descendants. A business that only operated in one generation might profit from overworking and underpaying human beings. A nation could not. Yet there was no nation of any importance that did not follow Britain's example.

Those who set out so gaily along that glittering road of accumulation failed to see to what it led. They did not grasp the moral truth, hidden from the utilitarians, that greed always overreaches itself. By enthroning it as the motivating principle of all economic activity, they set society on a downward declivity. At first the profits accruing to a man of enterprise, who under such a system was encouraged to apply his entire energies to their pursuit, could be great. Operating in a community in which wholesale exploitation had not hitherto been permitted, he was able to command the vigour, contentment, health and character of its people without paying anything towards the cost of these commercial assets—the accumulated legacy of former ages of sane and virtuous living and the real wealth of any continuing society. But with each generation the margin of available profit diminishes until the day arrives when the society under exploitation consists of debilitated, inefficient and resentful human beings without property, social cohesion or religion. The seven good years of the capitalist's policy are presently consumed by the seven lean. The exploiter is driven to seek new fields to succeed those already used up. And in these fields rival exploiters encounter each other, narrowing profits still further.

The peacemakers who assembled in 1919 could not see the flaw in the system. They were not bad men: only uninspired and, for all their entourage of experts, ignorant. They had none of the knowledge of far humbler men whom their great limousines passed marching on the dusty roads around Paris. They had not shared the soldier's crucifixion and his blinding, revealing vision. They could not therefore conceive a new world. They could only speak in the language of an old. They thought in terms of maps, political frontiers, racial rights and creeds, above all in markets and fields of profits for their bankers and industrialists. With infinite pains they re-erected the structure not of a co-operative but of a competitive world. They never saw the simple truth that for four years had been flashed nightly across the sky above the trenches in which millions of men who had no conceivable personal quarrel lived troglodyte lives to slay one another in the slime: that a competitive world ends in a warring world.

The peacemakers not only strove to reconstruct an impracticable system: they unconsciously aggravated it. They not only set the profit-makers and usurers of all nations in renewed competition with one another, they intensified and embittered that competition. There was little that was vindictive about the political terms of Versailles. It was just that France should regain her stolen provinces, Italy, Romania and Serbia their natural frontiers, and Poland and Bohemia their independence. It was only common sense that Germany should be disarmed and the claws of the Prussian bully cut. But it was madness deliberately to reshape the frontiers of central Europe in order to ensure the bankruptcy of German, Austrian and Hungarian producers and enrich their rivals in the victor states.[1] The British soldier in the trenches had fought only for one reason—to beat the Germans and teach them to keep their place. He had not endured that four years' agony in order to render future generations of workers poor and restless.

The German of 1919 was under no illusion as to who had won the war. He was cowed, humble and very hungry; he was fed up with imperialism and dreams of world conquest. He wanted to be what his ancestors had been before the Prussians had taught Teutons to dream of worldly domination and the financier and industrialist had made it seem a necessity—a home-loving, sentimental bourgeois smoking a pipe, swilling beer and imbibing music and philosophy. He had been taught his place.

There was no need, after thrashing him and taking his arms, to bankrupt him. It was suicidal, if a Germany was to remain part of Europe, to render it a financial cripple. As Maynard Keynes pointed out, during the half-century before the war Europe had become industrialised round the hard core of a manufacturing Germany. Instead of a continent of self-supporting agricultural states, manufacturing only for luxury, there had grown up an intensely complicated polity based on the industrialisation of the more advanced communities and a grouping of the others as customers and growers of their food-stuffs and raw materials. It might have been far better had no such economic alignment ever taken place. But since it had, any rearrangement of political frontiers that ignored it was bound to unsettle the life of millions.

For since capitalist Europe, in its search for industrial profits

---

[1] In a letter written in November, 1917, F. S. Oliver, then serving as secretary to a Cabinet Committee, described how the Foreign Office, the Board of Trade, the Treasury and the India Office were all thinking out "separate policies for doing in the Hun in the matter of his exports of manufacturer's imports of raw materials after the war." At the time of writing thousands of Englishmen were dying daily in the mud of Passchendaele.

and interest, had become interdependent, a regrouping of its provinces and people such as German aggression had rendered necessary was only practicable if accompanied by a divorce between national and economic sovereignty. Unrestricted political independence for its diverse races was, however dangerous, possible: but unrestricted economic independence set *laissez-faire* to operate in the conditions of a madhouse. For so long as sovereignty carried with it the right to raise tariffs and trade barriers along national frontiers, every transfer of industrial, mineral or agricultural territory involved the dislocation of existing industries and the unemployment and diminishing purchasing power of those dependent on them. The annexation of a province did not merely as in the past affront the pride of a few crazy nationalists and militarists. Under capitalist *laissez-faire* it entailed poverty and perhaps ruin on millions. It played into the hands of the very warmongers the treaties were designed to punish. For it offered for their discredited and antiquated notions a vast and hungry audience.

Since the countries who shared the same continent with industrial Germany were dependent for the sales of their primary products on the purchasing power of the German workers, the handicap imposed on her by anxious French statesmen created economic disturbance everywhere. It unwittingly sentenced the whole world to suffering. Already ruined by war and famine, men in all countries found themselves without former customers, markets or employment. Everywhere governments seeking to alleviate their sufferings and still their clamour were driven to create in a hurry new industries and markets to fill the hiatus. Artificial and perilous economic creations arose like the great armament industry of Czechoslovakia, cutting across the lines of natural economic development and arousing needless rivalries and animosities. A great geographical area like the Danube basin, which had formerly been an economic whole under the Hapsburgs, was cut up into unworkable trade-tight compartments.

In a world so anarchically devised that all nations were competitors for markets beyond their borders, nothing but the closest economic co-operation could have enabled their governments to safeguard the welfare of those for whom they were responsible. So long as a nation was dependent for its markets, credit and raw materials on forces outside its control, its people were subjected to fluctuations in prices and market conditions which rendered their life and employment uncertain. Only an agreement between nations to sacrifice part of their economic isolation, either in some internationally enforced system of multi-lateral clearing arrangements or in a low tariff group or economic union comparable to that formed by the States of the U.S.A. or the U.S.S.R., could have stabilised the trade conditions of a capitalist and politically divided continent. Only thus could the peacemakers have averted the fluctuations that devastated human society in the early 'thirties and, among other evils, carried Hitler to power on the flood-tide of central European misery and unemployment.

But in the bitterness of their aggravated racial feelings the Versailles statesmen, constant to the grooves of their vanished youth, deliberately discouraged international economic co-operation. The fiscal anschluss between republican Germany and the German rump of the old Austria was forbidden, as was a Danubian tariff union between the States which had constituted the Hapsburg Empire. Either permitted in time might have saved central Europe from ruin and Nazi domination. And with every year that passed any modification of economic barriers between the nations became harder because of the vested interests which grew up round even the most artificial and restrictive trade and financial channels. In the great slump of the 'thirties even generous Britain—fiscally the most liberal of all States—invoked her "most favoured" nation rights to prevent the formation of mutually beneficial low-tariff groups, first between the Scandinavian countries and then between Holland and Belgium.

For by a curious paradox the very insistence of Britain on the freedom of international trade now had the effect of restricting its free flow. A kind of intellectual petrification in its leaders caused them to insist on the retention of the identical form of commercial treaty employed in the days of Cobden. The "most favoured" nation clause, which the Foreign Office still rigidly inserted in every trade treaty, had been designed in a very different age to prevent countries which had not adopted free trade from obtaining concessions from which Britain was excluded. Its object, by making it impossible for any party to it to reduce its tariffs to another nation or nations without reducing them to every nation with which it had ever signed a treaty, had been to generalise tariff reductions and so make for greater freedom of trade.

Before mass production and cheap transport made it as easy to export to the far side of the world as to the next province, the universal use of the "most favoured" nation clause did not have the effect of subjecting a country, which wished to reduce tariffs to a favoured foreign customer, to dumping from the rest of the world. It merely lowered tariffs all round without interfering with that natural preferential and stable trade which existed between neighbouring countries. But once the world became for transport purposes a single unit and every nation, emulating Britain's example, started manufacturing for export, the operation of the clause made it dangerous and even impossible for any government to reduce tariffs at all. Though every nation needed stable trade and the reduction of fiscal barriers between itself and those with whom it normally traded, any agreement between two nations to this effect was impossible so long as this ubiquitous clause enabled others with lower wage and production costs[1] to claim equal rights and so flood the markets which they were trying to regulate and extend. Paradoxically the "most favoured" nation system meant that no nation could, under normal trading conditions, be favoured at all. It prevented by any but arbitrary and violent methods the formation of those larger and natural fiscal areas which alone could have rendered the capitalist system workable.

This unintended ossification of tariffs by the very measure which had been designed to reduce them had disastrous effects in the changed world of the 'twenties and 'thirties. By making the creation of planned and orderly international trade impossible, it subjected the peoples of every country to violent fluctuations which perpetually dislocated their employment and standards of living. Obstructing profits from stable trade, it drove investment into speculative channels and created a vast vested interest in fluctuating prices. Because capital could not earn assured returns from long-term investments, it sought them from forestalling rises and falls in stock exchange, currency and commodity prices. The ends of those who controlled capital became increasingly served, not by the steady development of the earth's resources, but by successive booms and slumps which brought recurrent uncertainty and unemployment to the workers

[1]Such, for instance, as Japan.

in all lands but whose intelligent foreknowledge offered favour-
ably-placed speculators and monopolists opportunities of
enormous profits.[1]

In countries like the U.S.A., Britain and France, which had
strong traditional social systems, reserves of wealth and access
to raw materials purchasable in their own currencies, such evils
could be endured for a time. Despite the sufferings of large
minorities they even could become—as the event showed—
accepted as a matter of course. In less fortunate countries,
especially those which had suffered defeat in war, they shook
the social system to its foundations. The broken nations of
Europe revolted against the misery of recurrent unemployment,
the burden of contractual usury and the waste of poverty in the
midst of potential plenty.

In place of these things there arose out of the fires of revolution monstrous and primeval tyrannies. For society in the throes
of rebirth fell inevitably into the hands of men who subordinated
all things to their struggle for power. To them violence, at first
a necessity of revolution, became an end in itself, power a con-
suming lust. The idealists, seeking to rescue mankind from its
cross of gold, conceived the ends of these revolutions; but it
was men more ruthless, violent and resolute who supplied the
means. Having gained power, they maintained it by the
centralising weapons of modern science. Murderers, torturers
and perjurers, they took their place on the thrones of kings.
The State became their tool and their will the law. In their
cruel hands creeds, which first arose as a human protest against
inhumanity, became far more harmful to man's happiness and
liberty even than the evil things they supplanted.

.   .   .   .

What happened in these less fortunate strongholds of Christian
civilisation did not occur in Britain. Her victory in the war,
her vast accumulated reserves of wealth won in her Victorian
hey-day, above all the greater strength of her political and
social institutions and the natural kindliness and good humour
of her people, enabled her to withstand the corrosion of a dis-

---

[1]How great such profits were can be seen from the fluctuating prices of commodities.
In the three years between 1935 and 1938 the variations in the maximum and minimum
prices of lead, zinc, copper, and rubber, were respectively, 176, 170, 152, and 132 per
cent. In 1938 wheat prices at Liverpool ranged between 58s. 4½d. and 24s. 6d. Such vast
variations in a world unified by science and cheap transport cannot be explained solely
by natural causes.

integrating system longer than any other European nation. Her ancient order and peace held. Her people shrank from the brutal remedies of their continental neighbours. They could not see the need for them. They loathed their practical expression.

But though the British fighting men had returned in 1919 to a land of ordered progress, in which many of the worst features of the industrial system were being constantly mitigated by the organised conscience of the community, business was still business. The soldier's dream of a decent and stable life for himself and his dear ones remained a dream. For in an island which had escaped the horrors of invasion, battle and famine, the old belief in the sanctity of profits and investments remained unshaken. Though a million of her bravest had fallen, *laissez-faire* had survived.

The soldier was expected to adjust himself to it. A government department was even set up to help him do so. But he soon found that, so far as commercial and professional success was concerned, he had merely lost four years. If he was a man of exceptional energy, in possession of good health and nerves and a little capital, he might have no great difficulty in making up the leeway. If, as was more often the case, he was spiritually and physically tired, he was soon at a disadvantage. After all his sacrifice this seemed unjust. But by the laws of *laissez-faire*, tempered though they were in kindly England by State charity, it was merely inevitable.

By such laws the men who had not shared the sacrifice of the trenches were, generally speaking, better off than those who had. They were established in their jobs and suffered no violent transition in their lives and habits. Whatever they had achieved in the past four years remained to their credit. If they had made money—and with soaring war prices and wages there had been unprecedented opportunities for doing so—it remained theirs. If they had invested it in government securities the State guaranteed them not only the capital but a safe five or even six per cent return on it for many years to come. And the man who in the nature of things was best off of all was the profiteer who had turned his country's necessity to glorious gain.

There was nothing in the economic morality on which Britain had based her commercial life for a century to make it wrong for a man to do so. The whole trend of finance and commerce had been to divorce the possession of money from that of civic virtue. By the mathematical rules of *laissez-faire* the two had nothing to do with each other except on the assumption that the accumulation of cash was itself tantamount to virtue. The war, with its contrasts between penniless V.C.s and hard-faced profiteers, had proved the falsity of this assumption. Yet the slick company promoter, with his untidy trail of bankruptcies and ruined concerns, the slum landlord, the conscienceless usurer were still allowed to render whole communities miserable and unstable. So, without realising it, were the *rentiers* and small savers who, under a system of joint-stock companies and giant trusts, lent the use of their money to those whom they could not control.

A man might be a fine craftsman, a self-sacrificing citizen, a gallant soldier, but in peace-time his virtues were worth only what they could earn in the market-place. They could not of their own buy him a house with a garden, a decent bed with clean sheets, goods and clothes for himself and his family. They could not even guarantee him a job or keep him in it. In such matters money alone spoke. If he was without it he was at a hopeless disadvantage in a community governed by contract instead of status. He could only with the greatest difficulty live a good life: it was almost impossible for him not to live a higgledy-piggledy one. He had to face the prospect of being workless, living on a dole insufficient to buy more than the barest necessities, sheltering from the weather with his family in a single verminous room in some dreary slum street without the slightest security of tenure and suffering the abasement which every man feels who has not the dignity of an assured craft and a home. The State, true to an enduring English tradition that had survived even the worst rigours of *laissez-faire*, saw to it that a workless man did not starve. But it did no more. It left him to the operation of economic laws which condemned him to a life of ceaseless discomfort and degrading squalor, enforced idleness and the absence of almost everything that can delight and ennoble man.

Instead of a world fit for heroes, let alone decent men and women, the corroding shame of unemployment and the degradation of urban poverty became the lot of millions. Nobody wished Englishmen to bear such suffering. It arose unavoidably out of the economic system and the circumstances of the age.

The masses who had been given unrestricted adult suffrage

could not see this. They supposed that the fluctuating numbers of the workless, which in reality depended on world factors outside the control of any single government, were due to the miscarriage of their politicians. Sometimes they blamed the Conservatives and sometimes the Socialists. It was all said to be Lloyd George's fault or Baldwin's or MacDonald's. This embittered public life, for unemployment and the poverty and wretchedness that went with it were such evils that they seemed a crime against the dignity of human nature. Whoever was responsible for them was obviously a criminal.

It was this, too, that explained the rapid rise of the Socialist Party which during the War had been discredited as a pacifist minority. For men felt that as the rich were so powerful and yet so impotent or unwilling to remedy such inhuman conditions, there must be something fundamentally wrong with the private possession of property. A political party that proclaimed this could not fail to win votes. Its two chief fields of recruitment were the masses who suffered under the industrial system and the intellectuals who sought remedies for it. The worse the suffering, the more insistent became the demand that the State should restrict the power of the rich by taxing and ultimately confiscating the wealth that was its source. No government, even the most conservative, dared oppose this. Though the project of a capital levy, much discussed in the first post-war years, was easily defeated through the influence of the great financial houses and trusts whose business it would have dislocated, high taxation of incomes and inherited estates was the toll which private wealth was made to pay for the manifest suffering and injustice of the social system. It was recognised as inevitable even by the most diehard.

So far as Socialism constituted an attack on the existing system, it thus received support from all but the stupidest and smallest minority. The alleviations which it proposed—unemployment insurance, increased social services, help to distressed areas—became part of the programme of all parties. Yet it never achieved a dominating hold on the British, far less on the English electorate. The English reacted against joint-stock capitalism because they did not want to be wage-slaves. They reacted against Socialism and still more against Communism because they did not want to be proletarians. By English individual standards of liberty a proletarian, whatever his status in the Marxian hierarchy, remained a kind of slave. For these philosophies of the omnipotence of the State with their rigid administrative machinery subordinated the freedom of choice and self-respect of the ordinary man to vast and tyrannic powers as effectually as did joint-stock capitalism itself. They left no scope for the English dream which was a free man's dream.[1]

Because of this, despite the obvious disabilities of the existing system, the British electorate, though largely composed of working men, even continued to send Conservative majorities to Parliament. But they probably would not have done so but for Baldwin. This kindly, liberal-minded and characteristically English politician so obviously shared the ordinary Englishman's humane ideal that when he told them that he was working to bring about a better England they believed him. They had no idea how he was going to bring it about, nor, it now seems, had he. The only thing that was certain—and he never tried to deceive them about this—was that it was going to take a very long time. For Baldwin, like his Socialist vis-à-vis, Sidney Webb, believed in the inevitability of gradualness. And it was just possible that by some miracle in the English mode the nation might ultimately have escaped the toils of its fatal economic disease by gradual methods and so have achieved what it was seeking.

But it was never given time. For the breakdown of the economic system on the Continent came too swiftly for the snail-like pace of Baldwinian evolution. So long as they could, the British people and their leader averted their eyes from the European scene. But presently it became impossible to do so. The strident dictators of hate who had emerged from the economic welter could not be ignored. Thereafter, rearming feverishly and desperately trying to avert their hateful doom and that of all mankind, the British people never removed their fascinated gaze from Europe until they were finally and inevitably drawn into the maelstrom.

For they knew instinctively that what was happening on the Continent could not be allowed to continue. However much they might loathe the idea of fighting a second war to end war, a

[1] The English answer to them was that of the Communist window-cleaner, who told a Tory that what he really wanted was a house and a garden of his own, with a high wall round it, and spikes in the top of it. It was because capitalist society denied him this that he was a Communist. He had still to realise that Communism would deny it him too. Most of his countrymen realised it already.

world Power like Britain, dependent on public confidence and peaceful dealing between nations, could not ignore the repeated challenge to international law and decency. As before in her history, she had to uphold public order in the world. A world without public order was not a world in which England could exist.

True to her past, her people took up the challenge. But even as they did so they knew instinctively that they were in some peril of fighting not only to destroy evil things but to preserve them. They were resolved to put an end to Hitlerism, for apart from their resentment at brutality and cruelty, they knew that their own frustrated dream could never be fulfilled by violence. In resisting it they were unconsciously protecting an unborn and gentler English revolution. But they did not want to destroy a false totalitarianism merely in order to make the world safe a second time for the system that passed, however unfairly, under the name of "Chamberlainism." The young men who, ill-equipped and abandoned by their allies, triumphantly and in the face of all expectation, fought their way intact to Dunkirk out of what threatened to be the biggest military disaster in British history, were not doing so for the sanctity of dividends or the continuance of profitable speculation in shares and commodities prices. They were fighting — though they still only knew it hazily—for the dream for which the forgotten dead had died a quarter of a century before.

. . . .

In a hundred years England had come full circle. The laws that govern human existence may seem inscrutable. Yet they possess one ruling principle—that of ultimate justice. This cannot be perceived by a generation that glorifies the individual at the expense of the living society. For it is not the guilty individual who is punished or rewarded but the commonwealth of which he is part. The rulers or electors who neglect eternal truth may escape retribution. Their innocent descendants cannot.

Because of an unbalanced obsession with the individual, private profit-making—formerly regarded merely as a means to the acquisition of that modest ownership that makes virtuous and free men—became accepted as an end itself. But for certain indestructible elements in the English character it might have become the only end. In the sphere of economics, covering nine-tenths of man's daily life, the test of every activity, increasingly came to be not "Is it just?" but "Does it pay?" There was only one check on that rule—the human conscience. With the gradual concentration of business in the hands of limited liability companies, even that check was removed. A limited liability company has no conscience. A priesthood of figures cannot consider claims of morality and justice that conflict with its mathematical formulas: it must live by its own rules. Man, who had once tried to model his life on the divine, came to take his orders from the lender of money and the chartered accountant acting in their purely professional capacity. That has been the story of the last century of civilisation. The age of enlightened selfishness begot plutocracy, and plutocracy begot the monstrous materialistic and pagan tyrannies we are now fighting to destroy. It was England that first unconsciously led the world into this morass. It is England—wisest and gentlest of the nations—that has now to discover the way out.

If, remembering all the kindly and virtuous men who in the course of their duty and livelihood minister to the modern economic and financial machine, the reader doubts this, let him ask himself this question. Can a bank, in the face of actuarial fact, grant credit to a man whose failure must cause far greater human misery and injustice than the imprudent under-writing of his overdraft could conceivably cause the bank's shareholders? To a modern mind, brought up in commercial principles, the very question has come to seem dishonest.

It is not the profit motive that is to blame. Free men have at all times sought profit from their labour. It is its enthronement to the exclusion of other motives far more important. Under any sane human system the first concern of a factory should be the production of goods to give the utmost use, pleasure, and wear to those who require them, and the satisfaction of the human needs of their makers. Under the present system the one is only considered indirectly, being subordinated to the prior ends of making the maximum profit on the year's trading or paying the rake-off—frequently an unnecessary one—of the middleman. The other is scarcely considered at all. Lack of satisfaction of the producer in his work—the supreme human need of our age—is embittering and sabotaging the whole industrial system. It is destroying the rhythm and vitality of life. It is of little avail for scientists to give man the wonderful tools of modern machinery if a system of accountancy makes it necessary to use them in such a way as to deprive him of pride and enjoyment in his labour and of stability in his life. For these are as essential to the well-being of man, as children and child-bearing to woman. A factory that does not afford them to its workers is a badly organised factory. Nearly all factories in the economy of mass production for profits are badly organised. So are those in the new despotic states organised for quantity of output.

Man should be master of his tools, not his tools of man. It used to be the glory of England that its craftsmen took pride in their work. Under the modern system the artisan is denied the joy of giving quality to his task and is usually employed on a temporary basis. He is at the mercy of forces over which he has no control. He is not truly that which his English instinct prompts him to be—a freeman. That is why many Englishmen found so surprising a degree of satisfaction amidst the perils, pain and discomfort of the last war. The army, for all its harshness, gave comradeship, pride in achievement and the assurance that a man who did his best would receive his reward. It was the same appeal that the iron totalitarian creeds later made to the starving and workless millions of capitalist Europe.

. . . .

Civilisation is the science of enabling men to live in society as free, virtuous and rational individuals. The cement of any such society must be justice. The utilitarians by setting the rule of figures above that of human equity gradually undermined Christian civilisation. Those who destroy civilisation leave men no other refuge but the herd. And the herd, as the totalitarians have proved, is cruel and irrational.

It is particularly unnatural for an Englishman to live in a world not governed by justice. That is why he is fighting to-day. An attack on the independence of a small people by a large is an obvious act of injustice which awakes the dormant conscience of every Englishman. But behind the barrage of figures which cloaks the pursuit of private profits, injustices have daily and unconsciously been committed against millions with almost as little equity as Hitler's rape of Poland and Czechoslovakia. There is not only a crying need for justice between nation and nation. There is a crying need for justice between man and man. Even in Franco's despised new Spain the law now compels the payment of seven continuous days' wages to manual workers employed by the day, on the ground that a man who works is entitled to his Sabbath's rest and his daily bread with it, whatever the logic of accountants may say.

It is an error in human mathematics to argue that any course which creates contented citizens can be economically unsound. Figures that prove anything so preposterous lie. A satisfied community will always find a way to exist. And a dissatisfied community, however sound its balance sheet, will invariably end in some social disaster—war, revolution, or national decay—which will nullify all its figures and profits. However learnedly accountants may reason that in a nation which looks after the money the men will look after themselves, the final account will always shatter their logic. Slums, social discontent, dole queues and war lie at the end of their avenues of promise; *si monumentum requiris, circumspice!* The truth, as England proved in her earlier past, is that, only in a nation which looks after the men, will the money look after itself.

Yet there are still some in this country who believe that economic *laissez-faire* will survive the war. They have long realised that a victory for the Dictators means the end of the right of man to invest his money as he pleases and of the sanctity of private investments. They have therefore, on the assumption that whatever the totalitarian states condemn must in itself be good, assumed that a victory for Britain must necessarily involve the re-consecration of the economic practice of the last century. At the expense of millions of lives the clock is to be put back to the paradisial hour of 1927 or even 1913.

Their system's inadequacy has once again been exposed in the hour of testing. In 1917 Britain was within an ace of starvation[1] because her people, in pursuit of profits from foreign trade, had become dependent to an unbalanced degree on foreign food. The same danger again threatens her because, in the very years when, recognising the imminence of a second war, she was spending £1,500,000,000 on re-armament, no provision was made for an adequate grain reserve for human and animal consumption, apparently because its purchase would have interfered with the customary profits of the middleman and speculator in foreign

[1]At one time, when the German submarines were sinking half a million tons of shipping a month, there was less than seventeen days' supply of food in the country. —Lord Lymington *Famine in England*.

foodstuffs.[1] In the same period the storage room for wheat in a dangerously overcrowded island was allowed to decline when every argument of prudence and patriotism dictated its urgent increase.

So also lack of care for the Empire has given needless hostages to the aggressor. Because foreign trade and investments brought bigger returns to the men of money, British lands that could have bred vigorous and healthy millions of our own race were neglected in favour of other lands. Canada, with an area equal to that of Europe, has still only a population of eleven millions. Australia, more than fifty times the size of England and the home of perhaps the finest natural fighters the world has ever seen, has hardly more white inhabitants than Portugal. After fifty years of British rule the two Rhodesias have fewer than Huntingdonshire. Those responsible for this blindness may have profited in their generation. But they helped to lose us the forty or fifty millions of our own allegiance and idealism who would otherwise be fighting by our side against Hitler. That the total population of all the British nations overseas is still less than that of Brazil or pre-war Romania is the price now being paid for a century of enlightened self-interest.

Because of a false philosophy that set the profits and comfort of the living generation above the needs and security of a continuing society, the happiness, health and character of the British people—so strongly founded in the past—has been jeopardised. Millions of men have been allowed to rot and eat out their hearts in idleness because bigger profits could be earned by buying from the foreign than from the home producer. Much of the finest farming country in the world, inhabited by the most skilful agricultural population, has been allowed to go out of cultivation—endangering the nation's vital security—because it paid vested interests better if Britain did her farming in the Argentine, Denmark, Poland and Cuba. Even the beauty of her countryside, an irreplaceable and spiritual heritage, has been subordinated to private enrichment. The criminal law forbids a man to obstruct an urban thoroughfare for a few minutes with a car. But it takes no account of such outrages on the permanent property of a great people.

---

[1]Even the usual economic argument of the expense involved did not apply in this case, since such a reserve of grain—war or no war—would constitute, like Disraeli's Suez Canal shares, a saleable and even profitable asset.

For a hundred years, in ever increasing measure, patriotism for the common man has been presented as a mere emotional affair of flag-wagging. That it has had anything to do with his daily life, his skill in his craft, his love of home and his care of his children, has been obscured. Yet slums and under-nourished men and women, verminous children and despairing dole queues are as much the concern of the patriot as the battlefield. It is as high a treason to undermine public morality and endanger the safety of the commonwealth for the sake of profits as it is to trade with the enemy or sell military secrets. In time of war nothing can save the State but the character of its people. The man who for selfish ends undermines it is the real fifth columnist.

Her capacity for making profits by foreign trade impaired by a continental blockade and her foreign investments mostly evaporated or frozen, Britain to-day has still two supreme assets—the character of her people and the lands of promise won for her in the past. Both have been neglected: both, despite defective leadership and lack of human vision, survive. The one is her guarantee of victory. The other is her opportunity for fulfilling the English dream. In the past many pursuing that vision have argued that it would be better if England ceased to be a world commercial power and became again a little land like Sweden or Holland, producing only for quality and the happiness of her people. But a nation, which has allowed its population to exceed its capacity for feeding it by more than half, cannot exist within its own narrow compass. Starvation and ruin for our densely populated millions have been the unthinkable price threatened for every attempt to discard the servitude and uncertainty of world *laissez-faire* trading conditions for a gentler and juster organisation of national life. Yet there remains an alternative. Canada and Australia, New Zealand and the Rhodesias are the life-line of the English future. There lies the appeal for the British people from the slum, the dole and the regimentation of the factory

.   .   .   .

Nations like men must reap what they sow. The justice that is visited upon the children's children is an inescapable law of existence. Yet there is another eternal principle governing the world. It is that of redemption. Man may learn from his mistakes and, when he has made atonement, raise his stature by self-regeneration. Here, also, he learns and acts not as an isolated individual but as a member of a continuing society of which his own birth and death as an individual are but a seasonal part. A great nation is a society that learns from its prior follies and in learning recreates itself.

England has always learnt her lessons from her past mistakes. That is why, in the last resort—on the Dunkirk beaches of her history—she is so great. She lost her first Empire by ignoring a great principle of human government. She kept her second by regarding it. She made war against the Boer burghers: she gave them freedom and self-dominion within ten years of their defeat. She denied nationhood to the Irish: she granted it ungrudgingly when the scales were lifted from her eyes. Her enemies have often recalled the crimes of England. Yet her true history is the record of how they were redeemed.

England is now learning again that neither wealth nor power nor comfort, whether for class or individual, are ends in themselves: that the wealth of a nation consists in nothing but the virtue of her children and children's children. That no profits, education, law, custom, or institution that does not contribute to their health and goodness is of any enduring value. That the proper test of all legislation, of every political programme and economic activity, is not "Does it pay?" or "Does it enrich this class or that?" but "Will it make better men and women?"

An island fortress, England is fighting a war of redemption not only for Europe but for her own soul. Facing dangers greater than any in her history she has fallen back on the rock of her national character. Her future and that of the world depend not only on her victory but on her ability to restate in a new form the ancient laws of her own moral purpose and unity. By so doing she may discover a common denominator for human reconstruction more glorious than anything in her long past.

THE END

INDEX